MW01103328

E-Government 2003

EDITED BY

Mark A. Abramson
IBM Endowment for
The Business of Government
and
Therese L. Morin
IBM

ROWMAN & LITTLEFIELD PUBLISHERS, INC.
Lanham • Boulder • New York • Oxford

ROWMAN & LITTLEFIELD PUBLISHERS, INC.

Published in the United States of America
by Rowman & Littlefield Publishers, Inc.
4720 Boston Way, Lanham, Maryland 20706
www.rowmanlittlefield.com

12 Hid's Copse Road
Cumnor Hill, Oxford OX2 9JJ, England

Copyright © 2003 by Rowman & Littlefield Publishers, Inc.

All rights reserved. No part of this publication may be reproduced, stored in a retrieval system, or transmitted in any form or by any means, electronic, mechanical, photocopying, recording, or otherwise, without the prior permission of the publisher.

0-7425-2796-4 (alk. paper)
0-7425-2797-2 (pbk.: alk. paper)

Printed in the United States of America

™ The paper used in this publication meets the minimum requirements of American National Standard for Information Sciences—Permanence of Paper for Printed Library Materials, ANSI/NISO Z39.48-1992.

E-Government
2003

IBM Endowment for
The Business of Government

THE IBM ENDOWMENT SERIES ON THE BUSINESS OF GOVERNMENT

Series Editors: Mark A. Abramson and Paul R. Lawrence

The IBM Endowment Series on The Business of Government explores new approaches to improving the effectiveness of government at the federal, state, and local levels. The Series is aimed at providing cutting-edge knowledge to government leaders, academics, and students about the management of government in the 21st century.

Publications in the series include:

2001
Transforming Organizations, *edited by Mark A. Abramson and Paul R. Lawrence*
E-Government 2001, *edited by Mark A. Abramson and Grady E. Means*
Managing for Results 2002, *edited by Mark A. Abramson and John M. Kamensky*
Memos to the President: Management Advice from the Nation's Top Public Administrators, *edited by Mark A. Abramson*

2002
Innovation, *edited by Mark A. Abramson and Ian D. Littman*
Human Capital 2002, *edited by Mark A. Abramson and Nicole Willenz Gardner*
Leaders, *edited by Mark A. Abramson and Kevin M. Bacon*

TABLE OF CONTENTS

PART I

The E-Government Challenge

CHAPTER ONE

E-Government: A Progress Report

Mark A. Abramson
IBM Endowment for The Business of Government

Therese L. Morin
IBM

Introduction

Two years ago, we published *E-Government 2001*. In that book, we attempted to chronicle the "early days" of e-government. The chapters in that book presented a "snapshot" in time as to where government—at the federal, state, and local levels—was in the year 2000 as it continued its march toward e-government. We wrote:

> While many of the accomplishments described in these chapters are impressive by today's standards and represent significant progress, they are likely to pale by comparison when reviewed by readers in the year 2005. Today, we are just at the beginning of the e-revolution in government. Significant breakthroughs lie ahead. (Abramson and Means, 2001).

Since the publication of *E-Government 2001,* the IBM Endowment for The Business of Government has continued to support a series of studies to examine various aspects of e-government and the state of its progress across the nation. This book contains 10 chapters presenting our second "snapshot" in time as we chronicle the public sector's continued march toward e-government. This chapter focuses on the major challenges now facing the public sector if e-government is to fulfill its potential over the course of the next five years.

How Do Government Websites Compare?

Today it has become commonplace and expected that all organizations—public, private, or nonprofit—will have a web address and a website. It has become the accepted way in which all organizations do business. While the reported demise of "bricks and mortar" proved to be premature, the advent of "clicks and mortar" has become a reality in nearly all organizations. Thus, the key question today is not whether organizations, including those in the public sector, have websites, but what is the quality of those sites and the scope of services currently being provided online.

In chapter two, Genie Stowers presents a "report card" on the state of federal government websites. Based on her review of websites in 148 different federal departments and agencies, she concludes, "Many federal agencies have made enormous strides in creating attractive, useful, and helpful content and services on their websites; others still face challenges in achieving the highest level of quality." Her study found that federal government websites were increasingly being designed and organized with the user in mind and that websites across government have become more content

Drivers of E-Government 2003

- **Clinger-Cohen Act of 1996:** This law delegates information technology spending to agencies and creates the position of chief information officer (CIO) in federal departments. The goal of the act is to improve government performance through the effective application of information technology.
- **Framework for Global Electronic Commerce:** Issued in July 1997 by the Department of Commerce, the framework provided strong policy support for impetus for the use of e-commerce by the federal government.
- **Government Paperwork Elimination Act of 1998:** This law requires agencies to provide citizens the alternative of submitting information or transacting public business electronically by October 2003.
- **National Defense Authorization Act for Fiscal Year 1999:** This law requires the Department of Defense to create a single electronic mall system for procurement.
- **Presidential Memorandum on Electronic Government:** Issued in December 1999, the document establishes the parameters and goals of e-government, including providing one-stop access to government services and putting the top 500 government services online by December 2000.
- **Electronic Signatures in Global and National Commerce Act of 2000 (ESIGN):** This act ensures that digital signatures would be recognized as legal across all 50 states.
- **President's Management Agenda:** Issued in August 2001, the agenda includes "Expanded Electronic Government" as one of its five major government-wide initiatives. The initiative resulted in an initial 24 separate "Quicksilver" projects to integrate key services across agency boundaries and organize them around the needs of targeted customers.

Adapted from Stowers, Chapter Two

and service oriented than the first wave of websites, which primarily provided one-way information.

The importance of user-friendly websites is emphasized by Stowers. In what she calls the "other digital divide," Stowers describes the lack of experience of many citizens in using computers or the Internet. Because of this divide, Stowers argues that federal websites should be designed with user-friendliness in mind and that all websites should have clear and accessible help features.

While the federal government has made great strides in recent years, Stowers argues that continued support for e-government is needed from top government leaders at the departmental and agency level. She found that top leaders often do not understand the issues or the potential of government on the web. She recommends continued effort be given to cultivating support for e-government and web initiatives as a vital part of the government of the future.

Just as Stowers evaluates the state of federal websites in chapter two, Diana Burley Gant and Jon P. Gant evaluate state government websites in chapter three. Using slightly different criteria than Stowers, Gant and Gant examined the functionality of all 50 state web portals across four dimensions: openness, customization, usability, and transparency. They found that while many states had made significant progress in recent years, many still lagged in the promise of "one-stop shopping."

In findings similar to those of Stowers, Gant and Gant found that states are providing an increased number of services online. In order to facilitate user access, many states are organizing their online services around events (such as vehicle registration) rather than the department in which the services are located. In addition to vehicle and driver license registration, other common transactions at the state government level include tax filing and online professional licensing.

While significant and dramatic progress has clearly been made at both the federal and state levels since the mid-1990s, clear challenges face the public sector in the remaining years of this decade if e-government is to fulfill its potential. Both the Stowers and Gant and Gant chapters identify legitimacy and accessibility as key future issues. Regarding legitimacy, Gant and Gant write:

> Do not assume that portal visitors will automatically trust the accuracy of portal content or the validity of transactions performed through the portal. Just like the dilemma faced by private sector organizations, state governments must earn the trust of portal visitors. To that end, state portals should include features such as security and privacy statements, content update procedures and dates, contact information for person or office responsible for web portal content, proper acknowledgment of transactions (receipts), and even independent third-party endorsements of the portal.

The Five Highest Rated Federal Websites

1. U.S. Patent and Trademark Office
2. Department of Health and Human Services
3. Department of Education
4. Department of the Treasury
5. Department of the Navy

From Stowers, Chapter Two

Key Characteristics of Effective Government Websites

1. Any site must deliver effective online information and services. Unless you build it, they will not come—at all.
2. The content and structure of the site should be organized so that those who are unfamiliar with government can find the services and information they need without having to understand how government agencies are structured.
3. Usability and help features must ensure that users can get around the site and find what they want and what they need.
4. Accessibility features must ensure that individuals with disabilities can use the site.
5. Legitimacy features must ensure users' confidence in the site as well as its content and services.

From Stowers, Chapter Two

Closely related to the challenge of legitimacy is the importance of privacy and security concerns. Based on her study, Stowers cautions that the information exchanged on many federal websites is personal and confidential. She writes, "Privacy and security policies, therefore, must be not only developed but clearly displayed as well. To fully meet users' needs, federal websites must create protected, private, and secure spaces for the mutual exchange of information."

The second major challenge facing public sector websites is accessibility. The two studies found significant shortcomings in this area. Both used the Bobby analysis to rate accessibility and found many sites receiving low ratings. Stowers found that many federal agencies were not in compliance with Section 508 regulations that require all federal electronic and information technology to be accessible to individuals with disabilities. Gant and Gant found a significant number of state portals that did not provide reasonable access to a large number of disabled users. They also found that most state portals did not include the capability for language translation. In addition, many states failed to include basic help features.

The highest rated federal government and state websites all received high accessibility scores. But many other sites fell short in this area. Based on her findings, Stowers recommends, "Web designers and web managers need to give more attention and priority to accessibility issues, including monitoring updates and changes to ensure that all content meets standards."

In chapter four, Julianne Mahler and Priscilla Regan examine federal intranet sites. Unlike the significant progress that the federal government

The Five Highest Rated State Government Websites

1. California
2. North Dakota
3. Maine
4. North Carolina
5. Pennsylvania

From Gant and Gant, Chapter Three

has made in developing and enhancing public websites for use by citizens, the federal government is lagging in the development of intranets for their own employees. They found that intranets did not receive the same level of attention and resources within their organizations as did their Internet siblings. Based on their case studies of five federal departments and agencies, Mahler and Regan conclude:

> Within federal agencies, more attention and energy is devoted to the agency's public access website than to its intranet. This is not remarkable given legislative and public support for online Government to Citizen interactions, the federal government's commitment to digital government, and the number of Internet champions both inside and outside the federal establishment.

Thus, the increased use of Government to Employee (G2E) initiatives is another e-government challenge confronting the federal government. While the federal government has made great strides in improving its ability and capacity to deliver online services to the American people via the Internet, as described by Stowers in chapter two, it appears that the federal government's use of intranets is not yet delivering a full portfolio of services to its own employees. The Mahler and Regan case studies in chapter four indicate that the federal government is providing limited online services to employees. Most departments and agencies examined provide information such as employee benefits online, but have developed only limited transaction capabilities. In addition to providing a series of findings from their research, Professors Mahler and Regan offer recommendations on actions that federal departments and agencies can take to more fully utilize the potential of intranets to improve services to their employees.

Five Ways to Improve State Government Websites

1. Emphasize customer service
2. Organize services by event rather than department
3. Allow for customization
4. Recognize the diversity of portal audiences
5. Include features that enhance the legitimacy of the portal

From Gant and Gant, Chapter Three

How Is E-Government Being Deployed?

In assessing the state of e-government today, it is important to examine e-government in action to see exactly how it is deployed by government agencies to improve the delivery of services to both citizens and its own employees. In chapter five, Barry Fulton presents 12 case studies of how the State Department is now using e-government technology as a crucial tool in enabling government managers to do their jobs more effectively and efficiently. Technology, according to Fulton, is not an end in itself but a tool for dramatically improving the performance of government activities.

There is an important lesson to be gleaned from chapter five. In analyzing the 12 State Department case studies, Fulton found that technology innovation occurred when technology executives and program managers forged close working relationships to implement a new e-government technology to improve the delivery of services. Thus, users were intricately involved in the development and implementation of the technology. The innovation did not occur when technology staff "pushed" a given technological initiative to program managers. It occurred by both groups working closely together to brainstorm on how a technology could respond to a specific problem or program need. Fulton writes:

> ... the most important lesson [from the 12 examples] is the need to ensure a close alignment between the user community and IT developers. The closest possible relation results when the two communities substantially overlap. Most of the innovations came from users who *also* have expertise in information technology. The most compelling example is from the Verification and Compliance Bureau, where senior IT staffers are required to be expert in arms control negotiations as a complement to their IT skills. Among the 12 examples, there is not a single case to be made for the separation of policy and IT competence.

M. Jae Moon in chapter six provides a specific illustration of both the use and potential of e-government in the public sector. Moon examines how state governments are using electronic means to improve the efficiency and effectiveness of their procurement activities. Based on a series of surveys over time, Moon concludes that state governments are increasing their use of e-procurement, specifically in the areas of posting solicitations and bids on the web, posting contract award information, electronic ordering, and the use of purchase cards. Particularly significant is the increase in the number of states that have passed legislation approving the use of digital signatures. Yet Moon concludes that e-procurement remains a promising alternative rather than an "instant panacea."

While Moon found that e-procurement initiatives provide significant potential for cost savings in contracting and purchasing, there are clear challenges to overcome in further implementing e-procurement in state government. While the early years of e-government saw many examples of "low-hanging fruit" in applying technology to the processes of government, such as procurement, the next set of challenges lie in developing responses to the many technical, financial, legal, and managerial issues raised by new ways of doing businesses. Moon concludes that state governments face the considerable challenge of finding the financial resources required to develop e-procurement systems. He recommends that state governments develop alternative strategic funding mechanisms for their e-procurement initiatives. These funding assessments should be based on the state government's financial condition, the projected number and amount of e-procurement transactions, as well as cost-efficiency and public-accountability considerations.

While these problems clearly can be overcome, it will require commitment and the development of innovative solutions to overcome many of the challenges. It will also require much technical expertise on the part of the government. Moon recommends, "State governments should develop and maintain technical personnel, in-house or contractual, who can manage automated procurement and administer statewide procurement transactions and related data."

In chapter seven, Robert Done also addresses the technological, legal, and social issues confronting government as it continues to move toward greater use of technology and the Internet. Done describes the use of Internet voting in the 2000 Arizona Democratic presidential primary election. By allowing voting over the Internet, the number of those voting increased dramatically from 12,884 in 1996 to 86,907 in 2000. Nearly 40,000 votes were cast via the Internet. Based on a survey of Arizona residents following the election, Done reports that both voter registration and voter participation is likely to increase with Internet voting. In addition to easing voter registration and increasing voter participation, Done reports that Internet voting could also improve the efficiency and effectiveness of elections.

Yet, there are clearly many issues to be resolved prior to expanding the use of Internet voting nationwide. On the technology front, Done concludes that while the technical issues are not likely to be insurmountable, they are significant. Done writes, "Under current technological conditions, remote Internet voting would create the greatest risk to the security and secrecy of votes, while kiosk and poll site Internet voting would create less risk with monitoring. Servers may be vulnerable to sophisticated viruses or simplistic denial of service attack." Equally challenging are the legal issues. While the Arizona election withstood legal challenges to that specific election, expansion of Internet voting is likely to face future legal challenges.

Internet voting during the 2000 Arizona presidential primary clearly succeeded. Done writes:

> The Internet was successfully used as a voting technology in the 2000 Arizona Democratic presidential preference election. This success was due in part to the considerable effort invested in voter outreach and education, and similar efforts would be important in future elections that include Internet voting. The Internet voting servers experienced no breach of security and only minimal downtime. The original goal of the Internet voting, voter participation, was clearly achieved.

Done recommends that state and local jurisdictions continue to experiment with Internet voting. Ideal candidates for experimentation would be local elections of limited scope, such as elections for school boards and city council members. Done also recommends that research continue on increasing Internet transaction security for elections.

What Are the Major Challenges Facing E-Government?

As seen in the case studies of e-procurement and Internet voting, there are significant challenges confronting the public sector as it moves to e-government. In chapter eight, Craig Johnson addresses a major challenge facing governments in moving faster toward an expansion of e-government activities: the financing and pricing of e-services. This is clearly a new frontier for government. Traditionally, government has relied primarily on appropriated funds. Johnson recommends that governments move to a new Internet model of funding based on the public sector's experience with infrastructure financing. He argues that web portal projects should be viewed as capital projects requiring *capital investments.* This will clearly require a dramatically new framework in which to view government websites and e-government in general. Further, Johnson recommends that websites be viewed as long-term investments that require long-term strategies for financing them.

It is clear from chapter eight that new ways of doing business will be required to fully implement e-government. Johnson found that few states conducted cost-benefit studies prior to undertaking the development of websites. While some states have experimented with the concept of "self-funded" or "vendor-financed" portals, Johnson concludes that government needs more experience in working with these new funding arrangements. Similarly, more experience is needed with "user charges" as an appropriate form of charging for certain portal services. There is also the potential, concludes Johnson, of government actually generating revenue from its online transactions.

A second major challenge facing government at all levels—federal, state, and local—is the challenge of information security. In chapter nine, Don Heiman presents a summary of a recent conference on security and critical infrastructure protection sponsored by the National Association of State Chief Information Officers (NASCIO). Heiman argues that the concept of security is clearly about more than just information technology. He also argues that IT governance should be a critical responsibility for the heads of government entities and should include all key stakeholders.

A third challenge for e-government is the adoption of new technologies. A prime example of such technology is wireless and mobile technologies. In chapter 10, Ai-Mei Chang and P. K. Kannan describe the potential of the third generation of wireless and mobile technologies. Chang and Kannan write, "With the advent of third generation (3G) wireless networks and broadband in the near future, wireless devices can be content rich, enabling transmittal of content-rich graphics, video, and other information at speeds up to 2Mbps." Given these expanded capabilities, Chang and Kannan argue that government must now begin to explore ways in which it can utilize wireless and mobile technologies to enhance the delivery of e-government both to government's own employees and to citizens.

What's Ahead for E-Government?

It is now appropriate to begin thinking about what themes are likely to be raised in *E-Government 2005*. The "early years" of e-government were characterized by the creation of websites that initially were designed to provide information to citizens about government activities and then began to provide an increased number of transactions that customers could undertake via the web. E-government focused on the application of information technology by individual agencies to a wide range of government functions.

However, it reinforced the existing structures and operations of government. Both *E-Government 2001* and *E-Government 2003* captured these important developments.

In *E-Government 2005,* we anticipate seeing a major emphasis on e-governance. While e-government focuses primarily on providing information and transaction-type services to "customers" of government, e-governance will likely focus increasingly on the public in its role as citizen. E-governance focuses on both modernizing and transforming government and developing a series of citizen-centric reforms. Innovative ways to engage and dialogue with citizens on the development of public policy will be tested. For example, the federal government is already using the web to enable citizens from across the nation to comment on government regulations via the web. New ways for government to dialogue with citizens will also be tested. Online polling at sites such as vote.com is likely to increase.

New ways—via the web—to make government more transparent will also be tested and implemented. By making information about government performance more accessible and transparent, the accountability of government to citizens will be dramatically altered and hopefully enhanced. The Council for Excellence in Government 2002 Hart-Teeter poll of citizen attitudes toward e-government found that making government more accountable was Americans' biggest hope for e-government. The survey also found that "Americans' belief in e-government's ability to improve government accountability has grown stronger over the past year—62 percent now say that e-government will make government more accountable, compared with 54 percent who said so a year ago." (Council for Excellence in Government)

The movement toward e-governance will include increased experiments in e-democracy. Robert Done in chapter seven describes the beginning of the movement toward voting on the Internet. Future developments in e-democracy also will likely see new ways for citizens to engage elected officeholders and to participate in the political process.

Finally, *E-Government 2005* hopefully will include case studies of how e-government has dramatically transformed public sector organizations. This transformation will likely be characterized by the increased use of new technologies and new ways of collaboration.

Thus, *E-Government 2005* will likely cover both the continued development of e-government to provide an increased number of opportunities for customers to undertake real transactions on the web and the expansion of e-governance as new ways are created for citizens to dialogue and participate in the nation's political process. We look forward to continuing to document and better understand these trends.

Bibliography

Abramson, Mark and Grady Means, *E-Government 2001* (Lanham, Md.: Rowman and Littlefield), 2001.

Council for Excellence in Government, *E-Government: To Connect, Protect and Serve Us* (Washington, D.C.: Council for Excellence in Government), 2001. (Available on the Council's website: http://www.excelgov.org/publication/polls.htm)

PART II

Government on the Web

CHAPTER TWO

The State of Federal Websites: The Pursuit of Excellence

Genie N. L. Stowers
Director and Professor
Public Administration Program
San Francisco State University

This report was originally published in July 2002.

The Federal Government on the Web

Introduction

This chapter provides an overview of federal e-government efforts, specifically elements of excellence in the websites that form the backbone of electronic government, or e-government. The top providers of those elements—including services, user help, service navigation tools, information architecture, legitimacy features, and accessibility—are described. Federal websites were examined for the prevalence of these features across 148 federal executive, legislative, and judicial sites with their own domain names. The federal megaportal, FirstGov.gov, was also examined, and then the top 12 federal government websites were identified.

The federal government has made great strides in providing e-government to its citizens in the past five years. In particular, the policy and regulatory framework in support of e-government has been expanding.

The Framework of Support

The following acts and policy initiatives, described in the order in which they were passed or promulgated, make up this framework.[1]

The **Clinger-Cohen Act of 1996** required the General Services Administration to provide online access to some kinds of information; in creating the office of chief information officer (CIO), the act also established the kind of leadership vehicle needed for sustained action, such as creating e-government and new agency websites.

A ***Framework for Global Electronic Commerce,*** issued by the Clinton administration in July 1997, provided strong policy support and impetus for the use of e-commerce by the federal government. Among other statements, this was followed by the National Defense Authorization Act for Fiscal Year 1999, discussed below.

The **Government Paperwork Elimination Act of 1998** (GPEA) instructed agencies, by October 2003, to allow (where practical) electronic maintenance, submission, and disclosure of information (this includes using electronic signatures). This act has played a critically important role in federal e-government, although it is possible that societal and governmental trends would have attained the same results, regardless. An effort by the U.S. General Accounting Office to determine, from early implementation plans, the progress being made suggested the following: "... although much potentially useful information was submitted in the October 2000 implementation plans, many omissions and inconsistencies were evident. Because electronic options for large numbers of activities were not planned until 2003 at the earliest or were not scheduled at all, many agencies may be at risk of not meeting GPEA objectives. Without more complete information collected in an integrated manner, agency progress in achieving GPEA's goals cannot be accurately assessed."[2]

The **National Defense Authorization Act for Fiscal Year 1999** required the Department of Defense to create a single electronic mall system for procurement purposes. This has had a profound impact on e-commerce applications like the Defense E-Mall—and on e-procurement in general.

The **Presidential Memorandum on Electronic Government** (December 17, 1999) established the parameters and goals of e-government, including providing one-stop access to government services. This provided the impetus for the FirstGov portal site.

The **Electronic Signatures in Global and National Commerce Act of 2000** (ESIGN) ensures that digital signatures (crucial for the expansion of e-commerce efforts) will be recognized as legal across all 50 states.

Together with the great efforts by federal employees and vendors, these policy initiatives have created a framework for today's results—the FirstGov portal and the 20,000 federal websites that currently exist. Much progress has been achieved.

A 2000 study on providing access for consumer complaints found that 90 percent of the 32 agencies studied used only a list of agencies' phone numbers and addresses, 65.6 percent included an e-mail link for users, and only 21.9 percent had a structured complaint form that could be used for complaints.[3] A January 2001 study surveyed 1,371 federal e-government initiatives. Of those, 809 dealt only with information dissemination, 88 had forms only, 460 included online transactions of some sort, and 56 encouraged transformation. Forty-one percent of these initiatives were government to citizen (G2C); the rest were roughly equally distributed (22.9 percent to 25.7 percent each) between government to employee (G2E), government to government (G2G), and government to business (G2B).[4] Also in 2001, West suggested that federal (along with state) sites had made good progress between 2000 and 2001 and that the federal government's sites, in general, provided more information and services than did their state counterparts.[5]

In February 2002, the Bush administration announced an e-government strategy that focused on 24 separate initiatives with 1,000 intragovernment and 5,600 government to business (G2B), government to government (G2G), and government to citizen (G2C) transactions to be put online.[6] These initiatives include a one-stop searchable database of recreation areas, online eligibility assistance, the streamlining of international trade processing, and consolidated health information. The Bush administration recognizes that spending for federal information technology will surpass $48 billion in 2002 and $52 billion in 2003; as the Clinton administration did, they are trying to focus those efforts toward goal-oriented e-government.[7] This chapter focuses on the websites themselves—the services they provide and how well they have been designed.

Challenges and Issues

Federal websites vary widely in the information they provide, the services they provide, how they provide services, and the way the sites are designed. The variations are attributable mostly to the vast differences among federal agencies, the missions that define them—and the many varied and unique issues they face. Here are some issues, challenges, and mandates federal web managers face:

- After the September 11th terrorist attacks on the World Trade Center and the Pentagon, federal web managers (as well as those of state and local governments) had to reassess the content on their sites and remove information that terrorists could use to harm the United States. In fact, even in 2000, the General Accounting Office was pointing out the potential harm in providing one site where users with damage in mind could easily access information. But those concerns have, of course, been severely heightened in light of the terrorist attacks.[8]
- After numerous hacker attacks against federal websites (FBI denial of service attacks and defacing of U.S. Senate and U.S. Department of the Interior sites, as well as others), the awareness of threats against the security of government websites was at an all-time high. Security gains importance as increased services are provided online to citizens and businesses—with potentially sensitive information being transferred across the Internet.
- The protection of citizens' and businesses' privacy is an important concern for public-sector web managers. More and more services are being conducted online, such as electronic filing of income taxes (http://www.irs.ustreas.gov/), buying stamps (http://www.usps.com/), applying for student financial aid (http://www.ed.gov/offices/OSFAP/Students/apply/express.html), replacing a Medicare card (https://s3abaca.ssa.gov/pro/imrc/imrchome.shtml), and applying for a job (http://www.usajobs.opm.gov/). All of these applications—and many, many more—require privacy and the ability to conduct secure transactions. To continue to enjoy the public's confidence, it is crucial that websites provide privacy and do not include sensitive information about private citizens, government employees, or contractors. In one instance in 2000, the U.S. Office of Management and Budget promulgated specific guidelines on the use of "cookies"[9] on the part of federal agencies to protect the privacy of individual users.

- It is very hard to tell that some federal websites are government sites because just as federal agencies differ in mission from purely public to quasi-public/quasi-private, so do their websites. The Amtrak, or National Railroad Passenger Corporation, site (http://www.amtrak.com/) and the site for the U.S. Postal Service (http://www.usps.gov/ and http://www.usps.com/), which even has both a .gov and a .com address, appear very unlike other public-sector websites and very like any other private-sector e-commerce sites. In terms of web design and management, this means, first, many models from which to choose, and, second, that all cannot be designed alike, even when they still have issues like privacy and security with which to deal.
- Federal law and policies structure web design and development to some degree. For example, sites are required to have privacy policies about issues like cookies, and they were required to make their sites accessible to individuals with disabilities (http://www.section508.gov/) by June 25, 2001.
- Federal websites (like those of other levels of government) are affected by the legal process. Several sites within the Department of the Interior were closed in early December 2001 due to a legal decision declaring that any sites containing Indian trust data had to be disconnected from the Internet. These sites were unavailable to the public for several months while this issue was resolved. (See http://www.doi.gov/indiantrust/ for more information about this controversy and its resolution.)

The issues described here illustrate just some of the complexity surrounding federal web management. Achieving excellence in providing online information and services must be seen in light of these complexities and challenges.

Providing Effective E-Government Service

Why is it important that the federal government aspire to excellence in e-government? Federal websites have to be accessible, in every sense, to individuals with varying understanding of government, computers, and the Internet. Even if individuals have access to computers and the Internet, can they effectively use what they find there? Can those without previous training and experience with government find the information they need and manipulate the system effectively enough to be on equal footing with early adopters and educated, trained individuals who came before them?

These concerns are particularly poignant for users of government websites, i.e., individuals who are seeking services from the government via technology. We already know that, in general, those who contact government tend to be middle class. The same individuals are the early adopters and have ready access to equipment and training in how to use the equipment.

This means that those without ready access already find it difficult to contact government and use services. These are also the individuals who tend to know the least about government, how government is organized, how to find information about and from government, and how to seek the correct services from government. Couple this with poorly designed websites—designed so that only those who really understand government and how it works can successfully navigate them—and another important barrier has been raised.

The Other Digital Divide

We can deem this the "other digital divide"—the gap between those who not only know how to contact government but understand enough about it to be able to sift and sort their way through a perhaps poorly designed government website—and those who not only have less access to computers and the Internet but also understand less about the agencies whose websites they are visiting. The result is another digital divide.

Bridging the divide does not mean just making computers available; it also involves making the websites easier to use—by removing barriers due to lack of experience with the Internet.[10] Designers and developers of public-sector websites must assume that those using their sites have limited training and experience and will need sites designed with usability and effective information architecture in mind. They must also consider that the design lessons developed for private sector e-commerce sites might not necessarily work for public sector sites. In fact, private sector sites have very different organizing concepts than public-sector websites have.

Removing usability barriers includes designing for important elements of public-sector website use:[11]

- Any site must deliver effective online information and services. Unless you build it, they will not come—at all.
- Effective information architecture, defined as how the information of a website is structured or organized, first presents information to the user of a website. Incorporated into this concept is the organization of the content and structure of the site, organized so that those who are unfamiliar with government can find the services and information they need—without having to understand how government agencies are structured.
- Usability and help features must ensure that users can get around the site and find what they want and what they need.

- Accessibility features must ensure that individuals with disabilities can use the site.
- Legitimacy features must ensure users' confidence in the site as well as its content and services.

The presence or absence of these features on public-sector websites can greatly affect the ability of a user to find and effectively use information and services available on the site.

Features That Bridge the Divide

These elements (online services, user help features, service navigation, site legitimacy features, and information architecture) clearly are part of any effective site. Here's how they ultimately help make e-government efforts effective.

Online Services

Providing online services to citizens, businesses, and other government employees is the most important part of an effective public-sector website. Content must be useful, generic services must be offered, and service provision mechanisms such as these must be extended consistently:

- Basic information
- Documents
- Communication with officials
- Downloadable forms
- Interactive forms
- Interactive databases
- Multimedia applications
- E-commerce applications
- Customizable content
- Mapping/GIS applications

Examples of these services include the downloadable tax forms at the Internal Revenue Service site (http://www.irs.treas.gov/), the interactive databases for government asset sales found at FedSales.gov (http://www.fedsales.gov/realpro.htm), the ability to purchase stamps online (http://shop.usps.com), and the ability to customize content on pages at MyGSA (found at http://www.gsa.gov/ or http://www.gsa.gov/Portal/common/registernewuser.jsp).

Services that are more specific to federal agencies can be provided online through the mechanisms listed above. Although other levels of government may provide them, they include specific types of federal information:

- Grant information
- Contracting/procurement information

- *Federal Register*
- Statistics
- Publications
- Employment information

Examples include the voluminous grant information available at the National Science Foundation (http://www.nsf.gov/) and the National Institutes of Health (http://www.nih.gov/), the price and other data available at the U.S. Department of Energy (http://www.energy.gov/), and the research and *Federal Register* information at the National Archives and Records Administration (http://www.nara.gov/).

User Help Features

In addition to the basic online services, governments must provide effective help so visitors to their sites can find information and services as well as their way around the website. They can do so through search engines and visible help features, including a help page, frequently asked questions (FAQs) about the site, site maps (pages that literally provide a map of the entire site), and tutorials on using the site.

Developers of public-sector websites must assume that those using their sites have limited training and experience and will need sites designed for ease of use. They must also consider that the design lessons developed for private-sector e-commerce sites might not necessarily work for public-sector sites. The 10 user help features identified and found on public-sector websites are listed in Table 2.1.

Table 2.1: User Help Features

Feature	Explanation
About the site	Link to information about the site
E-mail us	E-mail us for more information or for help with the site
FAQs	Questions frequently asked about the site
Feedback	Give us feedback about how the site works
Help	Agency-provided help with using the site
Index	Index of information, data, and agencies available on the site
Search	Facility to allow users to search the site
Site map	Visual representation of sections of the website
User tips	Helpful hints on how users can use the site
Other	Other user help features, including the use of other languages

Service Navigation Features

Designing a website for effective use also means thinking about the services, information, and other content with the user in mind—in the case of public-sector sites, citizens without in-depth knowledge of government and how it works. How can sites lead users right to the services they most want? Twenty-one possible ways of identifying useful services are listed in Table 2.2.

Accessibility Features

Accessibility features, those enabling access for individuals with disabilities, are also crucial. This is particularly true for public-sector websites, which must ensure equal access to all citizens. Accessibility features include having alternate versions of the site written in just text (and accessible with text browsers like Lynx), labeling all graphics with alternate text titles, labeling each frame clearly with text names, reducing animations, and otherwise making it easier for someone with limited vision to read information on a site.

Section 508 of the Rehabilitation Act of 1973, which was amended in 1998, required that all federal electronic and information technology be accessible to individuals with disabilities. As stated on the federal government's website dedicated to the topic:

> Inaccessible technology interferes with an individual's ability to obtain and use information quickly and easily. Section 508 was enacted to eliminate barriers in information technology, to make available new opportunities for people with disabilities, and to encourage development of technologies that will help achieve these goals. The law applies to all Federal agencies when they develop, procure, maintain, or use electronic and information technology. Under Section 508 (29 U.S.C. 794d), agencies must give disabled employees and members of the public access to information that is comparable to the access available to others.[12]

These requirements took effect June 25, 2001. Whether this standard has been achieved for a site can be determined in several ways, one being "Bobby Analysis." Bobby, a methodology developed by the Center for Applied Special Technology (CAST at http://www.cast.org/bobby/), is software that examines websites for the presence of design errors that could prevent individuals with disabilities from fully accessing the contents.

Features Adding to the Legitimacy of Websites

Finally, there are several features that serve to legitimize government websites:

- Endorsements of the site by outside parties

Table 2.2: Service Navigation Aid Features

Feature	Explanation
About	About the services available on the site
Answers a to z	Alphabetized listings of answers to questions
Calendars	Calendars of government events
Do you know/how do I … ?	List of questions organized according to major service areas from the citizen's point of view, stating "how do I do x or y?"
E-government services	Direct link from home page to all e-government services
Events	Link to information on major events
Facilities locator	Direct link to way to locate government offices
Featured link/spotlight	Many sites have featured programs or links
FOIA	Many federal sites have direct links to Freedom of Information Act information on their site
Hot topics	Link to information on what are considered currently important issues
In the news/news online/ press room	News items about the agency
Just for students/kids	Collection of links or information about the agency designed for use by children
Link to all agencies	Links to listings of all agencies
Link to contact information	Links to direct contact information
Maps	Link to maps relevant to agencies
Online public notice	Public notices are posted online
Most visited/frequently requested site	Links to or listings of the most frequently visited sites, indicating the importance of that information
Popular services/ major programs	Links to popular services or major programs
Special initiatives	Current, new, or special initiatives from the agency
Welcome	Welcoming statement from the director
What's new	Listing of new items posted on the site

- The presence of a visible security policy for the site
- A privacy policy that users can read and that informs users of the degree to which their privacy will be respected
- Disclaimer statements that inform users of the exact nature of the information available on the site—what is the product of the agency involved, what is not, and what other information is available through links
- Contact information so users know exactly how to ask the agency questions the site does not address
- The date the site was last updated, which tells users how current the contents are

Information Architecture Features

The information architecture[13] for a website organizes and labels information, particularly on the home page, or splash page. For government agencies, this is important because not all citizens have a good working knowledge of how government agencies are organized. A traditional method of organizing by the agencies in a department is not effective for all users. Table 2.3 briefly defines 11 types of information architecture for gov-

Table 2.3: Types of Information Architecture

Type of Information Architecture	Description of Site Organization
Audience/market	The needs of particular audiences or markets (for example, Firstgov.gov has information organized around online services for citizens, for businesses, and for governments)
Agencies/departments	Listings of agencies or departments
Branch of government	The various branches of government represented
Events	Events occurring in the life cycle of the agency
Metaphor	According to some metaphor
Officials	The main officials in the agency
Services/tasks/functions/processes	The services, tasks, or functions offered by the agency
Topics/issues	Various topics; often just miscellaneous listings of topics
Personalized/customizable	Customizable site; users can organize the site according to their own preferences, within certain limits
Newspaper listing	Listings of news items; newspaper-like in appearance
Hybrid site	Combinations of all of the above

ernment websites, including being organized like a newspaper, according to the services provided by agencies, and according to the needs of individual audiences and clienteles of particular agencies.

Evaluating Features on Federal Websites

All 148 federal websites were examined to determine which utilize desirable features and which do not. They were examined for the presence or absence of each of these features: online services, user help, service navigation, legitimacy, and degree of accessibility. The components of these features were identified for this project, their presence or absence on federal websites was coded, and some basic analysis was conducted. (See the Appendix for a detailed description of the methodology employed for this study.)

Figure 2.1 reveals the prevalence of numerous types of generic online services and of specific services that utilize numerous service delivery mechanisms. Clearly, basic information is the most prevalent (100 percent), followed by the provision of documents (95.3 percent) and communication with officials (85.8 percent). The more sophisticated and interactive mapping applications, customizable content, and e-commerce applications were the least seldom offered online services (2.7, 9.5, and 12.8 percent, respectively).

Of the specific services, employment information (85.1 percent) and publications (81.1 percent) were the two most widely found on federal websites. Information on grants (29.1 percent) and the *Federal Register* (33.8 percent) were found the least of the specific services.

Three user help features (Figure 2.2) were found in more than 50 percent of all federal websites: site-based search engines (89.9 percent), requests to "e-mail us" for assistance (66.2 percent), and site maps (52 percent). Frequently asked questions (FAQs) were included in approximately one-third and site indices were found in one-quarter of all websites; both of these features help users find agency services. Very few sites included user tips (2 percent).

Seven navigation aids to online services were found on at least 25 percent of all federal websites, indicating some convergence of these features across sites (Figure 2.3). They were the in-the-news feature (64.2 percent), about-the-site description (54.7 percent), the federal-only relevant FOIA information (52 percent), what's new (44.6 percent), links to agencies (38.5 percent), links to contact information (35.8 percent), and the just-for-kids feature (28.4 percent).

At least nine aids identified on public-sector sites were found infrequently, i.e., on less than 10 percent of all sites. These include online public

Figure 2.1: Online Services Provided by Federal Websites

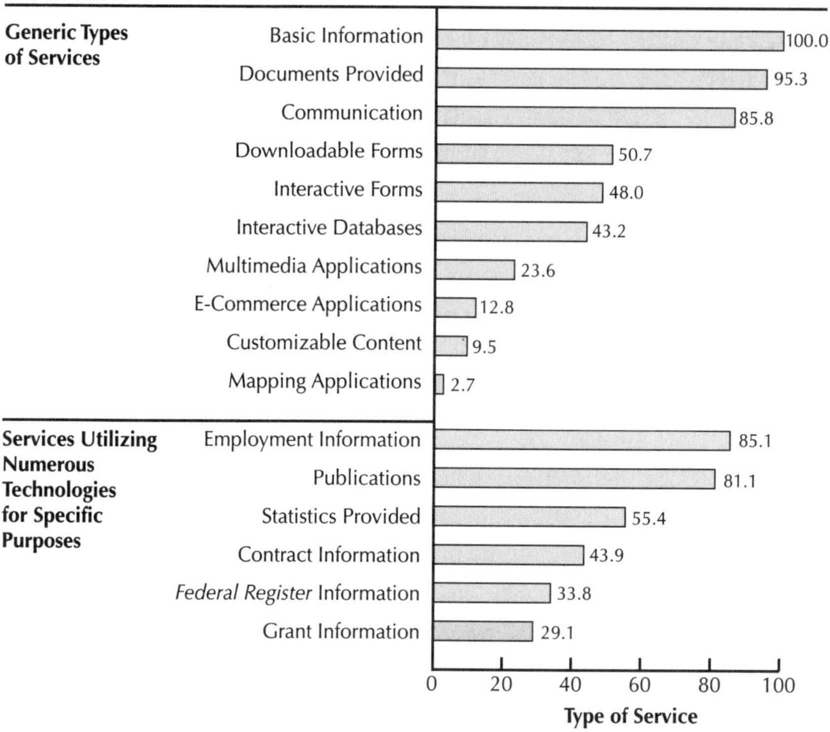

Figure 2.2: User Help Features Provided on Federal Websites

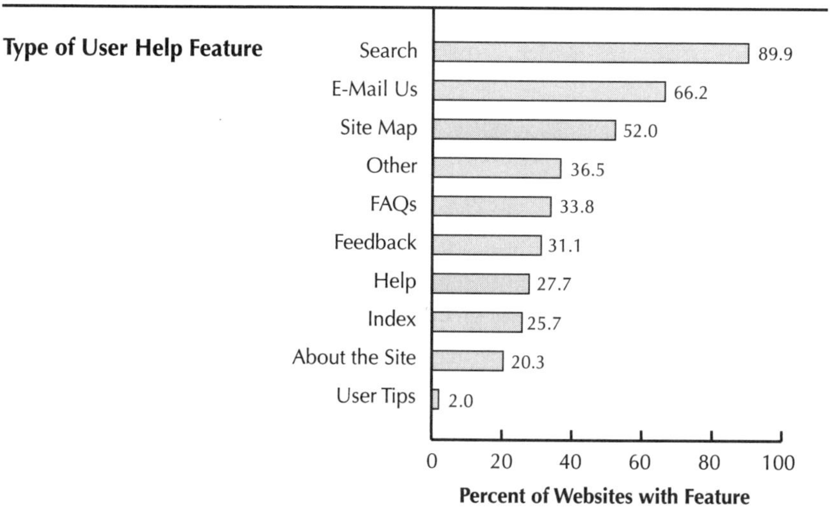

Figure 2.3: Service Navigation Aids on Federal Websites

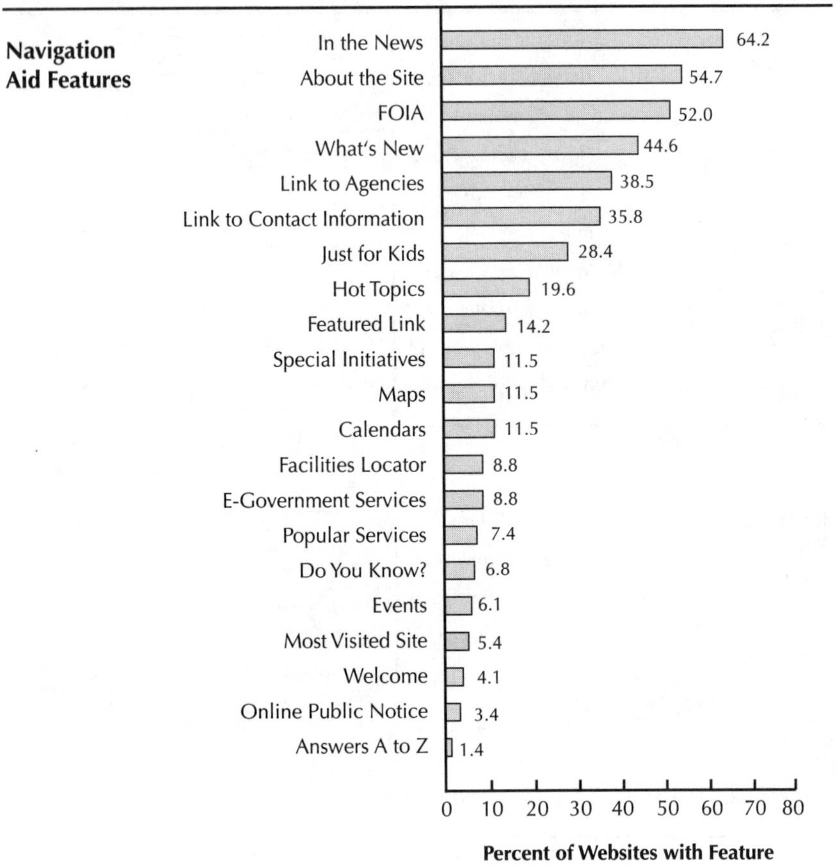

notices, welcome to the site, most visited sites, events, do-you-know?, links to popular services, direct links to all e-government services, answers a to z, and facilities locators.

Federal sites used legitimacy features consistently (Figure 2.4). Virtually all the websites (93.2 percent) had incorporated some kind of privacy policy; this comes as no surprise, given the emphasis placed on privacy by the Office of Management and Budget. A very high proportion of sites also had visible contact information (78.4 percent). A smaller proportion had a visible date when the site was last updated (43.9 percent), disclaimer statements (30.4 percent), or security policies (22.3). Hardly any sites (6.8 percent) had third-party endorsements, another indicator of site legitimacy.

Figure 2.4: Features on Federal Websites Contributing to Their Legitimacy

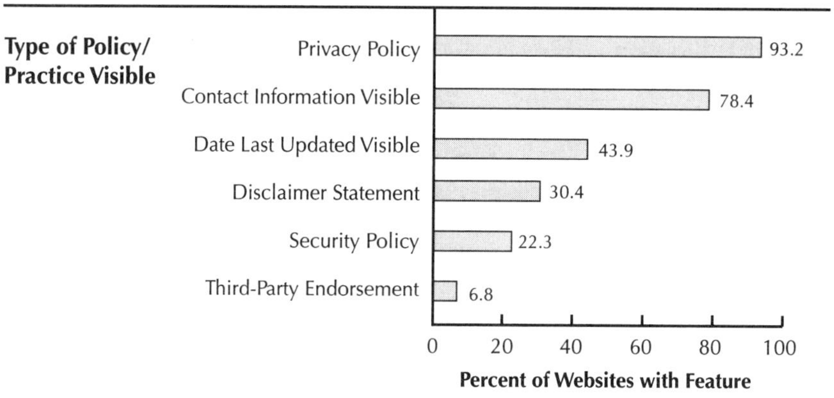

Figure 2.5: Number of Accessibility ("Bobby Analysis") Errors

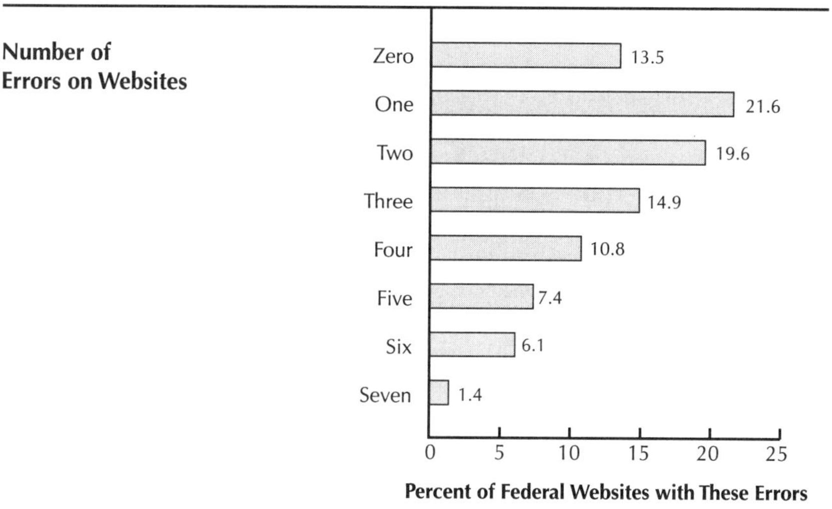

The Bobby Analysis of the accessibility of federal websites (Figure 2.5) revealed that only 13.5 percent of the 148 sites had zero errors, indicating that they could be considered "Bobby approved." Fifty-six percent of the sites had between one and three errors; many of these errors were simply the failure to provide text labels to all graphics and, when using frames, not labeling each frame with a text label. Twenty-five percent had between four and seven errors. Given that all federal sites were supposed to have

Figure 2.6: Federal Usage of Types of Information Architecture

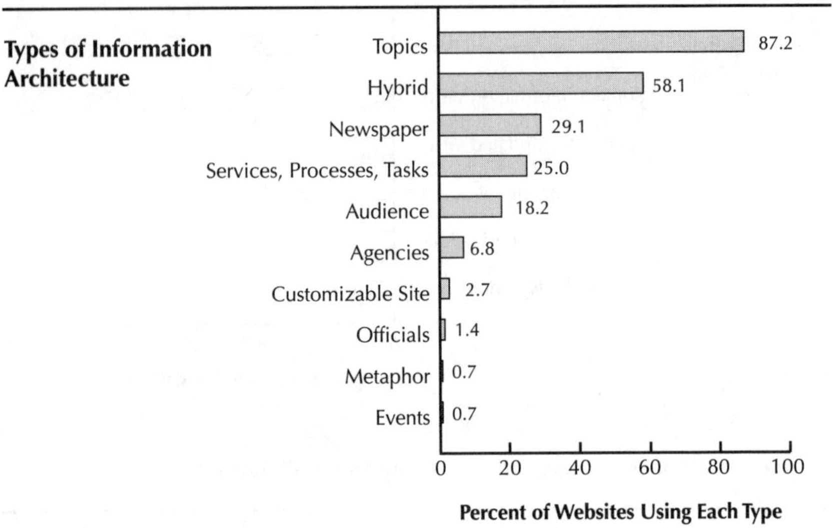

complied with Section 508 of the Rehabilitation Act of 1973 by June 25, 2001, this is a surprising finding.

A previous analysis in August 2000 by the U.S. Department of Justice, Civil Rights Division, indicated some progress between 2000 and 2002, although many of the same errors (lack of text labels for graphics) were still being made after the June 2001 deadline and up to 2002.[14]

Thoughtful information architecture on federal websites is very limited and consists largely of combinations and listings of various relevant topics with little regard to overall organization and structure (Figure 2.6). Practically 90 percent of all sites had only some type of topic listing (87.2 percent); 58.1 percent were hybrid combinations of various other types of information organization and architecture. Another 29.1 percent used a newspaper-type presentation of recent information and announcements. Only 25 percent used an organization that revolved around the actual services provided to help users find those services, or an audience-oriented structure (18.2 percent), which lists services based on the interests or needs of each type of agency clientele. These last two, arguably, are organized best for usability by the nonsophisticated in that they are structured according to users' understanding of government services rather than agency preferences.

Federal Websites Rated for Excellence

All the preceding elements were compared among the 148 federal websites and then combined into additive indices. Based on their excellence scores, the top five federal websites are presented below. Due to its immense influence as the federal portal, the FirstGov.gov site is described first. The methodology for determining the top sites is found in the Appendix.

The Portal Site: FirstGov.Gov

FirstGov, the federal megaportal, deserves special mention in any discussion of excellence in federal e-government (Figure 2.7). FirstGov became operational in September 2000 as a result of a presidential memorandum asking that access to government information be organized by type of service, not by agency.[15] The General Services Administration manages the site.

Recently redesigned, FirstGov serves as an efficient, effective gateway into the full range of federal information and services (according to the

Figure 2.7: FirstGov, the Federal MegaPortal (www.firstgov.com)

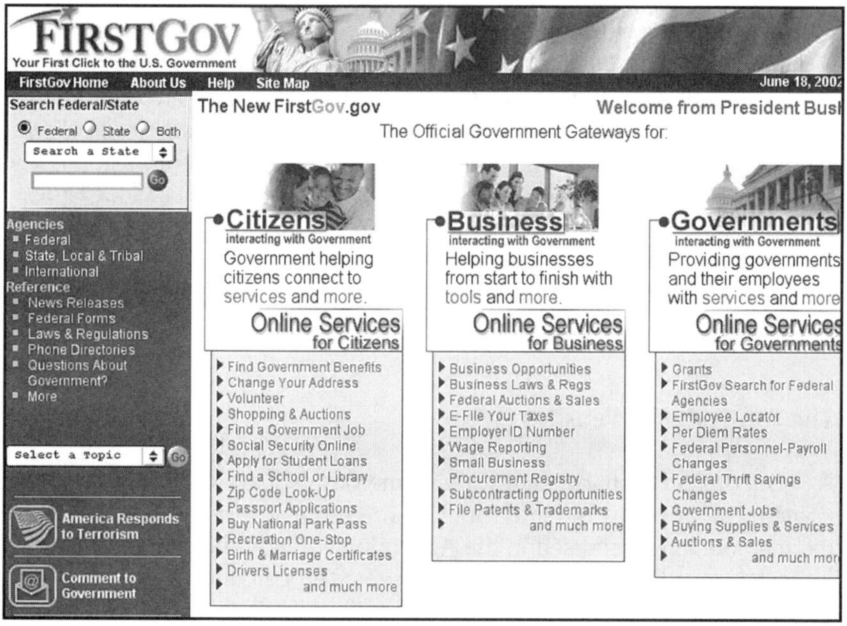

site, a full 51 million pages and 2,000 websites of information). And, complying with its mandate, the site organizes its information according to audience—online services for citizens, for businesses, and for governments—to help users who are unfamiliar with the site navigate according to their own interests and needs rather than those of the designers. Three main components make up FirstGov: the user interface, making it easy for users to find information; the database of federal web pages; and the search engine itself.

The user interface to FirstGov provides immediate access to the search engine, which is prominently displayed at the top of the site; users can search federal or state sites or both. The sidebar navigation structure features links to alphabetically listed agencies and basic references—news releases, forms, laws and regulations, phone directories, and questions about governments.

The site managers have made special efforts to gain citizens' input and to allow citizens to tailor the site to their own interests. A topical section includes a featured link to what appears to be a comprehensive compilation of how America responds to terrorism, covering everything from travel tips to benefits and assistance for victims, anthrax- and biochemical-related precautions, and terrorism training.

Strongly citizen focused, the site has a good comment-to-government section containing direct e-mail links to officials and a customer survey. Users can also customize access to e-mail newsletters on 23 topics (everything from a general FirstGov newsletter to newsletters on travel and tourism, government sales, and health care, as well as one for students).

The FirstGov office is undertaking several other initiatives. Working with the CIO Council's E-Government Subcommittee, they are coordinating a series of cross-agency portals. Currently, three are available: FedForms (http://www.fedforms.gov/), FirstGov for Seniors (http://seniors.gov/), and Students.gov (http://www.students.gov/). Others in development include FirstGov for kids (http://kids.gov/) and Disability Direct.gov (http://disabilities.gov/).

This site merits special consideration—not just because it is the gateway to federal information—but because of its thoughtful and effective design and content.

The Top Federal Websites

Once past FirstGov, there are numerous federal sites with excellent content, services, and user assistance. The top five, identified by means of the methodology discussed in the Appendix, are listed below, and Table 2.4 indicates an additional seven top websites. The calculation of total scores yielded several ties. While the ties were broken in terms of ranking the number of services, they did mean that instead of the top 10, the study

Table 2.4: Top Federal Websites

Rank	Website	Web Address	Total Excellence Score	Services	Help Features	Navigation	Legitimacy	Accessibility
1	U.S. Patent and Trademark Office	www.uspto.gov	31	10	7	10	5	-1
2	Health and Human Services	www.os.dhhs.gov	30	12	5	10	4	-1
3	Education	www.ed.gov	28	15	7	3	3	0
4	Treasury	www.ustreas.gov	28	13	5	6	4	0
5	Navy	www.navy.mil	28	12	6	7	4	-1
6	Agriculture	www.usda.gov	28	12	5	8	4	-1
7	Mine Safety and Health Administration	www.msha.gov	28	11	6	8	3	0
8	Indian Health Service	www.ihs.gov	27	12	5	8	3	-1
9	Veterans Affairs	www.va.gov	27	11	4	7	6	-1
10	Defense	www.defenselink.mil	26	11	6	5	5	-1
11	Small Business Administration	www.sbaonline.sba.gov	26	11	5	7	3	0
12	Railroad Retirement Board	www.rrb.gov	26	9	6	9	3	-1

named the top 12 sites. The top five sites, ranked in order of their total excellence scores, are:

- U.S. Patent and Trademark Office
- U.S. Department of Health and Human Services
- U.S. Department of Education
- U.S. Department of the Treasury
- U.S. Department of the Navy

First: U.S. Patent and Trademark Office

The U.S. Patent and Trademark Office (http://www.uspto.gov/) ranks as the top federal website in terms of services, user help, navigation, legitimacy, and accessibility. It provides a vast amount of useful content and a comprehensive set of aids to the user—all designed with the user in mind (Figure 2.8).

Site Services

Numerous services are available, including how to complete certain tasks (e.g., how to apply for a patent, http://www.uspto.gov/web/patents/howtopat.htm) and extensive information and resource listings about other aspects of the patent and trademark process. The site contains numerous searchable databases (existing patents and trademarks, published patent applications, patent and trademark applications) and even allows users to apply online for patents and trademarks (through the Electronic Filing System for patents, http://www.uspto.gov/ebc/efs/index.html, and the Trademark Electronic Application System, http://www.uspto.gov/teas/index.html). Through an e-commerce application, consumers can purchase

Scores for the U.S. Patent and Trademark Office

Rank	1
Web Address	http://www.uspto.gov
Services Score	10
User Help Features Score	7
Services Navigation Score	10
Site Legitimacy Score	5
Accessibility Score	-1
Total Excellence Score	**31**

Figure 2.8: The U.S. Patent and Trademark Office Home Page (www.uspto.gov)

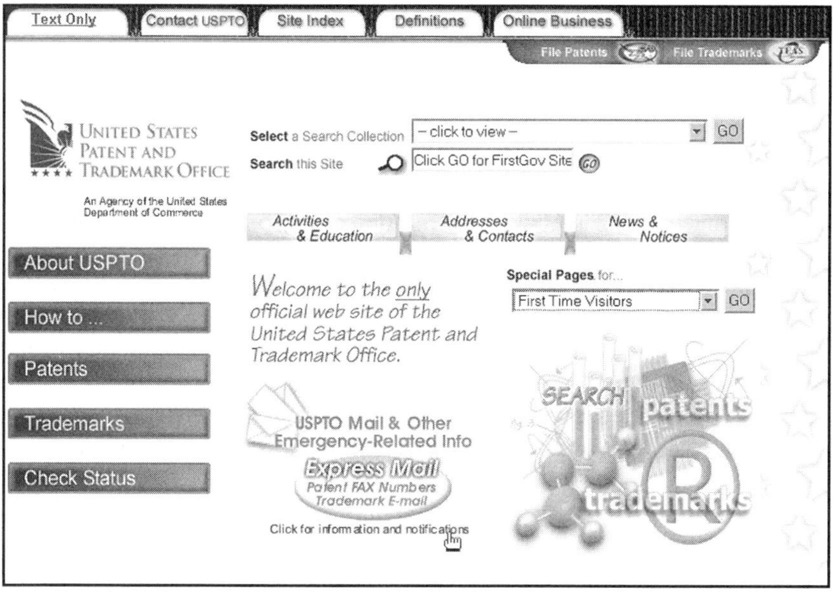

patent and trademark documents online (https://www3.uspto.gov/oems25p/index.html). After applying for patents or trademarks, users can check the status of their applications through the Office website (http://www.uspto.gov/teas/index.html).

The Director's Dialogues are another sign that this agency focuses strongly on their constituents. From reading these dialogues—transcripts of online discussions between high-level managers and the public—it is clear that these sessions, when happening in real time, enable citizens to get questions answered and government officials to have meaningful contact with the public.

Other interesting services include the Inventive Thinking Curriculum Project, curricular ideas for students on topics of invention, brainstorming, and innovative achievement. This section also includes a primer on patent, trademark, and copyright issues.

These Patent and Trademark Office services, very consumer and constituency driven, are immensely important to those interested in this area.

Usability, Accessibility, and Legitimacy

From a user's perspective, the U.S Patent and Trademark Office website is designed well. Users can choose from several means of finding information—a series of drop-down menus organized by perspective (the Special

Pages section, which includes everything from first-time visitors to vendors); the Search Collection drop-down menu (to search everything from patents to public comments to job announcements); or searching the entire site. They can also utilize the menu navigation system, which includes About USPTO, How To, Patents, Trademark, and Check Status. Three additional icons in the center of the splash page lead to Activities and Education (Director's Dialogues, Kids' Pages), Addresses and Contacts, and News and Notices. Five navigation tabs at the top of the page link to the text version of the site, to a site index, and to online business opportunities. One other helpful feature is a direct (and obvious) link from the splash page to contact information, mail, and other emergency-related information.

However, the site was not totally accessible, although a completely text-based version was clearly available by clicking an icon at the top of the screen. The site contained three accessibility errors, and the drop-down menus could cause accessibility concerns. The site has the second highest score possible for legitimacy, including privacy and security policies, contact information, the date last changed, and a disclaimer.

Overall, the site is filled with innovative content and services and with well-designed navigation and user help systems. Oriented toward the agency's multiple audiences and constituencies, it provides well-thought-out services for each.

Second: U.S. Department of Health and Human Services

Ranked second highest, the Department of Health and Human Services (http://www.hhs.gov/) offers useful information to multiple users with varying needs (Figure 2.9).

Scores for the U.S. Department of Health and Human Services

Rank	2
Web Address	http://www.os.dhhs.gov
Services Score	12
User Help Features Score	5
Services Navigation Score	10
Site Legitimacy Score	4
Accessibility Score	-1
Total Excellence Score	**30**

Figure 2.9: The U.S. Department of Health and Human Services Home Page (www.os.dhhs.gov)

Site Services

The site provides enormous amounts of information and types of services for many types of users. Each individual agency provides lots of information about services, grants, jobs, and resources (http://www.hhs.gov/agencies/). One useful service is GrantsNet (http://www.hhs.gov/grantsnet/), an Internet application designed by the Department of Health and Human Services to help those needing information about grant opportunities. A graphic approach is used to describe this process (Electronic Roadmap for Grants, http://www.hhs.gov/grantsnet/roadmap/index.html), which leads to information about funding opportunities, the application process, managing grants, and useful resources.

Another interesting program is KnowNet, an example of the new knowledge management trend (http://knownet.hhs.gov/). Although unfortunately fronted with a long Macromedia® Flash™ animation, the site introduces this initiative. This project seeks to provide just-in-time information and training on a variety of managerial topics electronically (Microsoft® PowerPoint presentations, online training opportunities, and other means), through several formats, including the Desk Reference Series—all available 24/7/365. As stated on their website, "KnowNet delivers reliable, timely and comprehensive information, instruction, integrated resources, collaboration capabilities, field expertise and performance support in the core business operations of the Federal Government of the United States of America 24/7. Quite simply, KnowNet is aggressively pursuing performance improvement."[16] The site also provides information on a wide variety of topics, including logistics, small businesses, and acquisition.

The Department also offers quick, handy, invaluable information to users through their 38 fact sheets, available at http://www.hhs.gov/news/facts/. Covering topics from aging to genetic testing, mad cow disease, and teen pregnancy, these sheets include statistics, data, trends, and additional resources.

Usability, Accessibility, and Legitimacy

The user-friendly site is organized with numerous help and navigation features, employing multiple modes of communicating information. Information can be accessed according to topic (such as adoption, disease prevention, Head Start, and substance abuse) from a drop-down menu, through an A-to-Z listing, and through the graphic icons available on the home page portal. In addition, a navigation icon provides a listing of the agencies that constitute the Department of Health and Human Services.

Top news items are highlighted on the home page. Special programs and events, with graphic icons, are also highlighted on the splash page—among them, high blood pressure, youth summit, organ donation, and Closing the Health Gap, a program about African-American health initiatives. The effect of all of these icons and pathways to information can overwhelm the casual user, however.

The site had a direct link to a text-based version, but because of its four accessibility errors, some design features should be reconsidered with the errors in mind. The site included a privacy policy, contact information, and the date last changed along with a disclaimer, but no security policy or endorsements.

Third: U.S. Department of Education

The Department of Education site is entered through a web portal titled No Child Left Behind (http://www.ed.gov/); users then go to the index page for the Department (http://www.ed.gov/index.jsp). This site had the highest services score of any of the sites studied as a result of offering every type of general service plus all but one of the specific types of federal services. It also contains links to numerous content areas and many user help and navigation features.

Scores for the U.S. Department of Education

Rank	3
Web Address	http://www.ed.gov
Services Score	15
User Help Features Score	7
Services Navigation Score	3
Site Legitimacy Score	3
Accessibility Score	0
Total Excellence Score	**28**

Site Services

The site organizes information well and in several ways, and individual users can create their own organization by means of the My.ED.gov portal service. Boxes throughout the splash page organize information and services into 10 categories:

- News
- Grants and contracts
- Policy
- Financial aid
- Research and statistics
- Education resources
- Education priorities
- Information for ... (various audiences of users)
- About ED (about the agency)
- My.ED.gov

Among the many resources available are the ERIC (Educational Resources Information Center) Digests, collections of research syntheses on a voluminous number of topics (http://www.ed.gov/databases/ERIC_Digests/index/). Other publications on a variety of educational and policy research topics are available throughout the site. The National Center for Educational Statistics (http://nces.ed.gov/) is a treasure trove of information for those interested in education; their database may be searched to find relevant data, most reports are available online, and statistics are easily available at EdStats at a Glance (http://nces.ed.gov/edstats/).

Usability, Accessibility, and Legitimacy

The boxes with the information in the preceding list are spread about the splash page in a somewhat confusing format because there are so many of them. Tabs at the top of the page lead to six of the topics listed above, plus the home page.

This information is organized by content (whether news, grants and contracts, financial aid, education resources, policy, or research and statistics) and by audience so that users can find what interests them (students, parents and families, teachers, principals, higher education administrators, and grantees and assistance providers). Also, users can choose among four areas of customizable content for their personal My.ED.gov page (subjects, audiences, levels of education, and resources). Once they have selected their personal preferences, a page appears with that information highlighted and it is automatically updated. Figure 2.10 illustrates a sample result.

Only two accessibility errors were found on this site. Contact information is listed on the home page, and privacy and security policies are also available.

Figure 2.10: My.ED.gov (Customizable Page from the U.S. Department of Education Website)

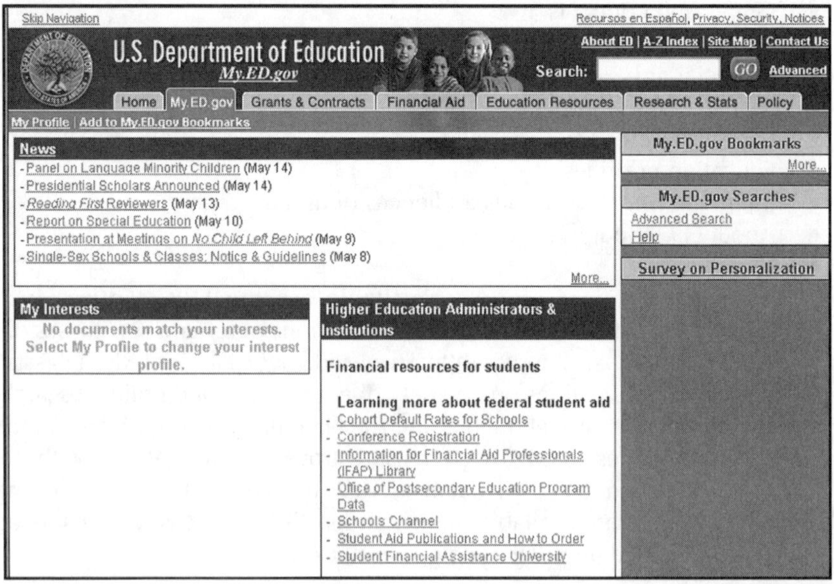

Fourth: U.S. Department of the Treasury

The Department of the Treasury site (http://www.treasury.gov/) ranked fourth among the 148 sites examined. Its deceptively simple splash page serves as the gateway to much content and information—and the second highest level of services. Recently, the site was totally redesigned with a busier splash page and better-organized content (Figure 2.11).

Site Services

Many services, particularly e-commerce services, are available. The various informational topics include current news and latest press releases, the federal budget, daily Treasury reports, statistics on the debt and financing, the war on terrorism, border protection, and the agencies within the Treasury Department.

From this site, users may buy savings bonds, T-bills, and notes through the Treasury Direct online service (or via telephone service or forms that can be downloaded from http://www.savingsbonds.gov/sec/sec.htm). Special coins and currency—like $10,000 worth of shredded U.S. currency, $1 Texas Lone Star notes, or $1 Year of the Horse notes—may be purchased through the Money Factory site (http://www.moneyfactory.gov/). Such e-commerce applications alone are a major service to consumers.

All kinds of forms can be downloaded from the Treasury Department and its multiple bureaus. Another important service for citizens is the ability to sign up for automatic e-mail notification concerning law enforcement actions, interest rate statistics, policy papers, and general press releases (http://www.ustreas.gov/ress/email/subscribe.html).

Scores for the U.S. Department of the Treasury

Rank	4
Web Address	http://www.ustreas.gov
Services Score	13
User Help Features Score	5
Services Navigation Score	6
Site Legitimacy Score	4
Accessibility Score	0
Total Excellence Score	**28**

Figure 2.11: The U.S. Department of the Treasury Home Page (www.ustreas.gov)

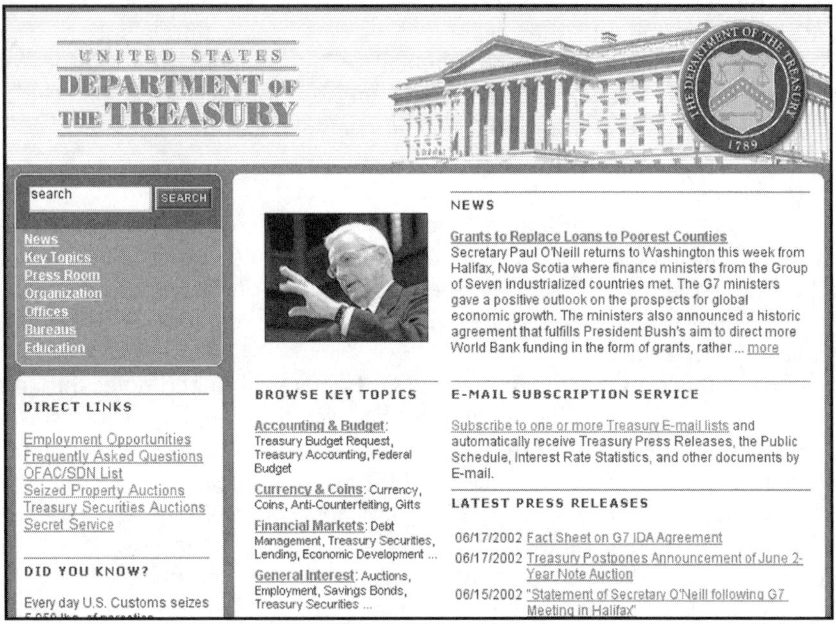

Usability, Accessibility, and Legitimacy

Users can find services and information in several ways on this site—through news on various topics, by browsing through a list of keywords (accounting and budget, currency and coins, financial markets, general interest, international, law enforcement, small business, taxes and technology), and through direct links to some services (Treasury service auctions, employment opportunities, seized property auctions, and other topics). The browse-key-topics area is quite useful, and users can always resort to the listing of agencies that is available through the navigation scheme.

The original site contained only two Bobby accessibility errors; perhaps because it was still being implemented, the redesigned site contained some basic errors, such as needing to include alternate text for all images, buttons, and frames. The site also contained a privacy policy, contact information, the date last changed, and a disclaimer.

Fifth: U.S. Department of the Navy

The very sparse splash page of the U.S. Navy website (http://www.navy.mil/) is the gateway to considerable content, user help features, and navigation features (what's new, search, site index, about this site, the Lifelines link to numerous organizational topics on military life, got a question?) as well as several interesting applications. See Figure 2.12.

Site Services

Enormous amounts of information are available here. For instance, the FactFile (http://www.chinfo.navy.mil/navpalib/factfile/ffiletop.html) and Navy Ships (http://www.chinfo.navy.mil/navpalib/ships/) provide information on the various types of missile systems, ships, submarines, and other portions of the Navy's mission, while Navy Organization (http://www.chinfo.navy.mil/navpalib/organization/org-top.html) details the organizational structure of the service. Status of the Navy (http://www.chinfo.navy.mil/navpalib/news/.www/status.html) provides up-to-date statistics on personnel, ships, and aircraft.

The site is also designed and used as an online reference source for Navy personnel and their families. An example is the All Hands Online manual (http://www.chinfo.navy.mil/navpalib/allhands/ah0197/contents.html) that includes basic information on being in the Navy.

One very useful service for military personnel and their families is the Lifelines site (http://www.lifelines2000.org/), which addresses quality of life issues. Among the vast amount of information available here are what to do when deployed, housing, legal assistance, pay and personnel, and relocation assistance, as well as links to thousands of service providers. Another section, e-courseware and games, provides games to test financial skills,

Scores for the U.S. Department of the Navy

Rank	5
Web Address	http://www.navy.mil
Services Score	12
User Help Features Score	6
Services Navigation Score	7
Site Legitimacy Score	4
Accessibility Score	-1
Total Excellence Score	**28**

Figure 2.12: The U.S. Department of the Navy Home Page (www.navy.mil)

skills for dependent children facing deployment, and skills for facing stress. A video on demand from the commandant of the U.S. Marine Corps, news reports, and other audio and video on demand are also presented. Links to ombudsman programs, numerous Navy and other military resources, daily news updates, and breaking news are also available. The section focusing on Navy careers incorporates multimedia in the guise of Macromedia Flash animations.

In the careers section is the Life Accelerator (http://www.navy.com/lifeaccelerator/index.jsp), an interesting application that uses a drop-down survey to match users' interests and goals to jobs available in the Navy. Results can be stored in a Navy "locker" along with details about particular career paths and personal information that would be needed to apply to join the Navy. A description of a pilot online training program (Task Force Excel) is also available (http://www.excel.navy.mil/).

The Navy's award-winning web application, the Virtual Naval Hospital (http://www.vnh.org/) is a well-organized health promotion tool. Its digital library of training and reference materials helps members of the service who might need medical expertise while at isolated duty stations.

Usability, Accessibility, and Legitimacy

The splash page for this site is quite simple—it begins with a graphic image of ships of several generations "slicing" through the ocean, and it lists topics on the far left of the page. The navigational scheme is not carried throughout the site, however, and the fair amount of animation and multimedia calls for the use of various plug-ins. The Navy site contained only two accessibility errors, and it stated privacy and security policies along with contact information and the date when last updated.

Overall, this is a content-rich site, designed to communicate to current employees as well as potential recruits, thereby addressing numerous constituencies. A more consistent navigation scheme would help in achieving this goal, but the overall quality cannot be ignored.

Overall Assessment

These top five sites are outstanding examples of what can be accomplished utilizing the World Wide Web as a creative means of providing services and information to citizens, businesses, and employees. The remaining top sites are also good examples of what can be achieved: (6) U.S. Department of Agriculture (www.usda.gov), (7) Mine Safety and Health Administration (www.msha.gov), (8) Indian Health Service (www.ihs.gov), (9) Department of Veterans Affairs (www.va.gov), (10) DefenseLink/ Department of Defense (www.defenselink.mil), (11) Small Business Administration (www.sbaonline.sba.gov), and (12) Railroad Retirement Board (www.rrb.gov).

Despite differing widely in approach and design, they are similar in providing outstanding content, good design, and useful user help and navigational features to citizens, businesses, and government employees. Government managers and web professionals should view them as models of effective content and services.

Recommendations

From this examination of federal websites and the lessons we have learned, we make the following recommendations:

1. Consider users' privacy and security concerns to be high priority.

The information exchanged on many federal websites is personal and confidential. Privacy and security policies, therefore, must be not only developed but clearly displayed as well. To fully meet users' needs, federal websites must create protected, private, and secure spaces for the mutual exchange of information.

2. Assure users that a website is the "real deal."

Managers and designers should communicate the legitimacy of a site by including contact information for the agency, the date the site was last updated (hopefully, a very recent date so that users know the information they are accessing is current), and the agency's policies on privacy and security. While most of the sites examined had the required privacy policy (93.5 percent), the other features were far less prevalent. Web managers need not only to make information available but to display it prominently.

3. Make accessibility an ongoing high priority.

The most surprising finding of this study was the relatively poor accessibility, according to the Bobby Analysis. Despite the mandate to comply with federal regulations by mid-2001, only 13.5 percent of the 148 sites examined had zero errors, and another 21.6 percent had one error. Even among our top five sites, only two had just one error, and the others had more than two. They continued to be counted among the top five since they had much higher scores on service delivery and on usability. The unresolved question is whether these sites adhered to the policy last year and have since "slipped" as a result of constant changes in content and design—or whether they ever complied with the requirements. Web designers and web managers need to give more attention and priority to accessibility issues, including monitoring updates and changes to ensure that all content meets standards.

4. Cultivate support by educating leadership about the Internet and its potential for public service.

Although support from leadership is essential for information technology, e-government, and web management success, managers and other leaders do not always understand the issues—or the potential—involved. Web managers and designers need to educate leaders about what is happening in these fields and how they have grown in order to cultivate support for e-government and web management initiatives in the future of public service.

5. Organize websites with the user in mind.

Web managers and designers need to organize sites for users who may know nothing about a particular government agency or its structure. Organization should therefore include ample and varied types of user help and clear navigational aids that direct users to services and specific types of information.

6. Design for content and services, not for glitz.

Federal and other public sector web managers and designers need not follow the path of many private-sector websites—high on concept and graphics and animation, low on content and services. Citizens from any audience need to be able to find their way *directly* to the appropriate services on federal websites. Rely on the audience or services information architecture approach, by the far the friendliest to users. Design for outside users, not for agency insiders.

7. Think outside of the box when considering web services and websites.

Current website development and e-government should not be reduced to an "add technology and stir" formula. Public-sector managers, web managers, and web designers have the opportunity to rethink how services should be provided. They should explore and expand their horizons—to create new applications, new ways of looking at government, and new ways of serving constituents. The potential for effective e-government is enormous, but the basics should not be forgotten as we move ahead in applying technology to deliver public-sector services.

Many federal agencies have made enormous strides in creating attractive, useful, and helpful content and services on their websites; others still face challenges in achieving the highest level of quality. The top five sites identified by this study can serve as examples for other agencies—examples of how to present information in helpful and useful ways—and, ultimately, of how to serve their users.

Appendix: Methodology and Resources

Methodology

In the research project discussed here, two reviewers conducted a cross-sectional comparison of federal websites, comparing results in order to validate their assessments.

The study included all federal websites of executive agencies (cabinet departments and agencies with their own domain names, and independent agencies), plus major legislative and judicial sites with their own domain names. Federal boards and commissions were not included, resulting in 148 federal websites. Because the period of the study, January to April 2002, unfortunately included the time during which three Department of Interior websites were offline due to legal difficulties, these sites were excluded.

Online services, user help features, navigation features, and the information architecture on each website were examined and coded as to presence or absence. The presence of online services was determined by examining the home page and links down to the third click (considered by many to be the farthest that users will go in their search for information). The presence of usability, help, navigation, and legitimacy features and information architecture was determined by examining the site's home page, the point where users need these features. Bobby Analysis (see http://www.cast.org/ for more information on this web accessibility analysis tool) was conducted on all sites, to links two levels down, to assess the degree of accessibility.

Both reviewers analyzed sites initially and later completed the same sites, in the middle and at the end of the project, for cross-comparison purposes. Then they were assigned their own to complete. The lead researcher reviewed all results to ensure validity.

To determine the highest number of "best" websites, the reviewers used four additive indices plus a scale for accessibility:

- An index of federal services (from one to 16)
- An index of help features (from one to 10)
- An index of service navigation features (one to a possible 22 features, although no site had more than 10)
- An index of legitimacy features (from one to six)
- A scale for accessibility (sites with zero errors received a +1, sites with only one or two errors received zero points, and sites with more than two errors had one point deducted from their total points, or -1

These four indices plus the scale added together yielded the total excellence score, which had a potential range from three to 55. The highest score any site received was 31.

Resources

A collection of the sites listed here and additional resources is available at http://bss.sfsu.edu/~mpa/faculty/facultyprojects/federalproject.htm.

Endnotes

1. U.S. General Accounting Office, *Electronic Government: Federal Initiatives Are Evolving Rapidly But They Face Significant Challenges,* GAO/T-AIMD/GGD-00-179 (2000). Available at http://www.gao.gov.

2. U.S. General Accounting Office, *Electronic Government: Better Information Needed on Agencies' Implementation of the Government Paperwork Elimination Act,* GAO-01-1100. (2001), 2. Available at http://www.gao.gov.

3. U.S. General Accounting Office, *Web-Based Complaint Handling,* GAO/AIMD-00-238R (2000). Available at http://www.gao.gov.

4. "Transformation" was defined as "government's taking a global focus, government involvement being minimal, and citizens not needing to know the government entity to obtain services." U.S. Government Accounting Office, *Information Technology: OMB Leadership Critical to Making Needed Enterprise Architecture and E-Government Progress,* GAO-02-389T (2002). Available at http://www.gao.gov.

5. Darrell M. West, *State and Federal E-Government in the United States* (2001). Available at http://www.InsidePolitics.org/egovt01us.html.

6. Mark Forman, "Achieving the Vision of E-Government" (2001). PowerPoint presentation. Available at http://www.egov.gov.

7. U.S. Office of Management and Budget, *E-Government Strategy: Simplified Delivery of Services to Citizens* (2002). Available at http://www.egov.gov.

8. U.S. General Accounting Office, *Electronic Government: Opportunities and Challenges Facing the FirstGov Web Gateway*, GAO-01-087T (2000). Available at http://www.gao.gov.

9. "Cookies" are defined by the General Accounting Office as "a short string of text that is sent from a Web server to a Web browser when the browser accesses a Web page." "Session cookies" last only as long as the current online session, while "persistent cookies" remain stored in the memory of a user's own computer for an indefinite period. U.S. General Accounting Office, *Internet Privacy: Implementation of Federal Guidelines for Agency Use of "Cookies,"* GAO-01-424 (2001). Available at http://www.gao.gov.

10. Jakob Nielsen, *Designing Web Usability: The Practice of Simplicity* (Indianapolis: New Riders Publishing, 2000). Louis Rosenfeld and Peter Morville, *Information Architecture for the World Wide Web* (Sebastopol, California: O'Reilly and Associates, 1998).

11. Jakob Nielsen, *Designing Web Usability: The Practice of Simplicity* (Indianapolis: New Riders Publishing, 2000). Eric L. Reiss, *Practical Information Architecture* (New York: Addison Wesley, 2000). Louis Rosenfeld and Peter Morville, *Information Architecture for the World Wide Web* (Sebastopol, California: O'Reilly and Associates, 1998).

12. Section 508.gov (2002). Available at http://www.section508.gov/index.cfm?FuseAction=Content&ID=3. More information on this topic is available at http://www.section508.gov/.

13. Defined earlier as how the information of a website is structured or organized, or how the information is first presented to the user on the website.

14. U.S. Department of Justice, *Information Technology and People with Disabilities: The Current State of Federal Accessibility* (2000). Available at http://www.usdoj.gov/crt/508/report/content.htm.

15. U.S. General Accounting Office, *Electronic Government: Opportunities and Challenges Facing the FirstGov Web Gateway,* GAO-01-087T (2000). Available at http://www.gao.gov.

16. U.S. Department of Health and Human Services, "About KnowNet" (2002). Available at http://knownet.hhs.gov/aboutKnowNet.htm.

CHAPTER THREE

Enhancing E-Service Delivery in State Government

Diana Burley Gant
Assistant Professor of Information Management
School of Information Studies, Syracuse University

Jon P. Gant
Assistant Professor of Information Management and Public Administration, Maxwell School of Citizenship and Public Affairs, Syracuse University

This report was originally published in January 2002.

Introduction

This chapter examines how state governments are using web portals to enhance electronic service (e-service) delivery. Until recently, state governments developed their web presence on an agency-by-agency basis with little tendency to develop an integrated website that linked all state resources to a central location. While this strategy allowed them to create websites quickly, it did little to serve the needs of an increasingly web-savvy public. Under growing pressure to be more responsive to citizen needs, state governments now are rethinking their web strategy and reconfiguring their existing websites into web portals.

At present, most state government portals provide basic information on state agency policies and access to a limited set of state services such as tax filing and car registration. However, as the public moves more of its daily activities online, expectations for online access to government information and services will also rise. Further, because over 167 million U.S. adults (Nielsen netRatings) from all demographic and geographic segments of the population use the Internet, state governments must simultaneously provide breadth and depth in the content they provide.

Thus, to truly serve all web constituents, state governments must build intelligent portals that include information on state policies, access to state agency services, and the ability to customize the information to meet their specific needs. It is not surprising, then, that state and local government spending on e-government initiatives totaled more than $1 billion in 2000 (*Governing Sourcebook 2001*). The challenge for policy makers and technology leaders is to find the right level of portal functionality while still maintaining fiscal responsibility.

Web Portals and E-Service Delivery: the Status of the States

The objectives of this research are to assess the level of functionality for each of the 50 U.S. state web portals and to provide a benchmark by which future developments in e-service can be judged. By combining an extensive content analysis of each of the portals with prior research on web portals, we characterize the content and structure of the portals along four dimensions: openness, customization, usability, and transparency. Taken together, these dimensions represent the key aspects of a portal's functionality.

Drawing upon prior research in e-government and discussions with key state government and technology industry officials, we identify the role that portals can and will play in e-service delivery. To illustrate how states use web portals to enhance service delivery, we discuss the five state web portals offering the most comprehensive level of e-service. These e-service leaders—

Defining Web Portal Services

A web portal serves as the integrated gateway into a state government website and provides visitors with a single point of contact for online service delivery within the state. Because portals integrate state e-service, they can improve access to government, reduce service-processing costs, and enable state agencies to provide a higher quality of service.

California, North Dakota, Maine, North Carolina, and Pennsylvania—not only provide online access to a variety of services through their portals, but they also promote open and equal access to government. These state web portals exemplify citizen-centric e-service delivery.

We then summarize key findings on the functionality of state web portals and their role in e-service delivery, and suggest recommendations for state web portal development based on these findings. Importantly, however, we must note that the findings presented in this chapter represent the status of state web portals during a single snapshot in time, during the spring of 2001. Given the ever-increasing demands of the public and the growing technological capabilities of the states, web portals remain in a constant state of development. Regardless of their current state of portal development, the findings presented here should provide some guidance for state officials as they work to deliver the highest level of e-service to their constituents.

E-Government

There has been growing interest in understanding ways in which public sector organizations can use information technology (IT), particularly applications delivered over the Internet, to improve service delivery and relationships with citizens. The search for more effective methods of delivering public services began in the early 1980s in most industrialized countries. In the United States, for example, the National Performance Review (NPR) recommended that government agencies "re-engineer government activities, making full use of computer systems and telecommunications to revolutionize how we deliver services" (NPR, 1993, p. v). The Access America Plan issued in 1997 strengthened this commitment to IT: "The NPR and Access America call for new IT-based information systems and improvements in the process by which they are managed to implement specific reforms in programs ranging from health care to law enforcement" (Heeks, ed., 2000, p. 232).

Heeks (2000) identified three main factors that have contributed to this phenomenon: (1) an unsustainable level of public expenditure that did not produce efficient public services (due to waste, delays, mismanagement, corruption, or poor organizational and management skills); (2) a resurgence of neo-liberal thinking emphasizing the efficiency of market competition and the need to make government more businesslike; and (3) the rapid development of IT and the increasing awareness of the value of information systems (IS).

Although governments use a variety of information technologies to support these initiatives, the use of integrated websites or web portals is increasingly becoming an important component of e-government. E-government refers to efforts in the public sector to use information and communication technologies to deliver government services and information to the public. E-government offers numerous possibilities to use the Internet and web-based technologies to extend government services online, allow citizens to interact more directly with government, employ customer-centric services, and transform operational and bureaucratic procedures.

The adoption of the World Wide Web by governments is the focus of a growing number of studies. Demchak, Friis, and LaPorte (2000) suggest that the adoption of the web for delivering government services will catch on rapidly as more websites are built with greater openness and effectiveness. West (2000) reports that while government organizations are adopting the web as a tool for delivering government services, government at all levels is not making full and effective use of commonly available information technology. And Hart and Teeter (2000) show that there is increasing public support for state governments to develop online government services further. These studies look at the web in general. We build on these earlier studies by focusing on the web portal and its relationship to the rest of the website for state governments and focus particularly on how web portals can be used to enhance government service delivery.

Web Portals

A web portal serves as the integrated gateway into a state government website and provides both external constituents and internal government personnel with a single point of contact for online access to state information and resources. State governments are complex organizations with hundreds of agencies, departments, commissions, and regulatory bodies. Portals are web-based front-end applications that allow state governments to access and manage all of their data and information, and to deliver it to its users. Through this gateway or main user interface, millions of web users can access the vast landscape of information, services, and applications available on state websites.

The Evolution of Web Portals

Web portals are web-based front-end applications that provide an integrated gateway into a website.

- The first wave of portals, in the early 1990s, was little more than a group of dressed-up search engines.
- The second wave of portals increased functionality by incorporating advanced search capabilities, enriched content, and increased user control.
- The third wave of portals now includes functions such as robotic crawlers that dynamically push categorized information onto the web page; tools that access integrated data from distinct enterprise applications and platforms; applications that customize website content; and communication features such as e-mail, calendars, instant messaging, and chat areas.

Since the mid-1990s, when the first portals appeared widely on the Internet, their features and functions have evolved significantly. Many refer to the first wave of portals as "dressed-up search engines." Commercial portal pioneers such as Yahoo!, Lycos, Excite, and AOL organized on a single web page a directory of interesting websites along with general interest information. These early portals matured quickly and increased their functionality by adding advanced search capabilities, enriched content, and increased user control. The latest portals do much more. Portals now have a robust collection of functions including robotic crawlers that dynamically push categorized information onto the web page; tools that access integrated data from distinct enterprise applications and platforms; applications that customize website content; and other key features such as e-mail, calendars, instant messaging, and chat areas.

Given the extraordinary potential for integrated, customized information delivery, portals are now being used by private sector firms, nonprofit organizations, and governmental agencies. In fact, governmentwide web portals are emerging as a key priority for government agencies as they develop their electronic government initiatives and create electronic relationships between government and citizens (G2C), government and business (G2B), government and its employees (G2E), and government and government (G2G). The portal is the centerpiece of enterprise approaches to e-government. The challenge for government organizations is to determine which features are most appropriate for creating high-functioning e-government portals.

The promise of the web portal as an integrated access point to all relevant information is undeniable. Because databases and existing departmental systems are often housed on different platforms, the World Wide

Web is a convenient infrastructure to use as the foundation for the transfer of data, statistics, and records across organizational boundaries. As a coordinated entryway into systems and shared databases, a web portal can provide significant cost and time savings. For example, a child welfare employee can, in less than one hour, check a juvenile's statewide history of school attendance, medical history, and interaction with the justice system prior to foster-home placement. Without this integrated system, the employee may have spent days or even weeks trying to contact the appropriate parties and access the information (IBM, 2001). This underlying system integration is one feature that distinguishes web portals from large-scale websites. The extent of the integration, in addition to a host of other factors, determines the level of functionality of the web portal.

Web Portal Functionality

High-functioning government web portals are designed to search, classify, and present relevant information, and to integrate applications at three levels of complexity: (1) information publishing and linking of existing websites, (2) single-agency transactions, and (3) transactions requiring integration of multiple agencies (IBM, 2001). High-functioning portals include tools to register, dynamically recognize, and classify users, thus giving agencies the ability to customize content, information access, and structure to meet the specific needs of an individual. When creating a high-functioning web portal, organizations use the portal features to promote open data access, customization of portal content, usability of portal features, and transparency of information.

State Portal Functionality

To assess the level of state government portal functionality, we conducted a comprehensive content analysis of the 50 U.S. state web portals in the spring of 2001. Using a 131-item portal evaluation questionnaire adapted from standard website evaluation questionnaires to incorporate both generic website evaluation criteria, as well as specific questions relating to public sector websites, we assessed the level of web portal functionality based on four dimensions: openness, customization, usability, and transparency.

Defined below, each of these dimensions represents a key aspect of portal functionality. Openness provides a comprehensive measure of service availability. Customization specifically addresses the role of web portals, as distinct from general-purpose websites, to provide targeted information and services to individuals and groups. Usability is a fundamental design issue for web development teams; and in no realm is general usability more important than in the public sector, where the fundamental role of e-government is to increase the access of all constituents to government services. Transparency indicates the extent to which governments are working to gain constituent trust online. Although the underlying concepts are discussed in a number of studies, we adapt the terms "openness" and "transparency" from Demchak et al.'s (2000) study on the role of the web in governance and democracy.

Based upon our assessment of the website evaluation literature used by public sector and library science researchers, we suggest that these dimensions accurately capture and categorize the key features of web portal functionality. We define high-functioning web portals as those portals that incorporate features in each of the dimensions. The more features included on the web portal, the higher its level of functionality.

Openness

Openness refers to the extent to which a government website provides comprehensive information and services, and maintains timely communication to all key public audiences (Demchak, et al. 2000). The more "open" a website, the more facts, figures, services, and other pieces of information are viewable either through direct reprint on the portal or a link to a website containing the information. In some cases the portal contains links to internal state government agencies. In other cases, the links redirect the portal visitors to an external website such as a federal government agency or a nongovernmental organization. The decision to reprint or link to data is often made based on portal space and design constraints, data availability, or the goals of the portal.

To measure the openness of each of the state web portals, we examined the availability of state information and services through the web portal. We recorded the number and types of services available, the number of steps required to perform these services, and the extent to which personal data followed users through their use of portal services.

One-Stop Service Shops

Openness is a key component of web portals as it underlies the idea of the portal as a one-stop shop for state government e-service. States design their web portals to serve as a main gateway to government information and services. As such, we found that all 50 state government web portals contain at least one direct link or search engine access to state agencies. Constituents can monitor pending legislation in their state legislatures

Table 3.1: Assessment of web portal functionality of U.S. state websites

State Name	Customization	Openness	Usability	Transparency	Overall Score	Rank
Alabama	None	Low	Medium	Not adequate	19.4	33
Alaska	None *	Medium	Medium	Not adequate	22.5	28
Arizona	None *	Medium	Medium	Not adequate	25.8	26
Arkansas	None *	Low	Low	High	31.3	15
California	High	Low	Medium	High	72.7	1
Colorado	None *	Low	Medium	Not adequate	19.6	31
Connecticut	None	Low	Medium	Not adequate	16.5	39
Delaware	None *	Low	Medium	High	41.3	9
Florida	None *	Low	Medium	Medium	29.0	16
Georgia	None	Low	Medium	Medium	29.0	16
Hawaii	None *	Medium	Medium	Not adequate	22.5	28
Idaho	None *	Medium	Medium	Not adequate	29.0	16
Illinois	None	Low	Medium	Not adequate	16.5	39
Indiana	None *	Medium	Medium	Not adequate	29.0	16
Iowa	None *	Medium	Medium	Not adequate	27.3	24
Kansas	None *	High	High	Medium	54.2	7
Kentucky	None *	High	Low	Not adequate	28.5	22
Louisiana	None *	Medium	Low	Not adequate	18.8	37
Maine	None *	Medium	High	High	60.4	3
Maryland	None *	Medium	Medium	Not adequate	25.6	27
Massachusetts	None *	Medium	Medium	Not adequate	29.0	16
Michigan	None	Medium	Low	Not adequate	19.2	36
Minnesota	None	Low	Medium	Not adequate	19.4	33
Mississippi	None *	Low	Medium	Not adequate	19.4	33
Missouri	None	Low	Medium	Not adequate	16.5	39
Montana	None	Medium	Low	Not adequate	15.8	45
Nebraska	None	Not adequate	High	Not adequate	16.7	38
Nevada	None	Not adequate	Low	Not adequate	0.0	49
New Hampshire	None	Low	Medium	Not adequate	16.5	39
New Jersey	None	Medium	Low	Not adequate	12.5	46
New Mexico	None	Not adequate	Medium	High	38.3	10
New York	Low	Medium	Low	Not adequate	27.1	25
North Carolina	High	Low	High	Medium	59.6	4
North Dakota	Low	High	High	High	71.9	2

continued on next page

Table 3.1: Assessment of web portal functionality of U.S. state websites (cont'd)

State Name	Customization	Openness	Usability	Transparency	Overall Score	Rank
Ohio	None	Medium	Low	Medium	34.6	12
Oklahoma	None *	Medium	Low	Medium	28.3	23
Oregon	None	Low	Medium	Medium	32.1	13
Pennsylvania	High	Low	Medium	Medium	57.1	5
Rhode Island	None *	High	Low	Medium	37.7	11
South Carolina	Low	Medium	Medium	High	55.8	6
South Dakota	None *	Not adequate	Medium	Not adequate	10.0	47
Tennessee	None *	Not adequate	Low	Not adequate	0.0	49
Texas	None *	Medium	High	Not adequate	31.7	14
Utah	None *	Low	Medium	Not adequate	16.3	43
Vermont	None *	Medium	Medium	Not adequate	29.0	16
Virginia	High	Low	Medium	Medium	44.8	8
Washington	None *	Low	Medium	Not adequate	19.6	31
West Virginia	None *	Low	Low	Not adequate	6.3	48
Wisconsin	None *	Low	High	Not adequate	19.8	30
Wyoming	None *	Low	Medium	Not adequate	16.3	43

** While the portal does not provide customized information, it does allow the user to link to a community of choice and access community-specific information.*
Each state is assigned a score in the table above that reflects the following hierarchy, from best to worst: high, medium, low, and not adequate.

through 46 portals. They can follow judicial proceedings through 38 state portals, and gain access to the executive branch through 45 state portals. In addition, 29 state portals provide access to nongovernmental websites that support state activities such as the Red Cross or United Way.

We found that 36 states allow web visitors to complete at least one state agency transaction online. The transactions most often supported through the web portals are tax filing, vehicle registration, and professional licensing. Other transactions include recreational licensing and fee payments.

Taxes

For a growing proportion of citizens, filing state taxes, obtaining tax information, and accessing tax forms online is a desired service. A full 42 of the state portals contain links to state tax websites through which users may download tax forms and tax instruction brochures, and 38 states offer online tax advice. Across all states, it takes an average of two mouse clicks

Web Portals as a One-Stop Service Shop

Thirty-six states allow citizens to complete at least one transaction online. The most popular e-service offerings are:

	Number of States
Taxes	
Form download	42
Tax advice	38
Tax filing in conjunction with mail filing	35
Complete online filing when refund expected	29
Complete online filing when payment necessary	23
Vehicle registration	
Form download	11
Complete online registration	16
Professional licensing	
Form download, information access	50
Partial online registration	25
Complete online registration	2

to go from the web portal to the state tax website to begin a session where the user can ask for information, obtain forms, and file taxes online.

Filing taxes online through the web portal is also a common function. In fact, 35 state web portals have links that allow users to file taxes online. Often, however, taxpayers must still complete their tax filing through the mail—either by sending a tax payment or a refund request. Only 29 states actually allow citizens to complete the transaction online when they expect a refund, and the number dwindles to 23 states when the tax filer owes tax money. Completing the tax payment online requires that the state web portal be equipped to handle credit card payments or some form of electronic payment.

Vehicle Registration

Nearly all of the state web portals have links that will carry the visitor to general information about vehicle registration laws and information. However, only 27 states actually allow car owners to register a vehicle through their web portal: 16 states allow car owners to complete the registration process online, the other 11 states require owners to download and mail the registration form. Web visitors find that it is relatively convenient to register a vehicle online. Across all 27 states, it takes an average of 1.4 clicks to start the vehicle registration process from the web portal.

Professional Licensing

Obtaining professional licenses is almost as common to do online as registering a vehicle, with 25 states allowing web visitors to start the process for obtaining a professional license online. The range of professional occupations varies considerably by state. Online license applications for cosmetologists, health professionals, engineers, and architects are the most common—available from all 50 state portals. Most states make it easy to download application forms, and to access information and instructions for their completion. Only Maine and California allow applicants to complete the entire registration process online for two or more occupations.

Customization

Customization refers to the ability to create user-specific content, layout, and display. All web portals provide generic content tailored to meet the needs of the average portal visitor. However, more sophisticated web portals give users the ability to create customized views that provide personalized content organized in a way that meets the direct needs of each user. The power of the web portal lies, to a large extent, in its ability not only to consolidate information but also to provide that information in a specialized manner.

We measure web portal customization based on the ability of web users to uniquely tailor views based on user registration data, to identify themselves with distinct user groups (for example, specific community members), and based on the extent to which the web portal dynamically recognizes these user groups and displays specialized content for them.

State Portal Customization

Surprisingly, only a small number of states give portal users the ability to personalize design and content. North Carolina, Pennsylvania, and California allow portal visitors to create personal profiles, to customize portal features and content based on these profiles, and to identify themselves with multiple constituent groups. Virginia's e-government portal also gets high marks for personalization and customization because its site allows users to create a personal profile and customize the portal content based on that profile. In fact, Virginia's portal is often used as a national example for providing targeted content to specific user groups. South Carolina and North Dakota also have limited personalization and customization capabilities on their portals.

Figure 3.1: California, http://www.state.ca.us/state/portal/myca_homepage.jsp

California claims the top ranking by successfully creating a customizable, one-stop service shop that gives users the ability to perform a host of tasks, from updating vehicle registration to making campsite reservations, through a uniquely tailored view of the portal features and content.

Usability

Usability refers to the ease with which users can access and navigate around the web portal. A well-designed portal delivers value to the user as a function of how accessible and usable the features on the site are. Well-designed portals have pleasant interfaces that are easy to use. It is also critical that the visual aspects use these features in a common design across the portal and linked pages so that the underlying interface elements are relatively constant.

Another determinant of web portal usability is the extent to which the portal is accessible to all constituents of the state. Unlike private companies, which can develop their web portals to meet the needs of a carefully defined target audience, states must develop their web portals to provide equal access for all. Constituent groups include permanent residents, temporary residents (students, for example), businesspeople, and tourists. Contained within each of these constituent groups are members who may be visually or hearing impaired, members for whom English is a second language, and members with other special needs. Some constituents may want to access the web portal with new wireless technologies such as Personal Digital Assistants (PDAs), while others may gain access through basic computers running early versions of web browsing software.

This wide range of development criteria is a challenge from both the technological and content perspectives. However, to effectively meet the needs of all of their constituents, it is vital that states develop their web portals in a manner that truly does provide equal access. We measure web portal accessibility using a content analysis of the state web portals and applying the Web Content Accessibility guidelines developed by the World Wide Web Consortium (W3C).

To measure the usability of the state web portals, we recorded features that increased the ease of use of the portal, making it easy to navigate and find necessary information. These features included intuitive menu systems, site maps, new information indicators, search tools, common state logo, uniform masthead, and dynamically generated list boxes. We also measured the level of accessibility of the portals by recording features such as help sections and FAQs.

In addition, we performed a Bobby analysis on each state web portal. Bobby is a web-based analysis tool, developed by the Center for Applied Special Technology (CAST), that identifies existing or potential problems with the structure and content of a website for a person with special needs. For example, a visually impaired user may need to have an audio soundtrack added to a video demonstration.

To become "Bobby approved" and earn the right to display a Bobby logo, the website must meet the criteria outlined in the W3C's Web Accessibility Initiative (WAI) Web Content Accessibility Guidelines. Included in these criteria are text equivalents for all images and multimedia items, black-and-white alternatives for colors, data table headers to facilitate line-by-line reading, chart and graph summaries, logical organization of content, alternative content for advanced technological features, and browser compatibility.

State Portal Usability

Portals deliver value to the user as a function of the accessibility and usability of the portal features. The seven most usable web portals include nearly all of the usability features discussed above. The states are Kansas, Maine, Nebraska, North Carolina, North Dakota, Texas, and Wisconsin.

Well-designed portals also ensure access to the portal for users of different skill levels and abilities. Users visiting the Alabama and South Carolina web portals are offered the most help and training. Other state portals that lend a helpful hand to users by offering good online help and new user training include Iowa, Kansas, Kentucky, Michigan, Nebraska, North Dakota, Texas, and Wisconsin. States such as Florida, New York, North Carolina, and

Indiana offer limited help features. Surprisingly, 16 state web portals do not offer any form of help.

A small number of state portals use multiple languages to communicate with the users. Four states—Iowa, North Carolina, Texas, and Virginia—give users the option to view content in languages other than English or provide an option for online language translation.

Based on the Bobby criteria, we found that only 34 of the 50 state web portals adequately serve users with disabilities. A total of 16 states have portals with features that do not provide reasonable access to a significant number of disabled users. These portals fail to include alternative image text to explain images to visually impaired users, often do not have table headers to facilitate reading, and have problems with content structure. States with the most egregious errors include Alabama and Louisiana. Table 3.2 lists the states that failed the Bobby test and the number and most frequent type of major errors found on these portals. It is also important to note that not even the 34 states that passed the Bobby test are error free. Many of these portals have minor problems relating to the use of graphic images.

We examined each web portal for features that allow users to interconnect with peripherals such as PDAs, other wireless applications, interactive voice response, and call center support. These technologies extend access to the portal beyond a computer and open up new opportunities to interact with state government. Virginia is the only state that allows users to download information from the state web portal to a PDA. North Carolina's web portal supports interactive voice response and call center support.

Transparency

Transparency indicates how easy it is for users to assess the legitimacy of the portal content. Information such as key agency personnel contacts, the person responsible for online content, feedback procedures, date of last update, and security and privacy policies is vital for users to trust the accuracy of portal content. Even government agencies must work to establish this trust online.

To measure web portal transparency we examined each portal for content and features designed to confirm the legitimacy of the portal and its interconnected websites, services, and information. We identified whether the user could easily determine the responsible authority for the portal and its content along with the accuracy, objectivity, currency, and coverage of the content and information published on the portal. We examined the portal for features and/or content that indicated the person or agency responsible for the portal, its content, and its technical support, as well as appropriate contact information.

Table 3.2: State web portals that failed the Bobby test of accessibility criteria for disabled users

State	Number of Bobby Errors	Most Frequent Error(s)
Azlabama	48	Need to provide alternative image text, potential screen flicker
Louisiana	43	Need to provide alternative image text, missing data table headers
Kentucky	27	Need to provide alternative image text
Montana	26	Need to provide alternative image text, missing data table headers
West Virginia	21	Need to provide alternative image text, provide color alternatives, extend image descriptions
Ohio	20	Need to provide alternative image text
Arkansas	18	Need to provide alternative image text, potential for screen flicker
Nevada	17	Need to provide alternative image text, provide color alternatives
Oklahoma	15	Need to provide alternative image text
New Jersey	14	Need to provide alternative image text
Michigan	10	Need to provide alternative image text
Rhode Island	5	Need to provide alternative image text
New York	3	Need to provide alternative image text
Tennessee	2	Need to provide alternative image text
South Carolina	1	Need to provide alternative image text
Iowa	1	Failure to include table headers

To gain public trust, high-functioning web portals should employ these transparency features. For instance, states can earn the confidence of constituents by incorporating typical aspects of offline transactions in the online environment. As with buying groceries, paying bills, or even registering a car with a department of motor vehicles office, each person completing a transaction online should be able to obtain a receipt or other certification. Surprisingly, this simple yet important feature of every offline transaction is supported by only eight states. Only citizens transacting business through the portals of Arizona, California, Delaware, Maine, New Mexico, North Carolina, North Dakota, and South Carolina are able to generate a receipt from a completed transaction.

Enhancing Web Portal Legitimacy

Only a few states effectively incorporate features to increase their online legitimacy.

	Number of States
Transaction receipts	8
Passwords	13
Security statement	10
Security statement and password	5
Privacy policy	32
Security statement and privacy policy	8

We also examined the security and privacy features contained on the web portals. Following the trend of high-quality e-commerce websites, we expected a state portal to post a statement of its security policy or an independent security certification, particularly if the web portal launches you into applications that require personal information. However, we found that only 10 of the state web portals currently post a security statement. Password protection for personal information was equally rare. We found that 13 states use passwords on their portals, and only five state portals—California, Kansas, Kentucky, Maine, and Maryland—use passwords and also post a security statement. A similar story exists for privacy statements. We found that 32 of the states include a privacy statement on their web portal. However, only eight states—California, Hawaii, Kansas, Kentucky, Maryland, Maine, New Mexico, and Utah—provide both a security and a privacy statement.

State Web Portals and E-Service Delivery

When states incorporate features from all four of the functionality dimensions—openness, customization, usability, and transparency—they create high-functioning web portals and enhance the value of these portals for e-service delivery. Based on the number of features included from each of the four dimensions, we ranked the states according to the level of web portal functionality. For purposes of this study, we treated all dimensions as equally important and calculated the state portal functionality score as the aggregate of the scores on each dimension. We then ordered the states according to this functionality score and ranked them accordingly. State portal performance on each dimension, overall portal functionality score, and rank are presented in Table 3.1 (see page 60).

Below, we discuss the states leading the way in e-service delivery. For each dimension of portal functionality, we describe the state portals and

Figure 3.2: North Dakota, http://www.state.nd.us or http://www.discovernd.com

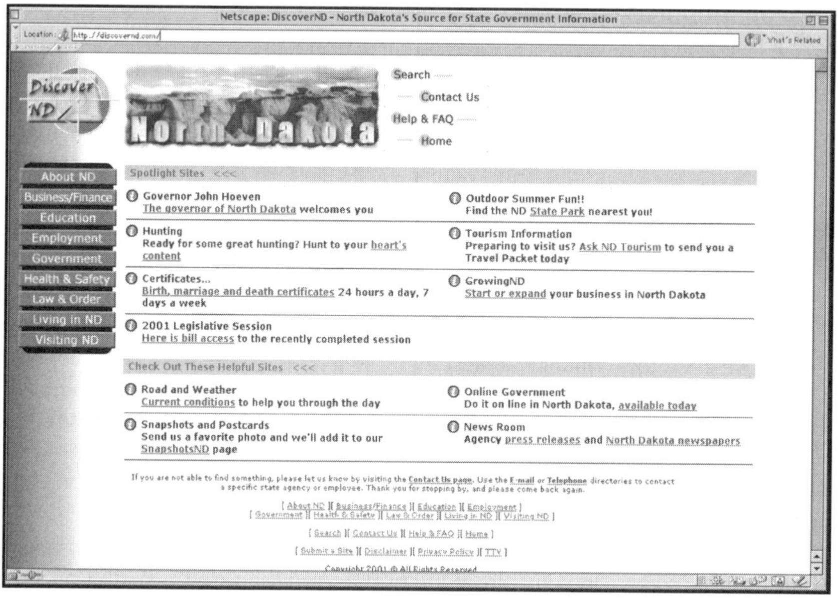

Top-notch in all aspects of functionality, the North Dakota portal is exceptional in its usability. Not only is the portal layout simple and easy to use, but the portal also provides comprehensive online help and searching capabilities, as well as new user training for inexperienced web users.

provide illustrative examples of how the states are using web portals to enhance e-service delivery.

E-Service Leaders: Summarizing Five High-Functioning State Web Portals

States leading the way in e-service not only provide online access to a host of services, but also have developed portals that increase the access to these services for all state constituents. California, North Dakota, Maine, North Carolina, and Pennsylvania use their portals to enhance e-service delivery by simultaneously providing customized content and equitable access to government.

Openness

These state web portals distinguish themselves by providing a comprehensive list of e-services. Through the portals, constituents can register cars, file taxes, and obtain professional licenses for a host of occupations including

> **One-Stop Service Shops**
>
> Leading state portals offer a variety of services including:
> - Car registration
> - Tax filing, form and instruction download
> - Professional licensing
> - Access to state regulations and pending legislation
> - Recreational licensing
> - Access to local municipalities, state, and federal agencies

accountant, architect, building contractor, and land survey engineer. Recreation seekers can secure licenses for fishing and camping, and citizens can monitor pending legislation and access many local and federal government agencies. In addition, portal visitors have access to a wide range of state facts and policy information.

Clearly, these states have successfully created one-stop service shops on their web portals. Not only are the services available, but they are also readily accessible—requiring, in some cases, three or fewer clicks to begin the transaction or get the relevant information. For instance, through the California and Pennsylvania portals, visitors are only two clicks away from registering their cars. North Dakota residents can begin their tax filings with one click from the portal. And Maine and North Carolina business owners are only three short clicks away from obtaining information on and submitting proposals in response to state requests for proposals.

Customization

Only a handful of states have portals that give users the ability to personalize either content or display, and, not surprisingly, the states offering this level of functionality are among the leaders in e-service. North Carolina, Pennsylvania, and California allow the greatest amount of customization. Visitors to these portals can create uniquely tailored views of portal features and content based on personal profiles.

On the California state portal, for example, users are encouraged to create a "My California" homepage that displays news, information, services, and links based on their specified community membership (tourist, resident, student, member of the press, businessperson, or state employee) and preferred online services. Users can choose from a list of online services and information on business practices, consumer and family affairs, education and training resources, environment and natural resources, government agencies, health and welfare agencies, California history and culture, labor and employment, transportation, and travel.

The Pennsylvania portal offers a similar service. Here users can create a "myPAPowerPort" homepage that contains information tailored to their preferences. The Pennsylvania portal also includes the capability for customized content delivery. Users can specify the order in which information

Figure 3.3: Pennsylvania, http://www.state.pa.us/PAPower/

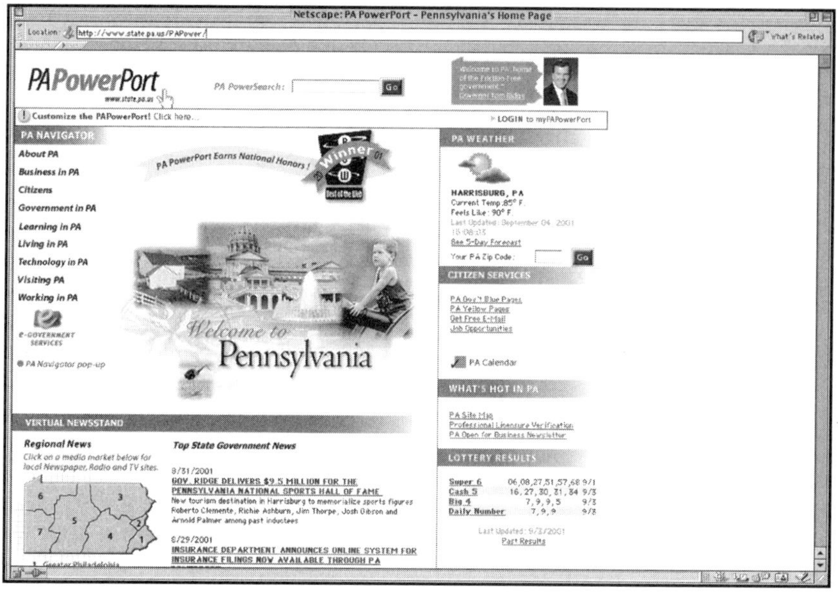

Pennsylvania's "PA PowerPort" is one of the top five portals and is distinguished by its level of customizability and advanced navigational features. Visitors to this portal gain access to business, citizen, vehicle, community, and educational services through a layout that enhances the user-friendliness and accessibility of the portal content.

should be displayed. Figure 3.3 shows an excerpt from the Pennsylvania portal. On this page, users can specify both the content and layout for their "myPAPowerPort" homepage.

Usability

E-service leading states are among the most usable web portals. Maine, North Carolina, and North Dakota rank at the top of the usability scale, and California and Pennsylvania provide a good level of assistance to users. One distinguishing feature of these portals is that they are accessible to users across a wide spectrum. At one end of the spectrum, these portals provide extensive help features for users with limited skills and abilities. For example, the North Dakota portal provides online help and searching capabilities as well as new user training. The Maine portal includes step-by-step demonstrations that walk users through the data-entry process for each of the services available online. The North Carolina portal offers help for inexperienced users and it gives non-English-speaking users the option for online translation of portal content. The Maine portal includes an innovative kids

Figure 3.4: North Carolina, http://www.state.nc.us

The North Carolina portal is a leader in both customization and usability. One of only three portals to allow users to create customized views based on personal profiles, the portal also provides a substantial level of help for inexperienced users, and it gives non-English-speaking users the option for online translation of portal content.

section that is designed to help young visitors learn about the state and its services. This page includes four sections: information about the state of Maine, information about the government, games and contests, and other general interest links.

For users at the other end of the spectrum, these leading portals facilitate flexible portal viewing. Many of the portals support advanced technologies. For example, California's portal constituents can gain access to state government information through wireless devices such as PDAs, cellular telephones, and pagers. Additionally, users can opt to receive e-mail notifications of traffic updates, energy alerts, press releases, and lottery results. Some of the portals include advanced navigation features. The Pennsylvania portal, for example, includes a pop-up navigation window that maintains one-click access to the primary online topic areas regardless of the user's clicking history.

Transparency

Without exception these leading portals provide enough information to allow visitors to feel at ease. The portals include basic contact information for agency personnel and for online content, and privacy statements. The online vehicle registration renewal service through the Maine state portal exemplifies how these portals maintain legitimacy with portal visitors. Maine residents completing the online vehicle registration process can access the portal privacy policy and a statement of fair credit card use online. Each page contains a link to the secretary of state's website, which includes contact information for key personnel such as e-mail, mailing address, and phone number. When the registration process is complete, users can print a receipt as proof of their transaction.

Benchmarking Future E-Service Development

Throughout this chapter we discuss web portals at different stages of development. At one end of the spectrum, e-service leaders such as California and Pennsylvania provide a wealth of services through their portals. Overall, the top states provide online access to services, contact information for key agencies, and well-developed portals that are usable by most of the constituents of the state. At the other end of the spectrum, we find state portals with more limited e-service offerings that are somewhat less accessible than their e-service leading counterparts. We recap the major study findings below.

Portal Functionality

Based on our assessment of the four dimensions of web portal functionality, we find that the five highest functioning state web portals are California, North Dakota, Maine, North Carolina, and Pennsylvania. These portals provide online access to services, include contact information for key agencies, and contain features that enhance usability for most of the constituents of the state. At the other end of the spectrum, New Jersey, South Dakota, West Virginia, Nevada, and Tennessee are more limited in their functionality.

One-Stop Service Shops

Although state web portals provide the promise of a one-stop shop, most states have not yet reached this goal. Even among states offering access to key transactions such as tax filing, car registration, and professional licensing online, most still require constituents to complete the transaction offline. This is particularly true for state portals in the early stages of development. States such as Nevada and South Dakota allow taxpayers to

Figure 3.5: Maine, http://www.state.me.us

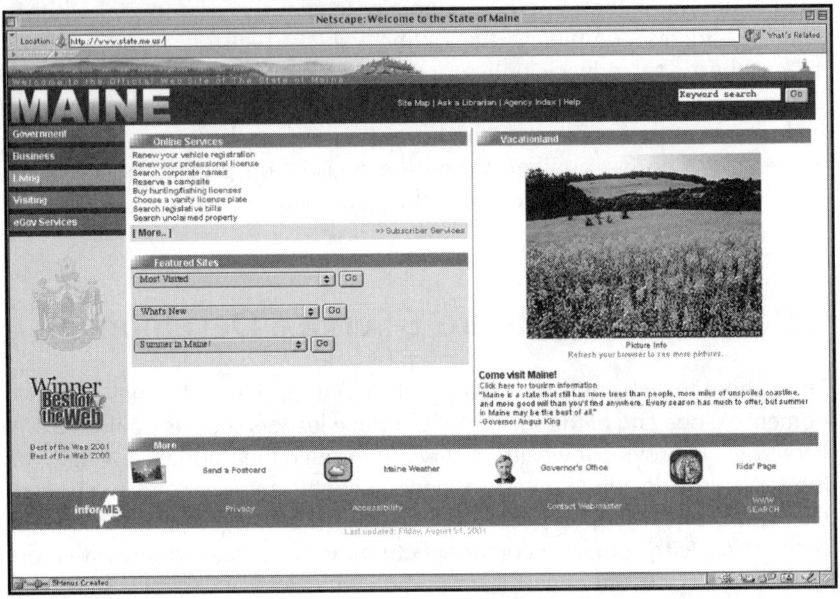

The Maine portal is notable for its high level of transparency. For instance, not only can Maine residents completing the online vehicle registration process access the portal privacy policy, personnel contact information, and a statement of fair credit card use, but they also can print a receipt as proof of their transaction. Although seemingly simple, this is an unusual feature among state portals—available through only eight state portals.

download forms and instructions, but then they must actually mail in their tax payments.

While most state e-government web portals publish information, link to existing websites, and enable users to perform single-agency transactions, some states are providing access to web-based transactions requiring the integration of multiple-agency data. Among these states, one growing trend is to organize services offered through the web portal around events.

For example, what if a citizen moves their residence and needs to update this information with all state agencies that require a current address? Without the integrated web portal, the citizen must first identify relevant agencies and departments to contact, and then complete and submit change of address forms for each. On the other hand, the integrated web portal allows citizens to reduce this cumbersome process to a single step. Because all agencies are linked to a centralized database accessed through the portal, this transaction (change of address) will be simultaneously updated in each agency. Currently,

28 state web portals organize e-government services around events. This is an emerging area of e-government application development; we expect to see more sophisticated examples of multiple-agency integration soon.

Accountability

Remarkably, it is not the lack of online service availability that limits the functionality of early-stage portals. Rather, usability issues hamper the value of the portals for e-service delivery. For instance, we found that many portals fail to include basic contact information. Surprisingly, many states develop sophisticated web portals with access to a host of information and services, but do not include basic information on whom to contact if the user has questions. If they are truly to enhance service delivery, these portals must convey a certain level of accountability. In other words, users need to believe that the portals are not only a convenient alternative method to access government services, but also that the portals are a fully integrated part of the government service delivery system held to the same standards as any other method. States receiving high ratings in this dimension (openness)—North Dakota, Kansas, Rhode Island, and Kentucky—simply provide telephone numbers, agency office locations, hours of operation, e-mail addresses, and even the names of key agency personnel.

Further, most state portals do little to instill constituent trust. Although privacy and security is a major concern for government portal developers, they do little to indicate this concern to portal users. Only eight states provide both a security and privacy statement on their portal. In addition, most states do not consistently provide receipts or other such acknowledgments of completed transactions. Users want a receipt, proof of the transaction. This is especially true with activities as important as tax payments and license registrations.

Accessibility

States have created their portals to reach the mainstream audience, but must adapt their portals to make them accessible to the wide range of constituents they serve. We found that 16 state portals contain features that do not provide reasonable access to a significant number of disabled users. These portals fail to include alternative image text that explain images to visually impaired users, and have structural issues that make it difficult for the less literate to read and understand the portal content.

In addition, we found that most state portals do not include the capability for language translation. Most surprisingly, however, we found that many states fail to include basic help features for portal users. The face of the Internet is changing. Constituents going online to access government services come from all demographics. State portal developers can no longer assume a certain level of comfort or knowledge of the technology. As a result, they must make the portals accessible to all constituents.

The Promise of Customized Content

Although the ability to display customized content is one of the key benefits of web portals, most states do not yet provide constituents with the ability to create customized views. Only seven of the 50 states allow portal users to create customized views and of these states, only three—California, North Carolina, and Pennsylvania—provide a high degree of customization. At these state portals, users can identify themselves with specific constituent groups such as students, tourists, or residents of a particular region. In addition, users can register and have their personal information follow them around the portal. This feature increases time savings and user satisfaction.

Conclusions and Recommendations

These findings represent the status of state web portals during a single snapshot in time. Given the ever-increasing demands of the public and the growing technological capabilities of the states, web portals remain in a constant state of development. Regardless of their current state of portal development, the findings presented here should provide some guidance for state officials as they work to deliver the highest level of e-service to their constituents. Accordingly, we make several recommendations to states in the midst of portal development based on the findings of this research.

1. *Emphasize customer service.* The benefit of e-service delivery via a web portal is that it provides more convenient access to state services and information for constituents. To that end, states should include features that facilitate portal use. Features such as help screens, agency contact information, and navigational site maps to help users manage their course through the portal should be readily accessible from every page. Questions, concerns, and problems related to portal content and services are inevitable. However, the goal of portal developers should be to make the answers—or the right person to contact to obtain answers—as easy to find as possible.
2. *Organize services by event rather than department.* Recognize that the average citizen does not understand nor care to figure out the bureaucracy of government. Structuring the portal around events rather than

agencies can provide better service to the user. For example, states should list professional license registration on the portal rather than a link to the secretary of state. A citizen who needs to renew his contractor's license will immediately click on "obtain professional license," but may not readily realize which state agency is ultimately responsible for the issue of professional licenses.

3. *Allow for customization.* The value of the portal for e-service delivery lies in its ability to provide easy access to relevant content. Residents want information on tax payments, while students want information on state financial aid policies, and vacationers want information on state parks and recreational permits. Two facts are clear: (1) the set of information and services provided by a state is vast, and (2) what is important to one constituent may be irrelevant to another. Thus, to efficiently present information to portal visitors, states should allow users to personalize both the display and content delivered through the web portal.
4. *Recognize the diversity of your portal audience.* As the Internet becomes a more widely used tool, states must recognize that the diversity of their portal visitors will continue to increase. Providing good e-service means creating a web portal that is accessible to all constituents of the state. And these constituents include members at both ends of the technological sophistication spectrum. State portals should include help features and demonstrations for novice users, alternative viewing options for users with special needs, and advanced capabilities for technologically sophisticated users.
5. *Include features that enhance the legitimacy of the portal.* Do not assume that portal visitors will automatically trust the accuracy of portal content or the validity of transactions performed through the portal. Just like the dilemma faced by private sector organizations, state governments must earn the trust of portal visitors. To that end, state portals should include features such as security and privacy statements, content update procedures and dates, contact information for person or office responsible for web portal content, proper acknowledgment of transactions (receipts), and even independent third-party endorsements of the portal.

Designing a web portal to effectively meet the demands of an ever-changing public is no small task. Government agencies are faced with the responsibility of simultaneously providing breadth and depth in their online content, while still maintaining fiscal responsibility. The findings of our research suggest that state e-government initiatives are well on their way to providing comprehensive service online. Our recommendations are designed to build upon the work currently underway in state IT departments. Taken together, these recommendations can help state governments use their web portals to further enhance e-service delivery and exceed the ever-increasing demands of the public.

Appendix:
State Portal Web Addresses

State Name	Standard Portal Address (URL)	Alternative Address (URL)*
Alabama (AL)	http://www.state.al.us	
Alaska (AK)	http://www.state.ak.us	
Arizona (AZ)	http://www.state.az.us	
Arkansas (AR)	http://www.state.ar.us	
California (CA)	http://www.state.ca.us	http://www.state.ca.us/state/portal/myca_homepage.jsp
Colorado (CO)	http://www.state.co.us	
Connecticut (CT)	http://www.state.ct.us	
Delaware (DE)	http://www.state.de.us	
Florida (FL)	http://www.state.fl.us	
Georgia (GA)	http://www.state.ga.us	
Hawaii (HI)	http://www.state.hi.us	
Idaho (ID)	http://www.state.id.us	
Illinois (IL)	http://www.state.il.us	
Indiana (IN)	http://www.state.in.us	
Iowa (IA)	http://www.state.ia.us	
Kansas (KS)	http://www.state.ks.us	http://www.accesskansas.org
Kentucky (KY)	http://www.state.ky.us	http://www.kydirect.net
Louisiana (LA)	http://www.state.la.us	
Maine (ME)	http://www.state.me.us	
Maryland (MD)	http://www.state.md.us	
Massachusetts (MA)	http://www.state.ma.us	
Michigan (MI)	http://www.state.mi.us	
Minnesota (MN)	http://www.state.mn.us	
Mississippi (MS)	http://www.state.ms.us	

* *The official web address for each of the 50 U.S. states is www.state.two-letterabbreviation.us, where "two-letter abbreviation" is replaced by the two-letter abbreviation for the state. Some states have established alternative homepage addresses for their web portals. To access these state web portals, users may enter either address.*

State Name	Standard Portal Address (URL)	Alternative Address (URL)*
Missouri (MO)	http://www.state.mo.us	
Montana (MT)	http://www.state.mt.us	http://www.discoveringmontana.com/css1default.asp
Nebraska (NE)	http://www.state.ne.us	
Nevada (NV)	http://www.state.nv.us	http://silver.state.nv.us
New Hampshire (NH)	http://www.state.nh.us	
New Jersey (NJ)	http://www.state.nj.us	
New Mexico (NM)	http://www.state.nm.us	
New York (NY)	http://www.state.ny.us	
North Carolina (NC)	http://www.state.nc.us	http://www.ncgov.com
North Dakota (ND)	http://www.state.nd.us	http://www.discovernd.com
Ohio (OH)	http://www.state.oh.us	
Oklahoma (OK)	http://www.state.ok.us	
Oregon (OR)	http://www.state.or.us	
Pennsylvania (PA)	http://www.state.pa.us	http://www.state.pa.us/PAPower/
Rhode Island (RI)	http://www.state.ri.us	
South Carolina (SC)	http://www.state.sc.us	
South Dakota (SD)	http://www.state.sd.us	http://www.state.sd.us/state/sitelist.cfm
Tennessee (TN)	http://www.state.tn.us	
Texas (TX)	http://www.state.tx.us	http://www.texasonline.state.tx.us
Utah (UT)	http://www.state.ut.us	
Vermont (VT)	http://www.state.vt.us	
Virginia (VA)	http://www.state.va.us	http://www.vipnet.org/portal/services/index.htm
Washington (WA)	http://www.state.wa.us	http://access.wa.gov
West Virginia (WV)	http://www.state.wv.us	
Wisconsin (WI)	http://www.state.wi.us	http://www.wisconsin.gov/state/home
Wyoming (WY)	http://www.state.wy.us	

Bibliography

Alexander, Jane E. and Tate, Marsha A. 1999. Web Wisdom: How to evaluate and create information quality on the web. Norwood, N.J.: Lawrence Erlbaum Associates, Inc.

The Council for Excellence in Government. September 2000, "E-Government: The next American revolution." http://www.excelgov.org/egovpoll/.

Demchak, Chris C., Friis, C., and LaPorte, T. M. 2000. "Webbing Governance: National differences in constructing the face of public organizations." In G. David Garson, ed. *Handbook of Public Information Systems*, New York, N.Y.: Marcel Dekker Publishers.

Heeks, Richard. 2000. *Reinventing Government in the Information Age*. London, England: Roultedge Press.

IBM. 2001. *Creating and Implementing an E-government Portal Solution: Requirements, solution options, and business model considerations*. IBM Global Industries. http://ibm.com/solutions/ government.

NPR. 1993. *Report of the National Performance Review*. Washington, D.C.: Government Printing Office.

Osborne, D. and Gaebler, T. 1992. *Reinventing Government: How the entrepreneurial spirit is transforming the public sector*. Reading, Mass.: Addison-Wesley.

Stowers, Genie N. L. 1999. "Becoming Cyberactive: State and local governments on the world wide web." *Government Information Quarterly*, 16, 2, 111-129.

West, Darrel M. September 2000. Assessing E-government: The Internet, democracy, and service delivery by state and federal governments. Brown University Report, http://www.brown.edu/ Departments/ Taubman_Center/polreports/egovtreport00.html.

CHAPTER FOUR

Federal Intranet Work Sites: An Interim Assessment

Julianne G. Mahler
Associate Professor, Department of Public and International Affairs, George Mason University

Priscilla M. Regan
Associate Professor, Department of Public and International Affairs, George Mason University

This report was originally published in June 2002.

Models of Intranet Use

Background

The growing interest in intranets is spurred by their usefulness as management tools to foster productive communication and coordination, manage information, and encourage self-organizing work teams. Business to employee (B2E) intranets in firms are developing rapidly because of their advantages in optimizing strategic communications. Allcorn (1997) identifies the "parallel virtual organization" composed of an intranet and organizational databases as the information and knowledge management model for the future. Curry and Stancich (2000) identify the advantages of the intranet for strategic decision making. Southwest Airlines is cited by the General Accounting Office as an exemplar of the uses of intranets for informal communication among employees at dispersed work sites to develop and maintain a culture of teamwork and pride (GAO/GGD-00-28).

Here we pose two principal questions about the intranet in federal government settings. First, what are the present capacities and designs of intranets in use? What features do they have and how are they used? The second set of questions concerns why agencies have developed their intranets, what they hope to get from them, and what work they would like them to do. Information about capacity and purpose will make it possible to know how to work with agencies to enhance their systems and to move from current designs to ones that will do more of the work staff would like them to do.

Use of Intranets

Intranets are part of the larger e-government landscape that includes Internet services for citizens and commercial applications for businesses to ease and speed their relationships. HUD notes in their 2001 website that e-government is the interchange of value, including services and information, through an electronic medium, and includes relationships between:

- Government and citizens
- Government and nonprofits
- Government and business
- Government and employees
- Government and government

Similarly, Stowers' study of e-commerce applications in the public sector distinguishes e-government operations that link governments to citizens (G2C), governments to business (G2B), and business to government (B2G). Government to citizen transactions online include a number of services allowing citizens to obtain copies of vital records, pay fees, renew licenses and registrations, file and pay taxes, and bid at government auctions (Stowers, 2001). Government to business e-linkages include opportunities to file taxes, obtain licenses and permits, and purchase government services. E-commerce applications between businesses and government include creating software to simplify purchasing and improve agency productivity. For example, the Department of Defense EMALL operation provides one point of entry for Defense customers to buy goods and services from commercial vendors and other government sellers. (Stowers, 2002, 26). Stowers also found applications of government to government e-commerce in Washington State's Central Stores Online, patterned after commercial online retail shopping sites.

In contrast to these applications, intranets are typically newer applications that emerged in the early to mid-1990s in the private sector and, based on our respondents' accounts, mainly after 1997 in federal government agencies. Intranets are websites within government agencies that connect the government agency to its employees and the employees to each other. In large multi-agency departments such as the Department of Transportation, intranets may be nested so that department-wide intranets and agency-specific websites operate simultaneously.

Information in bulky and expensive directories and manuals of policies and procedures can be provided in a more convenient, easy-to-find, and timely way in an internal web network. Intranets make it possible for employers to communicate quickly and efficiently and to save time and money in the dissemination of news and policy changes. Intranets may be principally portals linking employees to static information resources, or they may include interactive elements that provide human resources services such as the Employee Express payroll contract service. Some offer chat rooms where employees can communicate outside of formal channels, air grievances, and seek solutions.

We will describe cases in which the intranet has become a host for virtual meeting places for communities of interest that may yield program innovations or policy ideas. This communication function in at least one of the cases described here has spurred efforts to use the intranet as a vehicle for trying to foster the emergence of an agency-wide culture, not weakening the strong divisional cultures but encouraging an overarching mission and identity.

The scope and complexity of agency intranets appear to be somewhat more limited than those found in corporate settings. In corporations, applications range from functional web-based solutions for a single process such as travel arrangements to a multifunctional array of portals that create a personalized work setting for employees. In government agencies, single functional solutions, such as Employee Express, make it possible for employees to enter changes in payroll information directly without the intervention of human resources actors. We found no cases, however, of functional portals in which such web solutions fully covered an entire organizational process such as human resources (HR). Except for Employee Express, intranets were used to provide information to help employees find out how to request needed services from the HR offices.

In many cases we found that federal agencies were using intranets as "thin portals" to communicate news and policy changes to employees as well as offering a reliable, updated place to find information about existing programs and procedures. We did find cases of agencies working toward "fat portal" solutions by creating opportunities for the creation of self-organizing communities that could foster e-learning (see Figure 4.1). Similarly, we uncovered one case in which the department-wide intranet had been created to foster cultural unification; however, no evidence of success was noted by agency actors.

In the literature, a number of federal agencies have reported plans to use some form of intranet, but the extent of the content and the level of actual use in agencies vary widely. Before moving to the details of findings in this study, the efforts in other agencies might be noted. For example, intranets are central to the IRS reform efforts by providing a communications strategy for informing staff about changes in tax law, policy, and procedures, and for improving agency-wide communication (Letter Report, 04/21/2000, GAO/GGD-00-85). The National Resources Center, the IRS's intranet website, was created in 1998 to serve as a site for centralized guidance on policy and procedures, to disseminate answers to employee questions so that all staff would have the same answers, and to provide training for the provisions of the reform.

The difficulties the IRS had in setting up the National Resources Center are typical of the problems we found in intranet development. Many staff

Figure 4.1: How Organizations Are Using Intranets

Degree of Complexity			
	High	**Functional Portals** Deliver a single management function (e.g., HR, Finance)	**Fat Portals** Complex, multifunctional, enterprise site which creates a personalized work environment
	Low	**Functional Solution** A web application of a single management process (e.g., new hire, travel)	**Thin Portals** Delivers organization's information and provides linkages to other intranet sites
		Narrow	Wide
		Organization Scope	

(Diagram adapted from PricewaterhouseCoopers, Introduction to B2E and G2E Solutions, April 1, 2001)

did not have computers that could access the intranet and others were unaware of the site. These problems limited the success of reforms designed to bring consistency to procedures in the IRS.

Other examples of intranet uses for management are included in the GAO report on successful strategies by chief information officers for enhancing agency information and knowledge management (GAO/GAO-01-376G). In one case, the intranet at the Agency for International Development was used to make press clippings available to staff, a significant improvement in speed and cost from traditional methods. In the Veterans Health Administration, intranet access to performance information such as patient satisfaction data is used to encourage performance improvement (GAO/GAO-01-376G).

Many have noted the uses of intranets for speeding and personalizing human resources functions in organizations (Holz, 1997). GAO reports uses of intranets in private firms to foster human capital development that can serve as models for governmental agencies (GAO/GGD-00-28). Integrating human capital staff into management teams directly or via an intranet is seen as an exemplary development. GAO also reports on an exemplary use at Federal Express, where senior managers apply an automated intranet-based tool to assess the leader skills, potential, and development needs of mid-level managers so that new assignments and promotions can be made quickly and effectively.

How relationships between governments and employees can be facilitated through the use of intranets is the focus of the research here.

Field Research Questions and Hypotheses

Based on the development of intranets and e-government solutions in the federal government, we expected to find a range of intranet designs and purposes—from simple newscasts to sophisticated portals linking employees to sites for human resources needs, travel planning, training, and self-designed collaborative linkages. In fact, we found a narrower range of designs than expected. The reasons for this and other patterns in the development of intranets emerge from the individual case studies.

The examples are based on case studies in six agencies. We interviewed several individuals in the Department of Transportation, the Department of Housing and Urban Development, the Environmental Protection Agency, and the General Services Administration. We interviewed several respondents in different offices of the Departments of Commerce and Justice, which are multi-agency departments with complex intranet structures. We began to identify these agencies, and the offices and actors within them, from leads provided by the Chief Information Officers

Council, its E-Government Committee, and its Intranet Roundtable. Additional contacts were recommended by these actors. Our rationale for this approach to selecting cases was that we wanted to optimize our chances of finding the most advanced and sophisticated examples of intranets rather than a representative sample of all stages of intranet development in federal agencies. Case studies of agencies with little or no experience with intranets would not offer much guidance about the potential of intranets or the directions in which agencies want them to develop. The emerging vision of intranets as key management tools in government is more easily observed in agencies that are more advanced in their exploration of intranet use and its limitations.

We posed questions about the current state of agency intranets, their origins, and major changes to the site. In several cases we were able to document the design of sites at different stages of development. We questioned actors about the original purposes and motivations behind intranet creation. We tried to determine what pressures within the federal setting might encourage intranets. We also probed the sources and level of resources available for development. The composition and mission definition of intranet development teams were investigated. Agencies differed in whether the intranet was allocated its own team or had to share resources with Internet staff. Some agencies put web technicians at the head of projects while others placed managers in charge. As research progressed, we also became aware of the need for agencies to encourage intranet recognition and usage, and so we came to collect stories about how the intranet was marketed to agency staff. Finally, we investigated other factors that appear to have encouraged or impeded intranet development. We turn next to the details of these cases.

Design and Development of Intranets in Federal Government Agencies

Department of Transportation (DOT)

The director of the Department of Transportation intranet development team also heads up the Intranet Roundtable of the E-Government Committee of the Chief Information Officers Council. The director came to DOT after successfully creating an intranet at the Department of Housing and Urban Development (HUD). The task set for the director was to create a single intranet for DOT's 11 operating divisions, including the Federal Aviation Administration, the U.S. Coast Guard, and the Federal Highway

Figure 4.2: Department of Transportation Intranet Home Page

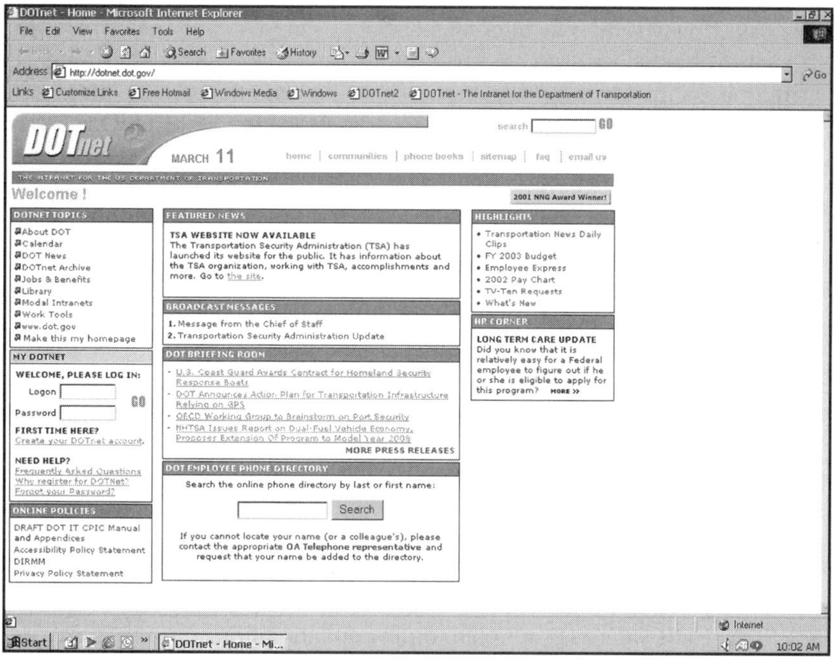

Administration. Each of these already had a functioning intranet, and the administration at DOT believed that strong cultural identities within some of these divisions prevented a single DOT ethos from emerging. It was hoped that the intranet could foster the development of an overarching DOT culture by generating strong linkages across divisions. There was strong top-level support for this objective from then DOT Secretary Rodney Slater.

In the summer of 2000, a reorganization created an e-government unit within the newly designed Office of the Chief Information Officer. There were few resources available for intranet development. Perhaps even more important, however, the intranet team was tasked with creating and maintaining both the department's Internet website and its new intranet. The intranet shared resources with the better recognized and established external website. The existing intranet was a static page with few features and low usage.

Shortly thereafter, in September 2000, a contract for a new intranet was negotiated, and a new prototype was tested in December. Then followed an intense period of consultations with managers and incorporation of their suggestions into the new site. Buy-in by the central and divisional managers was seen as key if the new agency-wide intranet was to be a success, given that there were already as many as 11 intranet sites within the department. In considering what new features might be appealing to department employees, the team director focused on crosscutting issues and services. Though in many cases human resources functions are crosscutting, here they were already decentralized into the divisions. Instead, the director considered what the central site could offer in the way of communication and information resources. Online communication, e-mail, chat rooms, and access to performance measurement databases were designed into the system. Design choices were made to use known terminology and management categories rather than requiring employees to master new website language. This simple principle was credited with contributing to the later success of the site.

Standard elements available on each employee home page include:

- Links to organization and budget information
- Breaking news features and access to online news services, news clippings, and specialized transportation publications
- Archives of past announcements
- Library resources, including links to the in-house library, online publications, policy statements, reference works, and other government document repositories including GPO [Government Printing Office] Access and FedWorld
- Work tools such as proprietary online collaboration software, databases and analysis software, and work-related forms
- Feedback links to intranet designers
- Department directory
- Department-wide human resources program information, including information about awards, benefits, wellness programs, job opportunities, training, and information about balancing work and family
- Department calendar

An important characteristic of the new site, and one that designers were particularly happy with, is that employees can personalize the content of their home page on the intranet. Each employee can create his or her own version of the elements listed above. The DOT intranet team had investigated the use of portal technologies but found them to be too expensive and decided to use existing software that enabled some level of personalization. A personally selected menu might include pages for:

- Personal calendar
- Administrative tools
- Modifying links to self-selected virtual groups and communities, as well as group sites
- Dictionary
- Weather
- Google

The next-generation intranet is now in design. It will feature interactive travel and training features for generating tickets and arranging for training rather than offering only forms and information about procedures and policy, as in the 2001 version.

Another important innovation at DOT is that employees can initiate online groups to collaborate about task issues or emerging program interests. Standardized templates for the groups make it easy to create a group and put up content on group spaces. Some groups have spawned subgroups interested in collaborating on particular problems or work issues. A page called "My Modules" offers tools for creating and altering the personalized home page, and for creating and altering content and membership on group pages. The content modification page offers a menu-driven method for:

- Creating, modifying, or deleting new content in groups
- Creating a new group
- Managing new group memberships
- Managing the group bulletin board
- Reviewing feedback on the site
- Creating a calendar event
- Creating a link to a group
- Creating an employee recognition article

There are few procedures, or barriers, for volunteers who want to join, create, or volunteer to head a community of interest. Groups can be open or private, and content can also be private to the group, encouraging use of the virtual groups for controversial or embryonic ideas. Documents and content can be uploaded to a bulletin board. Conversation takes place through chat rooms that can be open and public or password-protected and private. There is no group writing or special collaboration software such as Lotus Notes in use nor is it planned. Rather, access is kept simple and transparent. Open and closed groups can be created, and members can be limited and, in some cases, removed. The web administrator can also monitor a community and remove members. Groups form and disperse as needed.

The object, of course, of making it easy to form these groups and share information is to foster intra-agency communication and collaboration and thereby encourage a unified DOT-wide culture, or "One DOT." The organizational effects of fostering the online communities may be more complex and useful, however. These groups constitute a kind of self-organizing process that may lead to new multi-agency projects and smoother inter-divisional policy development. They may also spawn innovations in program ideas as agents from different sectors of the department chat, complain, or join forces to tackle problems.

While there has been no evaluation of whether a unified culture or self-organizing teams have emerged, there is evidence that the 2001 design changes have made the site far more attractive and useful than its earlier version. In May 2001, before the new design was online, there were 278,000 hits to the site, while in July 2001, after the changes, there were 2,700,000 hits. While these increases are large, they also represent a great deal of effort to prepare managers and staff for the changes and encourage them to use the site.

The intranet team leader attributes the relative success of DOTnet to at least three key factors:

- Putting managers in charge of design decisions
- Working with managers to identify useful Intranet functions
- Gaining the active support of top management in promoting the use of the site

Putting program and personnel managers rather than web technicians in the lead in design was important to the success of the DOT intranet, as it had been at HUD. Rather than allowing technical capacity to shape the design of functions, terminology, and layout, the intranet team leader gave managers, among whom she includes herself, the task of determining what information would be useful. Rather than making employees learn the web design program terminology, language already in use was employed. New ideas emerged from discussions with departmental managers and were pilot-tested with them.

Lessons Learned

- High levels of use and acceptance do not happen as a matter of course. High levels of use must be designed into to the site with self-consciously user-friendly terminology and functions that make sense to organization members and clearly contribute to their ability to do their work. Intranets built to demonstrate progressiveness through digital management do not convince members of their usefulness.
- Design decisions placed in the hands of managers make intranet applications that contribute to management tasks, especially communication and coordination.
- Group membership rises when employees are allowed to form their own groups and conduct group work with some autonomy and privacy (though actual contributions to management effectiveness and self-organization are not known).
- When intranets and the public access website must share design and maintenance teams, the intranet is likely to have a lower priority.
- Multiple divisional intranets make the creation and use of an umbrella intranet challenging.

Department of Housing and Urban Development (HUD)

The Department of Housing and Urban Development has had five iterations of its intranet beginning in November 1996. The first four, called "HUDweb," were referred to as "HUD's Internal Information Network." From 1996 to 2000, the HUDweb was modified on a yearly basis, with the goal of simplifying the website and making it more useful to employees. A major rethinking and revision of the website occurred in 2001 with the unveiling of a customizable intranet renamed "hud@work."

In August 1996, HUD decided to "add on" an intranet in response to perceived management problems, especially breakdowns in communication. The initial idea for an intranet came from the technical team who worked on the public access website, but management staff wanted to play a prominent role in its development and design. The intranet was viewed as a management tool to improve communications. The idea was that the agency could "work smarter, not harder, without paper." From the beginning, the intranet, or HUDweb, had support from HUD's leadership. Although not directly concerned about the management problems and the

Figure 4.3: hud@work Intranet Home Page

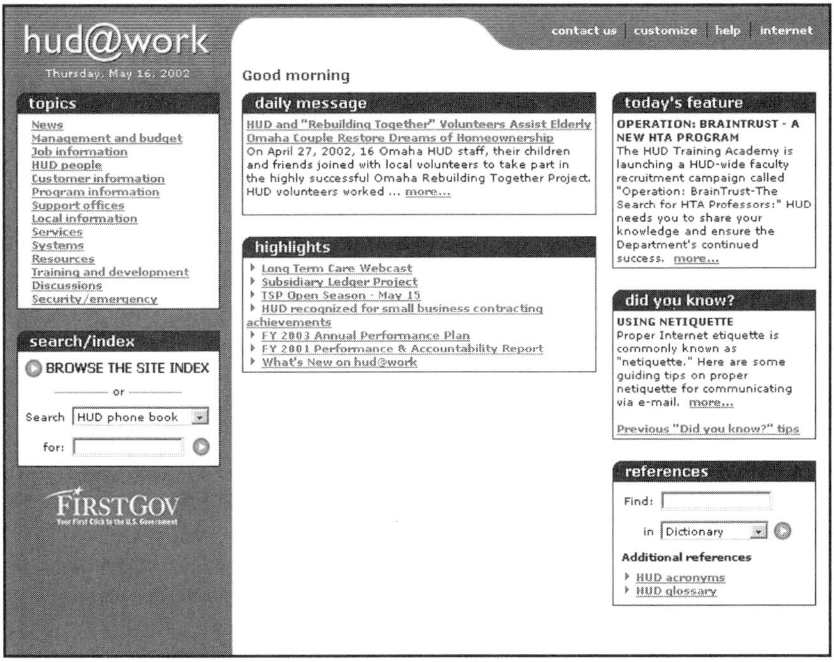

potential of an intranet for solving those problems, then Secretary Henry Cisneros was taken with the Clinton administration's vision of the Internet as a superhighway and understood that a HUD intranet might contribute to getting computers into public housing.

The technical team that worked on developing the intranet was dedicated to that project and separate from the technical team working on Internet projects. The intranet team recognized that the audiences for the two systems were also different. In developing the Internet website, staff needed to think about how citizens and nonprofit groups were likely to use HUD's website. In developing the intranet, the focus shifted to thinking about how staff were likely to use the intranet. The assumption was that staff would not access the intranet for things specific to their program, but would want to be able to do things that were general to HUD as an organization, such as human resource information and tasks.

From August through October 1996, the intranet team worked with managers in general administration on developing the conceptual content. The intranet team reported to the deputy secretary. In organizing the planning for the intranet, management learned from its experience in the development of the HUD public access website, which included staff volunteers on a working group at the planning stage. This resulted in a large working group of about 35 people, mainly people with technical skills and without a department-wide perspective. There was no working group for the intranet but instead a small team including both management and technical people.

The team asked managers what questions they were asked most often. Generally, their responses consisted of basic information questions that entailed information exchange rather than problem solving issues. The team developed broad topics using an almost intuitive common sense understanding of what should be accessible on the intranet. In November 1996, a prototype of the first HUDweb was launched. Top-level support was key at this stage. Indeed, the information technology director had a blank check to work toward the success of the prototype. The intranet team held briefings and worked through a network of staff to encourage use of HUDweb. Although the intranet had support at the secretary's level, managers within HUD often regarded it as the Internet's "baby sister" and saw the public access website as the primary electronic work site.

As is often the case in technological adoptions, exogenous events played a critical role. Shortly after the launch of the second version of HUDweb, Congress proposed abolishing HUD, and Secretary Cisneros decided that the intranet would be a good way to communicate with staff about the future of HUD. The resulting information campaign brought employees to the intranet on a more routine basis. When staff accessed the intranet, they first saw a message from the secretary in the center of the home page. During the tenure of Secretary Andrew Cuomo, there was further development of intranet content with particular attention to what was important to the staff. The intranet home page was organized by topics: What's New; Feature; Home Page; and Highlights.

The availability of information in both paper and electronic forms posed a problem in terms of generating and sustaining employee use of the intranet. If information was sent to all employees or posted on bulletin boards, then employees had less reason to access the intranet. A major boost in intranet use occurred when the Office of Personnel ceased printing vacancy announcements and posted them only on the intranet. When Secretary Cuomo announced there would be a cut in HUD staff from 12,000 to 7,000 and suggested that staff check HUDweb the following Monday for job announcements, the server crashed.

At the time of budgetary cutbacks, the intranet offered a chat room for staff to post comments anonymously. The purpose was to enable employees to discuss issues associated with managing change in the agency. The chat room was moderated by a chair, and both the secretary and deputy secretary participated for a while. There were 6,000 discrete users at one time. As the budgetary crisis passed, use of chat rooms diminished.

In 1998, there was a Web Awareness Day in Washington and in the regional offices to launch "two websites ➔ one hud" to teach staff the different benefits of HUD's public access website and intranet (see Figure 4.4). The message was that employees should use HUDweb—the intranet—to do their job; the deputy secretary's message was that the intranet was a "tool, not a toy." On the other hand, HUD's external website was designed for the public as a clearinghouse of information and services for consumers and business partners. As a result of this campaign, there was a doubling of intranet hits in six months, and that level of use was sustained for the next several years.

By 2000, HUDweb was four years old. With a consistent look and feel, it was used by employees in the field offices and Washington. It was operated by a small, centralized group. Employees' computers opened to HUDweb's home page with a focus and theme for the day. HUDweb was not personalized to each staff person.

One of the recurring problems in generating and sustaining employee use of HUD's intranet continued to be differentiating it from HUD's Internet website. The names of both were very similar: HUDweb and HUD.gov. The look and colors of the two websites were also very similar. In 2000 a contest was held to rename HUD's intranet. The new name, announced at a HUD Web Day, was hud@work. Red became the primary color for HUD.gov; for hud@work, it was green. The motto "if it's green, it can't be seen" was crafted to remind employees of the difference between the two sites.

As a result of focus groups with employees, hud@work added a customization feature. When employees booted up their computers, the

Figure 4.4: HUD Intranet Flyer

two websites one hud

HUDweb–What is it? (HUDweb.hud.gov)

HUD web is a management tool for communicating and doing work. It gives you what you need to do your job. It helps employees work smarter instead of harder. It's not optional–it's essential.

Who is it for?

HUD employees only.

What will I find?

- Important information to keep HUD staff up-to-date.
- Tools to help staff do their jobs.
- Business and Operating Plans for accomplishing HUD goals.
- Chat rooms to exchange ideas on important issues.
- HUD office homepages filled with information just for HUD staff.

Why is it important?

It empowers HUD staff by giving them the information and tools they need, when they need them!

HUD's Homes and Communities Page–What is it? (www.hud.gov)

HUD's Homes and Communities page is a clearinghouse of information and services for consumers and our business partners. It's not about HUD–it's about homes and communities.

Who Is It For?

The public.

What will I find?

- Easy to use information for citizens like "how to buy a home".
- Special pages on major HUD initiatives Webcasts of important training sessions and speeches.
- Databases and systems that let HUD partners work with us online.
- A whole section that teaches kids how to be good citizens.

Why Is It Important?

It empowers citizens by giving them what they need to solve their own problems 24 hours a day, 7 days a week.

hud

hud@work page appeared. Four items appeared on every employee's intranet home page:

- Daily message from the secretary
- Today's feature, which can be a news or personnel item
- Employee highlights including personnel announcements and an employee locator
- "What's New" feature, which includes personnel rule announcements and policy statements

Features that appear automatically in the left toolbar include:

- Chat
- Groups
- Handbooks and forms
- Headquarters offices
- Jobs and benefits
- Local offices
- Management
- Procedures
- Resources online
- Work online
- Suggestions
- Staff locator
- Search

Employees also have links to design the layout and content of the page. They can personalize other features they wish to include from five categories: hud@work tools, personal tools, working groups, Internet tools, and federal government tools.

The current iteration of HUD's intranet has virtual team technology whereby staff can exchange files, engage in real-time chat, teleconference, work together from different geographic locations, and set up meetings. Although managers are keen on this capability in concept, they seem reluctant to use it.

Lessons Learned

- Intranets should be designed to work in harmony with the culture of the organization. Intranet modifications should involve employees in design and solicit feedback from employees on what is, and is not, working for them.
- Support at the secretary's level is similarly important for the intranet to be a department-wide success. It is likely that various bureaus or field offices within a department will initiate their own intranets. But the value of a department-wide intranet is that it serves a department-wide service and function. Although there is often field office resistance to Washington oversight, there is no need for field offices to duplicate the departmental information and services offered by the department's intranet.
- Development of the intranet should be driven by management goals and involve management staff. It should not be driven by the technical team alone. Indeed, a technical perspective can limit the possibilities. If designers think in terms of what the technology can do, they are limited by the current hardware and software. Common sense and openness to new ideas appeared to be more important than a sophisticated understanding of the

technology. Indeed, the most successful development pattern involved management staff developing wish lists of applications and the technical people then determining the operational capabilities.

- Marketing the intranet within the agency is also key to success. Throughout the development and deployment of the five iterations of HUD's intranet, the intranet team was conscious of the need to involve staff and managers, and to promote the advantages of the intranet. Slogans such as "smart HUD employees work online" were typical of these promotions. Two marketing campaigns were especially important at HUD: the 1998 campaign "two websites → one hud" and the 2001 customizable hud@work, advertised as "HUD's Next Generation Intranet."

Environmental Protection Agency (EPA)

The EPA's intranet, EPA@Work, became available agency-wide in January 1998. The idea behind the intranet was to put information that is important to EPA employees at their fingertips: "Multiple sources of information to help EPA employees effectively do their jobs are just a click away." The latest iteration of the EPA intranet utilizes a new tasks and topics "portal" design by which EPA employees can quickly access agency processes and areas of interest by subject.

The first EPA intranet was not a spin-off from EPA's Internet site, but resulted from the realization that other agencies were developing intranets and that there would be value from an EPA intranet. A team of three, operating from the Office of Information Resources and Management but with support from the top of the agency, developed the prototypes of the intranet and oversaw its initial agency-wide deployment in January 1998. The members of the team all had some computer and technical background but were basically interested in information applications. In developing applications, team members interviewed managers of various programs to identify areas where the intranet might offer new opportunities. The intranet did not have its own budget; instead, funding came from the budget for the public access website.

Information was organized similarly on the EPA intranet and its Internet. In each case librarians catalogued metadata records using a hierarchy of control terms. In the case of the intranet, material was organized as text-based links under three main topics:

- Across the Agency—news from the EPA administrator, recent agency initiatives, contacts and work groups, news, and the calendar
- Management and Administration—employment and job openings, budgeting and purchasing, computers and networks, internal policy site, and employee services

Figure 4.5: EPA@Work Intranet Home Page

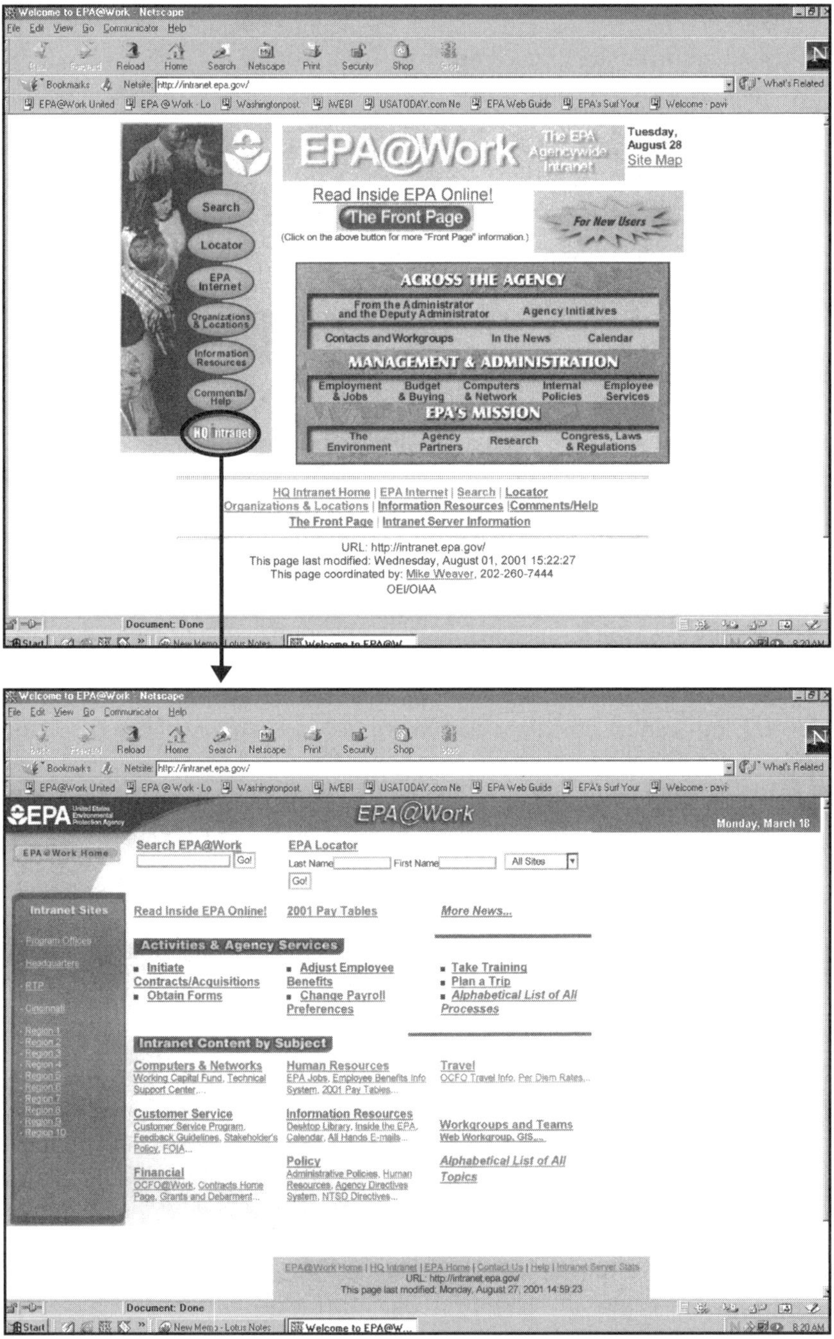

- EPA's Mission—including major recent research initiatives, Congressional action, and access to both summary and full text presentation of the laws and regulations under which the agency operates

The links from the EPA@Work front page include:

- Search and locator functions
- Link to the EPA external website (epa.gov)
- Organization and locations with charts of headquarters and regional offices
- Information resources, with calendar and e-mail
- Links for comments and help
- Link to the headquarters intranet, with features for making changes in personnel documents, travel information and forms, customer satisfaction program, contract forms, human resources, and a link to information on administrative policies

Several other components of EPA, including the regional offices, had intranets of their own. The goal for the agency-wide intranet was not to duplicate these but to provide information and functions that were common to all EPA employees.

About 70 percent of the EPA@Work content has been facilities-oriented including activities such as office cleaning, copying, and parking. One function that employees have consistently used and found valuable is the "EPA locator" by which staff can find contact information for other employees and contractors. This function has been prominent on all iterations of EPA@Work. Another popular function involves forms and information on travel. Forms can be downloaded and printed, but cannot yet be completed and submitted online.

The EPA intranet offers the capability of work groups, chat rooms, and collaboration through its license for Lotus Notes and Lotus Notes Mail. These more interactive functions have not yet been used widely in the agency because of training requirements, firewalls, and costs. The intranet team recently had a demonstration of the PeopleSoft portal, which would allow customization and more collaboration and flexibility; this may be the next iteration of EPA@Work.

Lessons Learned

- Marketing of the intranet to employees has been important throughout its developments and deployments. At various points, "Intranet Weeks" were held when the intranet team did a "dog and pony" show to illustrate the benefits and capabilities of the intranet. Although attendance tended to be low at such events, the team found these to be an important way of publicizing the intranet. For the launch of the September 2001 iteration, the intranet team designed a "power-up with EPA@Work" campaign using an "Empower Bar" theme to convey the idea that employees who are hungry for information can get "vital, up-to-date information" by starting their day with the "new and improved" agency intranet. This campaign involved posters, flyers, and bookmarks with the same slogans and images.

- The EPA intranet team believed it was important to expand the intranet as the technology became available to do more on it. The team tended to develop its own software and not be constrained by what was available "off the shelf." Money was a constraint and affected what the team was able to develop; for example, portal technologies were too expensive.

General Services Administration (GSA)

The GSA intranet, InSite, was developed in 1996 as a result of an initiative offered by David Barram, the GSA administrator during the second Clinton administration. Barram had come from private industry, had a close relationship with AOL, and was surprised at the lack of online activities at GSA. GSA had developed an Internet site in 1994 for citizen and business access, but the site was not accessible from within GSA. There were some small intranets operating within areas of GSA, but no agency-wide intranet. At a GSA information technology meeting in 1996, Barram proposed that he order GSA to offer employees Internet and intranet access within four months, by Flag Day (June 14, 1996). The chief financial officer shared the view that an intranet would enhance GSA's ability to conduct its business. However, others feared that if employees were able to browse the Internet, they might be distracted by other online activities.

In response to the GSA administrator's proposal, the chief information officer (CIO) worked with a small team to make GSA's computer network Internet accessible and to develop a vision for an intranet. GSA's intranet was "home-grown," largely based on the experiences of team members in navigating Internet sites. There were five major categories of features for the GSA intranet including travel and human resources. The administrator, who retained a close interest and offered several ideas from his industry experience, named the site "InSite." The Office of Communications marketed the rollout on Flag Day 1996 and planned the official announcement. The rollout highlighted GSA's desire to have a useful site for its employees and emphasized the practical aspects of how to browse the intranet and the "do's and don'ts" of using it.

It took over a year before intranet use took off. Key to its success was having it become a work site, not just a document site. The bulletin board area of the intranet, called "My 2 Cents," was a popular feature that brought employees to the intranet. This began as an anonymous, open bulletin board for the posting of questions and answers, but problems arose as the

Figure 4.6: GSA InSite Intranet Home Page

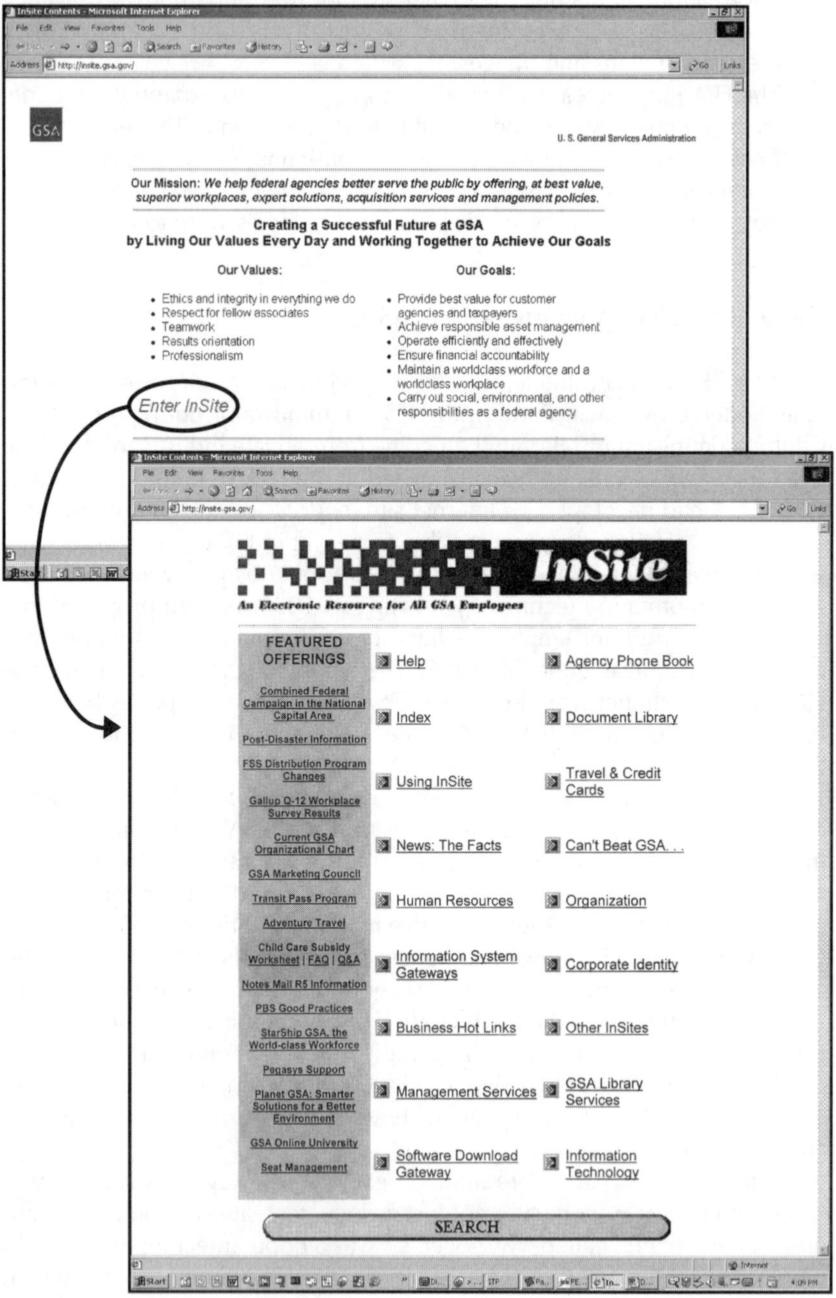

comments digressed and some users failed to understand "netiquette." The GSA administrator intervened by monitoring the bulletin board, responding to comments, and offering cash awards for suggestions. He also encouraged other top executives within GSA to participate, but some managers were reluctant to reply by name.

As the intranet became more robust and more of a tool, employees gravitated to the site. Basic features such as a telephone directory drew people to the site. The intranet team still struggles with making it more useful to the end users. At this time, there is no collaborative work space on the intranet, but there are some pilots under way. Other methods of knowledge sharing, such as Lotus Notes and Quick Place, are being investigated. One idea that is attracting interest is using the intranet as a tool of "knowledge management," but at this point the terms and labels are somewhat fuzzy to managers, who are more business oriented.

Lessons Learned

- Functionality is key to success. If the intranet offers useful services, employees will come to it.
- Although the GSA-wide intranet was initiated from the top of the agency, top management encouraged experimentation and further development by others in the organization when it became available. Experimentation by subunits had benefits in that employees had some sense of ownership over the intranet and were enthusiastic about its possibilities. But this strategy had costs because employees created subunit intranets and quickly became more attached to them than to the GSA intranet.

Department of Commerce

We were able to investigate intranet use at the Department of Commerce from two points of view. The Office of the Secretary houses the department's information resource management functions and supports the umbrella intranet for the entire department. The second perspective is from one of the seven operating units of the department, the U.S. Commercial Service, which maintains its own intranet. Like Transportation, the Department of Commerce is in some ways a holding company with separate divisions, each with its own strong identity, mission, and culture. This makes the development of an intranet challenging because it must overcome not only the typical resistance to new technologies, but also the insular tendencies of historically entrenched divisions.

Figure 4.7: Office of the Secretary, Department of Commerce Intranet Home Page

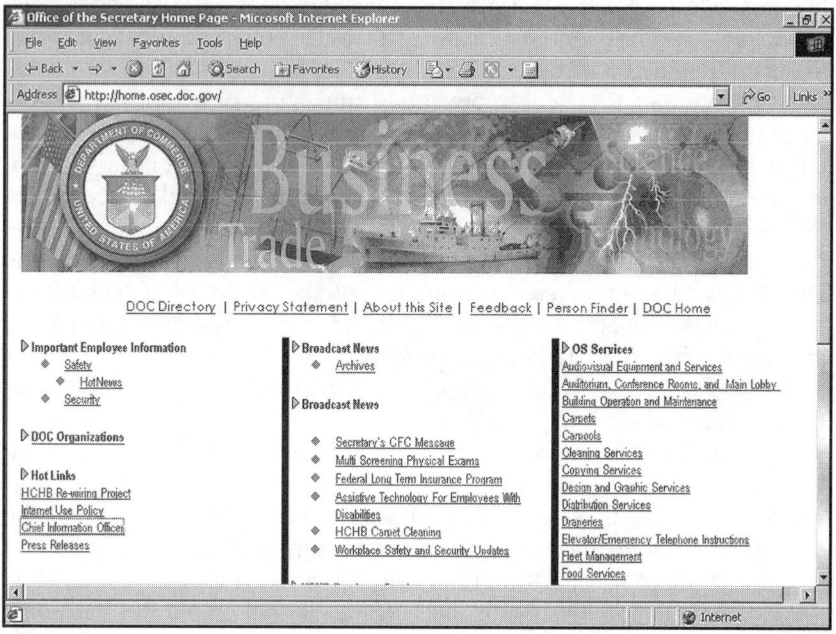

CS Intranet

The intranet for the Department of Commerce's Commercial Service (CS Intranet) is much more elaborate and sophisticated than its department-wide counterpart, which is more of a site map or portal. The present Commercial Service site is the third-generation design, and staff expects only cosmetic changes in the immediate future, although eventually they expect to add a search function. The CS site is not personalized, though security and authentication were recent issues, and the site is password protected.

The reasons behind the construction of the site appear to be most clearly tied to the need to share business process software. The core task in the CS is to match business opportunities to interested investors here and abroad. Databases for each, categorized in various ways, allow CS staff to help accomplish this commercial matchmaking. Business process software and databases are shared on the intranet. The software helps staff coordinate events for bringing businesses together and make arrangements for foreign trade missions. Teamwork is a key element of this commercial matching work. The final brokering of deals is done in person or by phone, but the information needed to know what deals are possible is made available with the software. A unified intranet makes it easier to communicate and coordinate information among the 287 offices outside of Washington, D.C. Intranet software has made it possible for staff to improve forecasts of event attendance, for example.

The current intranet was created by "one or two" outside contractors and CS agency people. Many of the programs and ideas for work elements on the intranet came from teams within CS who are able to get management support for their idea. The intranet development process was incremental. Ideas for applications emerged in response to problems in the field. There is only a limited level of support for project development, however, and there are more ideas than resources available. Projects must be readily seen to have value for them to get the needed in-house support. Not all ideas are successfully translated into applications, however. For example, staff wanted an interactive meeting scheduler for coordination among the remote offices, but found they could not do it even with a modest investment in new software.

Software expense is an issue. CS Intranet has acquired a shared document application, and uses instant chat and some large data sets. However, staff did not believe the division could afford desirable B2G software. Additional externally designed software is desired but seen as out of reach. Established government sites such as Employee Express are available from CS Intranet. Some of the material for the intranet also came from the Commerce Department's Internet site.

Seven main programs constitute the basic business processes. Menus for these programs are organized as follows on the site:

- eMenus, including applications to arrange trade events, make contacts, and obtain finance and product management
- Programs to match businesses with investors, arrange trade fairs, identify likely business and trading partners, provide access to market research and commercial news
- Marketing materials, including success stories and best practices, newsletters, and press releases
- Critical databases for market research, performance measures, and the Commercial Service Operations Manual
- Employee search programs
- News
- Personnel, including Employee Express, job announcements, and travel policies

Much of the software in these menus requires training to use. Descriptions of training opportunities, though not the courses themselves, are available online. Interview comments suggest that it has not been easy to get as widespread a use of the applications as desired. As the intranet content has become more valuable to staff, and more important within the organization, its use has increased.

Office of the Secretary, Department of Commerce Intranet

The intranet for the Department of Commerce as a whole was created as part of former Secretary William Daley's effort to quickly establish a digital capacity. He challenged the department to become a "digital department" in 45 days and built consensus for this with a series of town hall meetings. His vision was to have interactive features on the intranet permitting members to conduct international business, communicate, and make travel arrangements online, for example. Communication was perhaps the largest issue. With 50,000 employees to inform, a wide-reaching communications method was a necessity. In 1999, designers were challenged to come up with a home page to show quick success with e-government in line with the Clinton administration's priorities. Many of the individual program divisions, such as the Bureau of the Census and the Commercial Service, already had their own intranet, some largely based on their Internet websites. The current secretary has not yet focused attention on the department-wide intranet at this point, but staff expect this to happen.

Cultural consolidation of the seven program divisions of Commerce was not a top priority, so this mission for the intranet was not a driving force, as it was for Transportation. As a result, few general purpose applications have emerged. The focus so far has been as a source for important departmental documents, forms, policy statements, and information about building maintenance services and meeting spaces. Interactive features such as travel planning are considerations for the near future. Home access is an objective, and collaborative online work group programs have also been explored, but are not yet features of the intranet. A pilot project testing online collaboration found that face-to-face communication was preferred.

The site functions largely as a portal, but one designed to provide easy access to applications used with outside customers, with less attention placed on employee needs. The present site was created in the Public Affairs Office within the Office of the Secretary. Library staff and web technicians are represented on the design team. For the most part, the intranet site features information links, not interactive functions. The site contains links to a number of services:

- Major offices in the Office of the Secretary
- Department policy statements on administration, civil rights, security
- Department news and documents
- Employee services, including cafeteria information, forms, mail and telephone directories, and travel policy information
- Employee resources including links to Employee Express, the employee handbook, orientation
- Services for building maintenance

Some effort has gone into making staff aware of the site, but marketing has not been aggressive. Those who find the site are reported to like it. A demonstration at a town meeting in 1999 and one in the summer of 2000 introduced the site. Commitment to the site and its maintenance have been issues. Synergy between the intranet and Internet sites for the department is seen as the key to maintaining the site and keeping information up-to-date.

Resources have been a problem, too. The intranet and Internet sites share a technical staff and a common budget, but funds for either are scarce. In general, the intranets within the divisions are viewed as more sophisticated and are apparently better funded and maintained than the umbrella intranet, because they use applications that interact with the public.

Lessons Learned

- With more specialized and sophisticated software come barriers to use and the need for training that can impede the full use of the capacity of intranets.
- Intranets may be created in response to the mandate for digital government as well as in response to a specific need.
- Library-based designers, in contrast to design teams composed of management or technical members, tend to create information resource links rather than group collaboration or interactive applications.
- Cost-conscious agencies can create intranet sites, with minimal use of outside contractors, using incremental changes to existing platforms.

Department of Justice (DOJ)

The intranet at the Department of Justice, DOJnet, was created in 1998 as a spin-off of the formation of the department's Internet site, established earlier. The designers and technical systems staff were originally brought into the organization to determine how to respond to Freedom of Information Act requirements to make agency data available to the public. Another purpose was to serve the Clinger-Cohen Act requiring agencies to make information and services available online. The mandate by the Clinton administration to make a "Kid's" Internet page available at each agency was a third impetus. DOJ respondents believe the federal push has been first for the Internet to link clients and employees. The intranet emerged from the concerns of the department's chief information officer that an umbrella intranet was needed to provide information and better communication to the department as a whole. Some information was being copied and mailed to employees across the 36 components of the department. For example, a recently added subscription to an online news service linked to the intranet replaced in-house news clipping, copying, and distributing. Other news, administrative, and policy documents were being duplicated in the separate, divisional intranets. Like Commerce and

Transportation, the Department of Justice houses a number of agencies with separate identities and their own intranets.

Both the Internet and intranet sites at Justice are maintained and designed by the same staff group, composed of computer technicians and library information resource specialists. As the Internet site was developing, the technicians quickly realized they needed help with content, and the involvement of the library staff in web design evolved from that. The technicians work to maintain the server and write the html code. The intranet content is now a component of the DOJ library, which is developing an information resource management specialty. The library staff design the content of both the Internet and intranet sites including the appearance and the organization of the data. This placement of the web design function is seen to have affected both the library and the design process.

Funding for both the intranet and Internet sites comes from the same budget line. No particular level of resources is allocated to the intranet, and funds are tight. Cuts in the Department of Justice budget are more likely to come out of administrative funds than funds seen to affect crime fighting more directly. Only the first version of the intranet was designed by a contractor. Since then all work has been in-house.

Library staff determined the content of the site based on the types of reference information requests they receive in the library. Ideas for links were based first on the reference sources that employees ask for most often. Librarians also brainstormed about what information might be useful, examined other sites, and gleaned ideas from Intranet Roundtable participants. Other information support staff in personnel, litigation, and management offices were queried about what requests for information they receive most often.

The site is largely non-interactive at present. It offers links to the most recent department policy files and government sites such as Employee Express. Forms can be printed and mailed, but not filed online. The major categories of services and information sources on the departmental intranet site in October 2001 were:

- News and Events, including today's news clips
- People, Places, and Offices, employee organizations, shuttle bus routes, and commercial directories
- Research Resources, including library links, full-text legal decisions and manuals, asset forfeiture information
- Career Development, including job listings, résumé builder, training opportunities, e-learning
- Your Workplace, with links to ethics laws, EEO complaint forms, office supplies, personnel information
- Your Finances, with links to investments and savings plans, insurance information, payroll information, Employee Express, and retirement calculators

- Health and Welfare, including health benefits, employee assistance program, work life and flextime information, and leave bank
- Technical Information on web development training
- Travel and Weather

Categories as well as contents are much expanded from the previous version.

The next generation of the intranet is to be more interactive, but this will take a major change in architecture and represents a major investment. The information resource staff will depend on the Internet builders in the department for this advance. Overcoming security issues and including electronic signatures will mean that the system will be able to take time and attendance information online, making the site heavily used.

Virtual groups and collaboration are features of intranet work sites within the program divisions, where litigation work, such as briefs, may be shared. Many such work spaces are confidential and password protected. The department also sponsors extranets, cross-divisional work spaces, that are secure. They are used for work involving interdepartmental jobs such as between Treasury and the IRS. The DOJ-wide intranet itself does not yet have applications for collaborative work.

An example of one type of interagency intranet is the Consolidated Assets Tracking System, CATS. This system is used in five agencies in offices across the country to maintain an up-to-date inventory of assets seized under drug, money laundering, and racketeering statutes. Most offices in the Drug Enforcement Administration (DEA), Federal Bureau of Investigation (FBI), Immigration and Naturalization Service (INS), the U.S. Marshals Service, and the U.S. Attorney's offices have access to a computer dedicated to this system. The system itself is not interactive, but a special interagency e-mail links users. The system connects to the DOJ intranet from the Research Resources page. There has not been funding for marketing the program, and designers estimate that only about half of those eligible to use it know about it. Improvements planned include moving from a DOS-based to a Windows-based operating system.

Security issues in the department complicate the creation of an intranet considerably. The FBI and DEA have stand-alone computers not linked to other DOJ sites, including DOJnet. Separate computers available in some offices do link into the department-wide intranet, but the transition is awkward and inconvenient. These and other law enforcement divisions do have their own intranets. Because some of the information on the intranet may be sensitive, agency respondents asked us not to reproduce their home page.

Little has been done to explicitly market DOJnet, but its value has been recognized within the department. Its use has snowballed. One of the actions that helped popularize the site was to give it links to personnel functions and personal finance information. Highlights of news and new information items are also sent out by e-mail, making members aware of what is available at the site. E-mails also announce the existence of an archive of past items and provide a link to the archive on the intranet. At present, the Netscape home page for employees is the DOJ Internet website. DOJ is considering making the department intranet home page the home page for all employees. There is some reluctance to do this, however, because of the strong identity employees have with the divisions and divisional intranets.

Lessons Learned

- Once again we observe that when Internet and intranet sites are funded from the same budget and must share allocations, the Internet seems to get the larger share of funding.
- Funding for intranet and Internet sites, along with other administration-related functions, is more readily cut from tight budgets than other, more directly mission-focused work.
- Cost-conscious agencies must typically rely on in-house solutions and do not necessarily turn to outside consultants.
- Security issues in some agencies create challenging conditions for intranets since sensitive data must be protected from unauthorized access. This has meant stand-alone computers and the absence of linkages among intranets.

Human Resources Applications on Agency Intranets

Since intranet uses for human resources functions are often the most common and well developed of the uses of intranets, the human resources applications in the six agencies were examined in particular detail.

Department of Transportation

The department-wide intranet offers crosscutting human resources functions at the Department of Transportation, while HR procedures that are specific to a division are provided on the divisions' intranets. Most of the HR functions on the DOT-wide intranet are non-interactive, offering a central repository for information about awards, benefits—including long-term care options—job opportunities, and work-life balance. Centralizing this information was seen as offering major savings in time and labor, though the amount has not been quantified.

Department of Housing and Urban Development

In developing an agency-wide intranet at HUD, the assumption was that staff would not access the intranet for things specific to their program, but would want to be able to do things that were general to HUD as an organization, such as human resource information and tasks. The design team asked managers what questions they were asked most often, and generally the responses related to basic information questions that entailed information exchange rather than problem solving issues. A major boost in intranet use occurred when Personnel ceased printing vacancy announcements and posted them only on the intranet. One of four features that appear on each employee's intranet home page is Employee Highlights, including personnel announcements and an employee locator. Additionally, employees can select to personalize their page with features including handbooks, forms, jobs, and benefits.

Environmental Protection Agency

At EPA, one of three links from the EPA@Work front page is to Headquarters Intranet, with features for making changes in personnel documents, travel information and forms, the customer satisfaction program, contract forms, human resources, and links to information on administrative policies. One function that employees have consistently found valuable and regularly use is the "EPA locator" by which staff can find contact information for other employees and contractors. This function has been prominent on all iterations of EPA@Work. Another function that is popular involves forms and information on travel. Forms can be downloaded and printed, but cannot yet be completed and submitted online.

At EPA, most of the HR functions that are available interactively at this time are made possible through Employee Express and the Thrift Savings Plan (TSP). EPA is in the process of implementing HR Pro, the PeopleSoft enterprise software that is being customized for EPA. When that is in place, employees will have access to their personnel records and employee leave will be managed there. EPA also has an automated Employee Benefits Information System (EBIS) through which employees can receive a synopsis of their leave, TSP account holdings, and health and retirement benefits, either Civil Service Retirement System (CSRS) or Federal Employees Retirement System (FERS) as appropriate. Finally, EPA has an automated job database available on the public access site called EZHire (www.epa.gov/ezhire/), which will be linked from the intranet.

General Services Administration

InSite, the GSA intranet, includes five major categories of features including travel and human resources. As the intranet became more robust and more of a tool that employees could use, staff gravitated to the site. Basic features such as a telephone directory drew people to the intranet. Currently, there are two HR/financial applications available through InSite. One is FEDdesk, which is an application that handles time and attendance records, travel and miscellaneous reimbursements, and cash awards. Another is Pay and Leave Statements, a payroll application that renders employees' pay records and permits employees to change address and federal and state tax withholding information.

Department of Commerce

The department's intranet provides information to employees on a number of HR-related functions. It operates as a portal for information for employees such as directories, travel policies, occupational safety issues and reports, and information on health, retirement, and other benefits. These informational services, though not interactive, offer major savings in HR employee time and printing costs. Employee Express, the contract payroll service provider, is interactive and makes it possible for employees to make changes in payroll information online. This saves time for HR personnel who would otherwise have to handle these changes. According to the staff we interviewed, the greatest time savings from these intranet services is to the employees. No longer must they spend time trying to find the correct HR specialist to see, since the information is always available online. Such savings are needed because of major reductions in the size of the HR department over the past decade. It is not a matter of transferring HR specialists to new tasks so much as doing more with less.

Department of Justice

At Justice, the organization-wide intranet is also largely non-interactive. Information on health benefits, investments and savings plans, employee assistance programs, and work-life and flextime, as well as the leave bank, are all available from the intranet. As in Commerce, Employee Express allows employees to make changes in their payroll options without the intervention of HR specialists. While more interactive HR functions are desired, such change is expected to be expensive and had not been made six months after we first heard of their plans.

Overall, the respondents readily acknowledged that the HR functions, both the more typical non-interactive ones and the hoped-for interactive developments, are enormous timesavers for HR staff who otherwise spend enormous amounts of time responding to requests for information. Printing costs are also reduced through online provision of notices, rules, and directories. Many HR functions are still performed on an individual basis, however, including benefits changes and choices, as well as evaluations and rewards.

Findings and Recommendations

Findings

We can collate the lessons learned from each of the case studies into five overall observations.

Finding 1: In large multi-divisional departments, divisional or regional intranets predate the department-wide intranet and pose challenges for establishing a niche for an umbrella intranet.

In five of the six agencies examined—Transportation, EPA, GSA, Commerce, and Justice—divisional intranets existed prior to the creation of a department-wide intranet. In several agencies, employees in those divisions had become accustomed to using their divisional intranets in their day-to-day operations. This was particularly apparent for the Department of Commerce's Commercial Services Intranet—which has become integral to matching business opportunities and interested investors, the core function of the division—and for the Department of Justice's interagency intranet, the Consolidated Assets Tracking System. In both cases, much of the work of divisions was actually conducted on the intranet.

Not only did these agencies have small task-oriented intranets, but there were also robust divisional intranets. For example, at DOT, each of the 11 operating divisions had a functioning intranet. At EPA, each of the regional offices had intranets of their own. Within the Department of Justice, a number of agencies with separate identities and established functions, such as the FBI and INS, have their own intranets.

In several agencies, individual program or division intranets are regarded as more sophisticated and appear to be better funded and maintained than the agency-wide intranet. Three factors seem to account for this. First, over time these smaller intranets have been adapted to their users' needs and have developed a clientele through repeated experiences. Second, fewer people to appeal to and a more focused functionality have made it easier for these intranets to be responsive to their users. And, third, most of these divisions make a direct contribution to the public, and although the intranets are not accessible to the public, they do support the public service mission of the division.

The successes of divisional and regional intranets pose a challenge to the success of an agency-wide intranet. Within all the agencies examined, there is evidence of the usefulness of an internal, closed website for an organization. But it may be that there is an optimal size for the utility and functionality of an intranet. In most of the agencies examined, the agency-wide intranet was eclipsed by sub-agency (regional and divisional) intranets. In these instances, there was generally a link to the agency-wide intranet for department-level functions and information. But it would appear that most of the work of the department occurs in the smaller units and that the sub-agency intranets are more valuable to staff on a daily basis.

To be successful, a department-wide intranet needs to identify a role for itself that will draw employees. The Department of Transportation attempted to do this with some success. It viewed the department-wide intranet as a means to foster a common culture within the agency. Similarly, at EPA, the goal for the agency-wide intranet was not to duplicate the divisional and regional intranets but to provide information and functions common to all EPA employees. The Department of Justice is struggling with the same question. At present, the Netscape home page for employees is the DOJ public access website, but there is talk of changing that to the intranet home page. Still, there is some reluctance to do this because of the strong identity employees have with the divisions within Justice and employee links to their divisional intranet.

GSA has also experienced tension between sub-agency intranets and the agency-wide intranet. Within GSA, each service has now created its own intranet, which is used as the default home site for employees in that service. The regional offices have created their own intranets as well. To some extent, these entrepreneurial ventures were encouraged by the GSA intranet team, but the effect has been to relegate GSA InSite to the role of a holding company that is accessed from the other intranets. However, trying to consolidate and impose centralization on a decentralized organization is likely to be impossible given the organizational culture.

Finding 2: Top departmental support for and interest in the agency's intranet is especially critical in the initial planning for and launching of the intranet.

In virtually all of the agencies examined, support from the secretary or deputy secretary level was essential. Without such interest and support, an agency-wide intranet would not have developed. In three of the six organizations, support for a department-wide intranet came directly from the secretary.

- At HUD, both Secretary Cisneros and Secretary Cuomo were proactive in the development of the intranet and found opportunities to broaden its use. Cisneros, who was intrigued with the Clinton administration's vision of the Internet as a superhighway, supported the intranet as a concept and project. When Congress proposed abolishing HUD, Cisneros suggested using the intranet as a tool for communicating with employees. As a result of this initiative, more staff became accustomed to accessing the intranet. When he became secretary, Cuomo also supported the HUD intranet. On one occasion, after he announced the necessity of a staff cut and suggested that employees consult HUDweb for job announcements, there was so much traffic that the server crashed.
- GSA Administrator David Barram had come from private industry, had a close relationship with AOL, and was surprised at the lack of online activities at GSA. At a GSA information technology meeting in 1996, Barram proposed that he order GSA to offer employees Internet and intranet access within four months, by Flag Day.
- Commerce Secretary Daley challenged the department to become a "digital department" in 45 days and built consensus for this with a series of town hall meetings. His vision was to have interactive features on an agency-wide intranet, permitting members to conduct international business, communicate, and make travel arrangements online, for example. With 50,000 employees to inform, a wide-reaching communications method was a necessity. In 1999, designers were challenged to come up with a home page to show quick success with e-government in line with the administration's priorities.

In two of the case studies—the Departments of Justice and Transportation—support came primarily from the deputy secretary level. In these departments, the genesis for the intranet and staff support for its development came primarily from the chief information officer.

- At the Department of Justice, the intranet emerged from the concerns of the department's CIO that an umbrella intranet was needed to provide information and better communication to the department as a whole. It seemed unnecessary that in the electronic age much agency information was being copied and mailed to employees across the 36 components of the department. The intranet offered a way to more efficiently distribute information. For example, a recently added subscription to an online news service linked to the intranet replaced in-house news clipping, copying, and distributing.
- At the Department of Transportation, the e-government unit within the Office of the Chief Information Officer played the lead role in implementing an agency-wide intranet that would meet the goal of the development of a common DOT culture by generating strong linkages across divisions.

At EPA, the first intranet resulted from the realization that other agencies had developed intranets and that there would be value from an EPA intranet. A team of three, operating from the Office of Information Resources and Management but with support from the top of the agency, developed the prototypes of the intranet and oversaw its initial agency-wide deployment in January 1998.

Finding 3: Marketing of an agency-wide intranet is crucial to encouraging staff use.

Three of the six agencies examined had aggressive, and successful, marketing campaigns to generate staff interest and use. In general, these campaigns involved slogans and meetings, and accompanied the launching of each new iteration of the intranet.

- Marketing of the intranet to EPA employees has been important throughout its developments and deployments. At various points, "Intranet Weeks" were held when the intranet team did a "dog and pony" show to illustrate the benefits and capabilities of the intranet. Although attendance was often low at such events, the intranet team believed their publicity fostered more interest in and use of the intranet. For the launch of the September 2001 iteration, the intranet team designed a "power-up with EPA@Work" campaign using an "Empower Bar" (see Figure 4.8) theme to convey the idea that employees who are hungry for information can get "vital, up-to-date information" by starting their day with the "new and improved" agency intranet. This campaign involved posters, flyers, and bookmarks with the same slogans and images.
- At HUD, the intranet was viewed as a management tool to improve communication: "Work smarter, not harder, without paper." The slogan "smart HUD employees work online" was designed to encourage employees to use the intranet. In 1998, HUD made a concerted effort to differentiate its public access Internet site and its intranet for employees. A "Web Awareness Day" was held in Washington and in the regional offices to launch a "two websites → one hud" to highlight the message that the intranet was a "tool, not a toy." As a result of this campaign, there was a doubling of intranet hits in six months, and that level was sustained for the next several years. Some problems with differentiating HUD's intranet and public access website continued, and in 2000 a contest was held to rename the intranet. The winning name was hud@work. Again, slogans were utilized to catch employees' attention. "If it's green, it can't be seen" reminded employees that the primary color on HUD's intranet was green while its website color was red. Once more in 2001, when HUD added customization features to the intranet, this was advertised as "HUD's Next Generation Intranet."

- The GSA administrator named the agency's intranet "InSite." The Office of Communications marketed the rollout of the intranet on Flag Day 1996 and planned the official announcement. The rollout highlighted GSA's desire to have a valuable site for its employees. It also emphasized the practical aspects of how to browse the intranet and the "do's and don'ts" of using it.

Three departments—Transportation, Commerce, and Justice—have made more modest attempts at marketing their intranet sites. For example, the Department of Commerce introduced its intranet with a town meeting in 1999 and a demonstration in the summer of 2000. But in all cases, as employees become aware of the real value of the intranets, use increases.

Figure 4.8: EPA@Work EmpowerBar

Finding 4: Within federal agencies, more attention and energy is devoted to the agency's public access website than to its intranet.

This is not remarkable given legislative and public support for online Government to Citizen interactions, the federal government's commitment to digital government, and the number of Internet champions both inside and outside the federal establishment. Despite this focus on the Internet, all agencies are experimenting with transferring Internet technology and software, as well as the knowledge gained from developing and deploying Internet websites, to an internal agency intranet.

In most of the agencies examined, Internet and intranet staff and resources were shared. This was true in the Departments of Transportation, Justice, and Commerce. HUD has a separate staff dedicated to the intranet. Despite this, the intranet is still considered the Internet's "baby sister" and the Internet website is regarded as the primary electronic work site. At EPA, the intranet team members, all of whom had some computer and technical background but were basically interested in information applications, were separate from the Internet team. The EPA intranet did not have a separate budget; instead, funding came from the Internet budget.

Finding 5: In all the organizations examined, the development of the intranet has been an iterative process and is still very much evolving.

Agency personnel responsible for intranets are constantly evaluating how well their intranet is meeting the needs of employees and are looking for ways to improve it. None consider their intranet a finished product but instead see it as a work in progress. All agencies have had several iterations of their intranet.

- HUD has had five iterations of its intranet beginning in November 1996. The first four were entitled "HUDweb" and were referred to as "HUD's Internal Information Network." From 1996 to 2000, HUDweb was modified on a yearly basis, with the goal of simplifying the intranet and making it more useful to employees. A major rethinking and revision of the site occurred in 2001 with the unveiling of a customizable intranet renamed "hud@work."
- EPA's intranet was first available agency-wide in January 1998. Its latest iteration was launched in September 2001 and utilizes a new tasks and topics "portal" design by which EPA employees can quickly access agency processes and areas of interest by subject.
- The development of the Commercial Services Intranet within the Department of Commerce followed an incremental development process. Ideas for applications emerged in response to problems in the field.
- The Department of Justice's intranet is largely non-interactive at present. It offers links to the most recent department policy files and government sites such as Employee Express. Forms can be printed and mailed, but not filed online. The next-generation intranet is expected to be more interactive, but this will require a major change in architecture and a significant investment.

As part of this iterative process, chat rooms have been popular at particular times in a limited number of agencies. The use of chat rooms has been more episodic and hard to sustain for a long period of time.

- Within HUD, the chat feature on the intranet was used extensively by employees during the budgetary crisis under Secretary Cuomo. Both he and the deputy secretary encouraged the use of the chat room and participated in discussions about how best to manage changes associated with the financial problems. But as the budgetary crisis passed, use of the chat rooms diminished.
- At GSA, the bulletin board area of the intranet, named "My 2 Cents," was a popular feature and brought employees to the intranet. This began as an anonymous, open bulletin board for the posting of questions

and answers, but problems arose as comments digressed and some users failed to understand "netiquette." The GSA administrator intervened by monitoring the bulletin board, responding to comments, and offering cash awards for suggestions. He also encouraged other top executives within GSA to participate, but some managers were reluctant to reply by name.

Customization or personalization of intranets has also been a feature of the evolutionary development of intranets in a few agencies. This iteration generally occurs late in the process of development after employees have become accustomed to using the intranet and are seeking more innovation.

- DOT added a personalization feature for its intranet home page in its current iteration. Employees can now create their own version of the standard home page elements; establish links to online employee groups or communities, a weather site, an online dictionary, Google, and other features; and include their personal calendar.
- HUD's intranet added a personalization feature in 2001 with its hud@work iteration. In focus groups for the planning of hud@work, employees had requested such a feature.

Development of collaborative or shared work areas on intranets is another feature that has evolved in several organizations and is being planned in others. This has been more successful in some agencies than others.

- The DOT intranet offers the capacity to create and join interest-based virtual communities. This feature is one that employees value and use.
- HUD's current (2001) intranet includes virtual team technology that could be used for collaborative work through real-time chat, teleconferencing, and file exchange. Although managers favor the idea, they have been reluctant to use it.
- The EPA intranet offers work groups, chat rooms, and collaboration through its license for Lotus Notes and Lotus Notes Mail. These more interactive functions have not yet been used widely in the agency because of training requirements, firewalls, and costs. The intranet team recently had a demonstration of the PeopleSoft portal, which would allow customization and more collaboration and flexibility; this may be the next iteration of EPA@Work.
- At this time, there is no collaborative work space on GSA's intranet, but there are some pilots under way. Other methods of knowledge sharing, such as Lotus Notes and Quick Place, are also being investigated.
- The Department of Commerce has explored the possibility of collaborative online work group programs, but they are not yet features of the intranet. A pilot project testing online collaboration found that face-to-face communication was preferred.
- At the Department of Justice, virtual groups and collaboration are features of intranet work sites within the program divisions, where litigation

work such as briefs may be shared. These work spaces tend to be confidential and password protected. The agency-wide intranet does not yet have applications for collaborative work.

Recommendations

Our research offers a snapshot of intranet evolution as seen in the second half of 2001. The intranets we examined and those throughout the federal government are continuing to develop to better meet the needs of management and employees. Based on the analysis of the case studies, we offer three recommendations for enhancing intranet development in federal agencies.

Recommendation 1: A department-wide intranet requires a department-wide effort to be successful.

This recommendation encompasses three elements:

- *Upper management support is required.*
  If management wants employees to use the intranet, it must actively encourage employees to avail themselves of the options on the intranet. Managers should champion the intranet in their communications to employees. Their support should not be passive but active. Managers should be models to employees by using the intranet themselves. Manager support should be continual, not just at the point of the introduction of the intranet and subsequent iterations. For use of the intranet to be sustained, managers need to foster a behavioral change among employees.

  Finally, managers should make administrative decisions that require employees to use the intranet. For example, managers can discontinue paper copies of telephone directories and job announcements, the contents of which change frequently and can be easily updated online. Similarly, rules and regulations can be searched more easily in electronic form, making online versions more useful than paper copies.
- *Involvement of employees is essential.*
  To win employee support, employees need to be part of the decision-making process for designing the intranet. A top-down approach will not succeed. Rather, employees should be consulted about their work routines, their suggestions about how the intranet can make them more effective and efficient in their jobs, and their "wish lists" for additional features. In many of the agencies we examined, the intranet design teams held focus groups with employees and found such venues valuable sources of input.

- *Technical staff should not lead but must be active participants.* The development of an agency's intranet should not be directed by technical staff, but rather should be led by administrative staff and program managers. This helps to ensure that decisions are made based on what employees are likely to want and what functions are important to the agency as a whole. If decisions are driven by what is technically possible or innovative, then employees will need to readjust their work habits to suit the new technology. To be utilized and functional to the agency and staff, intranet technology should accommodate the needs and conventions of the employees and the organization. Moreover, if the technology drives intranet development, that development will be constrained by what is technically possible at that time. If management and staff needs drive development, new technical features may be created. Managers can challenge technical people to find appropriate solutions that may not be available with current technologies.

Recommendation 2: The more real value the intranet provides, the more employees will use it.

In all the agencies examined, as the intranet became more robust and more of a tool that employees could use, they gravitated to it. If the intranet offers useful services, employees will come to it. Functionality is key to success. Basic features such as a telephone directory or personnel notices draw people to the intranet. If employees can easily find there the information they use routinely in their jobs, then they will use the intranet. Once employees become accustomed to accessing it as part of their everyday routine, they will also begin to use more enhanced features on the intranet, such as collaborative work places. Sophisticated intranet software that requires training is less likely to be used by employees.

Recommendation 3: As intranets become more personalized and are used more for collaborative work, organizations will need to address issues of workplace surveillance and monitoring.

The organizations we examined are all in the early stages of designing personalized features into their intranets and using the intranet for collaborative work. As they offer these features, agencies encounter both enthusiasm and reluctance. The enthusiasm seems to result from the desire to be a part of a highly functional online environment. There appears to be a realization that there is great untapped promise from an intranet. At the same time, employees seem to recognize that if their online work spaces are personalized and if they participate in online collaboration, they will leave behind an electronic trail that managers can monitor and evaluate.

Thus, managers need to be proactive in explaining what substantive and transactional information will be captured as a result of intranet use, who will have access to that information, for what purposes the information will be used, and how long information will be retained. Managers should adopt policies that reflect the collection of the minimum amount of intranet information, should limit access to and retention of that information, and should restrict use of it. Moreover, employees should have the right to access any substantive and transactional information on the intranet, as well as the ability to redress any grievances that result from that information.

Appendix: Agency Personnel Interviewed

Environmental Protection Agency (EPA)

Pournima Soman
Computer Specialist
Information Services Branch
1200 Pennsylvania Ave., NW
Mail Code 2843 T
Washington, DC 20460
(202) 566-0693
fax: (202) 566-0685
e-mail: soman.pournima@epa.gov

Michael J. Weaver
Computer Specialist
Office of Environmental Information
Information Access and Analysis
1200 Pennsylvania Ave., NW
Mail Code 2843 T
Washington, DC 20460
(202) 566-0695
fax: (202) 566-0685
e-mail: weaver.mike@epa.gov

General Services Administration

Christopher F. Fornecker
Chief Technology Officer
U.S. General Services Administration
1800 F Street, NW
Room 3024
Washington, DC 20405
(202) 219-3393
fax: (202) 219-1249
e-mail: christopher.fornecker@gsa.gov

Dean T. Klein
Managing Director for Information
Office of the Chief Financial Officer
U.S. General Services Administration
1800 F St., NW
Room 2122
Washington, DC 20405
(202) 501-0329
fax: (202) 501-3310
e-mail: dean.klein@gsa.gov

Sally J. Perry
Division Director, Infrastructure Applications
U.S. General Services Administration
1800 F Street, NW
Room 1211
Washington, DC 20405
(202) 501-2871
e-mail: sally.perry@gsa.gov

Department of Commerce

Allan Betts
E-Business Development Counselor
U.S. Commercial Service
U.S. Department of Commerce
14th and Constitution Ave., NW
Washington, DC 20230
(202) 482-0287
e-mail: Al.Betts@mail.doc.gov

Karen F. Hogan
Deputy Chief Information Officer
U.S. Department of Commerce
1401 Constitution Ave., NW
Washington, DC 20230
(202) 482-2607
fax: (202) 501-1180
e-mail: khogan@doc.gov

Department of Housing and Urban Development

Candis Harrison
Departmental Web Manager for Field Operations
U.S. Department of Housing and Urban Development
HUD Tucson Office
160 North Stone Ave., Suite 100
Tucson, AZ 85701-1467
(520) 670-6237
fax: (520) 670-6207
e-mail: Candis_B._Harrison@hud.gov

Department of Justice

Susan L. Bronston
Manger/User Communications
Department of Justice
901 E Street, NW, Suite 101
Washington, DC 20530
(202) 616-1899
fax: (202) 616-0696
e-mail: sbronston@base2tech.com

Department of Transportation

Crystal M. Bush
DOT Intranet Manager
Office of the Chief Information Officer
U.S. Department of Transportation
Room 6100-J, NASSIF Building
400 Seventh Street, SW
Washington, DC 20590-0001
(202) 366-9713
fax: (202) 366-7024
e-mail: crystal.bush@ost.dot.gov

Phyllis Preston
Associate Chief Information Officer for E-Government
Office of the Secretary
U.S. Department of Transportation
400 Seventh Street, SW
Room 6432
Washington, DC 20590
(202) 493-0216
fax: (202) 366-7373
e-mail: phyllis.preston@ost.dot.gov

Bibliography

Allcorn, Seth. 1997. "Parallel Virtual Organizations: Managing and Working in the Virtual Workplace." *Administration and Society* 29:412-39.

Curry, Adrienne and Lara Stancich. 2000. "The Intranet—An Intrinsic Component of Strategic Information Management?" *International Journal of Information Management* 20 (4):249-68.

GAO. 2001. Executive Guide: Maximizing the Success of Chief Information Officers: Learning From Leading Organizations. Guidance, 02/01/2001, GAO/GAO-01-376G.

GAO. 2000. Human Capital: Key Principles From Nine Private Sector Organizations. Letter Report, 01/31/2000, GAO/GGD-00-28.

GAO. 2000. Tax Administration: IRS' Implementation of the Restructuring Act's Taxpayer Protection and Rights Provisions. Letter Report, 04/21/2000, GAO/GGD-00-85.

Holz, Shel. 1997. "Strategizing a Human Resources Presence on the Intranet." *Compensation and Benefits Management* 13:31-7.

PricewaterhouseCoopers. 2001. Introduction to B2E and G2E Solutions, Internal document. (April 1).

Stowers, Genie. 2001. "Commerce Comes to Government on the Desktop: E-Commerce Applications in the Public Sector." In *E-Government 2001.* Mark A. Abramson and Grady E. Means, eds. Lanham, MD.: Rowman and Littlefield Publishers, Inc.

PART III

E-Government in Action

CHAPTER FIVE

Leveraging Technology in the Service of Diplomacy: Innovation in the Department of State

Barry Fulton
Research Professor
School of Media and Public Affairs
The George Washington University

This report was originally published in March 2002.

Introduction: The Digital Challenge

I am determined that I'm going to get an Internet-accessible computer, with pipes to support it, at every desk in the State Department and every embassy in the world.

—Secretary of State Colin Powell, September 5, 2001

The Berlin Wall fell in 1989, and the remains of the Communist revolution disappeared in the early 1990s. The Information Revolution reached the tipping point as corporations embraced the new technologies and the Internet began its rapid diffusion throughout the industrial world. In the decade that followed, globalization has driven the world economy, new media have affected world politics, and private citizens have become increasingly engaged in international affairs.

The Department of State, while celebrating the end of the Cold War, was slow to apply the new technologies to the conduct of diplomacy. Indeed, in the last decade of the 20th century, decision making became more centralized, physical access more restricted, and information flow more inhibited. In frustration, a group of State Department officers issued a manifesto in which they wrote, "We are entering the uncharted waters of the 21st century in a rusted-out diplomatic hulk that is no longer seaworthy."[1]

This state of affairs has been richly documented by several studies including Reinventing *Diplomacy in the Information Age,*[2] *Equipped for the Future: Managing U.S. Foreign Affairs in the 21st Century,*[3] and *America's Overseas Presence in the 21st Century.*[4] In the first week of the George W. Bush administration, former Defense Secretary Frank Carlucci presented to Secretary of State Colin Powell a "resources-for-reform" proposal calling for the Department of State to undertake fundamental change, including upgrading information technology and adopting modern management practices. Co-sponsored by the Council on Foreign Relations and the Center for Strategic and International Studies, the review, *State Department Reform,*[5] represents a consensus among research institutions, scholars, and professionals that the time has come for action. "In short," the task force said, "renewal of America's foreign policy making and implementing machinery is an urgent national security priority."

A common element in practically all of a dozen recent studies is the State Department's failure to deploy modern information technology in support of diplomacy. As information acquisition, analysis, management, and dissemination are central to every aspect of diplomacy, it is no surprise that American diplomacy has lost its primacy in the conduct of foreign policy. This criticism does not necessarily reflect on the many able diplomats who serve in the American Foreign Service; it is meant to highlight the inadequacy of the tools that are available to them, especially in a period when diplomatic roles are rapidly evolving. In a world of ever increasing complexity, the national interest will suffer unless the professionals who serve in 180 countries are supported by the best available information technology.

Additional resources alone will not ensure success. Examples of colossal failures from both government and industry are plentiful. The U.S. Agency for International Development (USAID), for example, was forced to abandon a multi-million-dollar central accounting system several years ago when it failed to serve its employees. The Department of State's once planned three-enclave system, which required three computers at every employee's desk for full connectivity, would not have efficiently connected diplomats across borders or even within embassies.

If the status quo is unacceptable and can't be cured by money alone, what is required? As this study suggests, the answer is a combination of leadership and grassroots initiatives. Secretary of State Powell set the tone in his first week in office when he told employees that he lived on the Internet. These were words of appreciation for the innovators who were already using the new technologies, and words of encouragement for those who had been pushing for change.

Under Secretary for Political Affairs Marc Grossman told fellow diplomats that the revolution in information technology "is absolutely, utterly, and profoundly changing" the way diplomats do business. "Without the capacity to manage and master IT," he said, "we will not succeed." Under Secretary for Management Grant Green speaking of "e-diplomacy" at a George Washington University forum, promised to "create a desktop for diplomats with instant access to all the applications and information diplomats need to do their jobs." As new funding was made available, the State Department began deploying the Internet to every desktop and increasing its classified connectivity.

The Department of State identifies 57 major information systems[6] that it maintains to support its business practices. They range from an unclassified e-mail system to the Nuclear Risk Reduction Center system—and encompass an array of functions from communication to administration to the facilitation of diplomatic practices.

The single most important technological requirement for the State Department is secure communications between Washington and 250 embassies and consulates abroad. Legacy telegram systems continue to serve as the primary means of official secure communications, although an increasing amount of informal correspondence is carried over unclassified and classified e-mail systems.

Like most organizations, State's first use of data processing was in support of financial management and payroll operations supported by mainframe computers. Its initial foray into word processing was taken in the mid-1970s when it awarded a contract for the worldwide installation and maintenance of Wang word processors. Although State has been rightly criticized for holding on to the Wang technology for two decades, its initial decision was prudent, as Wang offered a reliable, low-maintenance system that offered efficiencies in word processing over the Selectric typewriters they replaced. E-mail and the World Wide Web were not candidates for diplomatic tools when the word processors were first installed.

Moving from stand-alone Wang word processors to Pentium-powered computers running on Local Area Networks (LANs) was a painful and time-consuming process because of budgetary limitations, personnel shortages, and security requirements. Modern computers operating on robust networks are now the norm. The last Wang word processors will soon be retired.

The purpose of this study was to look at recent initiatives that promise to transform the conduct of diplomacy. While examples of excellence are not widespread, there are a number scattered throughout the State Department that warrant recognition. Systems that support consular services, including the processing and issuance of visas, are very robust. Public diplomacy applications represent state-of-the-art technology. Refugee processing is being expedited by new IT applications. The study is intended to expand the circle of supporters by illustrating that information technology is already facilitating the conduct of diplomacy. By stimulating interest among diplomats, it is hoped that there will be a further incentive for internal reform.

Diplomacy and information technology intersect at three levels. The first is that which promotes efficiency in existing business practices including payrolling, accounting, and contracting. The second level directly supports the conduct of diplomacy including reporting, negotiation, representation, and advocacy. The third level is the substance rather than the practice of diplomacy. It includes U.S. negotiations to open telecommunications markets in China, analysis of the impact of software production in India, and advancement of telecommunications deregulation in the Caribbean. The State Department has applied its information technology predominantly at the first level, directed at improving administrative efficiency. The second level, with the exception of word processing and e-mail, has been largely ignored. The third level has commanded U.S. government attention, but is not a priority at the Department of State.

This study focuses on the second level—diplomatic support—by seeking and reporting examples of applications that advance the practice of diplomacy. Best practices were sought to illustrate the categories below:

- Knowledge management
- Database management
- Specialized intranets
- Multimedia reporting
- Customized hyper-linked virtual desktops

- Collaborative software
- Videoconferencing
- Digital imagery
- Presentation software
- Personal Digital Assistants (PDAs), cellphones, and wireless applications
- Language translation software
- Speech recognition software
- GPS (Global Positioning System)
- GIS (Geographic Information System)
- Remote sensing
- Digital communication systems
- Encryption

Research was conducted primarily through personal interviews, augmented by written exchanges and the examination of published accounts. Particular attention is given to the relation between the IT applications and the diplomats for whom (and by whom) they are designed. Have the systems enhanced the quality or efficiency of diplomacy? Are diplomats better prepared to cope with the requirements of the 21st century? Is the Department of State better prepared to communicate outside of traditional government-to-government channels? In short, can it be demonstrated that the national interest is served by the wise use of information technology?

The State Department's messaging systems, including a legacy cable system and classified and unclassified e-mail systems, are ignored in this study for two reasons. They are neither unique nor imaginatively integrated, so do not serve to illustrate the centers of IT excellence to which this study is directed. Likewise, the department's numerous administrative systems have not been examined, as the focus is on diplomatic practices.

Twelve examples have been selected to illustrate how information technology has been applied to enhance diplomatic practices. Ranging from refugee processing to the Dayton Peace Accords, the IT applications fall into three categories represented in the chapters that follow: diplomatic interaction, public access, and internal communication. None of the systems is universally used in the Department of State, and most are unknown except to the user community that developed the system.

To the extent that the cases illustrate excellence, this report may also serve to stimulate the transformation of American diplomacy, which would require changing its closed culture, reshaping core processes, and addressing third-level digital challenges.

Case Studies: Using Technology to Improve Diplomatic Interaction

Consular Consolidated Database (CCD)

The Consular Consolidated Database is a worldwide database of databases, consolidating data from every U.S. consular office in the world. The data is replicated in Washington and made available to consular officers around the globe.

Built on an Oracle database, it operates over the Department of State's sensitive but unclassified intranet known as OpenNet. All consular officers have had access to the CCD since mid-2001. Whenever an officer carries out any consular function—such as receiving data from a visa applicant or issuing a visa—these actions are recorded in the local database. Within five minutes selected data are available to authorized personnel worldwide.

The CCD serves several purposes critical to the efficient operation of American consular services. In the first instance, it provides a secure record of transactions in case local records are lost or destroyed or unavailable in an emergency. Equally important, it serves consular officers in sharing data with their colleagues at other posts, in responding to queries about the authenticity of questionable visas, and in allowing a check of prior information when a new visa application is received.

In case of emergencies, the CCD allows consular officers to continue services to American citizens through the central database or by downloading the data to a mobile site. The CCD also makes it much easier to share information with other agencies, as the data are already in a format that can be exported. The existence of the CCD has made it relatively easy for State to begin sharing all of its CCD-held visa information with the Immigration and Naturalization Service (INS) in the Department of Justice.

A separate but complementary system is the Consular Lookout and Support System, which automatically notifies the consular officer when an applicant has been previously turned down for a visa or when other lookout information is recorded in the system. This computerized system has been in existence since the mid-1960s, but was more extensively deployed by congressional mandate following the 1993 bombing of the World Trade Center. It also operates on the same intranet platform, OpenNet, which hosts the CCD.

Diplomacy is far more than government-to-government interactions. Increasingly it involves the interactions of officials and publics. As one Foreign Service officer said, "Being able to interact with the public as a representative of the United States and present official decisions of the United States concerning a foreign national's application for a U.S. government

Start Date: Fully operational in 2001

Originating Office: Bureau of Consular Affairs

Brief Description: Database aggregating data from all U.S. consular activities abroad including visa issuance, passport replacement, births and deaths of American citizens

service constitutes diplomacy. The more informed a consular officer is, the better the interaction will be, the better the service will be, the better perception the foreign public is going to have of the U.S. presence there. A lot of it depends on the consular officer's ability to express him or herself, but this gives the officer tools to make a more informed, authoritative decision."

Since its introduction, the Consolidated Consular Database has been well received by consular officers. The use of the CCD is intuitive and requires little or no training. A systems integrator designed the structure of the database and the replication system, created the consolidated database, and then created the web interface to the database. Since CCD's launch, consular officers have filed numerous unsolicited reports of the system's utility.

Other benefits to users are envisioned with the maturation of the system. Prior to the availability of the CCD, an ad hoc reporting tool (ART), based on Microsoft Access, was developed to enable consular personnel overseas to query their local consular databases. Because of its complexity and the inadequacy of training, ART did not enjoy the receptivity of CCD. As the CCD is not a data-mining tool, however, it cannot be easily queried for aggregate data. Although a small minority uses it for analysis, new analytic tools will be better crafted to satisfy user needs.

CCD now includes photographs of all visa recipients, and plans are under way to photograph all applicants, against which facial recognition software could be run to detect known terrorists and criminals. One-piece flat-screen computers are being procured so that consular officers can access relevant databases during the visa interview and record adjudications and informal notes directly into the database. Both of these enhancements represent changes in work practices that will be well received by some and resisted by others. Other future plans include eliminating paper files by scanning documents and generating workload statistics centrally instead of tasking each post to produce them.

Another related expansion of intranet use is interactive collaboration, which some see as a primary vehicle for consular officers to work with each other across distances. The question is how best to tap into the reservoir

Figure 5.1: Consular Section web page from the American Embassy in Paris

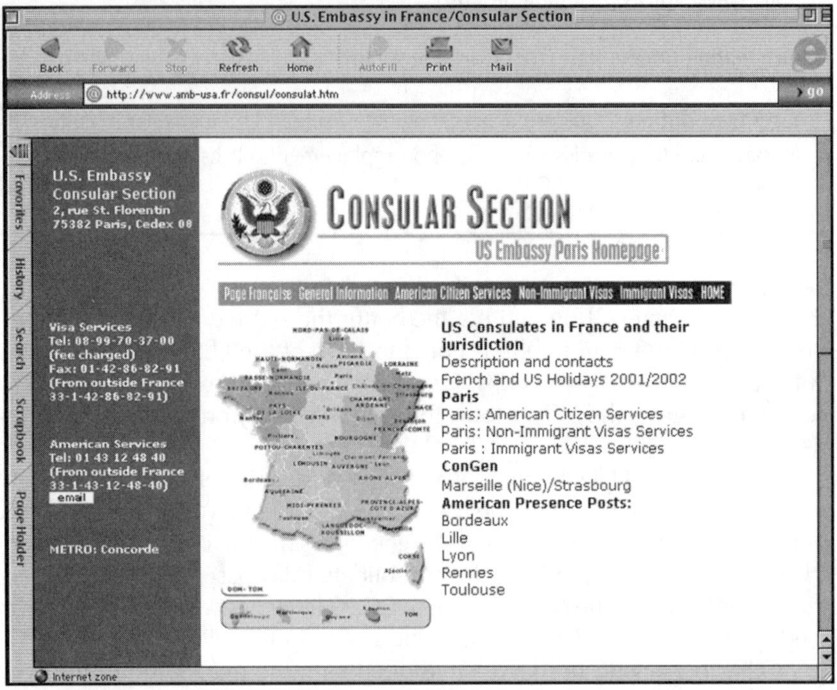

of knowledge held by experienced officers. Several newsgroups were established, but after a few comments, users stopped contributing. There was reluctance for officers to attach their names to documents going to an amorphous group, as well as a tendency not to read incoming postings. An ongoing experiment with an off-the-shelf collaboration tool, E-room, is showing mixed results. With projects or tasks moderated by a leader, collaboration has worked well. Collaborative groups that do not have the focus of a project have been less utilized. With well-defined tasks and increasingly heavy workloads, consular officers have been in the forefront of IT experimentation and adoption.

Lessons Learned

- *Simplicity, ease of access, and breadth of data are far more beneficial than tools that provide deeper, more flexible, more complex analysis.* Busy officers turn to the simpler systems. The experience in implementing CCD, as well as the Lookout System and ART, suggests it is better to introduce applications that are simple but effective, without bells and whistles. To the extent that routine processes can be automated, user satisfaction is axiomatic.

- *Systems, particularly in the introductory stages, should be built to accommodate existing work practices.* After the system is accepted it can be expanded to change existing work practices. A new system (e.g., CCD) can be thought of as a stepping-stone on which future development can be based.

Kosovo Repatriation Information Support (KRIS)

Among the many initiatives to assist Kosovar refugees after the withdrawal of Serbian forces in 1999 was a multi-agency effort in integrating information in a common geographical database. It was, in the first instance, an attempt to use Geographic Information System (GIS) software to catalog the extent of the humanitarian tragedy and to assist in the safe return of refugees. In the simplest terms, GIS is a means of displaying information on a map. Better defined, GIS is a database management system for the display and analysis of digital geo-spatial data. It combines mapping capabilities, databases of geographic and other relevant information, and spatial analysis to allow users to look at an area in relation to other areas, in relation to changes over time, and in relation to other relevant factors. By combining digital maps, satellite and aircraft imagery, and data collected from field workers on the ground, a GIS-based network can provide accurate and timely information for governments and nongovernmental organizations (NGOs) to respond to complex contingencies.

The State Department became involved in supporting a GIS system in Kosovo through the Office of the Geographer and Global Issues, although there were numerous other players including the National Imagery and Mapping Agency (NIMA), the Office of Foreign Disaster Assistance (OFDA) of the USAID, and the United Nations High Commissioner for Refugees (UNHCR).

The State Department's contribution was to assist in the development of the Kosovo Repatriation Information Support system (KRIS). The foundation for KRIS was the construction of an electronic base map by NIMA in 1998.

Start Date: Deployed in 1999

Originating Office: Office of the Geographer and Global Issues

Brief Description: Geographic information system deployed to support the repatriation of Kosovars after the withdrawal of Serbian forces from Kosovo

It included multiple data layers such as topography, roads, place names, and administrative units. OFDA commissioned a NIMA-produced "humanitarian-planning map" and distributed it in paper form to relief agencies working in Kosovo.

After the Yugoslav army withdrew from Kosovo following its spring 1999 offensive against the ethnic Albanians in Kosovo, UNHCR established a GIS unit in Pristina supported by a multi-agency team composed of U.N. agencies and OFDA. In June 1999, the State Department deployed the KRIS team to Macedonia. The team arrived with laptops loaded with GIS software and updated data from NIMA. Its purpose was to support UNHCR in developing data sets that would assist the repatriation process. The team was able to obtain and use U-2 photographic imagery depicting damage to homes in Kosovo.

The intention of using KRIS as a planning tool for repatriation was overtaken by the spontaneous return of the Kosovars. Nonetheless, KRIS databases assisted in coordinating repatriation activities and contributed to a survey by UNHCR of the damage to housing and other infrastructure in Kosovo within weeks after the Serb withdrawal. It served as a precursor to the U.N.'s Humanitarian Community Information Center (HCIC), which represented a major breakthrough in information sharing.

After repatriation, HCIC's role changed to supporting reconstruction planning and budgeting, election planning, and civil administration—all of which could be supported by the geographic databases that had been developed. The State officers who supported the initiative report that an effort "to develop a more systematic information-sharing regime for future complex contingencies has begun to gather momentum." USAID has issued a draft information-sharing plan that anticipates requirements for sharing geo-spatial data in future humanitarian assistance efforts.

Figure 5.2: GIS for repatriation planning

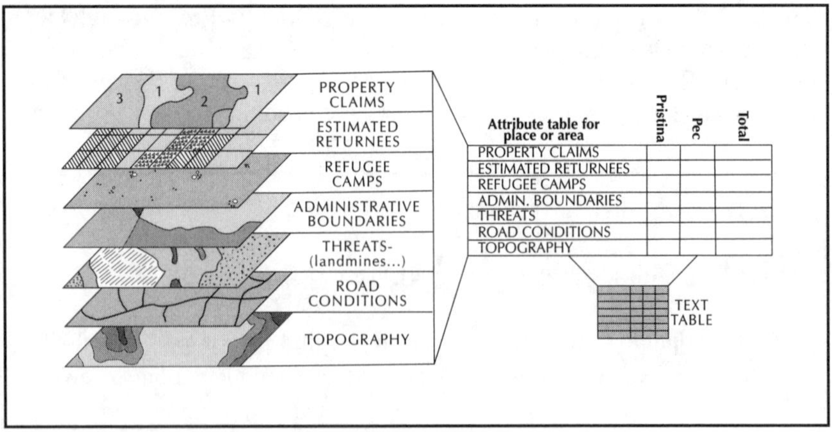

With scores of players involved in international humanitarian relief, coordination between civilian and military agencies, between government and nongovernmental organizations, between international organizations and numerous governments is always a challenge. If they can all contribute to, and draw on, a common data set, coordination is likely to improve markedly. GIS software provides the opportunity for unprecedented collaboration if the various actors can agree on common standards.

Lessons Learned

In a presentation at the U.S. Institute of Peace, Col. Michael Dziedzic and Dr. William Wood drew the following lessons from their experience in Kosovo:[7]

- *Develop a strategic information plan.* Use of GIS alone does not mean there is an information-sharing regime. An information strategy needs to be developed involving all major participating organizations to address data requirements, information security, and field constraints.
- *Designate an information-sharing coordinator.* Each organization should be responsible for developing and maintaining its own data sets, using common standards for the data and place names to ensure that the data sets can be integrated.
- *Build GIS foundation maps in anticipation of future complex contingencies.* This needs to be done by a technical agency such as NIMA in advance of a humanitarian intervention because of the time required.
- *Improve response time.* Major international relief organizations need to develop emergency response capabilities with the necessary GIS expertise, hardware, and communications equipment to facilitate the rapid establishment of information-sharing networks in the field.

Worldwide Refugee Admissions Processing System (WRAPS)

The Worldwide Refugee Admissions Processing System (WRAPS) supports a network of 15 Overseas Processing Entities (OPEs) that operate on contract with the Department of State through the Bureau of Population, Refugees, and Migration. From Havana to Moscow, the OPEs are the first point of contact for the 70,000 refugees that immigrate to the United States each year. WRAPS is a virtual private network for capturing information needed to process refugee applications, track movement, and, finally, to relocate refugees to the United States.

WRAPS also provides comprehensive information to volunteer organizations (e.g., Church World Service, International Rescue Committee, U.S. Catholic Conference) that help resettle the refugees in the United States after they arrive. WRAPS will provide access to case data on the refugees, so they can be efficiently assisted by the volunteer organizations. Each of

Start Date: First installation in 2001; additional sites to be completed in 2002

Originating Office: Bureau of Population, Refugees, and Migration

Brief Description: Web-enabled database to facilitate movement of refugees to the United States

the 10 volunteer agencies connected to the system have from 10 to 100 local affiliates, which also draw on the information. Other government agencies that require access to WRAPS include the Centers for Disease Control, the Department of Health and Human Services, and the Immigration and Naturalization Service. International partners with which interconnectivity will be possible in the future include the International Organization for Migration and the U.N. High Commissioner for Refugees.

Data is encrypted, transmitted over the Internet, and accessed through a web browser. Because so many users are external to the State Department, its proprietary connectivity has not been used to link the various system users. Necessary changes to the software can be made centrally from Washington, thereby minimizing maintenance at the OPEs and volunteer organizations.

This homegrown system was based on well-defined business needs, triggered by the uncertain guesswork of estimating the number of refugees arriving each month, the requirements for making airline reservations, and the need to comply with legislated ceilings. With thousands of employees involved from contract organizations, NGOs, government, and international organizations, it was impossible to plan and track refugee movement with precision. A host of logistical, personal, and medical problems had to be accommodated.

The project manager—whose expertise was in international relations, not information technology—proposed a real-time, centralized database. A consulting firm was engaged to develop baseline requirements, a timeline, and a budget, which were completed in 1998. Through a competitive bid, a contract was awarded to build the system. Both the consulting firm and the contractor had extensive and continuing contact with the end users at the 15 OPEs and with the stakeholders. During the process of system design, there were some organizational changes as well to better support the new processes.

WRAPS replaced a collection of disparate stand-alone systems that did not provide uniform data to those responsible for managing refugee resettlement. The new system was designed to allow a migration from uneven

Figure 5.3: Overseas Processing Entities for refugee admissions

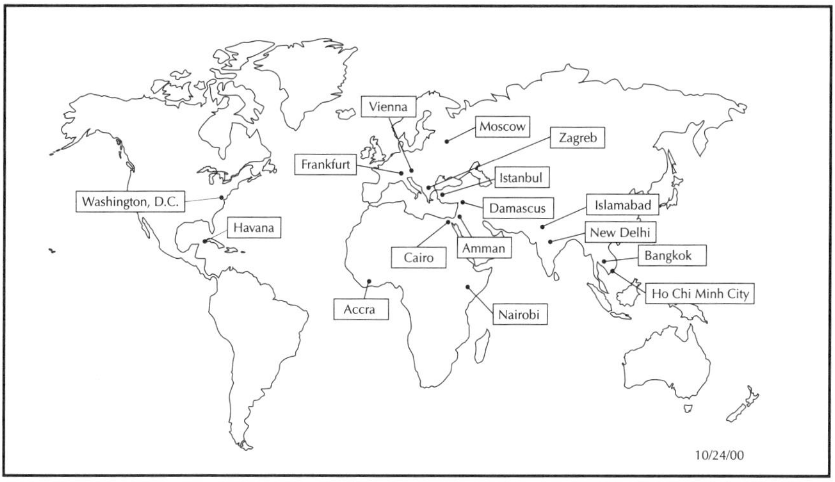

statistics and educated guesswork to a uniform database. It was first deployed in Russia in December 2001, at an OPE that processes some 16,000 refugees annually. The 100 Moscow employees welcomed the new system, which began full operation as scheduled, with only a few minor bugs. As of this writing, WRAPS remains to be deployed in the remaining 14 centers, scheduled for completion by December 2002. Refugee referrals from the UNHCR, which are currently processed manually, will also be electronically processed in another 18 months when the two systems will be fully compatible.

For system users, WRAPS is a welcome tool for processing applicants. The bottom-line benefit, however, is for the refugees themselves, who should experience fewer delays in being resettled in the United States. According to the project manager, "The whole procedure is shortened, and they get here faster. That's really been the goal of ours."

Lessons Learned

- *User involvement is key to building a successful system.* A user group was created to provide constant feedback as the system was being developed. A system was established for capturing, tracking, and responding to user comments. A website was established to allow users to track progress.
- *Likewise, stakeholder consultation is a key requirement.* Partners from the NGOs and government offices had to be carefully consulted to ensure that the information and statistics that WRAPS produces would satisfy their requirements.

- *Defining system requirements and writing detailed business rules for the programmers was far more complex and time-consuming than anticipated.* It's like building an addition on your house: It takes longer and costs more than you think. In the last analysis, users were well served because of the specificity of the business requirements.
- *Training is essential.* A training manual was written, trainers visited field offices, and field officers were brought to Washington for hands-on training and immediate feedback. A 16-hour-a-day help desk was established, and online help screens were developed.

Dayton Peace Accords

The virtual maps of Bosnia used by State Department negotiators leading up to the 1995 Dayton Accords represent the most widely chronicled use of information technology in the service of diplomacy. Although the Department of Defense managed the technology, its skillful use by State Department negotiators helped conclude a peace agreement that is still being maintained after more than six years.

The Defense Mapping Agency (now a component of the National Imagery and Mapping Agency) created a virtual-reality version of the Bosnian landscape that allowed negotiators to sit in front of a computer terminal and examine geographic features to a detail of two meters. The computer program that simulated the Bosnian countryside, the PowerScene terrain visualization system, was developed by Cambridge Research Associates of McLean, Virginia.

The negotiations took place November 1–21, 1995, at Wright-Patterson Air Force Base in Dayton, Ohio, for the purpose of forging a peace agreement and gaining agreement for a multi-ethnic Bosnian state. Territorial issues within Bosnia were among the most intractable decisions facing the negotiators. After years of bloodshed and centuries of ethnic rivalry, the stakes were extremely high. The three warring nations were represented in Dayton by Yugoslav President Slobodan Milosevic, Croatian President Franjo Tudjman, and Bosnian President Alija Izetbegovic.

Start Date: Used in peace negotiations in 1995

Originating Office: Department of State negotiators, with facilitation by DoD

Brief Description: Virtual mapping technology rendered three-dimensional views of disputed areas to assist in reaching agreement among warring parties

Figure 5.4: Digital map used in Dayton Peace Talks

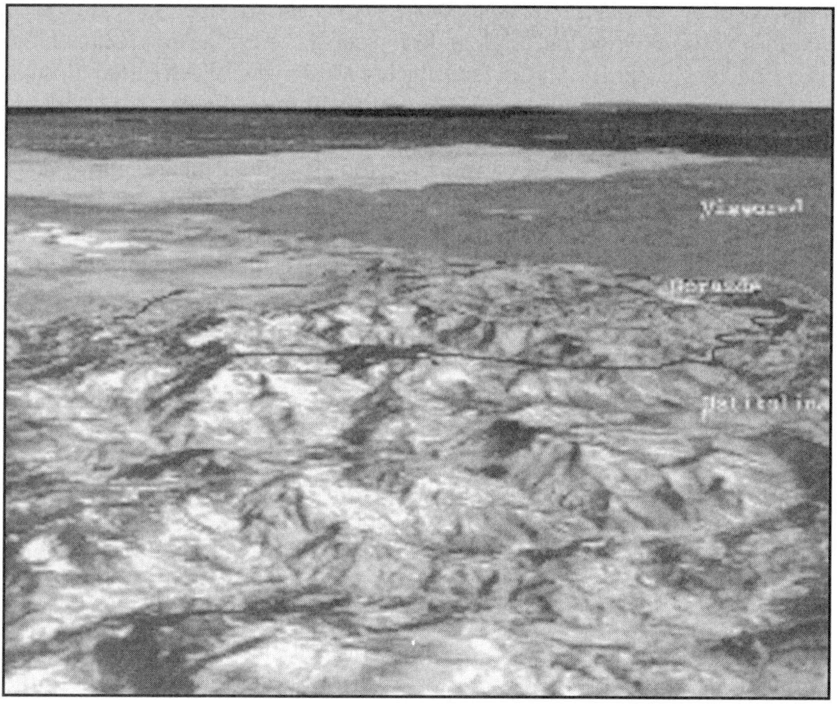

Assistant Secretary of State Richard Holbrooke headed the American negotiating team.

The virtual-mapping technology was supported by a team of 55 military experts and civilian contractors plus $4 million worth of map-making equipment. Bosnia had been completely filmed and stored to allow its virtual three-dimensional representation. The technology was originally developed for the Defense Department for use in Desert Storm.

One of the major challenges in Dayton was to convince all parties to agree to the same map and reach agreement on clear boundaries. Negotiators were able to pick a point on the map and simultaneously show on a split screen a color aerial image of the terrain. The principals were said to be astonished as they recognized familiar elements of the Bosnian landscape, including the ancestral home of one of the Balkan presidents.

Holbrooke was able to sit down with the principals and give them a virtual flight across disputed territories with the use of PowerScene. At one point, American officials brought Milosevic to a high-tech auditorium to show an aerial view of a disputed corridor of Serb-held territory between Sarajevo and

Gorazde. After seeing that his proposed two-mile-wide corridor was rendered impractical by the steep mountains, Milosevic agreed to widen the path to five miles. Holbrooke wrote that this high-tech video game played an important role in connecting Sarajevo with Gorazde, the last Muslim enclave in eastern Bosnia.

On a map scaled at 1 to 50,000, a slight shift may represent hundreds of yards on the ground, unintentionally separating communities and families. Bringing the landscape to Dayton by virtual means allowed all parties to understand without ambiguity the extent of their compromises and the precise nature of their agreement. The technology allowed the computation of the exact percentage of territory each side was given as various alternatives were considered. State Department negotiators were therefore in a position to build trust among the several parties. Technology removed subjectivity from the interpretation of the "facts on the ground." Any negotiator would benefit from having at his or her disposal an indisputable set of facts (i.e., an objective database) from which to forge agreement when emotions are running high.

Would the Dayton Accords have been reached without this technology? Holbrooke said: "It was very important, but I'm not going to sit here and tell you that we wouldn't have gotten a deal in Dayton without those computers. They made our job easier." As the technology itself was a reminder to the Balkan participants of America's technological edge, its impressionistic role may have been every bit as important as its facilitative role in establishing the Sarajevo-Gorazde corridor or computing the size of territorial divisions.

Holbrooke's masterful account of the negotiations in his book *To End A War* devotes two pages to the use of PowerScene at Dayton. In a 400-page volume, this brief summary may well represent a fair account of its value—useful but not critical. It is inconceivable that the peace accords could have been reached without the negotiating skills of a Holbrooke, but entirely plausible that PowerScene, as useful as it may have been, was not *the* element that made a difference between success and failure. Information technology, wisely deployed, can be a useful tool in negotiations, but is not a substitute for the skills of a negotiator.

Lessons Learned

- *As any negotiator knows, trust building is an essential element of success.* The maps, virtual and real, that were generated by the Defense Mapping Agency in Dayton served as an important confidence-building measure. While there were severe differences about where boundaries should be drawn, the technology helped settle disagreements about the facts on the ground. A 3-D virtual map manipulated by a joystick presents an image of verisimilitude that is impossible with a paper map.

- *The medium, as McLuhan asserted, is the message.* A reminder of America's high-tech capabilities at a peace conference may have had the unintended consequence of reminding the belligerents that America's power could be used in less benign ways. As participant Richard Johnson wrote, "Finding one's own house depicted on a tactical map at an air force base in a foreign country can be sobering, and knowing that anything on such a map can instantly become a target is even more unsettling."[8]
- *Although widely recognized by negotiators, it may be instructive for others to recognize that technology can strengthen the hand of an able diplomat, but cannot substitute for the skills he or she brings to the table.*

Case Studies: Using Technology to Improve Public Access

Kosovo Information Assistance Initiative (KIAI)

Following the liberation of Kosovo, USIA's Information Bureau (now the State Department's Office of International Information Programs, IIP) established Internet connectivity in the Kosovo Refugee Centers in Europe and the United States (e.g., Fort Dix, New Jersey). The Internet connectivity was established to facilitate communication among families who had been separated by the war and to provide Albanian-language news and information to refugees who had been forced out of their homeland.

After repatriation of the Kosovars, IIP set up Internet Cafés (or Community Internet Centers) in Pristina and seven other Kosovo cities to provide connectivity to the Internet and access to news and information about the outside world. The centers were equipped with donated hardware and software including computers from Silicon Graphics, Gateway, and

> **Start Date:** Initiated in 1999; concluded in 2001
>
> **Originating Office:** Office of International Information Programs (IIP)
>
> **Brief Description:** State Department initiated and supported program to bring Internet connectivity to Kosovars returning home after the withdrawal of Serbian forces from Kosovo

Figure 5.5: Pristina Internet Café

Apple. Each of the centers, with about 10 terminals each, had two-way high-speed satellite connectivity.

USIA gave a grant to the International Organization for Migration (IOM), which had offices on the ground in Kosovo, to fund the satellite equipment, satellite time, installation, and salaries of local staff. A contract network engineer made arrangements with the satellite provider, Hughes Network Systems, and a German subsidiary. His role was to negotiate physical space for the centers through contacts with the local IOM offices, ensure that they were refurbished and had electricity, and get equipment into the country. Because of local limitations and the mountainous terrain, it was not feasible to use ISDN lines, microwave relays, or combined satellite-telephone connections. The only practical option was two-way satellite connectivity. Each of the centers had its own connectivity, so they could operate independently of the others.

The centers attracted some 10,000 users a week, the majority of whom were teenagers and college-age students. Many had first used the Internet in the refugee camps. The opening of the centers was widely anticipated by word of mouth. When there were no phone lines between cities, the Internet Cafés allowed connectivity by Instant Messaging. Students used them for conducting research after the universities opened. Doctors used the centers to communicate with doctors outside of Kosovo. And journalists used them to download news for local broadcast. Since users were not paying, half-hour time slots were allocated. Still, there were far more demands than the centers could satisfy. The center in Pristina was booked three days in advance.

According to the contractor who oversaw the installation, "the technical part was the easy part. We did not deviate from our initial technical plan. It proved to be completely viable. The difficult part was logistical—getting the equipment, getting the facilities, getting the power, getting back and forth, traveling to the cities, getting the subcontractor in to set up the antennas, getting technicians in the country, and getting them from place to place." The IIP representative arrived in September 1999 and opened the first center in Pristina just before Christmas, which he described as "one of the most worthwhile things we could have done." The last of the seven centers was opened in Mitrovica in May 2000.

By August 2000, CNN reported that there were at least nine Internet Cafés in Pristina and 20 in Kosovo region, charging $2 an hour and still attracting crowds. "I have 15 computers now, and if I could buy another 15, they would all be busy," said Luan Oruqi, one of Kosovo's homegrown entrepreneurs, who is connecting Kosovo's ethnic Albanians to the world.

The centers set up by the State Department were transferred to local NGOs or closed in 2001 when the original grant was exhausted and commercial alternatives had materialized. Even with limited access, the Internet had played a role in keeping Kosovars informed, from the day when they were first forced out of Kosovo until they returned. The Internet Cafés demonstrated, particularly to young people, the importance of information, the power of free speech, and the role of technology as liberating forces against tyranny.

Lessons Learned

- *Most importantly, understand the complexity of the environment in which you are operating.* IIP's representative on the ground said that everything took three to four times longer than estimated, in part because of a shoestring budget that caused delays and compromises.
- *Technology is the easy part; logistical and bureaucratic considerations are far more difficult.* The most difficult part was getting the equipment into the country. USIA had all the equipment, but had to wait several months for shipment by sea freight. Even the satellite equipment was slow to arrive because of limited shipments into Kosovo.
- *Do contingency planning to shorten the lead time in establishing similar centers in the future.* By following the Defense Department's (DoD) lead, computer and satellite equipment could be containerized for immediate shipment. The Kosovo experience showed that it took too long to assemble the package from scratch.

Digital Videoconferencing (DVC)

Digital videoconferencing between Washington and American embassies began in 1993 at a handful of overseas posts. The purpose was to conduct expert exchanges in support of public diplomacy objectives. When American experts were unavailable to travel abroad to meet with foreign publics, digital videoconferencing appeared to be an alternative—less expensive than travel and far less expensive than the broadcast-quality one-way Worldnet video programs that had been in use for nearly a decade by USIA.

Digital videoconferencing requires an ISDN line or broadband IP line (Internet connection) between two remote points to exchange video and audio signals. Although the signal is not broadcast quality, many prefer this medium to one-way broadcast quality video, because they can see their interlocutors. Conversation flows much more readily, and the interaction approximates a face-to-face conversation. First-time users are frequently surprised at how natural their conversation becomes—unlike one-way studio experiences, where the audience cannot be seen. Overseas participants can sit in a small conference room in front of a 27-inch monitor or view the exchange in an auditorium on a large screen projection.

Twelve units were purchased by USIA in late 1992 at a cost of $60,000 each and were installed at several major overseas locations including London, Paris, Tokyo, and Hong Kong. During this early experimental stage, there was only one DVC per month. After a few years, the number began to increase, so that by the end of 2001, the Office of International Information Programs was averaging three DVCs per day. And that doesn't include the videoconferencing that is taking place in State's other 20 locations, or in other government offices like the Office of the U.S. Trade Representative that have since obtained their own equipment. Based on experiences with IIP's system, NGOs are also installing similar systems. A recent example is the Middle Eastern Institute in Washington, which adopted the technology after one of its members participated in a State Department program.

Three factors account for the growth. The cost has decreased from $60,000 a unit in 1992 to $6,500 for a unit made by Polycom. ISDN lines are available in many more locations, although their costs have decreased

Start Date: Initiated in 1993; continually upgraded and expanded since then

Originating Office: Office of International Information Programs (IIP)

Brief Description: Digital expansion of public diplomacy program designed to create an opportunity for dialogue between American experts and foreign publics

Figure 5.6: Videoconference between Washington and Kiev

only slightly. Finally, users are increasingly satisfied with the results as the picture quality and reliability of circuits have increased.

It is axiomatic that busy people whom the State Department may wish to engage as expert speakers abroad can more easily spare an hour or two in a studio than the several days required for travel to an overseas post. On the other hand, no one would suggest that the experience of meeting one on one can be completely duplicated by a videoconference. There is always a tradeoff between the ideal and the practical. After eight years' experience it is clear that the effort has paid off. From several posts in 1993 to 168 overseas sites today, videoconferencing is now accepted as a standard tool in the conduct of public diplomacy.

As the manager of the IIP facility said, it's always a people issue. "The sooner you get people meeting each other and exchanging ideas, that furthers diplomacy. You may not be able to get them at the same table, but this is a good way of starting." Most of the exchanges are between an American expert speaking on American policy or society and an international audience, but the medium has served other causes as well. For example, former U. S. Trade Representative Charlene Barshevsky used the facility in a working meeting with the South African minister of finance. On another occasion, a forensic scientist visiting the United States testified by DVC at a trial in Durban, South Africa, concerning an apartheid-era murder.

The staff finds its continuing interaction with experts to be a side benefit of the job. Expert participants, as well, find that the digital conferences leave them better informed through their interactions with international audiences. Since this operation began in a single room in 1993, small studios have been installed throughout the State Department at nearly 20 different locations. With no centralized coordination, each office manages its own conferencing, although no others have a dedicated staff or the frequency of the IIP operation. In a new development, the Office of Verification and Compliance is currently testing a high-definition video connection between Washington and Geneva for use by American arms control negotiators. And G-8 principals have expressed an interest in using videoconferencing in lieu of travel to frequent preparatory meetings.

IIP was planning to use Internet connections early in 2001 to transmit the DVCs, but has been at least temporarily restricted because of fire-walls that block video signals. When and if that option becomes available, sharply decreasing transmission costs will undoubtedly spur even greater usage.

The next phase, if the current firewall prohibitions are removed, is to allow the interconnection of posts with ISDN lines and IP lines through a gateway, thereby adding even more flexibility to an operation whose growth seems ensured. Plans are also under way to add video clips from the DVCs to IIP's overseas website. As long as new technologies are incorporated into the operation, its utility appears to be guaranteed.

Lessons Learned

- *Understand the environment.* The informality of the medium—which promotes conversation—must not sanction inadequate preparation or less than professional standards. In the early years there were numerous problems to overcome including unreliable ISDN lines, poor video and sound quality, and inadequate translation facilities. Overseas employees were occasionally untrained, speakers were poorly briefed on the use of the medium, and planning was inadequate.
- *Ensure that adequate resources are available.* Because the medium was perceived as relatively inexpensive and less than professional (compared to broadcast quality video), the operation has been shortchanged, from equipment to staff. As a consequence, in its early years quality suffered. Since then, the staff has upgraded its studios, routinely tests connectivity well before the scheduled conference, establishes contingencies to ensure audio connections if the video circuits fail, and otherwise promotes a professional production.

- *Innovators must hold on to their convictions until a new medium matures.* Because of the constraints of quality and cost, there was relatively little usage in the early years. As equipment costs decreased and quality improved, the early champions of digital videoconferencing have proven to be prescient. Digital videoconferencing has become a powerful medium.

FOIA Electronic Reading Room

The Department of State website looks like many others in the federal government. But, one distinguishing characteristic is the Freedom of Information Act (FOIA) collection, particularly as it concerns key aspects of the U.S. government's conduct of foreign affairs.[9] Its Electronic Reading Room makes available to the public Department of State records that have been declassified and released under the Freedom of Information Act.

With a full- and part-time staff equivalent to 136 full-time employees, the department considers several thousand requests each year at an annual cost of more than $11 million. The staff includes scores of retired Foreign Service officers who meticulously review each document before release. The office is supported by an online archive of electronic diplomatic communications, a case tracking/imaging/electronic redaction system, and several Internet and intranet websites. The archive includes more than 25 million records.

The Electronic Reading Room receives 70,000 hits per day, a measure of public interest in the government's diplomatic relations. A well-indexed archive provides documents by subject and date in PDF format through a Verity search engine. The system is exceedingly responsive, even with a standard dial-up modem.

The current index of electronic documents includes CIA Creation Documents, El Salvador Churchwomen Documents, Guatemala Collection, Raoul Wallenberg Collection, El Salvador Collection, and the Amelia Earhart Collection. The most extensive files are those on U.S.–Chile relations

Start Date: 1997

Originating Office: Bureau of Administration, Office of IRM Programs and Services

Brief Description: Web-enabled online database established to provide public electronic access to State Department documents

Figure 5.7: Declassified document from FOIA Electronic Reading Room

·MEMORANDUM

THE WHITE HOUSE
WASHINGTON

(non-log)

~~SECRET/SENSITIVE~~

ACTION
September 17, 1970

MEMORANDUM FOR THE PRESIDENT

FROM: Henry A. Kissinger HK

SUBJECT: Chile

Unless we establish tight control and professional guidance, the covert action program approved by the 40 Committee for Chile will not work. It is going to be a long-shot as it is; if we have to face the additional handicaps of well-meaning but unprofessional activism, of lack of coordination and of bureaucratic resistance, we will be dangerously exposed.

The situation is as follows:

-- State is timid and unsympathetic to a covert action program; it will not be able to provide either the imaginative leadership or the tight coordinated overview we need.

-- Ambassador Korry is imaginative, but he is an "unguided missile." He is acting now as his own project chief and is trying to construct an operation all by himself. This is dangerous from a professional intelligence-operations point of view, and inefficient because there are so many inhibitions on his capacity to operate. He is too exposed and visible to do this kind of thing, and it may even affect his objectivity and analysis.

-- But Korry does not trust his staff and will not use it; most of his key officers, including the CIA Station Chief, have been cut out of the operation.

-- Only Korry is doing any real reporting, and while it is voluminous, it is inconsistent and contradictory. We cannot be sure of what the situation really is and how much Korry is justifying or camaflouging.

-- CIA is unhappy at the modus operandi, but does not feel it can impose discipline on Korry; it certainly cannot do it through its present Station Chief.

-- There is no consensus among agencies here concerning the full scope of operations and some lack of enthusiasm for overall planning. Hence, the bureaucracy is simply reacting to what happens in Santiago.

-- The 40 Committee does not have the time for this kind of close, detailed supervision, and the time-lag would make it impossible anyway.

~~SECRET/SENSITIVE~~

DECLASSIFIED
Authority

from 1968 to 1991, which include a total of 17,413 documents. This collection of cables, memoranda, letters, and testimony includes documentation on relations with the Pinochet government and the 1976 car bomb assassination of Orlando Letelier and Ronni Moffitt in Washington.

The Electronic Freedom of Information Act Amendments of 1996 (E-FOIA) established the requirement for all agencies to make available "copies of all records, regardless of form or format, which have been released to any person ... and which, because of the nature of their subject matter, the agency determines have become or are likely to become the subject of subsequent requests." Among other requirements, E-FOIA grants the public access to government documents via computer telecommunications. One of the amendments required that the first documents to be made available were those released since November 1, 1966. It also required that an index of such documents be made available electronically by December 31, 1999. The Department of State's FOIA website, which was launched in 1997, was one of the first FOIA sites available electronically in the federal government. And it may well rank as the best.

There was a time when diplomats could assume that their confidential communications would remain closed to the public. With the passage of FOIA, individuals could request to examine any materials whose disclosure would not compromise national security or violate privacy restrictions. Nonetheless, there were impediments including costs and time delays. Delays are still common, but once a search has been done, the documents are now available to anyone with an Internet connection and a web browser.

That diplomats know their reporting will someday be public may restrain their candor or, more likely, will ensure the thoroughness of their documentation and the quality of their analysis. Furthermore, those members of the public who care about an issue will be able to examine its diplomatic nuances—and, in the last analysis, hold the government accountable for wisely representing the national interest.

When the Chile documents were released, for example, the National Security Archive at George Washington University credited State Department officials with a strong commitment to using declassified U.S. documents to advance the cause of human rights abroad and the American public's right to know at home.

Lessons Learned

- *The most important lesson to be learned by the FOIA Electronic Reading Room is that it never would have happened without legislation.* The average cost of processing a single request is close to $4,000. Only one-hundredth of one percent of the costs is collected in fees. The administrative disincentive to offer such a service to the public is enormous.

- *By posting these materials on the web, the business of government is now much more broadly shared with interested citizens.* The residual effect on trust building may be well worth the investment in opening these files to public scrutiny. A better-informed citizenry will strengthen the conduct of diplomacy.
- *It requires subject specialists to review the documents to ensure that their release does not compromise national security.* Although aided by information technology, there is no substitute for reading each document and exercising professional judgment on the merits of its release.

Liquid State (Content Management System)

Liquid State is the latest step in the State Department's continuing modernization of the Washington File and associated digital products developed by the International Information Program Office. The Washington File is a daily multi-language product directed at foreign publics to explain American foreign policy and American society. It consists of speeches, texts, interviews, and summaries of U.S. issues produced in regional editions in print and web formats. Since it began in 1994, its web-based version[10] has garnered numerous accolades including *U.S. News & World Report*'s recent list of top sites and the *Library Journal*'s citation that "the State Department's International Information Program site is the best gateway to the various federal agency responses, both domestic and international, to terrorism and the September 11 attacks."

Liquid State is a three-part initiative consisting of: a content management system for web and print publications; a digital asset management system to provide access to photography, video, and sound; and the global graphics initiative to provide standards and technology for image manipulation, page layout, web design, and electronic distribution.

The purpose of its key element, the content management system, is to "let writers write and designers design." Liquid State is a concept, a proce-

Start Date: Initiated in 2002 to improve public access to numerous existing information services

Originating Office: Office of International Information Programs (IIP)

Brief Description: Content management system to enhance production of public diplomacy website, other electronic products, and print publications

Figure 5.8: Washington File

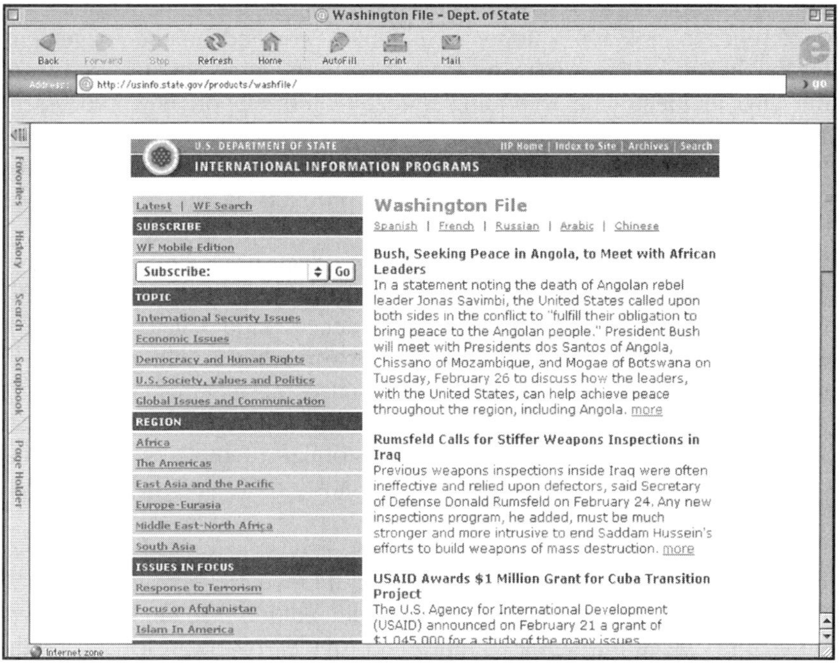

dure, and a process wherein producers focus on the content rather than the product per se. Writers enter text into a web-based content management system from which a variety of products—from print to electronic—can be produced, depending on the public diplomacy requirements in different regions or countries. Hence, the raw copy might form the basis for a press release, a pamphlet, a CD-ROM, an electronic file, or a web-based product. The content management system can be accessed by writers from their desks at the State Department, from their homes, or through an Internet terminal abroad. It not only allows faster input, but also eliminates the need for the writer or an associate to rewrite in HTML.

The content management system selected by the State Department for this application is eGrail. Using object-based architecture, eGrail offers content flexibility, rapid development, and website uniformity. It allows users to manipulate distinct "objects" at a granular level (such as text, graphics, XML files, whole or partial client/server scripts, applications, etc.). With its point-and-click control, content management is nearly automatic. Its object-based, database-driven architecture allows writers to update pages quickly and easily, thereby ensuring that information is current. XML files, instead of PDF files, allow post-by-post customization.

The initiative was undertaken to provide more tools to the producers and more flexibility to the overseas missions. Attending a Seybold publishing conference to look at private sector initiatives provided the encouragement for this initiative. The focus was not just on introducing new technologies, but also in identifying technologies that would support new processes. While IIP's predecessor bureau in USIA had been one of the first in the foreign affairs community to use the World Wide Web, it was now time to adopt new technologies to support older products as well. Print has not been replaced by the Internet.

IIP's focus on electronic delivery of its products has left many American missions in the developing world without the print assets to communicate with publics who do not yet have Internet access. Liquid State, through the content management system and associated technologies, will give to overseas missions not only the content, but also the technical and design resources necessary to produce customized products. The information stored in eGrail can be poured into customized templates to produce print and electronic products that better satisfy different requirements in different countries.

Even as IIP looked at legacy products, it was looking ahead to new media including Personal Digital Assistants (PDAs). An early adaptation of the Washington File was to produce a mobile edition that can be accessed on a Palm device through a commercial provider, AvantGo. It has already enjoyed some early successes.

Lessons Learned

- *Stay on top of industry developments.* The developers have maintained close contact with commercial innovations by attending trade shows and professional meetings. They understand that in order to be competitive, they must stay in touch with emerging standards and anticipate where the industry will be by the time a project is finished.
- *Focus on the requirements of the users—the writers and designers who produce the daily products—not on the hardware or software.* The designers first went to the users and said, "Would you want to do this? What do you think about this? What is the feedback?" To be sure to get buy-in from the users, the new process must actually provide a benefit to the user.

Case Studies: Using Technology to Improve Internal Communication

Treaty Information Portal (TIP)

The Treaty Information Portal (TIP) is the latest upgrade to the Arms Control Treaty Negotiations Database, where negotiators and analysts can log on to a single network to access multiple databases containing all current arms control treaty records. It is managed by the Verification and Compliance Bureau of the Department of State, formerly part of the Arms Control and Disarmament Agency (ACDA) until consolidation in 1999. The Treaty Information Portal incorporates 12 libraries, including the official negotiating record archives; inspection reports related to the Conventional Forces in Europe (CFE) and the Strategic Arms Reduction Treaty; and treaty exchange data from CFE, the Organization of Security and Co-operation in Europe (OSCE), and Confidence and Security Building Measure (CSBM) data sets (including the global exchange of military information). Another library contains weapons photos that account for existing treaty-limited equipment. The photos are used to resolve disputes over weapons disposition.

The Treaty Portal also incorporates public affairs archives of signing ceremonies and numerous unclassified photos of weapons systems. (This is the place to go if you need a World War I picture of a horse in a gas mask; see Figure 5.9).

By far the most important database is the Negotiation Record Database. The usefulness is evident. Negotiators in Geneva or Vienna can refer back to the intent of the original negotiators. Even if the treaty language itself is vague, the negotiation record usually speaks to the intent of the negotiators—10, 20, or 30 years after the fact.

The data repository is managed in-house by a team of data administrators who input data using high-speed scanners and electronic feeds from the cable network. Programmers and engineers work on links to existing databases outside of the State Department. Databases from DoD and other

Start Date: Initiated in 2000 to improve staff access to numerous existing databases

Originating Office: Verification and Compliance Bureau

Brief Description: Web-based classified portal consolidating numerous databases containing all current arms control treaty records members of the arms control community are indexed within the State system to provide one-stop shopping for users.

The volume of new data exceeds 50,000 pages annually, not all of which is in English. In the past, there were numerous sources of translation, which occasionally led to confusion. Now, through interagency coordination, all documents are translated by one agency and shared by all. TIP, through indexing, provides capabilities to all user agencies to access their own data plus the data of others to the extent that the originator allows. An important element of TIP is the software to provide differentiated access. Data providers are less willing to collaborate if access to their data is unrestricted.

In 1982, Congress mandated that ACDA maintain a complete archive of the negotiating record to provide the basis for accurate and effective treaty negotiations. An interagency body, the Arms Control Coordinating Research Committee, decided to field two systems: ACCORD (Arms Control Online Research Database, an unclassified system accessed through a dial-up modem) and a classified system called ARENA (Automated Recourse to Electronic Negotiation Archives). The dial-up speed was slow, and the data structures didn't lend themselves to analysis. So, the system was underutilized, and most users simply requested paper copies.

The Conventional Forces in Europe negotiations, which required exhaustive data exchange among parties, created the next impetus for change. After some debate within the arms control community, it was decided that ACDA would become the official repository of the exchanged data, inspection reports, and notifications—on the condition that it would be made available online. Subsequent legislation required ACDA to maintain both paper and electronic records of treaty texts, negotiation records, research, and related arms control information.

Plans to migrate from a dial-up modem to a network system based on Internal protocol (IP) were completed in 1999, using Excalibur RetrievalWare. The proof of concept developed for the Y2K project gave the Verification and Compliance Bureau a head start in building the data repository search engine for the Treaty Information Portal. New data sharing agreements were signed with NATO, the On-Site Inspection Agencies, and other members of the arms control community.

The availability of DoD's classified SIPRNET was a key element in the success of the project. It provided adequate bandwidth and the ability to share classified data. With a common web interface and graphical front end, SIPRNET was ideal for this application.

The key attribute of the Treaty Information Portal is providing *timely* and *accurate* information. It also eliminates duplication of effort among the thousands of people who work on arms control by providing data from all the data sets that are maintained and indexed. It makes everyone more efficient and eliminates unnecessary duplication of cost.

Figure 5.9: WWI picture of horse in gas mask

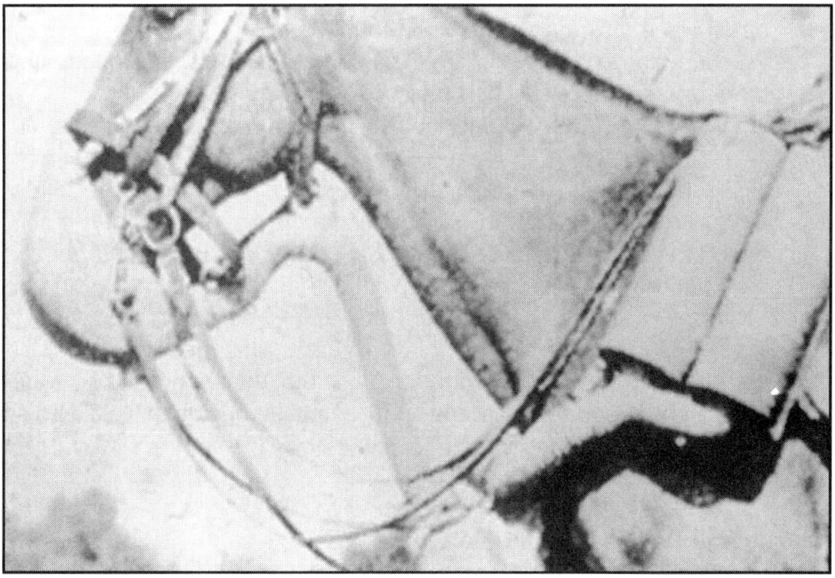

Prior to this system, arms control specialists were unable to share data with other agencies in real time. If an analyst at the Pentagon needed to know the U.S. position on a particular topic, he would call and ask for a data search. Then ACDA would send the data over by classified pouch, with a delay of a few days. Now the analyst searches the database in real time. The State Department is more efficient as well. By spidering all of the sites from a single interface, there is no need to duplicate data held by other agencies.

With the Treaty Information Portal functioning well, the staff is now building expertise on, and testing, high-definition video systems between Washington and Geneva. Given the care that is evident in the deployment of the new system, secure videoconferencing between policy makers in Washington and negotiators overseas will likely be commonplace before long.

Lessons Learned

- *There are several important lessons to be learned from the operation of this complex, classified interagency system, but none more important than the insistence of the leadership that all senior members of the IT staff be also expert in arms control.* Diplomacy and information technology must be tightly aligned if the latter is to serve the former. "I tell my guys, if you're not good enough to go work in the policy office, you're not good enough to work here. If you can't go work in the chemical weapons office or the nonproliferation office, that means you don't know enough to do your job here."[11]

- *The IT office must choose its core competencies.* As the demands are so great, it has to decide what is most important, specialize in that, and ignore the rest. "We succeed because we've chosen to ignore 90 percent of things we were doing, but do a few things and try to do them extraordinarily well."[12]
- *When working with the interagency community, draw up access agreements with great specificity, so that each agency will have the confidence that its data will not be misused or end up with unauthorized users.* Otherwise, agencies are reluctant to share their data.
- *Economies of scale can be found when related elements are supported by a common IT shop.* This is not an argument that the support of business functions should be centralized, but that common business functions can be supported by a single office large enough to have expertise in several related functions.

Worldwide Remote E-mail Network (WREN)

The Worldwide Remote E-mail Network is a mobile Local Area Network, or LAN, designed to support the Secretary of State during foreign travel. It provides classified communications to the Secretary and his immediate party from any point in the world through encrypted messaging on ISDN lines, a dedicated V-SAT satellite, or leased time on a M-4 InMarsat satellite. Connectivity to the V-SAT is through a 1.5-meter dish carried on the Secretary's plane; the InMarsat connection is through an even smaller mobile antenna. The systems, operated at a speed of 256 Kbps, provide secure communications to the State Department's Operation Center—and from there to any embassy in the world.

The system, from laptops to generators, is completely self-contained, so it can function in remote locations. While worldwide connectivity is

Start Date: 2000

Originating Office: Executive Secretariat

Brief Description: Mobile high-speed Internet connectivity enabled by satellite technology to allow broadband communications for the Secretary of State during international travel

Figure 5.10: Worldwide Remote E-mail Network

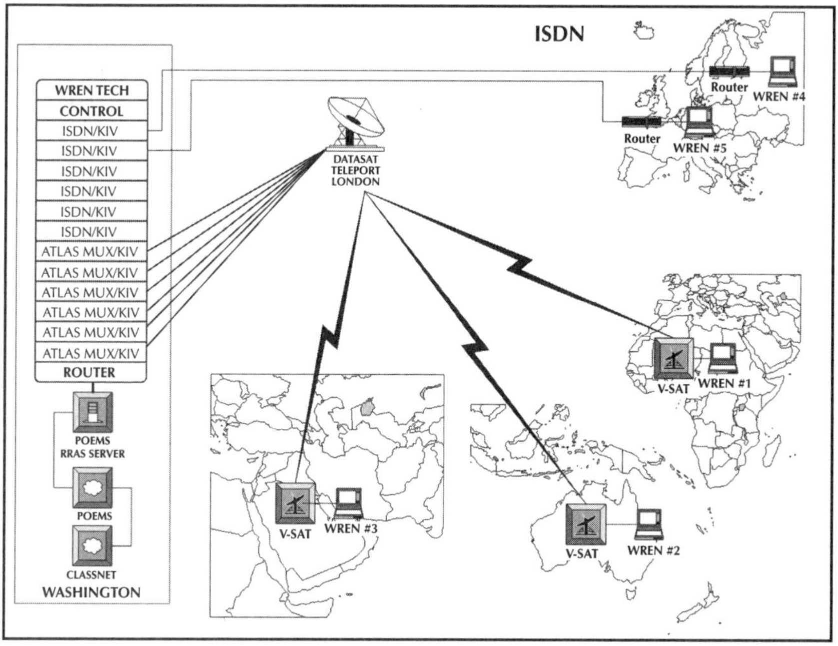

hardly a novelty in the 21st century, it is only recently that secure, high-speed, e-mail connectivity between Washington and any remote location was routine. In fact, the system was inaugurated in 2001 during Secretary of State Albright's official visit to Pyongyang. Its use has since become standard operating practice.

WREN had its origins in Y2K preparations when older systems were subject to careful scrutiny. Legacy cable systems and classified fax were used to connect the Secretary with the Department of State, each requiring several steps of processing, along with the attendant staff support. The Department's Executive Secretariat proposed an upgrade using secure computers and networking sufficiently robust to satisfy the government's highest security requirements—without the intermediate delays inherent in the legacy systems.

As cables had been circulated by e-mail within the Secretary's inner office for several years, extending the same system to a mobile LAN did not represent a sharp departure from standard practice. To the contrary, information access on the road was the same as in the State Department itself. The change in technology resulted, as well, in minor organizational changes to better synchronize technical support with the operational requirements of the Secretary of State. Routines that were developed to support Secretary Kissinger during the Nixon and Ford administrations have been abandoned.

With WREN, the Secretary and his traveling party have much faster access to information than with its predecessor systems that required several intermediate processing steps before reaching the principals. For both strategic and humanitarian reasons, minutes lost may make a difference when the Secretary is on the road. WREN has been designed to ensure that information is available in real time.

In addition to classified e-mail, WREN also provides full access to the State Department's classified intranet—and through it to Defense Department and intelligence community networks. It offers periodic briefing materials and other information prepared in Washington to support the Secretary's travel. The occasional fax that is still sent is being replaced by e-mail attachments. Secure videoconferencing is a planned future application over the network. For efficiency and thoroughness, plans are also under way to replace e-mail messaging with e-mail alerts that will be hyperlinked to HTML pages accessible through a browser.

WREN was designed to support the Secretary of State and his immediate staff during official travel abroad. That it does well. Additionally, it also supports the many others in the Department of State who are responsible for keeping the Secretary informed and for collaborating, advising on policy, and acting on instructions. While the system would not surprise anyone familiar with modern communications, it represents a significant advance over the legacy system that it replaced. As one officer in the Executive Secretariat said, "It is much, much faster." It is also easier to use.

Lessons Learned

- *The primary lesson learned is the need for the IT developmental staff to be close to business practices.* Despite its centrality to policy making, the innovation did not come from the department's central IT office, but from immediate users. While centralizing infrastructure, network management, and standards may be advantageous, decentralizing IT applications is often the wiser course. To centralize all IT support is to put at risk the innovation that comes from those who are responsible for business practices.
- *Innovations built on systems familiar to users tend to reduce the resistance that often accompanies change.* The Secretary and staff were comfortable with information provided in familiar packages. The only change they saw was greater speed and greater depth in what they could access. Familiarity with the look and feel of the system output is particularly important when there is little or no latitude for error. WREN feels comfortable to users.

ChinaNet

The American Consulate General in Hong Kong has transformed the way it does business by moving many of its routine functions to Web-based applications. They include innovations in financial management, human resources, and procurement—the usual focus of technological change in the State Department. But changes have also been developed in the Public Affairs section, the Economic-Political section, and the Protocol section. The key to this profusion of innovation was a functioning real-time network and the availability of Web-based software. The transformation began in 1999 with the arrival of a computer-savvy administrative officer who joined with a forward-looking computer systems manager and talented local staff to demonstrate that the Consulate General could develop across-the-board efficiency gains. They exploited Internet-based software innovations to develop new applications based on Web browsers (e.g., Netscape Navigator, Internet Explorer) that were already familiar to officers and staff.

In addition to increasing the efficiency of administrative functions, the move to Web-based applications has directly supported several diplomatic requirements. The Public Affairs section is better managing its database of press guidances, thereby making them more useful to officers throughout the mission. The Economic-Political section put its biographic files online and substituted searchable, electronic record-keeping for traditional paper files. The Protocol section maintains a Consulate-wide contact list, searchable by staff, joined with an automated system to manage Consulate representational events. The Public Affairs and Administrative sections collaborated with the Foreign Broadcast Information Service (FBIS) to replace the cable distribution of FBIS news summaries and translations, press briefings and media reactions with a single searchable database. This Web-based application is now routinely accessed by Missions throughout Asia and by interested officials in Washington. In the words of the Consul General, "The entire institution is transforming the way it does business."

Over the past decade the Department of State has been coping with an increasing workload in the face of reduced staffing. Long hours are

Start Date: 1999

Originating Office: American Consulate General in Hong Kong

Brief Description: Web-based diplomatic and administrative applications to improve efficiency at the Hong Kong Consulate General

Figure 5.11: American Consulate General in Hong Kong

accepted as routine. Since the introduction of word processors more than two decades ago, there are few documented examples of new information technologies improving staff efficiency. The Hong Kong consulate is one of the exceptions. The result has been the elimination of needless steps, a reduction in paper use, and a much greater sharing of information.

Templates have been developed and networked to make forms easily available and ensure consistency in their completion. Directories, contact lists, and biographic files are shared across offices. Training has been made widely available.

One of the new applications, ChinaNet Procurement, has attracted interest outside of Hong Kong by demonstrating that a Web-based application could enhance productivity. Partly as a result, the State Department is now developing Web-based software for numerous other applications.

Many IT innovations result from the leadership of an individual whose passion for change is strong enough to overcome bureaucratic resistance. The introduction of new IT practices at the American Consulate General in Honk Kong was no exception. The State Department acknowledged that the post's administrative officer, Jay Anania, made the difference, for which he was awarded the Innovation in the Use of Technology Award for the year 2000. It was his leadership and inspiration that transformed the Hong Kong Consulate General.

In recommending him for this recognition, the Consul General wrote: "Jay has been a catalyst for change. He brought to his job a deep knowledge of processes and an eye for how they could be improved by advanced technology. Equally important, he recognized that his staff had the capability to generate substantial improvements on their own. He therefore devoted his energies not only to hands-on exploration of opportunities for innovation, but to leading his staff, channeling their energies, and inspiring their creativity. Despite some initial resistance, he drove through the idea that we would transform the way we do business in Hong Kong, and share that with our colleagues in the region."

Lessons Learned

- *The first lesson learned from the Hong Kong experience is the key role of an IT champion who has the vision and force of personality to inspire, cajole, and lead the transformation of work practices.* With the predictable resistance to change, it takes a knowledgeable and persuasive champion to introduce change successfully.
- *The second lesson is that change agents must understand the business practices well enough to demonstrate that the recommended changes will improve efficiency or quality.* And the advocate must offer training to give the new users the confidence that they can perform the new routine at or beyond their personal standard of excellence. The technologies that were introduced were built to fit the user, not vice-versa. As the Consul General wrote: "If you build it, and show them how to use it well, they will come—in droves."
- *A third lesson is that success breeds success. Hong Kong's IT innovations, having received recognition, are being propagated to other American missions.* This summer the officer responsible for these innovations is being transferred to a senior position in Washington, where his abilities and experience can be further exploited.

Foreign Affairs Systems Integration (FASI)

Knowledge management (KM) systems have come into vogue in the last decade to permit large enterprises to share intellectual knowledge among their employees. If the New Delhi office of an international consulting firm solves a local problem for a client, it may benefit other consultants in the firm to apply the solution elsewhere or, conversely, to learn what has not

Start Date: Prototype tested in 2001; pilot to be tested in 2002

Originating Office: Information Resource Management Bureau (IRM)

Brief Description: Web-based initiative to provide knowledge management tools to all government agencies operating in American embassies and consulates

worked. While the line between information and knowledge is sometimes blurry, knowledge management systems are more than information management systems. It may be helpful to think of knowledge as what you have in your head, in contrast to information, which you keep in your file cabinet. Knowledge management systems allow you to efficiently store, retrieve, and exchange knowledge. And knowledge management systems tend to be collaborative.

At one level, the Department of State can be thought of as a mega-knowledge management system—ceaselessly gathering, processing, and acting on information; building a reservoir of knowledge about nations, alliances, agreements, and threats; sharing knowledge with other elements of government and other nations.

Indeed, sophisticated messaging systems as well as routine meetings and conferences have served the purpose of exchanging knowledge. But, such exchanges are often inefficient or even non-existent. What is known to a Second Secretary in Buenos Aires may never influence policy making in Washington. If he takes his knowledge with him when he departs post, it won't even influence his successor. Knowledge management systems are designed to give decision makers what they need to know to make wise decisions and to filter out that which is irrelevant.

If the business of diplomacy is representation, negotiation, and advocacy, it follows that diplomatic skill is a function of knowledge: knowledge of the issues, knowledge of the environment, knowledge of one's adversaries. It would be foolish to proceed to a diplomatic assignment without a thorough knowledge of the issues and personalities that one will confront.

The question is whether KM systems can be designed to improve either efficiency or quality—or perhaps even substantially change one's conduct of diplomacy. There will necessarily be an investment in hardware, software, and training. Will the return to the diplomat warrant the resources (particularly time) that are required to design, manage, and operate the KM system that purports to assist in the management of knowledge?

The Department of State has recently initiated the design of a worldwide, multi-agency knowledge management system designed to serve

Figure 5.12: FASI Knowledge Management Project

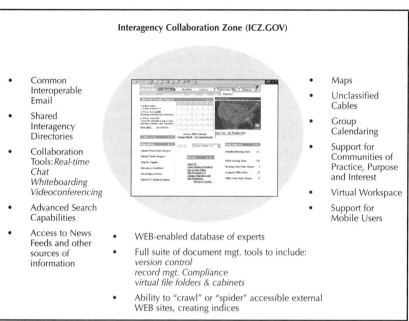

Interagency Collaboration Zone (ICZ.GOV)

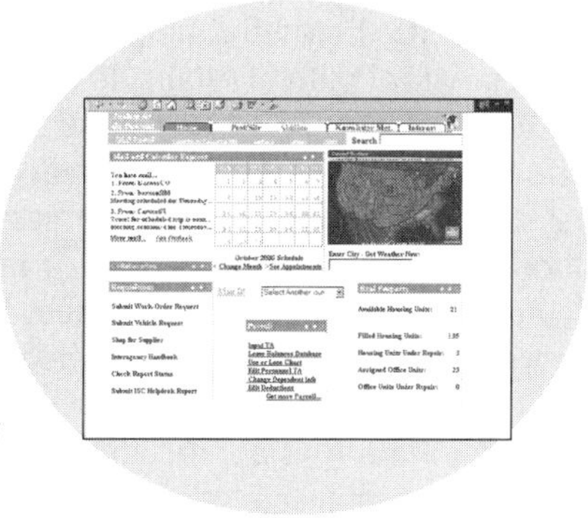

- Common Interoperable Email
- Shared Interagency Directories
- Collaboration Tools: *Real-time Chat Whiteboarding Videoconferencing*
- Advanced Search Capabilities
- Access to News Feeds and other sources of information

- Maps
- Unclassified Cables
- Group Calendaring
- Support for Communities of Practice, Purpose and Interest
- Virtual Workspace
- Support for Mobile Users

- WEB-enabled database of experts
- Full suite of document mgt. tools to include:
  version control
  record mgt. Compliance
  virtual file folders & cabinets
- Ability to "crawl" or "spider" accessible external WEB sites, creating indices

State Department employees as well as the overseas employees of some 40 U.S. government agencies. The system, managed by Information Resource Management's (IRM) Office of Foreign Affairs Systems Integration (FASI), grew out of a 1999 recommendation by the Overseas Presence Advisory Panel. The panel wrote that "management of knowledge must be a central focus of IT upgrades ... to create a system that not only distributes information but also captures and securely stores it for future retrieval...."

A preliminary system design was completed by IRM in the spring of 2001 with the advice of outside experts including KPMG, CSC, and Gartner group. Five vendors were invited to propose solutions. From their submissions, three industry teams were selected for the prototype phase, which is under way as this is being written. Members of the three consortia include SAIC, PricewaterhouseCoopers, SRA International, IBM, Accenture, General Dynamics, and Booz Allen Hamilton. After comparative testing, one of the three teams will be selected for a more exhaustive pilot test. It is scheduled to involve up to 2,400 employees working in Washington, India, and Mexico. If the pilot is successful and funding is available, worldwide deployment will begin in 2003 and will be completed in two to three years. Designed to reach the desktops of 30,000 State Department employees in

180 countries with a full suite of software including video, the FASI knowledge management project is an exceptionally ambitious undertaking.

Meanwhile, smaller KM initiatives have been initiated, driven by the business processes that they are designed to support. They include the Collation for Anti-Terrorism (CAT) Matrix, developed with the encouragement of the Under Secretary for Political Affairs, to support the international coalition put together by Secretary Powell after the September 11 terrorist attacks. Also, with the support of the Under Secretary for Management, a demonstration KM system to support the G-8 process is under development. Not quite a thousand flowers, but knowledge management systems are clearly at the blossoming stage in the Department of State.

Unlike the other systems that have been described, KM systems are still in their pilot phase at the State Department. With a 70 percent failure record in industry, the risk of failure is appreciated. Yet, the risk of postponing a decision in a knowledge-intensive organization is also significant. As everyone who has used a phone in the last several years knows, automated phone-answering systems save time for the corporation, but seldom for the caller. KM systems must either save time or improve the quality of diplomatic work. No matter how sophisticated the system, it must enhance the conduct of diplomacy to be judged a success.

Lessons (to be) Learned

- The Department of State faces the same question as every large enterprise: Are new systems best built from the top down or from the bottom up—or is there an intermediate step that combines the virtues of both? The FASI Knowledge Management system, with deployment costs estimated to approach $300 million, will be an expensive failure if it does not improve the efficiency or the quality of diplomacy. On the other hand, boutique applications like the CAT Matrix and G-8 KM system, even if precisely tailored to the business needs, may not be scalable or adaptable to other diplomatic requirements. The lessons from these approaches remain to be learned as the systems are deployed over the next several months and years.

Lessons Learned

Despite its reputation as a laggard in the deployment of information technology, the Department of State deploys a sophisticated array of computer and communications technology to collect, analyze, archive, and disseminate information. It maintains secure connectivity with embassies in practically every country in the world. From issuing visas to negotiating treaties, it is responsible for managing the foreign policy of the United States.

This study was undertaken to examine the introduction of information technology that has directly advanced the conduct of diplomacy (thereby excluding an examination of systems for personnel, financial, and administrative management). Current diplomatic practices were examined in search of applications ranging from database management to geographic information systems. It was no surprise to find that most diplomatic practices have changed little in the past decade, with the exception of the dramatic growth of e-mail within the Department of State.

With little central direction, e-mail messaging is competing with, and in many ways supplanting, State's legacy cable system. During this transitional period, where new practices are being consolidated, it is premature to say that the conduct of diplomacy has been enhanced by the introduction of e-mail. It has, nonetheless, introduced dramatic changes in business practices, producing positive consequences that will likely be manifest in the near future. Until then, the advantages of speed have been tempered by the excesses of distribution and the lack of connectivity among internal systems.

From the 12 discrete systems described here, there are several lessons to be learned in designing future applications. Table 5.1 shows the common features of the 12 innovations.

The key findings drawn from Table 5.1 are:

- Most of the innovations were driven by forces exterior to the Department of State, including the 1993 bombing of the World Trade Center, the fear of Y2K systems meltdown, and budget reductions requiring great efficiencies.
- Practically all of the innovations were initiated and developed by individuals who were part of the user community that they were designed to serve.
- Most of the applications were developed in areas of the Department of State traditionally thought to be out of the mainstream of political and economic analysis and policy making.
- Most of the innovations cannot be considered "mission critical"—that is, their development was not driven by an expressed need to improve the practice of diplomacy, even if that subsequently was the result.

Among the lessons identified for each of the 12 innovations, there are several that appear frequently enough to warrant particular mention:

- During the developmental stages, the user community and the IT developments *must* be very closely aligned. System development must be driven by the business needs, not by the hardware or software.
- In addition to the technology, developers *must* understand other environmental constraints including logistical problems and bureaucratic resistance.

Table 5.1: Common Features of the 12 IT Innovations to Improve Diplomacy

	Outside Catalyst	Internal Champion	Non-traditional	Mission Critical
Consular Consolidated Database	√	√	√	√
Kosovo Repatriation Information Support	√	√	√	
Worldwide Refugee Admissions ProcessingSystem	√	√	√	√
Dayton Peace Accords	√			√
Kosovo Information Assistance Initiative	√	√	√	
Digital Videoconferencing		√	√	
FOIA Electronic Reading Room	√	√	√	
Liquid State		√	√	
Treaty Information Portal	√	√	√	√
Worldwide Remote E-mail Network		√		√
ChinaNet		√		
Foreign Affairs Systems Integration	√	√		

- Planners *should* be generous in estimating the time and cost of systems development and deployment. It's like building an addition on your house; it takes longer and costs more than you think.
- In the early stages of deployment, systems *should* be built to accommodate existing work practices in order to overcome resistance to change.
- Effective training *should* be offered to give users confidence in the new systems.
- Contingency planning *should* be undertaken to allow diplomats to respond swiftly to unforeseen events including natural disasters and hostilities.
- Interagency agreements *should* be carefully crafted to ensure that all parties are using compatible systems and common standards.

Drawing on these examples, the most important lesson is the need to ensure a close alignment between the user community and the IT developers. The closest possible relation results when the two communities substantially overlap. Most of the innovations came from users who *also* have expertise in information technology. The most compelling example is from the Verification and Compliance Bureau, where senior IT staffers are required to be expert in arms control negotiations as a complement to their IT skills. Among the 12 examples, there is not a single case to be made for the separation of policy and IT competence.

Given the responsibility of leveraging technology to support core diplomatic activities, what can the Department of State learn from its current practices? The lessons suggest that the most favorable circumstance is one in which:

- The diplomatic requirement (i.e., business need) is well defined and well understood.
- There is a champion (e.g., project manager) within the user community who is also competent in information technology.
- There is a catalytic force (e.g., crisis) outside of the Department of State that drives action.
- Attention is given to inertial constraints (e.g., employee resistance) through incremental deployment, reorganization, and training.
- Planning anticipates the real costs and time required for effective deployment.

The Department of State remains a backwater in the deployment of information technology, but the underlying requirements for change are present: IT-savvy leadership and an organizational restlessness with the status quo. The innovations illustrated do not yet form the critical mass that ensure success, but are certainly of sufficient consequence to encourage widespread innovation in the service of diplomacy.

Recommendations

The Department of State has received more attention in its use of information technology than most areas of government. That it fell behind the curve is no secret in Washington. That it is moving forward is both a consequence of the attention it has received from outside *and* a determination from within to leverage technology in the service of diplomacy. The recommendations that follow are not specific to the Department of State, but to any comparable organization that needs to regain its information edge in support of its core functions.

Based on State's experience, the recommendations should apply as well to other foreign ministries, to other governmental organizations involved in the conduct of foreign affairs, and to NGOs with international responsibilities. Although they may apply more broadly, since the lessons were drawn from the support of foreign policy, it is to that discipline that the recommendations are directed. Furthermore, they are restricted to what were identified as second-level functions that directly support the conduct of diplomacy. Financial management, logistical support, and administration are not included within the scope of the study, although each is critical to the support of diplomacy.

First, it should be understood that information technology is no panacea, that it has no business in the workplace unless it supports core functions. Experience has shown that the payoff for new IT is slow, that new systems are subject to high failure rates. So, the first recommendation is to review and, if necessary, restate core business functions with clarity. Answer the question: What product do we make? Or: What service do we provide? Without clarity at this stage, it is difficult to design supportive IT systems.

Second, before deploying information technology, ask how existing business processes might be improved to yield greater *efficiency* or higher *quality.*

Third, apply information technology.

It is the third step in which the State Department's experience may be of value. How one applies new information technology is not, however, as clear as the need to keep core business functions in focus. For example, even if a diplomat understands clearly that his or her role is to issue visas, and to ensure that they are issued expeditiously to applicants who satisfy specified legal requirements, it is not self-evident how information technology is to be applied.

Should a central IT office manage it all to ensure efficiencies of scale? Or, should each consular officer be given a laptop and asked to figure out how to improve his or her work? The second solution is obviously inefficient. Although less obvious, for a large enterprise the first solution may be only marginally better. A hybrid solution, respecting efficiencies of scale, the uniqueness of different diplomatic functions, and the hands-on innovation of diplomats is suggested by the 12 cases that have been reviewed.

The five key recommendations for introducing information technology in support of diplomacy are:

Recommendation 1: Centralize common requirements such as network architecture, equipment procurement, security requirements, and software standards.

IT specialists should design and maintain stable networks that serve a variety of different user needs. That is, a central IT office should keep one step ahead of users by rapidly adopting industry standards to ensure that the networks are sufficiently robust to support new requirements. Because of the lead time for evaluating new technologies, ensuring compliance with security requirements, and contracting, government IT managers must remain current with industry developments and move rapidly to adopt new technologies to satisfy users at the working level.

Recommendation 2: Decentralize the development and support of IT applications.

For example, the unique technology requirements of consular affairs should be supported by consular affairs IT specialists, the requirements for arms control verification by arms control IT specialists, and so on. While central networks and standards must support these and other unique diplomatic practices, it is the diplomats themselves who best understand the requirements of diplomacy. As this study has demonstrated, many of the State Department's diplomatic applications have originated with the users—when funds, equipment, and networks were available.

Recommendation 3: Encourage a cadre of IT-literate diplomats, officers whose specialty is foreign affairs with IT competence.

These are officers whose IT expertise—whether the result of serendipity or design—is recognized as an asset in the conduct of diplomacy. They are the boundary spanners who work across the lines of diplomacy and technology. IT literacy should not be a requirement for most, but the State Department should recruit and train a cadre of skilled diplomats who have the confidence to drive IT innovation. The more diplomatic practices can be enhanced by information technology, the more time officers will have to attend to the core elements of diplomacy.

Recommendation 4: Share learning by encouraging user groups that function across institutional lines.

For example, ensure that political officers understand how consular officers have deployed technology to satisfy their diplomatic requirements. Encourage one area's success to be adapted by others. The Department of State has long encouraged such sharing, although most of the applications have been in support of administrative practices. The next step is to encourage the sharing of IT innovations in the practice of diplomacy. In a profession where there are few textbook solutions to unique diplomatic challenges, the more sharing of IT solutions, the more agile will be the practice of diplomacy.

Recommendation 5: Promote innovation by funding pilot projects and recognizing excellence.

As the examples have shown, the State Department recognizes excellence through its awards and funds pilot projects to test their merit. Both have undoubtedly encouraged the IT breakthrough that is under way. Nonetheless, more should and can be done. As the lead foreign affairs agency, the Department of State must become the preeminent agency in the deployment of information technology—not because it is trendy, but because the raw material of analysis and advocacy is information. To ensure the quality and speed of its information, the department should expand its recognition of innovative technology.

The Department of State should not wait for crises, which have driven some technological developments, or rely on individuals to champion them. It needs to aggressively create the conditions that reward innovation. To this end, it may wish to consider a planning office which operates at the intersection of diplomacy and technology. Staffed by policy officers, IT specialists, and outside academicians, it could accelerate the deployment of information technology in support of diplomacy.

To repeat, information technology is not a panacea. On the other hand, it is not an option in today's competitive environment. If diplomats do not have real-time connectivity to stay informed, if they do not have powerful tools to assist in analysis, if they do not have the means to improve their productivity, then those who do will best them. That will include not only diplomats from other nations, but also colleagues from other areas of government and competitors from the NGOs.

Neither the Office of Management and Budget nor the General Accounting Office currently gives the State Department high marks on its use of information technology. But, with its current leadership and the new funding it has received, buttressed by a new focus on diplomatic requirements, a turnaround within 24 months is a strong possibility for the Department of State. It is, indeed, a plausible candidate to assume a leadership role in the use of information technology in the foreign affairs community.

Appendix: Glossary

ACDA	Arms Control and Disarmament Agency
CCD	Consolidated Consular Database
CFE	Conventional Forces in Europe
CSBMs	Confidence and Security Building Measures
DARPA	Defense Advanced Research Projects Agency
DoD	Department of Defense
DVC	Digital Videoconference
FASI	Foreign Affairs Systems Integration
FBIS	Foreign Broadcast Information Service
FOIA	Freedom of Information Act
GIS	Geographic Information System
GPS	Global Positioning System
HCIC	Humanitarian Community Information Center (United Nations)
HTML	Hyper Text Markup Language
IIP	Office of International Information Programs (State Department)
IOM	International Organization for Migration
IRM	Information Resource Management bureau (State Department)
Kbps	Kilobits per second
KIAI	Kosovo Information Assistance Initiative
KRIS	Kosovo Repatriation Information Support
NGO	Nongovermental Organization
NIMA	National Imagery and Mapping Agency
OFDA	Office of Foreign Disaster Assistance (USAID)
OPE	Overseas Processing Entity
OSCE	Organization for Security and Cooperation in Europe
PDA	Personal Digital Assistant
PDF	Portable Document Format
SIPRNET	Secret Internet Protocol Router Network (DoD)
START	Strategic Arms Reduction Treaty
TIP	Treaty Information Portal
UNHCR	United Nations High Commissioner for Refugees
USAID	United States Agency for International Development
USIA	United States Information Agency
USIP	United States Institute of Peace
USTR	United States Trade Representative
WRAPS	Worldwide Refugee Admissions Processing System
WREN	Worldwide Remote E-mail Network
XML	Extensible Markup Language

Endnotes

1. *SOS for DOS: Call for Action,* an appeal to the Secretary of State signed by some 1,500 employees of the Department of State, January 2001. http://www.afsa.org/c-street/topicPF.cfm?ThreadID=8#12

2. Center for Strategic and International Studies, *Reinventing Diplomacy in the Information Age.* Washington: Center for Strategic and International Studies, 1998. www.csis.org/ics/dia

3. Henry L. Stimson Center, *Equipped for the Future: Managing U.S. Foreign Affairs in the 21st Century.* Washington: Henry L. Stimson Center, 1998. http://www.stimson.org/pubs/ausia/ausr1.pdf

4. Department of State, *America's Overseas Presence in the 21st Century.* Washington: Department of State, 1999. http://www.state.gov/www/publications/9911_opap/rpt-9911_opap_instructions.html

5. Council on Foreign Relations, *State Department Reform.* New York: Council on Foreign Relations, 2001. http://www.cfr.org/p/resource.cgi?pub!3890

6. http://www.foia.state.gov/MajorInfoSys.pdf

7. Michael J. Dziedzic and William B. Wood, "Kosovo Brief: Information Management Offers a New Opportunity for Cooperation between Civilian and Military Entities," Washington: United States Institute of Peace, August 9, 2000. http://www.usip.org/oc/vd/vdr/dziedzic-wood.html

8. Richard G. Johnson, *Negotiating the Dayton Peace Accords through Digital Maps.* Washington: United States Institute of Peace, 1999. http://www.usip.org/oc /vd/vdr/rjohnsonISA99.html

9. http://foia.state.gov

10. http://www.usinfo.state.gov

11. Glen Johnson, Director of Verification Operations, interview by the author, December 31, 2001.

12. Ibid.

Bibliography

Arquilla, John and David Ronfeldt. *The Emergence of Noopolitik*. Santa Monica: Rand, 1999. http://www.rand.org/publications/MR/MR1033/

Center for Strategic and International Studies. *Reinventing Diplomacy in the Information Age*. Washington: Center for Strategic and International Studies, 1998. http://www.csis.org/ics/dia

Cooper, Jeffrey R., "The CyberFrontier and America at the Turn of the 21st Century: Reopening Frederick Jackson Turner's Frontier," *First Monday,* July 2000. http://FirstMonday.org/issues/issue5_7/ cooper/index.html

Council on Foreign Relations. *State Department Reform*. Task Force Report by the Council on Foreign Relations and the Center for Strategic and International Studies. New York: Council on Foreign Relations, 2001. http://www.cfr.org/p/ resource.cgi?pub!3890

Department of State. *America's Overseas Presence in the 21st Century.* Washington: Department of State, 1999. http://www.state.gov/www/ publications/9911_opap/rpt-9911_opap_instructions.html

Dizard, Wilson, Jr. *Digital Diplomacy: U.S. Foreign Policy in the Information Age*. Westport, Conn.: Praeger, 2001.

Dziedzic, Michael J. and William B. Wood, "Kosovo Brief: Information Management Offers a New Opportunity for Cooperation between Civilian and Military Entities," Washington: United States Institute of Peace, August 9, 2000. http://www. usip.org/oc/vd/vdr/dziedzic-wood.html

Fulton, Barry, ed., "Diplomacy in the Information Age," *iMP: Information Impacts,* July 2001. http://www.cisp.org/imp

Fulton, Barry, "The Information Age: New Dimensions for U.S. Foreign Policy," *Great Decisions 1999*. New York: The Foreign Policy Association, 1999, pp. 9-18.

Henry L. Stimson Center. *Equipped for the Future: Managing U.S. Foreign Affairs in the 21st Century.* Washington: Henry L. Stimson Center, 1998. http://www.stimson.org/pubs/ausia/ausr1.pdf

Henry, Ryan and C. Edward Peartree. *The Information Revolution and International Security.* Washington: Center for Strategic and International Studies, 1968.

Holbrooke, Richard. *To End a War.* New York: Random House, 1998.

Information Age Diplomacy: a symposium organized by the National Defense University and Northwestern University, April 5-6, 2001 http://www.ndu.edu/ndu/nwc/Public/SymposiumWebsite/symposium_main.htm

Johnson, Richard G. *Negotiating the Dayton Peace Accords through Digital Maps*. Washington: United States Institute of Peace, 1999. http://www.usip.org/oc/vd/vdr/rjohnsonISA99.html

Moose, Richard M., "From U2 to URL: Technology and Foreign Affairs," *Georgetown Journal of International Affairs,* Summer/Fall 2000, pp. 15-22.

National Foreign Intelligence Board. *Global Trends 2015: A Dialogue About the Future with Nongovernment Experts*. Washington: National Foreign Intelligence Board, December 2000. http://www.cia.gov/cia/publications/globaltrends2015/index.html

Nye, Joseph S., Jr. and William Owens, "America's Information Edge," *Foreign Affairs,* March/April 1966, pp. 20-36.

Ronfeldt, David and John Arquilla, "What If There is a Revolution in Diplomatic Affairs?" United States Institute of Peace, Virtual Diplomacy Series No. 4, February 2000. http://www.usip.org/oc/vd/vdr/ronarql-SA99.html

Rosenau, James N., "States, Sovereignty, and Diplomacy in the Information Age," United States Institute of Pace, Virtual Diplomacy Series No. 5, February 2000. http://www.usip.org/oc/vd/vdr/jrosenauISS99.html

Rothkopf, David J., "Cyberpolitik: The Information Revolution and U.S. Foreign Policy," summary of a presentation at the Carnegie Endowment for International Peace, March 22, 2000. http://www.ceip.org/prgrams/info/rothkopf.htm

Solomon, Richard H., Walter B. Wriston, and George P. Shultz, Keynote Addresses from the Virtual Diplomacy Conference. Washington: United States Institute of Peace, 1997. http://www.usip.org/pubs/pworks/virtual18/vdip_18.html

CHAPTER SIX

State Government E-Procurement in the Information Age: Issues, Practices, and Trends

M. Jae Moon
Assistant Professor
George Bush School of Government and Public Service
Texas A&M University

This report was originally published in September 2002.

Introduction[1]

There have been a great deal of criticism and negative perception that public procurement management is neither efficient nor effective at present. One study shows that the government spends about 5.5 cents to administer every procurement dollar while its private counterparts spend only 1 cent to do the similar procurement task (JTFIT, 1996). State governments spend about $75 to $100 administering a single transaction (JTFIT, 1996), which is perceived to be very inefficient. Such criticism and negative public perception force governments to find new and innovative approaches for promoting better, more efficient procurement management.

In the meantime, as information technology (IT) has become a possible solution for many administrative problems in the public sector, e-procurement has emerged as an innovative alternative to achieve a better, more cost-efficient system. E-procurement is defined as a comprehensive process in which governments either establish agreements for the acquisition of products/services *(contracting)* or purchase products/services in exchange for payment *(purchasing)*, using IT systems.[2] E-procurement achieves these ends through various means, such as electronic ordering, purchasing cards, reverse auctions, and automatic accounting/procurement systems, among others.

Reflecting the dramatic emergence of IT applications in the information age, society has been flooded with literature based on various IT-related studies of business, sociology, and economics. Despite the wealth of information on IT-related issues and the increasing significance of IT for management and policy, surprisingly little research has been conducted in the field of public administration. Some studies suggest that public organizations, which tend to be late adopters of new technology, are perpetually behind in the technology diffusion curve. As this pessimistic view of the public sector suggests, such specific IT applications as e-procurement are neither well explored nor advanced in present studies.

Procurement management has had ample opportunities to improve through the phenomenal popularity of e-commerce (activities related to selling, transferring, and buying products and services using IT systems) and the availability of electronic transaction systems in the private sector. As large buyers, state governments search for managerial alternatives to streamline procurement procedures and reduce overhead costs. Often, IT is one of the most attractive alternatives. Of the many functional initiatives of e-government employed by state governments, this study is specifically designed to survey IT usages in e-procurement management.

State governments are the focal governmental unit of this study. Many state governments have adopted e-procurement management, following the federal government example and the compelling rhetoric of e-procurement. State governments are a good unit of analysis because of the wide variation in their practical implementation of e-procurement. Also, the experience of state governments represents a possible laboratory for local governments, which increasingly are interested in new alternatives for managing procurement.

The study explores general IT applications in the public sector from the perspective of e-government, specifically examining the evolution of e-procurement tools at the state level. Then state governments' adoption and implementation of various e-procurement technologies are examined. This is followed by several case studies of innovative initiatives that suggest the potential effectiveness of e-procurement practices in state governments. The study uses data collected by the National Association of State Procurement Officials (NASPO) in 1998 and 2000 and by the author in a 2001 follow-up survey. Overall, this study seeks to increase our practical understanding of and assess the future implications of e-procurement by surveying the current practices of state governments.

Information Technology and the Move toward E-Government[3]

IT appears to be the most significant technological factor in amplifying social (electronically networked society), economic (e-commerce), political (e-politics, e-campaigning), and governmental (e-government) dynamics through its unique properties of networked communication, data processing, and data management. In particular, e-commerce has become an increasingly popular practice for commercial transactions, thanks to the development of electronic transaction systems and Internet-based businesses. These practices have been reshaping the operation and content of businesses in the private sector.

Echoing the IT applications in the private sector, e-government has become a major reform buzzword for future governance in the public sector. A study by Hart-Teeter (2000) shows that both public and private managers are generally excited and positive about the prospects of e-government, though they raise some security and privacy concerns. IT has opened many possibilities for improving the internal managerial efficiency and the quality of public service delivery to citizens. For example, IT has contributed to dramatic changes in politics (Nye, 1999; Norris, 1999), bureaucracy (Fountain, 1999; 2001), performance management (Brown, 1999), reengineering (Anderson, 1999), red tape reduction (Moon and Bretschneider, 2002), democracy (Musso et al., 2000), and public service delivery (West, 2001) during the last decade. As part of the National Information Infrastructure (NII) initiative, the Clinton administration attempted to visualize electronic government as a means through which the government overcomes the barriers of time and distance in administering public services (Gore, 1993).

The Clinton administration believed that IT would enhance both the efficiency and the effectiveness of public organizations by simplifying administrative procedures and instituting reliable accountability mechanisms. On June 24, 2000, President Clinton delivered his first webcast address to the public and announced a series of e-government initiatives. A highlight was the establishing of an integrated online service system that put all online resources offered by the federal government on a single website, www.firstgov.gov. The initiative also attempted to build one-stop access to roughly $300 billion in grant and $200 billion in procurement opportunities (White House Press Office, 2000). This initiative reflected continuing governmental efforts to advance e-government at the federal level. For instance, the federal government has improved their websites and provided web-based services to promote better internal procedural management and external service provision (Fountain, 2001; West, 2001; Moon, 2002).

E-government includes four major internal and external aspects: (1) the establishment of a secure government intranet and central database for more efficient and cooperative interaction among governmental agencies; (2) web-based service delivery; (3) the application of e-commerce practices for more efficient transaction activities, as in procurement and contracts; and (4) digital democracy for more transparent accountability of government (Government and the Internet Survey, 2000). Various technologies support these unique aspects of e-government, including electronic data interchange (EDI), interactive voice response (IVR), voice mail, e-mail, web service delivery, virtual reality, and public key infrastructure (PKI).

For instance, after introducing Electronic Filing Systems (EFS) with custom-designed software that incorporates encryption technology, the U.S. Patent and Trademark Office (USPTO) substantially reduced the amount of paper the agency handles by allowing inventors or their agents to send any documents to the USPTO via the Internet (Daukantas, 2000). Due to various web technologies, 40 million U.S. taxpayers were able to file their 2000 returns via the web, while 670,000 online applications were made for student loans via the web-based system of the Department of Education (Preston, 2000). Some governments have also promoted virtual democracy by pursuing web-based political participation, such as online voting and online public forums.

In their research, some scholars have reacted to the introduction of IT and the evolution of e-government. Some early research (Bozeman and Bretschneider, 1986; Bretschneider, 1990; Cats-Baril and Thompson, 1995) attempted to understand distinctive managerial principles and unique characteristics of the public management information system (PMIS). Other research focused on information resource management at various levels of government (Caudle, 1988, 1996; Fletcher, 1997; Norris and Kreamer, 1996). Recently some scholars have researched the evolution of e-government (Weare, Musso, and Hale, 1999; Musso, Weare, and Hale, 2000; Fountain, 2001; Layne and Lee, 2001; West, 2001; Moon, 2002). Overall, we have a better understanding of the scope and volume of IT applications and advances in e-government, although not of how various aspects of IT affect specific administrative functions within government. This calls for a new set of studies to go beyond the impact of IT on governmental performance and examine the actual effects of IT on specific areas such as e-procurement.

As an e-government initiative, e-procurement has been widely pursued by many governments as a means of becoming "smart buyers." Public managers believe e-procurement both enhances the overall quality of procurement management through savings in cost and time and leads to a more accountable procurement system. The evolution of e-procurement will be explored in great detail in the next section.

The Evolution of E-Procurement

Procurement management is significant within governmental actions in terms of its monetary volume and managerial implications. Unfortunately, though, perceived as inefficient and wasteful in procurement practices, governments have suffered a decline in public confidence and trust in their performance. Even though state and federal governments have applied rigid procedural standards to prevent procurement abuses and enhance procurement management, the results have not always been successful—leaving room for further improvements in procurement management.

A study suggests that the total procurement cost to federal and state governments for purchasing from the private sector is an estimated $1 trillion. In fact, the federal government spent about $550 billion in 2000 (Neef, 2001). According to statistics from the General Services Administration (GSA), the federal government made about 28 million purchases during the 1998 fiscal year, and about 98 percent were valued at $25,000 or less. The sheer volume of transactions represents a great opportunity to use e-procurement methods for contracting and purchasing products or services because IT-based transactions can be processed much easier, faster, and cheaper. In particular, the government has fundamentally changed the old paper-based procedures and other forms of conventional management by introducing various elements of IT into procurement practices.

The Federal Acquisition Streamlining Act of 1994 required the federal government's procurement management to evolve into a more expedient process based on EDI[4] (Schriener and Angelo, 1995). This forced the federal government to develop the Federal Acquisition Computer Network (FACNET), which is the government's version of the EDI system. FACNET enables the federal government to disseminate its contracting information via online channels. President Clinton issued a presidential memorandum introducing the EDI system to all the federal government's contracting offices as a primary means for purchases in the $2,500 to $100,000 range. The initiative was taken to make federal procurement faster, more efficient, and more discretionary for federal agencies and employees in purchasing information technologies. Although FACNET's mandated use was repealed by a recent legislative action, many government and civilian agencies currently use it as a primary means of their procurement activities.

The Office of Management and Budget (OMB) has a strategic plan to incorporate e-commerce practices into government procurement management by reforming the buying and payment processes. Many public institutions are adopting innovative purchasing card systems, which are often credited with improving the procurement process for federal agencies and many state governments. Several states have participated in joint cooperative e-procurement systems to promote efficiency. Furthermore, state governments use IT in the form of financial models to support budget allocation, budget forecasting, and other related procurement management activities.

Following the federal and state model, San Diego County has practiced a similar e-procurement mechanism in which the county posts solicitation/bids and contract-award information on the web and integrates purchasing and accounting systems. To deal with increasing workloads and promote better procurement management, e-procurement allowed purchasing transactions under $100,000 through simplified procedures (Wood, 2000). To promote this system, the Purchasing and Contracting Office of San Diego County developed BUYNET, "a system that would integrate the existing online requisitioning system and the accounts payable system" (p. 38), with the technical assistance of the Department of Information Services. Wood (2000) reports that BUYNET represents a win/win situation to the county's procurement management by providing better information to suppliers, simplifying procurement procedures, reducing the workload of procurement specialists, and saving money for the county government.[5]

Proponents of e-procurement argue that it brings not only monetary savings to governments but also a more accountable, effective, and faster way to manage procurement. Figure 6.1 compares the prospective strengths and challenges of e-procurement. It also summarizes changes in a procurement manager's roles when procurement practices shift from paper-based to electronic.

Neef (2001) suggests that the various prospects of e-procurement are: (1) lowering transaction costs, (2) faster ordering; (3) greater vendor choices, (4) more efficient and standardized procurement processes, (5) more control

Figure 6.1: Prospects and Challenges in E-Procurement Management

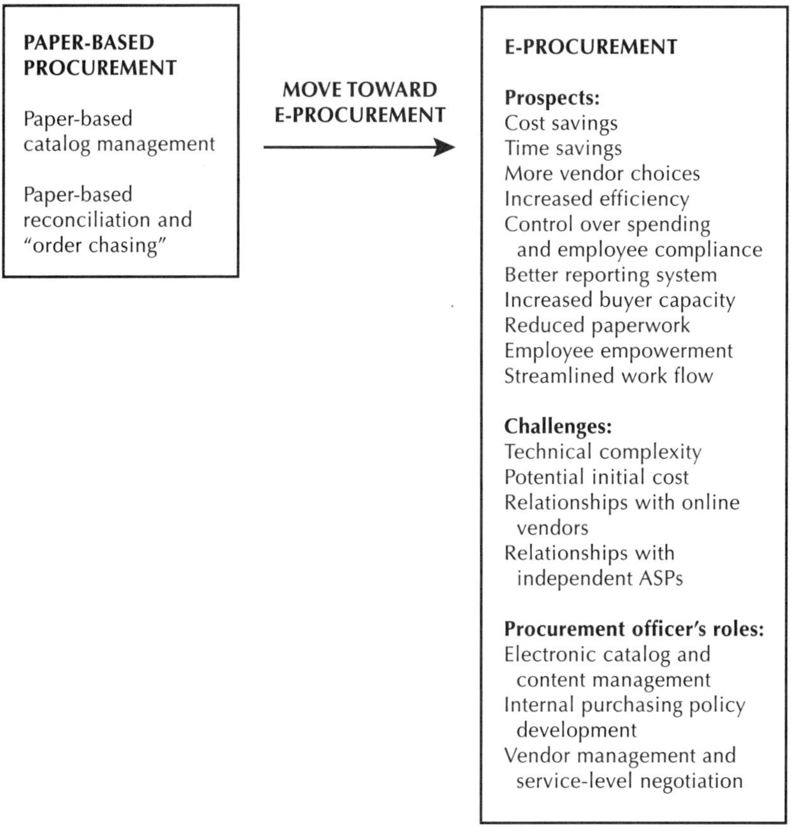

PAPER-BASED PROCUREMENT
Paper-based catalog management
Paper-based reconciliation and "order chasing"
MOVE TOWARD E-PROCUREMENT
E-PROCUREMENT
Prospects:
Cost savings
Time savings
More vendor choices
Increased efficiency
Control over spending and employee compliance
Better reporting system
Increased buyer capacity
Reduced paperwork
Employee empowerment
Streamlined work flow
Challenges:
Technical complexity
Potential initial cost
Relationships with online vendors
Relationships with independent ASPs
Procurement officer's roles:
Electronic catalog and content management
Internal purchasing policy development
Vendor management and service-level negotiation

Adopted from Neef (2001), e-Procurement: From Strategy to Implementation, *p. 58.*

over procurement spending (less maverick buying) and employee compliance, (6) more accessible Internet alternatives for buyers, (7) less paperwork and fewer repetitive administrative procedures, and (8) reengineered procurement work flow. Despite these positive aspects, government must still cope with technical, legal, and managerial challenges. These challenges include technical complexity, the potential financial burden involved in the initial investment, security issues, and sustainable relationships with vendors.

Moving toward e-procurement from traditional paper-based processes also brings great challenges to procurement officers. They need new technical and managerial skills, such as managing electronic catalogs, building relationships with online vendors and independent ASPs (portal site providers), and developing strategic team-based purchasing with other purchasing entities, among others. To sustain the evolution of e-procurement, state governments must provide appropriate technical training and assistance to procurement officers and develop closer working relationships with vendors and various government buyers (state agencies, local governments, others).

Architectural Models

Models of e-procurement differ based on who is the focus of the procurement system (sell-side or buy-side), who manages the electronic catalog (suppliers, buyers, or third parties), and the types of portal sites (one-to-many model or many-to-many model), among others (Neef, 2001). Neef (2001) presents various models including the sell-side one-to-many model, buy-side one-to-many model, independent portal model, and auction model.

The sell-side one-to-many model is a vendor-designed e-market Internet site that allows potential buyers to browse and purchase specific products from the site. As Figure 6.2 shows, public agencies can access the vendor-designed e-commerce site and make purchases. This model is designed mainly to meet vendors' interests and to promote the marketing activities of vendors. The buy-side one-to-many model is closer to the generic e-procurement concept than the sell-side one-to-many model, which is closer to the concept of e-commerce.

As Figure 6.3 illustrates, a government can establish a buy-side one-to-many model in which the government invites many vendors and provides electronic catalogs for potential purchasing. Previously, buyers often designed and maintained in-house electronic catalogs of many vendors for various items. The buy-side one-to-many model incorporates electronic purchase order, electronic invoice, electronic fund transfer, and enterprise resource planning (ERP) elements into the system to enhance procedural efficiency and convenience (Neef, 2001).

The independent portal model shown in Figure 6.4 represents both e-commerce and e-procurement elements by having multiple vendors and multiple buyers in a portal site that makes both electronic order and payment transactions.

The independent portal site is a central place where buyers and vendors are integrated to make online transactions. Current e-procurement practices have shifted from the sell-side one-to-many model to the independent portal model. Many ASPs are third parties who design and provide portal sites for web-based shopping malls, web-based auctions, and other web-based marketing- and procurement-related services (Neef, 2001).

Figure 6.2: Sell-Side One-to-Many Model

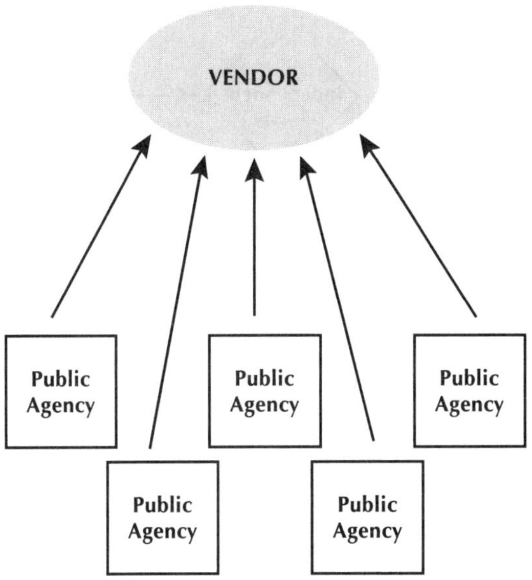

Adopted from Neef (2001), e-Procurement: From Strategy to Implementation, *p. 76.*

Figure 6.3: Government Buy-Side One-to-Many Model

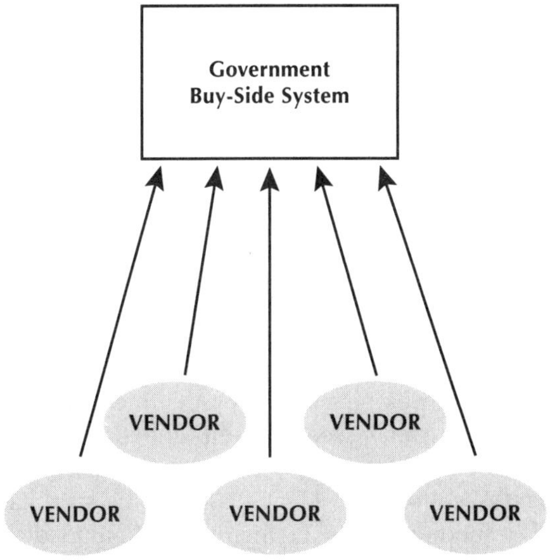

Adopted from Neef (2001), e-Procurement: From Strategy to Implementation, *p. 78.*

Figure 6.4: The Independent Portal Model

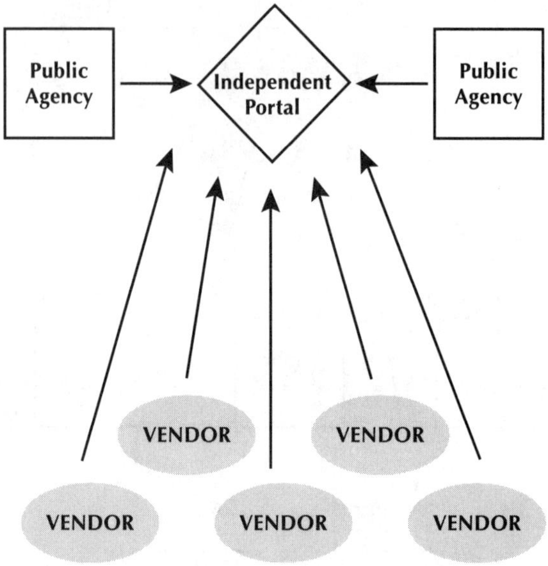

Adopted from Neef (2001), e-Procurement: From Strategy to Implementation, *p. 81.*

Many governments have favorably adopted this independent portal model, thanks to the potential benefits from the infrastructure that a private ASP readily provides. Many governments favor this model because, with low initial costs and little technical capacity, they can take advantage of commercial ASPs. Independent ASPs often proactively approach governments and develop e-procurement portal sites for them with an expectation of profitable business opportunities in the future.

Funding Approaches

Various funding approaches[6] have been presented and introduced by state governments for developing state e-procurement systems: (1) exclusive state-funded approach (Tennessee); (2) self-funded approach/ reverse revenue approach (Texas, Connecticut, Colorado, and Utah); and (3) combined approach (Washington) (NECCC, 2000b). If a state has a designated revolving fund or funding flexibility, then the state-funded approach might be a good option. The state can then charge transaction fees to vendors and use them partially to fund the system.

Many state governments prefer the self-funded approach because it requires no initial funding. Private vendors often host the system and charge fees for providing e-procurement services, such as registration/subscription, ordering transaction,bidding transaction, and catalog service (NECCC, 2000b). The combined approach combines the self-funding approach with a government's paying partially for the system's initial development costs. As state governments and ASPs face substantial financial challenges with the exclusive state-funded approach or the self-funded approach, many states seem to prefer the combined approach (Sarkar, 2001b).

Governments need to consider legal and policy aspects in determining their funding mechanisms for e-procurement. States with statutory spending and revenue limitation (i.e., TABOR in Colorado) should deal with systems that charge a fee to the vendors, in the context of their statutory revenue limits. Limits on spending and revenue challenge the legal ability of state agencies to function like commercial entities. Also, they potentially could affect governments' efforts to provide equal opportunities to small businesses (NECCC, 2000b). There are several fundamental questions regarding funding sources of e-procurement systems: (1) Who should maintain the ownership of the system? (2) Who should be in charge of raising necessary funds? and (3) Who should pay the acquisition cost? To answer these questions, governments must deal with another set of legal, political, technical, and policy issues, such as a rigorous business and cost model, a fee-enforcement mechanism, a policy stating the mandated or optional use of the e-procurement system, political support, budget office support, and technical support (NECCC, 2000b).

Standardization

Standardizing e-procurement is another challenging task for both governments and vendors who want more efficient, more effective e-procurement systems. Standardization already has been an issue in terms of e-commerce practices, such as ordering integration with EDI, eXtensible Markup Language (XML), Open Buying on the Internet (OBI), as well as Vendor Centric Standards with XML and xCBL (NECCC, 2001b). Now, standardization includes several supplier concerns, such as catalog creation, external integration (punch-out,[7] channel consideration for co-branding, etc.), internal integration (supply chain automation), and order status as well as electronic invoicing and payment. It also incorporates specific commodity codes, such as National Institute of Governmental Purchasing (NIGP)[8] and the United Nations Standard Product and Services Code (UNSPSC),[9] among others.

In particular, EDI, a critical element of e-commerce, ensures the security of data transfer. EDI is often used between vendors and manufacturers when dealing with purchase orders, purchase order changes, invoices, and requests for proposals. Long used in the transportation industry, EDI has been adopted by many other industries. Its benefits include saving costs—reducing the amount of paper by transmitting electronic documents instead—improving quality through keeping better records and saving time, reducing inventory, and providing better information for decision making (Kalakota and Whinston, 1997). Among the standards for EDI are International Telecommunication Union (ITU) standards, the ANSI X.12 standard, and the United Nations EDIFACT standard (Gunyou and Leonard, 1998). Steps such as purchase order, purchase order confirmation, booking request, booking confirmation, advance ship notice, status report, receipt advice, invoice, and payment represent the basic EDI transactions (Kalakota and Whinston, 1997, p. 379).

Although closely associated with efficient, speedy adoption of e-procurement by governments and suppliers, standardization and interoperability still face many obstacles. Standardization often requires resources for training in such technical details as typography, lexicon, and structure. Considering the various standards currently used for state e-procurement systems, governments and vendors will have to give more attention and more resources to the difficult task of achieving a uniform standardization of e-procurement.

State E-Procurement in Practice

At the state level, NASPO along with the National Association of State Information Resource Executives (NASIRE) and the National Association of State Directors of Administrative and General Services (NASDAGS) conducted joint research and presented a white paper in 1996 to promote innovative procurement management. Their recently published report, "Buying Smart: State Procurement Reform Saves Millions," suggests managerial solutions and best practices based on a detailed examination of various procurement challenges.

Many state governments have already implemented some innovative procurement measures by reengineering the procurement process—reducing purchasing time, streamlining layers of review, allowing more discretion for small purchases, broadening relationships with vendors, and awarding bids based on best value (JTFIT, 1996). The joint study suggests five reform agenda items, in which e-procurement is emphasized as the future of procurement management:

- Simplifying the procurement of commodity items and services
- Building an infrastructure for electronic commerce

- Procuring based on best values
- Developing beneficial partnerships with vendors
- Solving problems with solicitations

A report by NECCC (2000b) summarizes the scope of e-procurement in state governments by presenting its six major elements: (1) passive bid solicitation systems, (2) web-based publication of state contracts and price agreements, (3) bid solicitation distribution systems, (4) catalog systems without bidding capability, (5) catalog systems with internal quote and bidding capability, and (6) catalog systems integrated with the state's accounting systems (p. 5). These elements reflect the evolution of e-procurement from the elementary stage—one-way, passive communication to disseminate public notices of bid solicitation—to the intermediate stage—proactive bid solicitation through the electronic mailing system—and onward to the highly sophisticated stage of integrating e-procurement into accounting systems. Some states (Connecticut, Washington, Colorado, and Utah) actually require that e-procurement systems be integrated with their existing accounting systems (NECCC, 2000b). As state governments take their technically sophisticated, extensive e-procurement systems to a higher level, they face multiple technical, legal, and managerial challenges.

Based on these preliminary observations, the next section surveys several e-procurement initiatives and presents innovative approaches for e-procurement market integration: single-state systems, two-state systems, a multistate system for horizontal integration, and a local-state system for vertical integration. The current status of various e-procurement applications among state governments is discussed, based on the three surveys conducted in 1998, 2000, and 2001.

Single State E-Procurement Initiatives

North Carolina (NC E-Procurement @ Your Service)

In February 2001, North Carolina initiated an extensive e-procurement system for all public organizations in the state, including state agencies, schools, municipalities, and communities. Accenture (2001) reported on the initiative, suggesting that it would be introduced over three years following a four-year business model, with a total budget of about $60 million.

Unlike many of its counterparts, the North Carolina e-procurement system is mandatory for all state agencies. Two private companies, Accenture and Epylon Corporation, developed the system. Its comprehensive online features include requisitioning, purchase order transmission, notification of electronic quotation requests, electronic quote response for informal bidding, and receipt of goods (for more information, see www.ncgov.com/eprocurement/asp/section/index.asp). The state also plans to integrate the e-procurement system with its financial system. Officials estimate cost savings to be about $50 million a year (Sarkar, 2001c). North Carolina chose a self-funding system, charging a 1.75 percent marketing fee to future vendors. Despite the bold e-procurement initiative, fewer online transactions have been made than the state and vendor expected, which puts more financial constraints on the self-funding model. This is an example of the unexpected obstacles that can follow the implementation of an e-procurement system in a favorable atmosphere and with great rhetoric on the part of a state government.

Virginia (eVA)

Leading an e-government initiative, Virginia's governor highlighted an e-procurement program with Executive Order 65 in May 2000. To actualize the state's e-procurement system, the Department of General Services collected information and feedback from vendors concerning the best design. The state organized a focus group to invite more specific input from vendors and then solicited designs of e-procurement systems, finally selecting American Management Systems Inc. (AMS) as the vendor (Sarkar, 2001c).

Virgina's system, namely eVA (www.eva.state.va.us), was designed to facilitate the automating and streamlining of procurement (Atwater, 2001). In addition to automated procurement procedures, it includes electronic receiving and invoicing as well as reverse auctions. The eVA system provides various procurement information services for public use, as well as exclusive information and services for registered vendors and agencies. Virginia charges $25 per transaction or an advance fee of $200 for registration, online access, vendor catalog posting, and other services such as electronic receipts and online bid submissions. Vendors also pay a 1-percent transaction fee per order, not to exceed $500. The eVA system is expected to benefit government buyers through better selection, buying, processes, and decisions. It benefits participating vendors through simplified administrative procedures, more opportunities, better processes, and better support services. Local governments and school districts in the state, as well as state agencies, can use the system for procurement.

Maryland (eMaryland M@rketplace)

Maryland initiated the eMaryland M@rketplace (www.eMarylandmarketplace.com) program and has been pushing e-procurement as part of an overall effort to become "the digital state." The state launched the program in 2000 and has already seen some progress. According to Pete Richkus, secretary of the Department of General Services:

> [The eMaryland M@rketplace] is already delivering significant savings for the State and our public sector partners. For example, Anne Arundel County saved almost $12,000 on 27 bid solicitations in its first month as a participating buying entity. Our eMaryland M@rketplace vendors are also realizing financial and resource efficiencies. In March 2000, Maryland began to move its $6 billion in annual purchasing to the Internet by taking a totally innovative approach: no new funding, no new bureaucracy, no multimillion dollar program development contract. The process begins with a creative, multistep request for proposal (RFP), well defined by requirements, and an aggressive outreach program to vendors throughout Maryland as well as to state and local government agency buyers. In its first year, eMaryland M@rketplace posted more than $10 million in purchases on its website, enrolled close to 3000 companies, and trained over 250 buyers (Maryland Department of General Services, 2001, p. 2).

Commenting on the eMaryland M@rketplace, Major Riddick, Jr., the governor's former chief of staff and chairman of the Maryland Information Technology Board, said that the new e-procurement system will "save money, time, and eliminate duplicated efforts and our vendors can recover many of these same costs for themselves" (Maryland Department of General Services, 2001, p. 3). The annual report prepared by the Maryland Department of General Services (2001) for the eMaryland M@rketplace (2001) provides some evidence of growing popularity among public buyers in the state. The cumulative catalog-usage-by-dollar amount had jumped to $140,000 in March 2001 from $60,000 in March 2000, while the cumulative catalog-usage-by-transaction number had reached 175 in March 2001 from 25 in March 2000. As of March 2001, 262 government buyers (state agencies, municipalities, schools) and 280 vendors were participating in the eMaryland M@rketplace program.

Initiatives for Horizontal and Vertical Market Integration

Several states' innovative, collaborative e-procurement approaches demonstrate both horizontal (interstate) and vertical (intergovernmental) e-procurement collaboration for market integration. In horizontal market integration, two or more states combine their purchasing power to obtain better pricing and a more cost-efficient procurement system. In vertical market integration, local and state governments and quasi-governmental organizations collaborate by using the same electronic catalogs and the same e-procurement system. Figure 6.5 illustrates horizontal and vertical e-procurement.

Colorado and Utah Joint E-Procurement: A Cooperative System

In the 2000 meeting of the Western State Contracting Alliance, the governments of Colorado and Utah exchanged ideas about developing a cooperative e-procurement system that takes advantage of existing e-commerce and first-rate suppliers. Advancing the idea, the two states established a five-year contract for the joint system. They contracted with the NIC Commerce—a subsidiary of a nationally known portal vendor with 13 state portal implementations, including Hawaii and South Carolina—which has e-procurement catalog systems with NASA, the U.S. Air Force, and the Houston-Galveston Area Council of Governments (Utah Division of

Figure 6.5: Horizontal and Vertical E-Procurement Market Integration

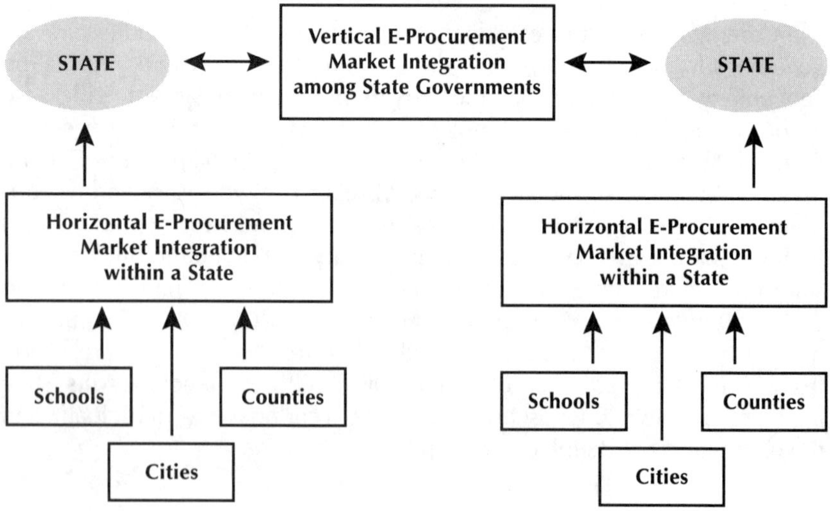

Purchasing and General Services: www.purchasing.state.ut.us/eps/description.htm). The contract stipulates that the two state governments are not responsible for the development cost and that the NIC Commerce recovers its cost through a 1-percent transaction fee to successful vendors. Other states are allowed to join the system later.

This joint e-procurement system was designed to provide Colorado and Utah with a single catalog system for requisitioning and ordering small purchases, such as office supplies, computers and other commodities, as well as services on state price agreements and catalogs from other vendors in the NIC trading community. The system promotes various goals, as offered in its mission statement: (1) automating procurement processes, (2) collecting comprehensive expenditure data, (3) reducing procurement time with appropriate procurement oversight, (4) seeking improved pricing and cost savings, and (5) enhancing supplier exposure to state purchases (Utah Division of Purchasing and General Services: www.purchasing.state.ut.us/eps/welcome%20page.htm). Following a 270-day pilot phase, the system was to be fully implemented (Sarkar, 2001a). Unfortunately, the two states decided not to implement the joint e-procurement system because they viewed the pilot objectives (particularly in terms of demonstrated efficiencies and prospects of reduced costs through broad supplier adoption) as not having been met. Although Colorado and Utah did not see the tangible benefits of proceeding to full-scale production as outweighing the resource costs and risks involved, their joint effort offers a great possibility for future collaborative efforts between states.

Multi-State EMall™ Initiative: A Horizontal/Interstate Market Integration

To take advantage of the scale of economy—similar to better price deals at wholesale markets—several states joined the Multi-State EMall™ pilot project that the Operational Services Division of Massachusetts initiated at the end of 1997. Its private ASP, Intelisys Electronic Commerce (whose name was later changed to Metiom), was selected and asked to offer the applications of various e-procurement-related technical elements, including authentication and authorization, requisitioning, order processing, and receiving functionality.

In 1998, Massachusetts made online transactions for a statewide procurement contract. The pilot was later expanded to include four other states (Idaho, New York, Texas, and Utah) in the project. The Multi-State EMall team produced a comprehensive evaluation in 1999, suggesting the project to be successful and to exemplify the possibilities of online multistate cooperative procurement processes. In the report presented by the Multi-State EMall team (2000) to the NASPO 2000 Marketing meeting, the team forecasted its cost savings for the year to be between \$4.3 million (conservative calculation) and \$8.1 million (optimistic calculation). Despite its positive prospects, this initiative currently faces serious challenges as its ASP, Metiom, filed bankruptcy under Chapter 11 in May 2001 (www.state.ma.us/emall/). Despite the unexpected interruptions and challenges, the Multi-State EMall provides information and services via its own website (www.state.ma.us/emall/), and its executive committee plans to sustain the initiative.

State and Local Government Collaboration: A Vertical/Intergovernmental Market Integration

As seen in the eVA and Multi-State EMall initiatives, many single state e-procurement systems pursue vertical (intergovernmental) market integration to take advantage of economies of scale by combining the purchasing powers of local and state governments. California, Massachusetts, North Carolina, South Carolina, and Virginia invite local governments, school districts, and various quasi-public organizations to participate in their e-procurement systems and obtain price and procedural benefits. For example, the North Carolina e-procurement system attempts to generate a statewide vertical market integration to take advantage of cost savings by incorporating various vendors and buyers, including state agencies and institutions, universities, community colleges, public schools, and local governments.

Advances in State E-Procurement

Much of the following information was obtained from an e-mail survey designed by the author and from mail surveys conducted by NASPO, a non-profit organization of 50 directors from the 50 states' central purchasing offices. The NASPO surveys were conducted in 1998 and 2000 by the NASPO Research and Publication Committee, and their results were published in 1999 and 2001, respectively.[10] In 1998, 47 states[11] responded to the NASPO survey and provided their procurement information, while 43 states[12] responded to the 2001 survey.[13]

The NASPO surveys collected comprehensive information, including procurement authority, bidding practices, ethics codes, environmental issues, purchasing information technology, use of technology, automated procurement systems, purchasing cards, travel cards, and utility deregulation. In a follow-up (conducted by the author in October and December 2001) to update the 2001 NASPO survey, e-mail surveys were sent to procurement officers in 50 states. Thirty-five states[14] responded concerning the use of technology, automated procurement systems, and purchasing cards—information that helps us understand current e-procurement practices among the states.

This study basically combines the author's 2001 follow-up e-mail survey and the 2001 NASPO survey. The 2001 follow-up survey updates the 2001 NASPO survey and adds information for states that did not respond originally: Alabama, Delaware, Oregon, and Wisconsin. The combined 2001 data (the follow-up survey and 2001 NASPO survey) are analyzed and compared with the 1998 NASPO survey data to identify any particular trends in the adoption of e-procurement practices. It should also be noted that the 2001 surveys include much more detailed information than the 1998 survey regarding e-procurement, though many items overlap in the two surveys. The 2001 follow-up e-mail survey by the author includes questions regarding the effectiveness of e-procurement practices.

Adoption of Web Technology

Public agencies have adopted web technology widely in recent years. Agencies typically post a wealth of information regarding their missions, functions, contacts, public relations, and answers to frequently asked questions. Web pages for procurement offices often have more sophisticated and technical applications, such as electronic request for proposals, electronic ordering, vendor information, electronic catalog, reverse auction, and Internet-based bidding.

Despite variation in functions, as well as in degrees of sophistication and extensiveness, all state governments offer websites for procurement management. (The web addresses and major contact information are summarized in Appendix I.) According to the 2001 NASPO survey, all state governments utilized e-mail systems to support communication with vendors and internal buyers, but their computer systems are not well linked with other communication systems. For example, only 15 out of 43 states responded that they have integrated fax systems in which a fax is linked with central procurement's computer system. Only eight states (Arizona, Arkansas, California, Iowa, Nebraska, South Carolina, South Dakota, and Virginia) responded that they received incoming faxes via this system. This indicates that communication systems are not well integrated, although state procurement offices are fairly well equipped with various communication tools.

According to the 2001 combined survey data, while respondent states have their own web pages for their central procurement office, 42 states post solicitation/bid information and 41 states post contract-award information on the web. More state governments have come to rely on the web as a means of disseminating information for public notice. In 1998, for example, 39 states responded that they upload RFP information and 35 states responded that they post contract-award information on the web.

Posting Solicitation/Bids on the Web (2001)

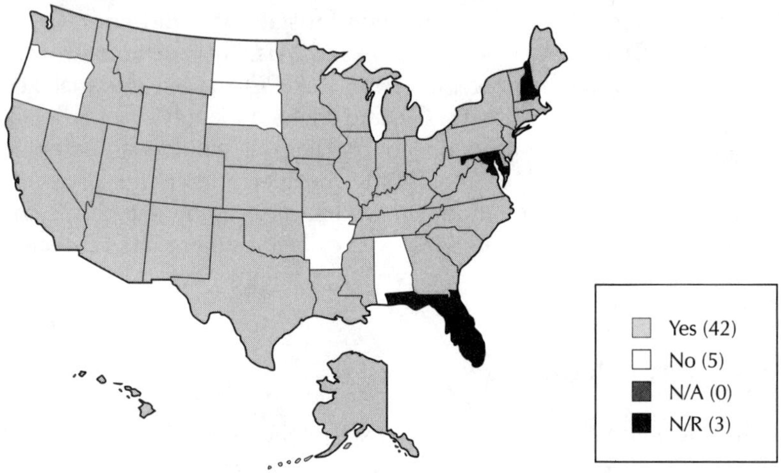

Posting Contract Awards on the Web (2001)

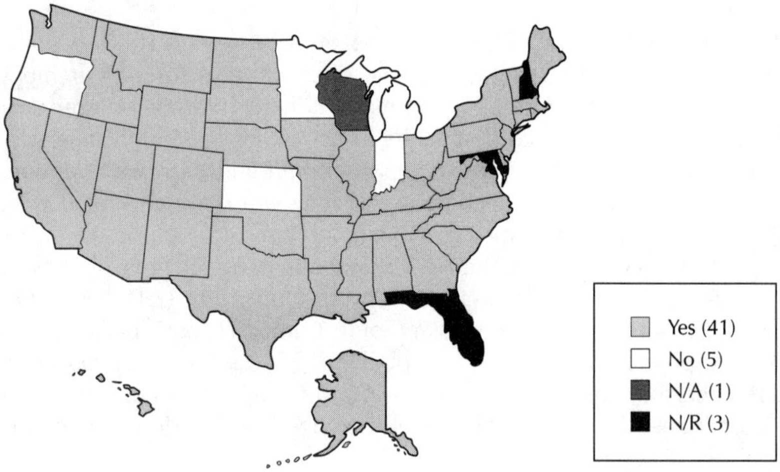

Adoption of Digital Signature

Digital signature is an electronic means of signing electronic documents that provides sender authentication using public-key encryption. Digital signature supports e-procurement and e-commerce by facilitating online financial and documental transactions. The authentication procedure of digital signature includes (1) combining private key and specific document and (2) computing the composite (key + document) and generating a unique number (digital signature).[15]

In 2001, only 31 states had enacted digital signature laws to facilitate online financial transactions. Only eight states (Illinois, Kentucky, Louisiana, Minnesota, New Mexico, South Carolina, South Dakota, and Tennessee) responded that their procurement management offices use digital signature to route and approve documents internally. Only seven states (Idaho, Maine, Minnesota, Pennsylvania, Tennessee, Texas, and Washington) responded that they accept as legally binding digital signatures from the vendor community on procurement documents.

The number of state governments enacting digital signature legislation, though, has increased. In 1998, only 21 states responded that they had digital signature legislation, and six states (Arizona, Maryland, Michigan, Nevada, Tennessee, and Texas) responded that they approved digital signature for internal documents. Only four states (Maryland, Ohio, Pennsylvania, and Washington) responded that they accepted digital signature for procurement documents.

Digital Signature Legislation (2001)

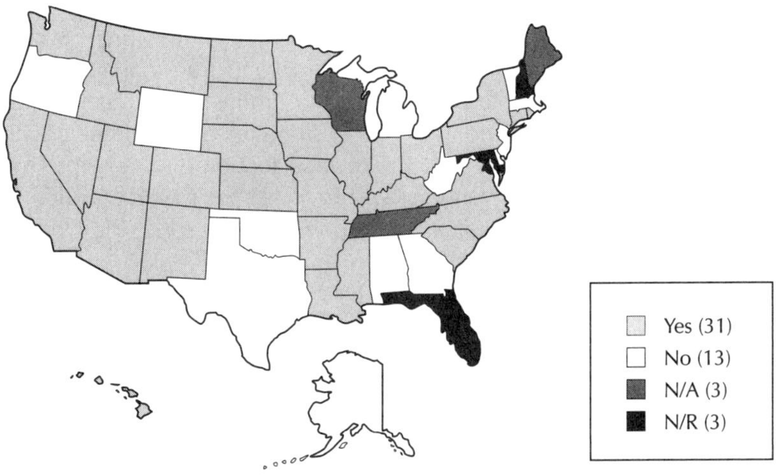

Digital Signature for Procurement Documents (2001)

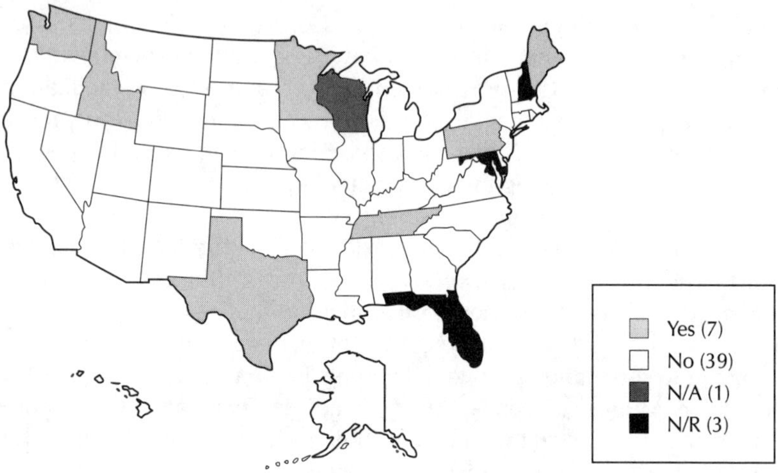

Internet-Based Bidding and Reverse Auction

Internet-based bidding, using e-commerce through online auctions, has become common practice. The practices of Internet-based bidding and even reverse auctions increasingly are being introduced to governments. For example, governments can specify the products they want to purchase with specific prices in a reverse auction, and vendors of these products compete to offer the best prices. At the federal level, the GSA's Federal Technology Service has introduced reverse auction through the Buyers.gov portal site. Often, bidders can bid more than once with their identities unknown to each other, which ensures dynamic competition and true market pricing (O'Hara, 2001). The Minnesota Department of Administration recently initiated reverse auction by allowing vendors to simultaneously compete with each other online for state contracts. The reverse auction system helps governments save costs because vendors tend to lower their bidding price to win the contracts. In fact, in its first auction on June 21, 2001, the Department of Corrections saved about $35,000 by buying 500,000 pounds of aluminum for license plates through MaterialNet (www.materialnet.com) (Morehead, 2001).

Despite the prospective benefits and rising popularity of Internet-based bidding systems and reverse auction in the private business area, they have not been widely introduced to state governments. Only 10 states (Colorado, Idaho, Maine, Minnesota, Missouri, North Carolina, Pennsylvania, South Carolina, Texas, and Wisconsin) have developed procedures or

Governing Procedures for Internet Bidding (2001)

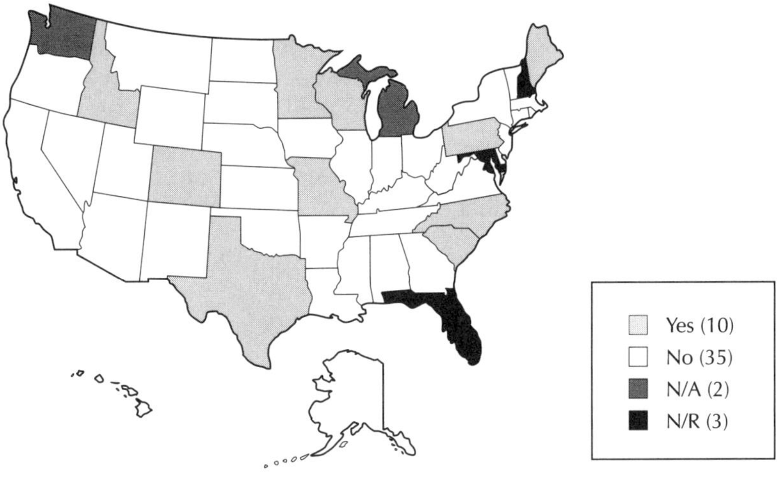

Reverse Auction (2001)

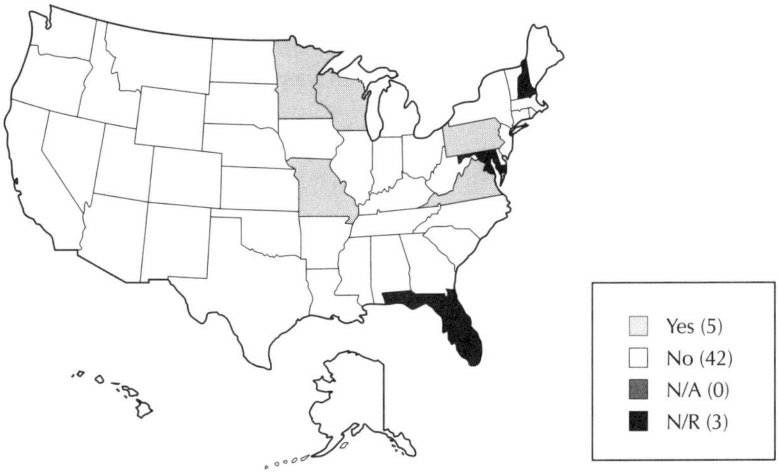

statutes governing Internet bidding, while 13 states (Idaho, Kentucky, Maine, Massachusetts, Michigan, Minnesota, Missouri, North Carolina, Pennsylvania, South Carolina, Texas, Virginia, and Wisconsin) responded that their central procurement office has conducted electronic bidding. Only five states (Minnesota, Missouri, Pennsylvania, Virginia, and Wisconsin) currently conduct reverse auctions for their procurement. The 1998 NASPO survey did not survey the status of Internet bidding and reverse auction in state governments because they had not been widely introduced to state procurement management at that time.

Electronic Ordering

Like e-commerce practices in the private sector, electronic ordering—which governments can use to make purchase orders electronically—is a fundamental element of e-procurement. About 32 states have electronic ordering systems as part of their e-procurement systems. Of them, only four states (California, Ohio, Pennsylvania, and Virginia) responded that their systems are maintained by state governments, whereas 25 states responded that the systems are maintained by vendors. Four states (Idaho, Kentucky, Massachusetts, and Wyoming) responded that their systems are maintained jointly by the state and vendors.

The management of electronic ordering systems and procurement portal sites is often initiated, developed, and maintained by private businesses. This fact suggests two conflicting points. On the one hand, state govern-

Electronic Ordering (2001)

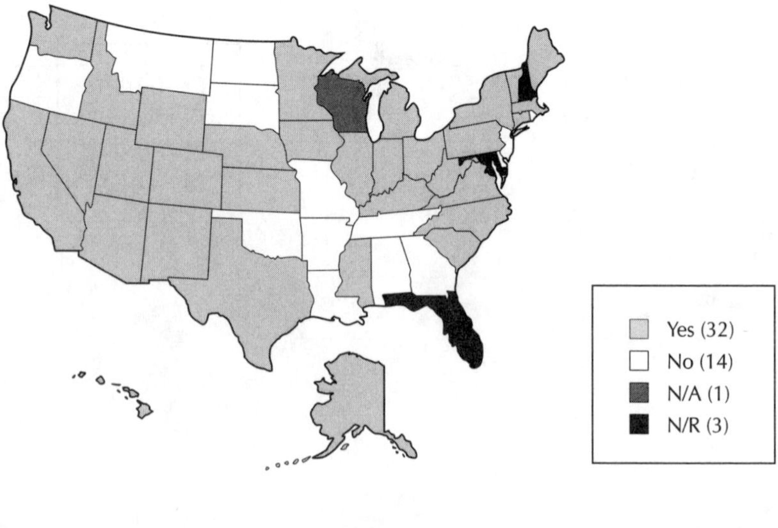

Electronic Ordering System Maintainer (2001)

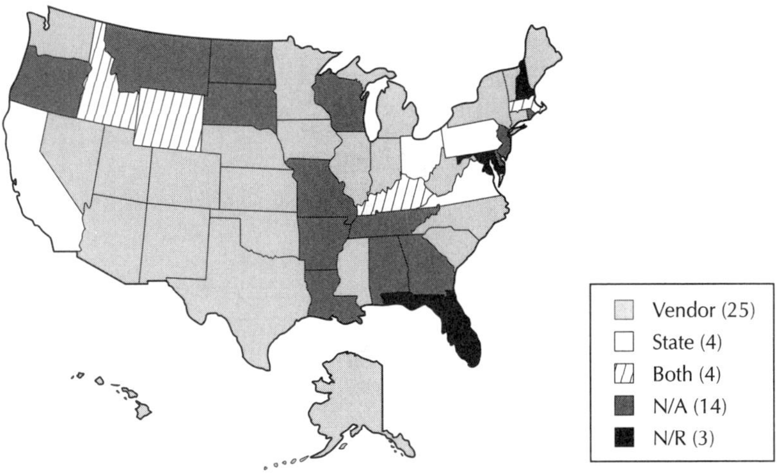

ment have actively taken advantage of the existing private sector capacity to maximize the utility of e-procurement; on the other hand, a strong business interest exists in the e-procurement implementation process, which may cause concerns about potential accountability problems.

Electronic ordering has been rapidly diffused to many states over the last three years. According to the 1998 NASPO survey, only 21 state governments responded that they had an electronic ordering system. Similarly, a majority of the electronic systems (16) are maintained by vendors; the system is maintained by state governments in six states. The Florida state procurement office responded that the system was maintained jointly by vendors and state government.

Maintenance of Procurement Records

Strong managerial and technical capacities for maintaining and tracking procurement-related records—which allow the state to assess and audit its procurement decisions and cost-effectiveness—are critical to the overall quality of procurement. Many state governments seem to have a centralized record-keeping system in that central procurement offices maintain records of the overall dollar volume of purchases. According to the 2001 data, 31 state governments responded that they maintain those records in central procurement offices, while eight states responded that the records are maintained by other state agencies. Thirty-three state governments responded that their central procurement offices are able to track dollars spent by type

Record Keeping (Total Amount) by Central Procurement Office (2001)

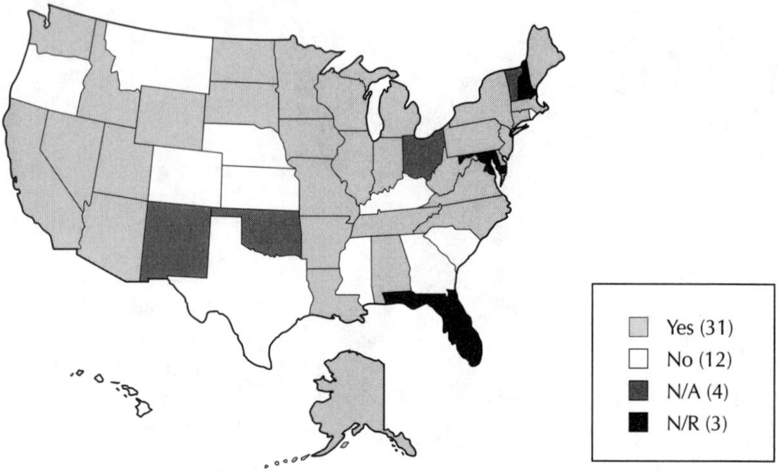

Tracking Records for Amount by Commodity (2001)

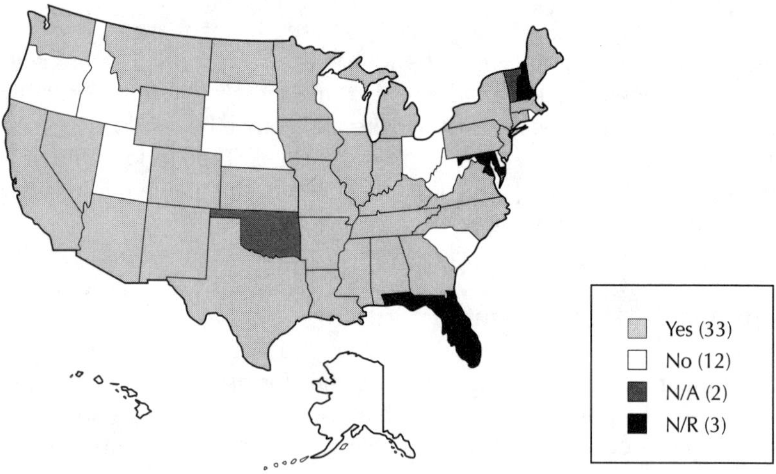

of commodity or service, while 36 states responded that they are able to track dollars spent according to vendor.

Little has changed in procurement record-keeping systems. The 1998 survey indicates that 30 states, specifically, their central procurement offices, recorded and maintained the overall dollar amount of purchases. Thirty-two state governments responded, in 1998, that they could track the dollars spent by type of commodity, while 36 state governments responded that they could track dollars spent according to vendor.

Automated Procurement Systems

Automation of the procurement process enables the state to make procurement decisions at the user level by providing vendors' information and catalogs on the web. The automated system often decentralizes procurement management, making the organization flatter, or less hierarchical. The system also helps save time and reduce total cost by providing comprehensive views of state procurement decisions and multiple procurement choices. Automated procurement systems offer various functions, from such simple services as provision of vendor's performance and order forms to such sophisticated services as lead-time analysis and asset management support.

In the 2001 survey, many states (42) responded that central procurement offices have automated procurement systems, but few states responded that they are equipped with a full range of capacities, such as

Automated Procurement Systems (2001)

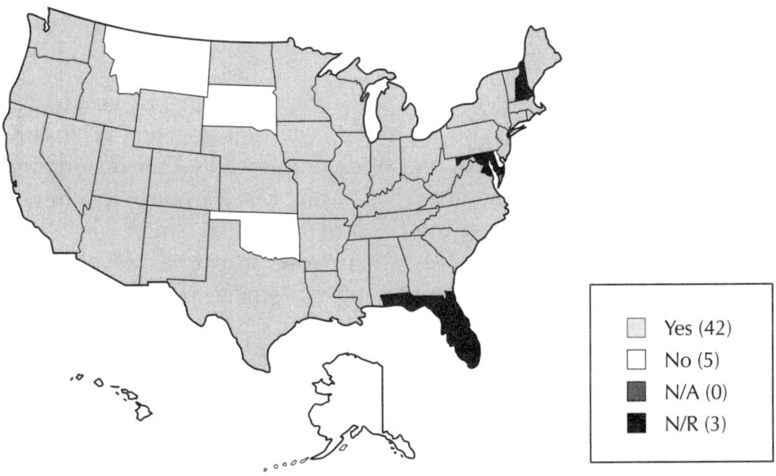

Automated Procurement Systems Integrated to E-Commerce (2001)

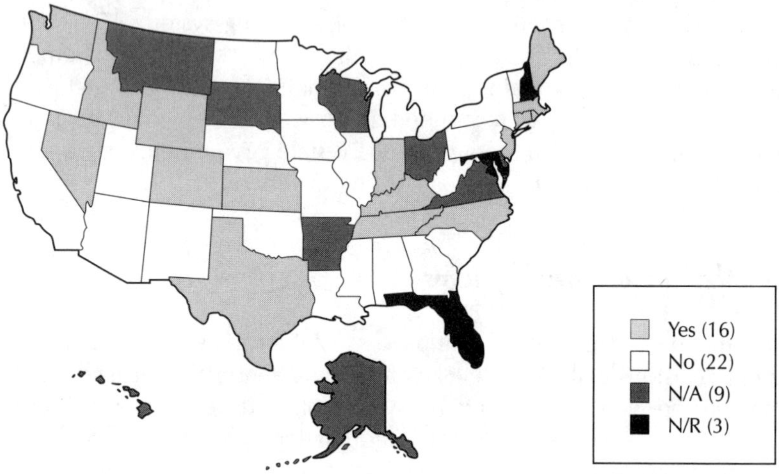

automatic purging, selection of vendors, vendor performance screens, lead-time analysis, and asset management. For example, 16 states have the capacity for lead-time analysis, and 18 states incorporate the EDI element in their procurement system. Sixteen state governments integrate their procurement system with the e-commerce system, and 26 have added asset management functions to the automated procurement system. These aspects of e-procurement were not included in the 1998 survey, so no comparison is made here.

Purchasing Cards

An electronic payment system (EPS) is defined as "a financial exchange that takes place online between buyers and sellers" (Kalakota and Whinston, p. 153). In fact, EPS is the critical part of e-commerce that enables online financial transactions. EPS includes electronic cash, electronic checks, online credit-card-based systems, the point of sale (POS), smart cards, and purchasing cards, among others. The federal government has developed a system to link e-procurement (ordering) and e-payment (paying) for goods and services. For example, an innovation from the GSA automatically links purchasing information and accounting information (Robinson, 2001).

E-procurement systems widely use purchasing cards, in particular, for small but frequent purchases. Many states have adopted purchasing cards to reduce processing costs and to enhance the quality of record keeping. It is common for the cards to be issued by major credit companies (such as Visa, MasterCard, or American Express) so that public employees can purchase various goods and services directly through vendors. A recent NASPO (2001b) report highlights benefits that purchasing cards bring to procurement management, including administrative cost reductions, productivity increases, vendor flexibility, reporting improvement, and employee empowerment and convenience, among others.

> Presently, more than 50 percent of the items procured through purchasing cards are under $1,000. Quite often, these items can represent up to 80 percent of a government's transactions but less than 20 percent of that government's purchasing dollar. Using a government rule-of-thumb number that each purchase order costs $75 to $100 to issue, the potential cost avoidance for governments is substantial. Some users report up to a 90 percent reduction in processing costs (118).

In the 2001 survey, seven states (Alabama, Arkansas, Hawaii, Illinois, Indiana, Rhode Island, and Tennessee) responded that they do not use purchasing cards yet, although many states have flexible policies under which purchasing cards are optional. Forty, out of 47, states responded that they use purchasing cards as a tool for their procurement management. Most states that use purchasing cards have some sort of limit, such as a single purchase (often $1,000 or $2,500), daily purchase, or cycle purchase limit, to prevent abuse of the cards. Many states do not allow state employees to use purchasing cards for alcoholic beverages and travel. States vary greatly

Purchasing Cards (2001)

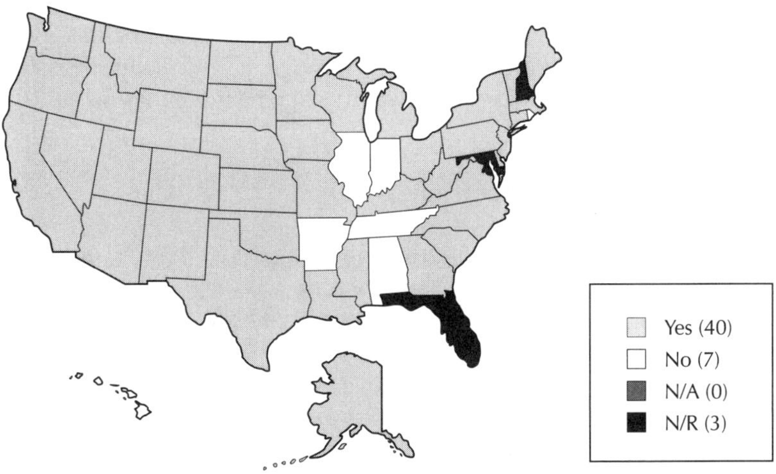

Purchasing Cards for Statewide Contracts (2001)

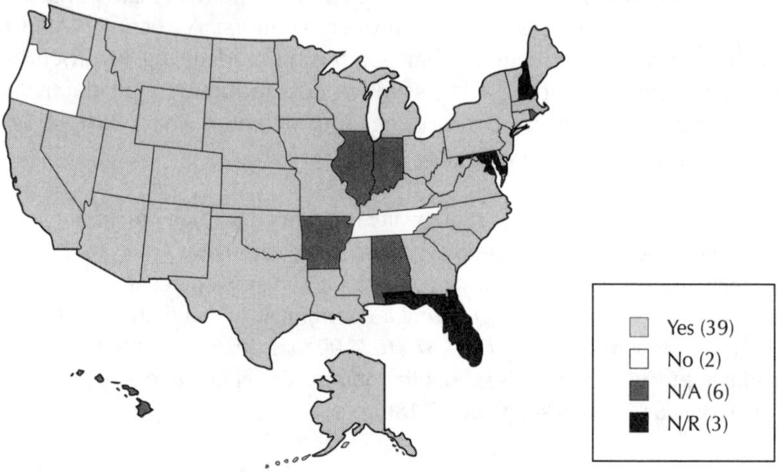

in monthly transaction volumes with, for example, South Carolina having monthly card transactions of $35,000 and Washington spending $2.5 million per month on average.

Thirty-nine state governments use purchasing cards for statewide contracts and fleet management. Only five states (Arizona, California, Iowa, Pennsylvania, and West Virginia) responded that their purchasing cards are funded through a fee-based cost recovery. Only 17 state governments post purchasing-card transactions to their accounting systems.

Purchasing cards appear to be the major development in state procurement over the last three years. According to the 1998 survey, only 32 state governments indicated that they used purchasing cards for state procurement, 29 state governments used purchasing cards for statewide contracts, and 35 state governments had fleet management purchasing cards.

Assessment of Systems' Effectiveness

The 2001 follow-up e-mail survey by the author asked the states' chief procurement officers to indicate whether e-procurement management had yielded cost-saving and time-saving benefits. Only 13 states[16] out of 35 respondents indicated cost savings, while 11 states[17] indicated having saved time. Massachusetts indicated having saved $52–$108 per procurement transaction and having realized a 72-percent reduction in the time spent for procurement management. Despite rhetoric and some indication of positive

Cost Savings through E-Procurement (2001)

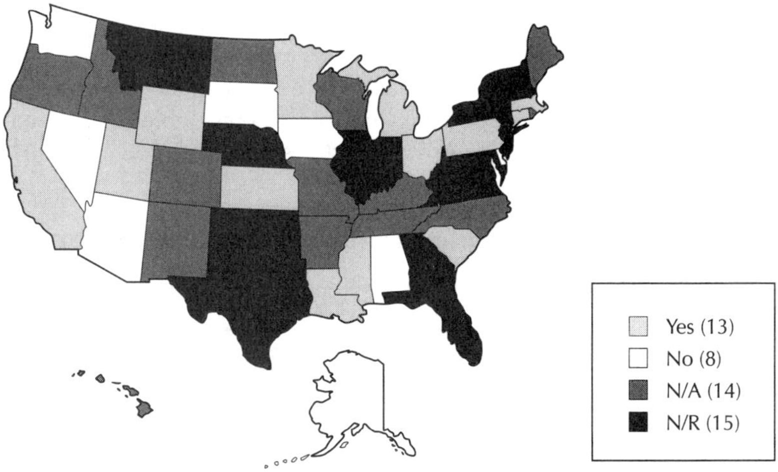

Time Savings through E-Procurement (2001)

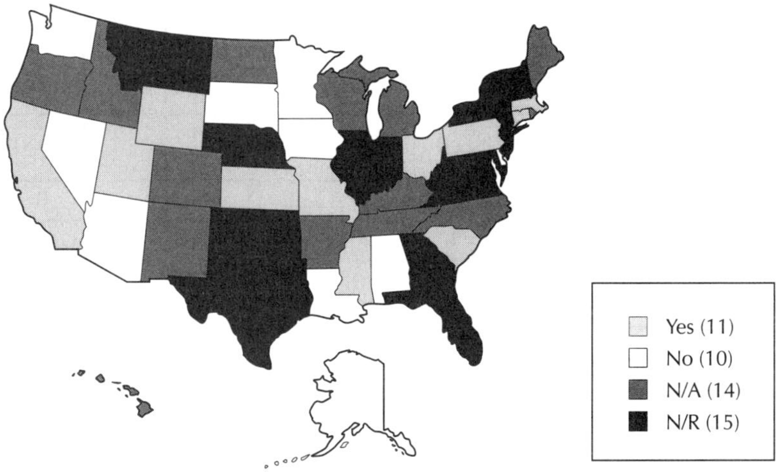

outcomes, however, not many state governments could offer their specific, rigorous information about cost and time benefits. State governments, it seems, lack this information and cannot prove specific utilities of their initiatives because e-procurement is still new and experimental. As indicated above, however, many state governments have made steady progress in advancing e-procurement by adopting various elements. Table 6.1 summarizes the changes in state e-procurement practices between 1998 and 2001.

Table 6.1: Changes in State E-Procurement Practices between 1998 and 2001

	1998*			2001**		
	Yes	No	N/A	Yes	No	N/A
Posting solicitation/ bid on the web	**39**	8	0	**42**	5	0
Posting contract award information on the web	**35**	12	0	**41**	5	1
Digital signature legislation	**19**	28	0	**31**	13	3
Approving digital signature internally	**6**	41	0	**8**	35	4
Accepting digital signature for procurement documents	**4**	43	0	**7**	39	
Governing Internet-based bidding procedures***				**10**	35	2
Practicing Internet-based bidding***				**13**	33	1
Reverse auction***				**5**	42	0
Electronic ordering	**21**	26	0	**32**	14	1
Automated procurement system***				**42**	5	0
Purchasing cards	**32**	15	0	**40**	7	0
Purchasing cards for statewide contracts	**29**	18	0	**39**	2	6
Fleet management purchasing cards	**35**	12	0	**39**	6	2
Cost-saving benefit***				**13**	8	14
Time-saving benefit***				**11**	10	14

** Forty-seven state governments responded to the 1998 NASPO survey.*
*** Forty-seven state governments are included. The data from the 2001 NASPO survey and the 2001 follow-up e-mail survey by the author are combined.*
**** The question is asked only in the 2001 e-mail follow-up survey, to which 35 state governments responded.*

Conclusions and Recommendations

Conclusions

E-procurement, as an e-government initiative, is perceived to be an innovative alternative that leads to better, more efficient, and more effective procurement management by overcoming many traditional paper-based procurement problems. Based on this outlook, many state governments have implemented e-procurement initiatives to improve their procurement management, some even attempting to pursue horizontal and vertical e-procurement market integration.

Many state governments have adopted various e-procurement techniques: (1) posting solicitation and bids and contract-award information on the web, (2) electronic ordering, (3) automated procurement system, and (4) purchasing cards. Several others have also been implemented but less widely: (1) digital signature legislation and accepting digital signature as legally binding for procurement documents, (2) Internet-based bidding, and (3) reverse auction. E-procurement remains in the experimental stage, however, and most state governments have not reached the mature point of realizing benefits from their e-procurement practices.

A promising alternative rather than an instant panacea, e-procurement leaves state governments facing many technical, financial, legal, and managerial challenges. The following challenges should be resolved in order to sustain e-procurement as an initiative and obtain the prospective benefits and utilities.

1. Financial Issues

State governments often face considerable challenges in finding the financial resources required to develop e-procurement systems. With funding being a common problem, the exclusive state-funded approach is not being widely adopted. Many state governments rely on private companies' participation and private resources in developing the technical systems, and support a financial arrangement in which the private companies later recoup their investment by charging various fees. Accordingly, many e-procurement systems are developed, provided, and maintained by vendors and ASPs, which leads to the potential problem of private business interests overruling public interests. E-procurement systems driven by private businesses could be corrupted when those private interests lack appropriate accountability mechanisms.

Nor has the self-funded model met with success, as we saw in the North Carolina case. Sarkar (2001b) also reports that the private funding model has not been successful. A hybrid model has become more popular, one in which state governments invest some money and vendors recover their own costs through transaction fees. But state governments must continue to pay careful attention to the nature of funding mechanisms for e-procurement systems.

2. Technical and Standardization Issues

Lack of technical capacity is a major obstacle to e-procurement and other e-government initiatives. Procurement officers need such specialized technical skills as managing electronic catalogs, electronic ordering, Internet-based bidding, reverse auction, digital signature, purchasing cards, and automated procurement systems. Managing e-procurement demands a more comprehensive range of skills because the automated procurement system is often linked to budgeting and accounting systems. Similarly, standardization and interoperability pose continuing challenges to state governments as they pursue better, more efficient, and more effective e-procurement systems.

3. Vertical and Horizontal Market Integration

Collaborative initiatives for e-procurement market integration that several state governments have undertaken have failed to succeed. They face technical and managerial difficulties, and many local governments are not equipped with either the necessary technical capacities or the e-procurement officers. States have not acquired tangible benefits of horizontally integrated e-procurement systems partially because the potential for gaining efficiencies and reducing costs through broad supplier adoption are outweighed by the costs and risks involved.

4. Legal/Accountability Issues

Because there have been legal challenges with respect to digital signatures, state governments should have an appropriate legal arrangement that specifies when a digital signature is accepted as a legally binding signature for procurement documents. Posting RFP information on the web should also be treated as a legitimate public notice. Because, for instance, purchasing cards have been abused by many public officials who use them for inappropriate purposes (GAO, 2001), state governments need strong accountability mechanisms to reduce the possibilities of abuse, fraud, and mismanagement of the e-procurement system.

5. Internal/External Management Challenges

E-procurement offers various internal and external management challenges to state procurement offices. Internally, states should develop—and govern according to—policies that offer comprehensive institutional outlines for e-procurement decisions and processes, institute clear procedures and functions as well, and develop closer, more strategic relationships with vendors. Externally, state governments need to communicate with vendors and ASPs to update procurement items and prices and to negotiate with them for better options and prices.

Recommendations

1. Develop Strategic Funding Mechanisms

In pursuing long-term, sustainable benefits of e-procurement, state governments should carefully assess both weaknesses and strengths of alternative funding models (exclusive state-funded approach, self-funded approach, and hybrid approach) and cost-recovery models. Assessments should be based on the governments' financial condition, the projected number and amount of e-procurement transactions, as well as cost-efficiency and public accountability.

2. Provide Technical Assistance and Pursue Standardization

State governments should develop and maintain technical personnel, in-house or contractual, who can manage automated procurement and administer statewide procurement transactions and related data.

State governments should continue to introduce advanced e-procurement elements that are less diffused to governments, including Internet-based bidding and electronic ordering.

State governments should provide more technical training opportunities to state procurement officers and public/quasi-public officers who use advanced e-procurement systems.

3. Promote Vertical and Horizontal E-Procurement Market Integration

State procurement offices should continue to carefully pursue e-procurement market integration, vertical and horizontal, and to form specific cooperative institutional arrangements.

They should invite more vendors to participate in e-procurement systems based on mutual interests, and they should also provide more technical assistance to local governments and other quasi-public organizations.

4. Institute Legal/Accountability Mechanisms

State governments should enact digital signature laws and should proactively define announcements made via the web to be legitimate public notices.

State governments should institute strong accountability mechanisms to reduce the possibilities of abusive, improper, and fraudulent e-procurement activities.

State governments should promote accountability and efficiency by establishing and maintaining record-keeping systems and by integrating procurement systems with accounting systems to allow for systematic tracking and checking of procurement data.

5. Establish Collaborative Relationships with Vendors, ASPs, and Government Buyers

State governments should develop statewide procurement policies and procedures that govern many e-procurement activities, including electronic ordering, Internet-based bidding, and reverse auctions, among others.

Central procurement offices should develop closer, more strategic relationships among government buyers, vendors, and ASPs in order to build more cooperative relationships and ensure more updated price information and better price negotiation.

State governments should establish a systemic procurement arrangement for better prices with specific vendors through purchase agreements.

E-procurement offers both opportunities and challenges to state governments. To accomplish sustainable e-procurement, state governments should cope with these challenges proactively and strategically by enhancing appropriate technical and managerial capacities, improving the quality of systems, and establishing cooperative inter-sectoral and intergovernmental relationships among central procurement offices, state agencies, local governments, vendors, and ASPs. Such efforts will turn the rhetoric of e-procurement into real administrative results in the near future.

Appendix I: Web Addresses and Contact Information for State Procurement Offices

Alabama
http://www.purchasing.state.al.us/
Director: Ran Garver (Acting)
Division of Purchasing
Department of Finance
P.O. Box 302620
100 N. Union Street, Ste. 192
Montgomery AL 36130
Phone: 334/242-7250
Fax: 334/242-4419
rgarver@purchasing.state.al.us

Alaska
http://www.state.ak.us/local/akpages/ADMIN/home.htm
Director: Vern Jones
Division of General Services
Department of Administration
P.O. Box 110210
333 Willoughby Road
Juneau AK 99811-0210
Phone: 907/465-5684
Fax: 907/465-2189
Vern_jones@admin.state.ak.us

Arizona
http://sporas.ad.state.az.us/
Director: John Adler
State Procurement Office
Department of Administration
15 South 15th Avenue, Suite 103
Phoenix AZ 85007
Phone: 602/542-5308
Fax: 602/542-5508
John.Adler@ad.state.az.us

Arkansas
http://www.accessarkansas.org/dfa/purchasing/index.html
Director: Joe Giddis
Office of State Purchasing
Department of Finance & Administration
1509 West 7th Street
P.O. Box 2940
Little Rock AR 72203
Phone: 501/324-9312
Fax: 501/324-9311
joe.giddis@dfa.state.ar.us

California
http://www.pd.dgs.ca.gov/
Director: Ralph Chandler
Procurement Division
Department of General Services
1823 14th Street
Sacramento CA 95814
Phone: 916/445-6942
Fax: 916/324-2009
Ralph.Chandler@dgs.ca.gov

Colorado
http://www.gssa.state.co.us/
Director: Richard Pennington
Division of Purchasing
Department of Personnel
225 East 16th Avenue, Ste. 802
Denver CO 80203-1613
Phone: 303/866-6100
Fax: 303/894-7445
richard.pennington@state.co.us

Connecticut
http://www.das.state.ct.us/busopp.asp
Director: Jim Passier
Procurement Services
Department of Administrative Services
P.O. Box 150414
165 Capitol Avenue
Hartford CT 06106
Phone: 860/713-5086
Fax: 860/713-7484
jim.passier@po.state.ct.us

Delaware
http://www.state.de.us/purchase/index.htm
Director: Blaine Herrick
Division of Purchasing
Department of Administrative Services
Wilmington Avenue,
Gov. Bacon Grounds
P.O. Box 299
Delaware City DE 19706
Phone: 302/834-7081
Fax: 302/836-7642
bherrick@state.de.us

District of Columbia
Director: Jacques Abadie, III (Interim)
Department of Administrative Services
441 4th Street, NW
Suite 800 S
Washington DC 20001
Phone: 202/727-0252
Fax: 202/727-6827
abadiej@ocp.dcgov.org

Florida
http://fcn.state.fl.us/fcn/centers/purchase/
Director: David Minacci
Division of Purchasing
Department of Management Services
4050 Esplanade Way, Suite 335M
Tallahassee FL 32399-0950
Phone: 850/488-3049
Fax: 850/414-6122
hosayr@dms.state.fl.us

Georgia
http://www.doas.state.ga.us/
Director: Debra Blount (Acting)
Statewide Business Services
Department of Administrative Services
200 Piedmont Avenue, Suite 1304
W. Floyd Building
Atlanta GA 30334
Phone: 404/657-6000
Fax: 404/655-4528
rdkissel@doas.ga.gov

Hawaii
http://www.state.hi.us/icsd/dags/spo.html
Director: Aaron Fujioka
State Procurement Office
P.O. Box 119
1151 Punchbowl Street, 230-A
Honolulu HI 96813
Phone: 808/587-4700
Fax: 808/587-4703
Aaron_Fujioka@exec.state.hi.us

Idaho
http://www2.state.id.us/adm/purchasing/index.htm
Director: Jan Cox
Division of Purchasing
Department of Administration
5569 Kendall Street
P.O. Box 83720
Boise ID 83720
Phone: 208/327-7472
Fax: 208/327-7320
jcox@adm.state.id.us

Illinois
http://www.state.il.us/cms/purchase/default.htm
Director: Robert Kirk
Procurement Services Division
Dept. of Central Management Services
801 Wm. G. Stratton Building
Springfield IL 62706
Phone: 217/785-3868
Fax: 217/782-5187
robert_kirk@cms.state.il.us

Indiana
http://www.ai.org/idoa/index.html
Director: Rebecca Reddick
Division of Procurement
Department of Administration
Government Center South
402 W. Washington St., Rm. W468
Indianapolis IN 46204
Phone: 317/232-3032
Fax: 317/232-7312
rreddick@idoa.state.in.us

Iowa
http://www.state.ia.us/government/dgs/Purchase/business.htm
Director: Patricia Schroeder
Customer Service, Admin. and Purchasing
Department of General Services
Hoover State Office Building, Level A
Des Moines IA 50319
Phone: 515/281-8384
Fax: 515/242-5974
Patti.Schroeder@dgs.state.ia.us

Kansas
http://da.state.ks.us/purch/
Director: John Houlihan
Division of Purchases
Department of Administration
Landon State Office Building
900 S.W. Jackson Street, Room 102N
Topeka KS 66612
Phone: 785/296-2376
Fax: 785/296-7240
John.Houlihan@state.ks.us

Kentucky
https://ky-purchases.com/
Director: Mike Burnside
Division of Purchases
Finance & Administration Cabinet
Room 367, Capitol Annex Building
Frankfort KY 40601
Phone: 502/564-4510 ext. 248
Fax: 502/564-7209
Mike.Burnside@mail.state.ky.us

Louisiana
http://www.doa.state.la.us/osp/osp.htm
Director: Denise Lea
Office of State Purchasing
Division of Administration
P.O. Box 94095
301 Main Street, 13th Floor
Baton Rouge LA 70804
Phone: 225/342-8057
Fax: 225/342-8688
dlea@doa.state.la.us

Maine
http://www.state.me.us/purchase/homepage.htm
Director: Richard Thompson
Division of Purchases
Department of Administrative & Financial Services
State Office Building
State House Station #9
Augusta ME 04333-0009
Phone: 207/624-7332
Fax: 207/287-6578
Richard.B.Thompson@state.me.us

Maryland
http://www.dgs.state.md.us/overview/procure2.htm
Director: Mark Krysiak
Purchasing Bureau
Department of General Services
301 W. Preston Street,
Room M6
Baltimore MD 21201
Phone: 410/767-4430
Fax: 410/333-5482
gpwcmg@dgs.state.md.us

Massachusetts
http://www.state.ma.us/osd/osd.htm
Director: Ellen Phillips
Operational Services Division
John W. McCormack Office Building
One Ashburton Place, Room 1017
Boston MA 02108
Phone: 617/727-7500 ext. 260
Fax: 617/727-6123
ellen.phillips@state.ma.us

Michigan
http://www.state.mi.us/dmb/oop/
Director: Kathy Jones
Office of Purchasing
Department of Management & Budget
P.O. Box 30026
530 W. Allegan, Mason Bldg.,
2nd Floor
Lansing MI 48909
Phone: 517/373-0300
Fax: 517/335-0046
jonesk@state.mi.us

Minnesota
http://www.mmd.admin.state.mn.us/
Director: Kent Allin
Materials Management
Department of Administration
112 State Administration Building
50 Sherburne Avenue
St. Paul MN 55155
Phone: 651/296-1442
Fax: 612/297-3996
kent.allin@state.mn.us

Mississippi
http://www.mmrs.state.ms.us/Purchasing/
Director: Don Buffum
Office of Purchasing & Travel
1401 Woolfolk Bldg, Suite A
501 North West Street
Jackson MS 39201
Phone: 601/359-3912
Fax: 601/359-2470
buffum@dfa.state.ms.us

Missouri
http://www.oa.state.mo.us/purch/purch.htm
Director: Jim Miluski
Division of Purchasing & Materials Mgmt.
Department of Administration
P.O. Box 809
301 W. High Street, HST Bldg. #580
Jefferson City MO 65101
Phone: 573/751-3273
Fax: 573/526-5985
MilusJ@mail.oa.state.mo.us

Montana
http://www.mt.gov/doa/ppd/index.htm
Director: Marvin Eicholtz
Procurement & Printing Division
Department of Administration
P.O. Box 200135
Helena MT 59620-0132
Phone: 406/444-3318
Fax: 406/443-2212
meicholtz@state.mt.us

Nebraska
http://www.das.state.ne.us/materiel/
Director: Don Medinger
Material Division
Department of Administrative Services
301 Centennial Mall South
P.O. Box 94847
Lincoln NE 68509
Phone: 402/471-2401
Fax: 402/471-2268
dmeding@notes.state.ne.us

Nevada
http://www.state.nv.us/purchasing/
Director: William Moell
Purchasing Division
Department of Administration
209 E. Musser, Room 304
Carson City NV 89710
Phone: 775/684-0170
bmoell@govmail.state.nv.us

New Hampshire
http://www.state.nh.us/das/purchasing/index.html
Director: Wayne Myer
Bureau of Purchase & Property
Department of Administrative Services
State House Annex, Room 102
25 Capitol Street
Concord NH 03301
Phone: 603/271-3606
Fax: 603/271-2700
wmyer@admin.state.nh.us

New Jersey
http://www.state.nj.us/treasury/purchase/
Director: Janice DiGiuseppe (Acting)
Procurement & Contracting
New Jersey State Purchase Bureau
Department of Treasury
33 W. State Street, CN-230
Trenton NJ 08625-0230
Phone: 609/292-4751
Fax: 609/292-0490
formica_j@tre.state.nj.us

New Mexico
http://www.state.nm.us/clients/spd/spd.html
Director: Lou Higgins
Purchasing Division
Department of General Services
1100 St. Francis Drive
Joseph Montoya Building
Santa Fe NM 87501
Phone: 505/827-0480
Fax: 505/827-2484
lou.higgins@state.nm.us

New York
http://www.ogs.state.ny.us/purchase/default.asp
Director: Paula Moskowitz
Procurement Services Group
Office of General Services
Mayor E. Corning, 2nd Tower, Room 3804
Albany NY 12242
Phone: 518/474-6710
Fax: 518/486-6099
customer.services@ogs.state.ny.us

North Carolina
http://www.doa.state.nc.us/PandC/
Director: J. Arthur Leaston
Division of Purchase & Contract
Department of Administration
305 Mail Service Center
Raleigh NC 27699-1805
Phone: 919/733-3581
Fax: 919/733-4782
john.leaston@ncmail.net

North Dakota
http://www.state.nd.us/csd/
Director: Linda Belisle
Central Services
Office of Management & Budget
600 East Blvd., Dept. 188
Bismarck ND 58505-0420
Phone: 701/328-3494
Fax: 701/328-1615
lbelisle@state.nd.us

Ohio
http://www.state.oh.us/das/gsd/pur/pur.html
Director: Mark Hutchison
General Services Division
Department of Administrative Services
4200 Surface Road
Columbus OH 43228-1395
Phone: 614/466-2375
Fax: 614/466-7525
Mark.Hutchison@das.state.oh.us

Oklahoma
http://www.dcs.state.ok.us/okdcs.nsf/
Director: Tom Jaworsky
Central Purchasing Division
Department of Central Services
2401 N. Lincoln Blvd., Ste 116
Oklahoma City OK 73105
Phone: 405/521-2115
Fax: 405/522-6266
Tom_Jaworsky@dcs.state.ok.us

Oregon
http://tpps.das.state.or.us/purchasing/
Director: Dianne Lancaster
Purchasing Services Division
Department of Administrative Services
1225 Ferry Street, SE
Salem OR 97310
Phone: 503/378-3529
Fax: 503/373-1626
Dianne.Lancaster@.state.or.us

Pennsylvania
http://www.dgs.state.pa.us/purch.htm
Director: Joe Nugent
Department of General Services
414 North Office Building
Harrisburg PA 17125
Phone: 717/787-4718
Fax: 717/783-6241
jnugent@state.pa.us

Rhode Island
http://www.purchasing.state.ri.us/home.html
Director: Peter Corr
Associate Director/Purchasing Agent
Division of Procurement Materials & Information Management
Department of Administration
One Capitol Hill
Providence RI 02908-5855
Phone: 401/277-2142 ext. 123
Fax: 401/277-6387
pcorr@purchasing.state.ri.us

South Carolina
http://www.state.sc.us/mmo/mmo/
Director: Robert Voight Shealy
Materials Management Officer
Office of General Services
1201 Main Street, Ste. 600
Columbia SC 29201
Phone: 803/737-0600
Fax: 803/737-0639
VShealy@ogs.state.sc.us

South Dakota
http://www.state.sd.us/boa/pp.htm
Director: Jeff Holden
Office of Purchasing & Printing
Division of Central Services
Bureau of Administration
523 East Capitol
Pierre SD 57501
Phone: 605/773-3405
Fax: 605/773-4840
jeff.holden@state.sd.us

Tennessee
http://www.state.tn.us/generalserv/purchasing/
Director: George Street
Department of General Services
Third Floor, Tennessee Tower
312 Eighth Avenue North
Nashville TN 37243-0557
Phone: 615/741-1035
Fax: 615/741-0684
gstreet@mail.state.tn.us

Texas
http://www.gsc.state.tx.us/
Director: Jim Railey
General Services Commission
P.O. Box 13042 Capitol Station
Austin TX 78711
Phone: 512/463-3444
Fax: 512/463-7994
jim.railey@gsc.state.tx.us

Utah
http://www.purchasing.state.ut.us/
Director: Douglas Richins
Division of Purchasing
Department of Administrative Services
3150 State Office Building, Capitol Hill
Salt Lake City UT 84114
Phone: 801/538-3143
Fax: 801/538-3882
pamain.drichins@state.ut.us

Vermont
http://www.bgs.state.vt.us/PCA/index.html
Director: Peter Noyes
Division of Purchasing
General Services Department
128 State Street, Drawer 33
Montpelier VT 05633-7401
Phone: 802/828-2211
Fax: 802/828-2222
peter.noyes@state.vt.us

Virginia
http://159.169.222.200/dps/
Director: Ron Bell
Division of Purchases & Supply
Department of General Services
P.O. Box 1199
805 E. Broad Street, 4th Floor
Richmond VA 23218-1199
Phone: 804/786-3846
Fax: 804/371-7877
rbell@dgs.state.va.us

Washington
http://www.ga.wa.gov/vendor.htm
Director: Bill Joplin (Acting)
Office of State Procurement
Department of General Administration
201 General Administration Building
P.O. Box 41017
Olympia WA 98504-1017
Phone: 360/902-7404
Fax: 360/586-2426
bjoplin@ga.wa.gov

West Virginia
http://www.state.wv.us/admin/
purchase/
Director: David Tincher
Purchasing Division
2019 Washington St., East
P.O. Box 50130
Charleston WV 25305
Phone: 304/558-2538
Fax: 304/558-4115
dtincher@gwmail.state.wv.us

Wisconsin
http://vendornet.state.wi.us/
vendornet/
Director: Leo Talsky (Acting)
Bureau of Procurement
Department of Administration
101 E. Wilson Street,
6th Floor
P.O. Box 7867
Madison WI 53707-7867
Phone: 608/266-0974
Fax: 608/267-0600
Michael.Cornell@doa.state.wi.us

Wyoming
http://ai.state.wy.us/GeneralServices/
procurement.asp
Director: Mac Landen
Purchasing Section
Department of Administration
& Information
Emerson Building,
Room 323E
2001 Capitol Avenue
Cheyenne WY 82002
Phone: 307/777-7253
Fax: 307/777-5852
MLANDE@state.wy.us

Source: National Association of State Procurement Officials (NASPO)'s website (http://www.naspo.org/directory/index.cfm#anchor236482), accessed April 22, 2002.

Appendix II: Summary of the Surveys

Table 6.A.1: 1998 NASPO Survey

State	Web Solicitation	Contract Award on Web	Digital Signature	DS for Internal Document	DS for Procurement Document	Electronic Ordering	EO Maintainer	Record: Total Amount	Record: Amount by Commodity	Record: Amount by Vendor	Purchasing Card	PC for Statewide Contract	Fleet Management	PC for Travel
Alabama	n	n	n	n	n	n	n/a	n	n	n/a	n	n	n	y
Alaska														
Arizona	y	y	y	y	n	n	n/a	y	n	n/a	y	y	y	n
Arkansas	n	n	n	n	n	y	vendor	n	n	n/a	n	n	n	y
California	y	y	y	n	n	y	vendor	y	y	y	y	y	y	y
Colorado	y	y	n	n	n	n	n/a	n	n	y	y	y	y	y
Connecticut	y	y	n	n	n	y	state	y	y	y	y	y	n	y
Delaware	n	y	n	n	n	y	vendor	y	n	n/a	y	y	n	y
Florida	y	n	y	n	n	y	combo	y	y	y	y	y	y	y
Georgia	y	y	y	n	n	n	n/a	y	y	y	y	y	y	y
Hawaii	y	n	n	n	n	n	n/a	n	n	n/a	n	n	n	n
Idaho	y	n	y	n	n	y	vendor	y	y	y	y	y	y	y
Illinois	y	y	y	n	n	n	n/a	y	y	y	n	n	y	y
Indiana	y	y	y	n	n	n	n/a	y	y	y	n	n	y	n
Iowa	y	y	n	n	n	y	state	y	y	y	n	n	y	y
Kansas	y	y	y	n	n	n	n/a	n	n	n	y	y	y	y
Kentucky														
Louisiana	n	n	n	n	n	n	n/a	y	y	y	n	n	y	y
Maine	y	n	n	n	n	y	vendor	y	y	y	y	y	y	y
Maryland	y	y	n	y	y	n	n/a	y	y	y	y	y	y	y
Massachusetts	y	y	n	n	n	y	state	y	y	y	y	y	y	n
Michigan	y	n	n	y	n	n	n/a	y	y	y	y	n	y	y
Minnesota	y	y	y	n	n	y	state	y	y	y	y	y	y	n
Mississippi	n	n	y	n	n	y	vendor	n	n	n	y	y	y	y
Missouri	y	y	n	n	n	y	vendor	y	y	y	y	n	y	n

Table 6.A.1: 1998 NASPO Survey (continued)

State	Web Solicitation	Contract Award on Web	Digital Signature	DS for Internal Document	DS for Procurement Document	Electronic Ordering	EO Maintainer	Record: Total Amount	Record: Amount by Commodity	Record: Amount by Vendor	Purchasing Card	PC for Statewide Contract	Fleet Management	PC for Travel
Montana	y	y	y	n	n	n	n/a	y	n	y	y	y	y	y
Nebraska	y	y	n	n	n	y	vendor	n	n	n	n	n	n	y
Nevada	y	y	n	y	n	n	n/a	y	y	n	y	y	n	y
New Hampshire														
New Jersey	y	y	n	n	n	n	n/a	y	y	y	y	y	n	y
New Mexico	y	y	y	n	n	n	n/a	y	y	y	n	n	y	y
New York	y	y	n	n	n	y	vendor	n	y	y	y	y	y	y
North Carolina	y	y	y	n	n	n	n/a	y	y	y	y	y	y	y
North Dakota	n	n	n	n	n	n	n/a	n	n	n	n	n	y	n
Ohio	y	y	n	n	y	y	state	y	y	y	y	y	n	y
Oklahoma	y	y	n	n	n	n	n/a	y	y	y	n	n	y	y
Oregon	y	y	y	n	n	y	vendor	y	y	y	y	y	y	y
Pennsylvania	y	y	n	n	y	y	state	n	y	y	y	y	y	y
Rhode Island	y	y	y	n	n	n	n/a	n	n	y	n	n	n	n
South Carolina	y	n	y	n	n	n	n/a	n	n	y	y	n	y	y
South Dakota	n	y	n	n	n	y	vendor	y	n	y	y	y	y	y
Tennessee	y	y	n	y	n	n	n/a	y	y	y	n	n	y	y
Texas	y	y	n	y	n	n	n/a	n	y	y	y	y	y	y
Utah	y	y	y	n	n	y	vendor	y	y	y	y	y	y	y
Vermont	y	y	n	n	n	y	vendor	n/a	n/a	n/a	n	n	y	n
Virginia	n	y	n	n	n	n	n/a	n	y	y	y	y	y	y
Washington	y	y	y	n	y	n	n/a	n	y	y	y	y	n	y
West Virginia	y	y	n	n	n	n	n/a	y	y	y	y	y	y	y
Wisconsin	y	y	y	n	n	y	vendor	y	y	y	y	y	y	y
Wyoming	y	n	n	n	n	n	n/a	n	y	y	n	n	n	y

Table 6.A.2: 2001 Combined Procurement Survey—The 2001 NASPO Survey and 2001 Follow-Up E-Mail Survey

State	Web Solicitation	Contract Award on Web	Digital Signature Legislation	DS for Internal Approval	DS for Procurement Document	Governing Internet Bidding	Internet Bidding	Reverse Auction	Electronic Ordering	EO Maintainer	Total Amount	Amount by Commodity	Amount by Vendor	Automated Procurement System	Lead-Time Analysis
Alabama	n	y	n	n	n	n	n	n	n	n/a	y	y	y	y	n
Alaska	y	y	n	n	n	n	n	n	y	vendor	y	n	n	n	n/a
Arizona	y	y	y	n	n	n	n	n	y	vendor	y	y	y	y	n
Arkansas	n	y	y	n	n	n	n	n	n	n/a	y	y	y	y	y
California	y	y	y	n	n	n	n	n	y	state	y	y	y	y	n
Colorado	y	y	y	n	n	y	n	n	y	vendor	n	y	y	y	n/a
Connecticut	y	y	y	n	n	n	n	n	y	vendor	y	y	y	y	n
Delaware	y	y	n	n	n	n	n	n	n	n/a	y	n	y	n	n/a
Florida															
Georgia	y	y	n	n	n	n	n	n	n	n/a	n	y	y	y	n/a
Hawaii	y	y	y	n	n	n	n	n	y	vendor	n	n	n	n	n/a
Idaho	y	y	y	n	y	y	y	n	y	combo	y	n	y	y	y
Illinois	y	y	y	y	n	n	n	n	y	vendor	y	y	y	y	y
Indiana	y	n	y	n	n	n	n	n	y	vendor	y	y	y	y	y
Iowa	y	y	y	n	n	n	n	n	y	vendor	y	y	y	y	n
Kansas	y	n	y	n	n	n	n	n	y	vendor	n	y	n	y	n
Kentucky	y	y	y	y	n	n	y	n	y	combo	n	y	y	y	n
Louisiana	y	y	y	y	n	n	n	n	n	n/a	y	y	y	y	y
Maine	y	y	n/a	n/a	y	y	y	n	y	vendor	y	y	y	y	n/a
Maryland															
Massachusetts	y	y	n	n	n	n	y	n	y	combo	y	y	y	y	y
Michigan	y	n	n	n	n	n/a	y	n	y	vendor	y	y	y	y	n
Minnesota	y	n	y	y	y	y	y	y	y	vendor	y	y	y	y	y
Mississippi	y	y	y	n	n	n	n	n	y	vendor	n	y	y	y	n
Missouri	y	y	y	n/a	n	y	y	y	n	n/a	y	y	y	y	y

Table 6.A.2: 2001 Combined Procurement Survey—The 2001 NASPO Survey and 2001 Follow-Up E-Mail Survey (continued)

State	Web Solicitation	Contract Award on Web	Digital Signature Legislation	DS for Internal Approval	DS for Procurement Document	Governing Internet Bidding	Internet Bidding	Reverse Auction	Electronic Ordering	EO Maintainer	Total Amount	Amount by Commodity	Amount by Vendor	Automated Procurement System	Lead-Time Analysis
Montana	y	y	y	n	n	n	n	n	n	n/a	n	y	y	n	n/a
Nebraska	y	y	y	n	n	n	n	n	y	vendor	n	n	n	y	n
Nevada	y	y	y	n	n	n	n	n	y	vendor	y	y	y	y	y
New Hampshire															
New Jersey	y	y	n	n	n	n	n	n	n	n/a	y	y	y	y	y
New Mexico	y	y	y	y	n	n	n	n	y	vendor	n/a	y	y	y	y
New York	y	y	y	n	n	n	n	n	y	vendor	y	y	y	y	n
North Carolina	y	y	y	n	n	y	y	n	y	vendor	y	y	y	y	y
North Dakota	n	y	y	n	n	n	n	n	n	n/a	y	y	y	y	n
Ohio	y	y	y	n	n	n	n	n	y	state	n/a	n	n	y	n/a
Oklahoma	y	y	n	n	n	n	n	n	n	vendor	n/a	n/a	y	n	n
Oregon	n	n	n	n	n	n	n	n	n	n/a	n	n	n	y	n
Pennsylvania	y	y	y	n	y	y	y	y	y	state	y	y	y	y	n/a
Rhode Island	y	y	y	n	n	n	n	n	n	n/a	n	n	n	y	y
South Carolina	y	y	y	y	n	y	y	n	y	vendor	n	n	y	y	n
South Dakota	n	y	y	y	n	n	n	n	n	n/a	y	n	y	n	n/a
Tennessee	y	y	n/a	y	y	n	n	n	n	n/a	y	y	y	y	y
Texas	y	y	n	n	y	y	y	n	y	vendor	n	y	y	y	y
Utah	y	y	y	n	n	n	n	n	y	vendor	y	y	y	y	n
Vermont	y	y	n	n	n	n	n	n	y	vendor	n/a	n/a	n/a	y	n
Virginia	y	y	y	n	n	n	y	y	y	state	y	y	y	y	y
Washington	y	y	y	n/a	y	n/a	n/a	n	y	vendor	y	y	y	y	n
West Virginia	y	y	n	n	n	n	n	n	y	vendor	y	n	n	y	n
Wisconsin	y	n/a	n/a	n/a	n/a	y	y	y	n/a	n/a	y	n	n	y	n/a
Wyoming	y	y	n	n	n	n	n	n	y	combo	y	y	y	y	n

Table 6.A.2: 2001 Combined Procurement Survey—The 2001 NASPO Survey and 2001 Follow-Up E-Mail Survey (continued)

State	EDI Element	Integrated to E-Commerce	Asset Management	Purchasing Card	PC for Statewide Contract	PC for Travel	Cost Recovery for PC	PC Linked to Accounting System	Fleet Management	Cost Saving	Time Saving
Alabama	n/a	n	y	n	n/a	y	n/a	n/a	y	n	n
Alaska	n/a	n/a	n/a	y	y	y	n	y	y	n	n
Arizona	n	n	n	y	y	y	y	n	y	n	n
Arkansas	y	n/a	y	n	n/a	y	n/a	n/a	n/a	n/a	n/a
California	n	n	n	y	y	y	y	n	y	y	y
Colorado	y	y	n	y	y	y	n	n/a	y	n/a	n/a
Connecticut	y	y	n	y	y	y	n	y	n	y	y
Delaware	n/a	n/a	n/a	y	y	y	n	n	y	n	n
Florida											
Georgia	n/a	n	n	y	y	y	n	n/a	y		
Hawaii	n/a	n/a	n/a	n	n/a	n	n	y	n	n/a	n/a
Idaho	y	y	y	y	y	y	n	y	y	n/a	n/a
Illinois	n	n	n	n	n/a	y	n/a	n/a	y		
Indiana	y	y	y	n	n/a	y	n/a	n/a	y		
Iowa	n	n	y	y	y	y	y	n	y	n	n
Kansas	y	y	n	y	y	y	n	n	y	y	y
Kentucky	y	y	y	y	y	y	n/a	y	y	n/a	n/a
Louisiana	n	n	n	y	y	y	n/a	n	y	y	y
Maine	y	y	n	y	y	y	n/a	y	n/a	n/a	n/a
Maryland											
Massachusetts	y	y	n	y	y	y	n	n	y	y	y
Michigan	n	n	n	y	y	y	n	n	y	y	n/a
Minnesota	y	n	n	y	y	y	n	n	y	y	n
Mississippi	n	n	n	y	y	y	n	n	y	y	y
Missouri	n	n	y	y	y	y	n	n/a	y	n/a	n

Table 6.A.2: 2001 Combined Procurement Survey—The 2001 NASPO Survey and 2001 Follow-Up E-Mail Survey (continued)

State	EDI Element	Integrated to E-Commerce	Asset Management	Purchasing Card	PC for Statewide Contract	PC for Travel	Cost Recovery for PC	PC Linked to Accounting System	Fleet Management	Cost Saving	Time Saving
Montana	n/a	n/a	n/a	y	y	y	n	y	y		
Nebraska	n	n	n	y	y	y	n	n	y		
Nevada	y	y	y	y	y	y	n	n	n	n	n
New Hampshire											
New Jersey	y	y	n	y	y	n	n	y	n		
New Mexico	y	n	n	y	y	y	n	n/a	y	n/a	n/a
New York	n	n	n	y	y	y	n	y	y		
North Carolina	y	y	y	y	y	y	n	y	y	n/a	n/a
North Dakota	n/a	n	n	y	y	n	n/a	y	y	n/a	n/a
Ohio	n/a	n/a	n/a	y	y	y	n	n	y	y	y
Oklahoma	n	n	n	y	y	y	n	n	y		
Oregon	n	n	n	y	n	n/a	n	y	y	n/a	n/a
Pennsylvania	y	n	n/a	y	y	y	y	y	y	y	y
Rhode Island	n/a	y	y	n	n/a	y	n/a	n/a	y	n/a	n/a
South Carolina	n	n	n	y	y	y	n	n	y	y	y
South Dakota	n/a	n/a	n/a	y	y	y	n	y	y	n	n
Tennessee	n	y	n	n	n	y	n	n	y	n/a	n/a
Texas	y	y	y	y	y	y	n	n	y		
Utah	n	n	n	y	y	y	n	y	y	y	y
Vermont	n	n	n	y	y	y	n	n	n		
Virginia	y	n/a	y	y	y	n	n	n	n		
Washington	y	y	n	y	y	y	n/a	n/a	y	n	n
West Virginia	n	n	n	y	y	y	y	n	y		
Wisconsin	n/a	n/a	n/a	y	y	y	n/a	y	y	n/a	n/a
Wyoming	n	y	y	y	y	y	n	y	y	y	y

Appendix III: Survey Instrument for the 2001 E-Mail Follow-Up Survey

Survey instrument is adopted from the 2001 NASPO survey to update information and fill in missing information.

1. Is the central procurement office posting solicitation/bids on the Web?
2. Is the central procurement office posting contract award information on the Web?
3. Has the state enacted digital signature law?
   1) If yes, what is the citation?
   2) If yes, please provide a summary of the law.
4. Does the state use digital signatures to route and approve documents internally?
5. Is the state accepting digital signatures as legally binding signatures from the vendor community on the procurement documents?
   1) If yes, which documents?
6. Has the state central procurement office developed procedures or have statutes governing Internet bidding?
7. Has the state central procurement office conducted bids via the Internet?
8. Has the state central procurement office conducted reverse auctions?
9. Does the state utilize electronic ordering?
   1) If yes, is the ordering system state or vendor maintained?
10. If the ordering system is state maintained:
    1) What standard do you use?
    2) What service provider does the central procurement office use?
    3) Is there a vendor fee or a fee to the customer?
11. Does the central procurement office maintain records of the overall dollar volume of purchase issued by central purchasing and delegated agencies (Yes, No, Other agency)?
12. Can the central procurement office tracks dollars spent by type of commodity or service (Yes, No, Other agency)?
13. Can the central procurement office track dollars spent by vendor (Yes, No, Other agency)?

Automated Procurement System

14. Does the central procurement office have an automated procurement system?

If yes, please indicate if the system supports the following capabilities:

1) a) Vendors automatically purged
   b) Vendors automatically selected
   c) Notice distribution of Invitation to bids and Requests for proposal via E-mail, Fax, Hard copy, or Other?
2) On demand electronic distribution of Invitation for Bids and Requests for Proposals (via Fax on demand, Internet download, Other)?
3) Vendor performance (via Vendor notes screen, Vendor performance screen, or Linked vendor notes and performance screens)?
4) a) Can purchase order form be easily modified?
   b) Do purchase orders look as they are printed?
   c) Can blanket purchase orders or contract be used?
   d) Can contracts be searched for goods and services?
5) a) Are Invitation to Bid templates available?
   b) What standard PC Suites software can be used in Invitation to Bid?
   c) Do you have the ability to use standard terms and conditions language in an Invitation to Bid?
   d) Do you have the ability to choose standard language for each Invitation
   e) Can the Invitation to Bid be downloaded from the Internet?
   f) Can the system handle sealed bids?
6) a) Can appropriate terms and conditions be copied to purchase orders and contracts?
   b) Can purchase order and contract be printed at remote location?
   c) Capable for online requisitioning from the agency customer?
   d) Is the system capable of electronic routing and approvals?
7) Is the system capable of workload assignment and status?
8) Will the system document purchasing process milestones or timelines?
9) Will the system provide lead-time analysis?
10) Will the system record and prompt for pending action?
11) Does the system have commodity code capability?
12) Does the system have keyword search?
13) Which commodity codes are utilized?
14) Does the program allow for forms to be downloaded?
15) Is the system EDI capable?
16) Does the system support online receiving?
17) Does the system provide integrated electronic commerce?
18) Does the system support delegated authority?
19) Is the system integrated with an asset management system?

Purchasing Cards

15. Does the state have a purchasing card?
16. What are the typical dollar limits placed on the card (Single limit, Daily limit, Cycle purchase limit)?
17. Does the state allow purchasing cards to be used for purchasing from statewide contracts?
18. What is the estimated monthly transaction volume using the purchasing card?
19. Which credit card and bank is the state using?
20. Does your state use a credit card for travel?
    1) If yes, is it the same credit card as for general procurement?
21. Is use of purchasing cards optional?
22. Does the state fund the purchasing card program through a fee-based cost recovery? If yes, what is the fee?
23. What products/services are disallowed for use with the purchasing card program?
24. Do the purchasing card transactions electronically post to your statewide accounting system?
25. Does the state remit monthly payments via wire transfer/ACH?
26. Do you have a fleet management purchasing card?
    1) If yes, what fleet card processor is the state using?
27. Is there a state travel office?
28. Is the travel office within the CPO? If no, where is it located?
29. Does the travel office administer contract for Travel Agency Service?
    1) If no, how are these services provided to the agencies?
    2) Does the state administer contracts for air fares?
30. Does the state administer contracts for car rental?
31. Does the state administer contracts for hotel/motel?
32. Have you made any cost saving through e-procurement?
    1) If yes, how much cost did you save last year?
33. Have you made any time saving through e-procurement?
    1) If yes, how much time did you save last year?

Endnotes

1. This research is supported by a generous grant from The PricewaterhouseCoopers Endowment for The Business of Government. The author wants to thank the excellent research assistance of Jwa Young Poo, Deserai Anderson-Utley, Hae Won Kwon, and Jongyun Ahn.

2. Definitions of related terms are available at the website of National Electronic Commerce Coordinating Council: http://www.ec3.org/InfoCenter/02_WorkGroups/2000_Workgroups/eprocurement/definitions.htm.

3. This section builds on a previous paper (Moon, 2002). Some parts of the paper reappear in revised form in this section.

4. EDI standards have been established to promote any commonly used data (documents) found in routine business transactions.

5. BUYNET can be accessed via the Purchasing and Contracting website: www.co.san-diego.ca.us/cnty/cntydepts/general/prchcntr/newfctns.hts.

6. Advantages and disadvantages of each model are well summarized in NECCC (2001a), *Electronic Procurement: Funding Models and Measurement to Success*. Also see Johnson (2002), "Financing and Pricing E-Service." In Gant, Gant, and Johnson, *State Web Portals: Delivering and Financing E-Service*. The PricewaterhouseCoopers Endowment for The Business of Government.

7. Punch-out includes product selectors and product configurators. Product selectors refer to the technical applications that allow buyers to figure out specific applications of a product based on detailed characteristics of the product. It helps and supports selecting an appropriate product for a given application. Product configurators are a little different from product selectors in that they are equipped with the capacity to customize particular products within given criteria. For more details, see NECCC (2001b), p. 8.

8. There are 3-digit (class), 5-digit (item), 7-digit (group), and 10-digit (detailed item description) codes. For example, 615-45-29-028 is a 10-digit code. 615 indicates general office supplies, 45 is for file folders (regular, legal, and letter sizes). 615-45-29 indicates file folders, double tab, legal size, manila, standard height (overall 14-3/4 in. x 9-1/2 in.). 615-45-29-028 is file folders, one-third cut, 9-1/2 point, 100/box. The 3-digit level code does not require licensing but 5-digit and more upper-level codes require licensing. For more details, see NECCC (2001b), pp. 14–15.

9. The UNSPSC is accepted as the universal standard by the Electronic Commerce Code Management Association (ECCMA) and can be used without any licensing fees. There are four levels in the code hierarchy (segment, family, class, and commodity). Each hierarchical level has two to three digits for the code. For more details, see NECCC (2001b), pp. 15–17.

10. The NASPO surveys are summarized in NASPO Survey of State and Local Government Purchasing Practices (1998) and NASPO Survey of State and Local Government Purchasing Practices (2001a).

11. Nonresponding states are Alaska, Kentucky, and New Hampshire.

12. The seven states that did not respond are Alabama, Delaware, Florida, Maryland, New Hampshire, Oregon, and Wisconsin.

13. It should be noted that the 2001 NASPO survey reflects state e-procurement from 2000 since the survey was conducted in 2000 and published in 2001.

14. Nonresponding states are Florida, Georgia, Illinois, Indiana, Maryland, Montana, Nebraska, New Hampshire, New Jersey, New York, Oklahoma, Texas, Vermont, Virginia, and West Virginia.

15. For more details, see Kalkota and Whinston (1997), p. 142.

16. They are California, Connecticut, Kentucky, Louisiana, Massachusetts, Michigan, Minnesota, Mississippi, Ohio, Pennsylvania, South Carolina, Utah, and Wyoming.

17. The states include California, Connecticut, Kentucky, Louisiana, Massachusetts, Mississippi, Ohio, Pennsylvania, South Carolina, Utah, and Wyoming.

Bibliography

Accenture, *State of North Carolina E-Procurement Due Diligence Final Report.* January 26, 2001.

Anderson, Kim. "Reengineering Public Sector Organizations Using Information Technology." In *Reinventing Government in the Information Age,* New York, Routledge, 1999, pp. 312–330.

Atwater, Kristin. "Virginia Revolutionizes Virtual Sphere of Procurement." *Government Procurement,* June 2001, pp. 7–10.

Bozeman, B. and S. Bretschneider. "Public Management Information System: Theory and Perception." *Public Administration Review* (46) 1986, pp. 475–487.

Bretschneider, S. "Managing Information Systems in Public and Private Organizations: An Empirical Test." *Public Administration Review* (50) 1990, pp. 536–545.

Brown, Douglas. "Information Systems for Improved Performance Management: Development Approaches in US Public Agencies." In *Reinventing Government in the Information Age,* ed. Richard Heeks. New York, Routledge, 1999, pp. 113–134.

Cats-Baril, W. and R. Thompson. "Managing Information Technology Projects in the Public Sector." *Public Administration Review* (55) 1995, pp. 559–566.

Caudle, Sharon. "Federal Information Resource Management after the Paperwork Reduction Act." *Public Administration Review* (4) 48, 1988, pp. 790–799.

Caudle, Sharon. "Strategic Information Resources Management: Fundamental Practices." *Government Information Quarterly* (1) 13, 1996, pp. 83–97.

Daukantas, Patricia. "PTO Starts E-government Shift." *Government Computer News* (33) 2000, p. 198. http://www.gcn.com/vo119_no33/news/3327-1.html. Accessed September 7, 2001.

Fletcher, P. "Local Government and IRM: Policy Emerging from Practice." *Government Information Quarterly.* (14) 1997, pp. 313–324.

Fountain, J. "The Virtual State: Toward a Theory of Federal Bureaucracy." In *democracy.com? Governance in Networked Word,* ed. Elaine Ciulla Kamarck and Joseph S. Nye. Jr., New Hampshire, Hollis Publishing Company, 1999.

Fountain, Jane. *Building the Virtual State: Information Technology and Institutional Change*. Washington, D.C., Brookings Institution Press, 2001.

General Accounting Office (GAO). *Purchasing Cards: Control Weaknesses Leave Two Navy Units Vulnerable to Fraud and Abuse*. Washington, D.C., 2001.

Gore, Albert. *Creating a Government That Works Better and Costs Less: Reengineering Through Information Technology.* Report of the National Performance Review, Washington D.C., U.S. Government Printing Office, 1993.

Government and the Internet Survey. "Handle with Care." *The Economist* (8176) 355, 2000, pp. 33–34.

Gunyou, John and Jane Leonard. "Getting Ready for E-commerce." *Government Finance Review* Vol. 14, No. 5, 1998, pp. 9–12.

Hart-Teeter, Inc. *EGovernment: The Next Revolution.* Washington, D.C., Council for Excellence in Government, 2000.

Hiller, Janine and France Bélanger. *Privacy Strategies for Electronic Government.* The PricewaterhouseCoopers Endowment for The Business of Government, 2001.

Joint Task Force on Information Technology of the National Association of State Purchasing Officers and the National Association of State Information Resource Executives (JTFIT). *Buying Smart: State Procurement Saves Millions.* White paper. National, 1996. http://www.naspo.org/whitepapers/buyingsmart.cfm. Accessed October 13, 2001.

Johnson, Craig. "Financing and Pricing E-Service." In Gant, Gant, and Johnson. *State Web Portals: Delivering and Financing E-Service.* The PricewaterhouseCoopers Endowment for The Business of Government, 2002.

Kalakota, Ravi and Andrew Whinston. *Electronic Commerce: A Manager's Guide.* Reading, Addison Wesley Longman, Inc., 1997.

Layne, Karen and Jungwoo Lee. "Developing Fully Functional E-Government: A Four Stage Model." *Government Information Quarterly* (2) 18, 2001, pp. 122–136.

Maryland Department of General Services. *eMaryland @ Marketplace 2001 Annual Report.* 2001.

Moon, M. Jae. "Evolution of Municipal E-Government: Rhetoric or Reality." *Public Administration Review* (4) 62, 2002, pp. 400–409.

Moon, M. Jae and Stuart Bretschneider. "Does the Perception of Red Tape Constrain IT Innovativeness in Organizations? Unexpected Results from a Simultaneous Equation Model and Implications." *Journal of Public Administration and Research and Theory* (2) 12, 2002, pp. 273–292.

Morehead, Nicholas. "Minnesota Tests Reverse Auctions." *Civic.com.* July 18, 2001.

Multi-State EMall™ Team. *Pilot Project Evaluation: A Multi-State Cooperative Procurement System on the Internet.* Office of the Comptroller, Operational Services Division, October 12, 1999.

Multi-State EMall™ Team. *Multi-State eMall: Procurement Powered by Intelisys.* Presented at NASPO 2000 Marketing Meeting. http://www.state.ma.us/emall/. Accessed April 10, 2002.

Musso, Juliet, Christopher Weare, and Matt Hale. "Designing Web Technologies for Local Governance Reform: Good Management or Good Democracy." *Political Communication* (1) 17, 2000, pp. 1–19.

National Association of State Procurement Officials. *NASPO Survey of State and Local Government Purchasing Practices.* 1998.

National Association of State Procurement Officials. 2001a. *NASPO Survey of State and Local Government Purchasing Practices.* 2001.

National Association of State Procurement Officials. 2001b. *NASPO State and Local Government Purchasing Principles and Practices.* 2001.

NECCC. 2000a. *Electronic Payments Primer.* National Electronic Commerce Coordinating Council Symposium 2001. Presented at the NECCC Annual Conference. Las Vegas, Nevada, December 13, 2000.

NECCC. 2000b. *Funding E-Procurement System Acquisition.* National Electronic Commerce Coordinating Council Symposium 2000. Presented at the NECCC Annual Conference. Las Vegas, Nevada, December 13, 2000.

NECCC. 2000c. *E-Government Strategic Planning: A White Paper.* National Electronic Commerce Coordinating Council Symposium 2000. Presented at the NECCC Annual Conference. Las Vegas, Nevada, December 13, 2000.

NECCC. 2001a. *Electronic Procurement: Funding Models and Measurement for Success.* National Electronic Commerce Coordinating Council Symposium 2001. Presented at the NECCC Annual Conference. Las Vegas, Nevada, December 10–12, 2001.

NECCC. 2001b. *Is the Lack of E-procurement Standards…a Barrier to Implementation? A Government and Supplier Perspective.* National Electronic Commerce Coordinating Council Symposium 2001. Presented at the NECCC Annual Conference. Las Vegas, Nevada, December 10–12, 2001.

Neef, Dale. *eProcurement: From Strategy to Implementation.* Upper Saddle River, New Jersey Prentice Hall, 2001.

Norris, Donald and Kenneth Kreamer. "Mainframe and PC Computing in American Cities: Myths and Realities." *Public Administration Review* (6) 56, 1996, pp. 568–576.

Norris, Pippa. "Who Surfs? New Technology, Old Voters, and Virtual Democracy." In *democracy.com? Governance in Networked Word,* ed. Elaine Ciulla Kamarck and Joseph S. Nye, Jr., New Hampshire, Hollis Publishing Company, 1999, pp. 71–94.

Nye, Jr., Joseph. "Information Technology and Democratic Governance." In *democracy.com? Governance in Networked Word,* ed. Elaine Ciulla Kamarck and Joseph S. Nye, Jr., New Hampshire, Hollis Publishing Company, 1999, pp. 1–18.

O'Hara, Colleen. "GSA Moves Ahead with Reverse Auctions." *Federal Computer Week*, June 6, 2001.

Preston, Morag. "E-government US-style." *New Statesman* (4517) 129, Special Supplement, 2000.

Robinson, Brian. "Down Payment on E-Procurement." *Federal Computer Week,* August 20, 2001.

Sarkar, Dibya. 2001a. "States Team up for E-Buying." *Civic.com.* August 22, 2001.

Sarkar, Dibya. 2001b. "States Premature on E-Procurement." *Government e-Business.* September 3, 2001.

Sarkar, Dibya. 2001c. States Buy into E-Buying." *Civic.com.* April 2, 2001.

Schriener, Juday and William Angelo. "Procurement Going Paperless." *ENR.* October 2, 1995, p. 13.

Sprecher, Milford. "Racing to E-government: Using the Internet for Citizen Service Delivery." *Government Finance Review,* (5) 16, 2000, pp. 21–22.

The Virginia Governor's Task Force on Procurement Assessment, 2000. *Report of the Governor's Task Force on Procurement Assessment: Recommendations to Improve Virginia Government's Procurement Systems.* February 3, 2000.

Utah Division of Purchasing and General Services. Description of the Utah/Colorado E-Procurement System. http://www.purchasing.state.ut.us/eps/description.htm. Accessed October 22, 2001.

Ventura, Stephen. J. "The Use of Geographic Information Systems in Local Government." *Public Administration Review,* (5) 55, 1995, pp. 461–467.

Weare, Christopher, Juliet Musso, and Matt Hale. "Electronic Democracy and the Diffusion of Municipal Web Pages in California." *Administration and Society,* (1) 31, 1999, pp. 3–27.

West, D.M. *E-Government and the Transformation of Public Service Delivery.* Presented at the American Political Science Association Annual Meeting. San Francisco, August 30–September 2, 2001.

White House Press Office. "President Clinton and Vice-President Gore: Major New E-Government Initiatives." *US Newswire.* June 24, 2000. http://web.lexis-nexis.com/universe...d5=0f245defaacf01afe17703e5dfd7da67. Accessed September 7, 2001.

Wood, Lawrence. "The Beginning of the End of Paper Procurement." Government Finance Review. June 2000, p. 38.

CHAPTER SEVEN

Internet Voting: Bringing Elections to the Desktop

Robert S. Done
Assistant Research Professor of Management and Policy
Eller College of Business and Public Administration
University of Arizona

This report was originally published in February 2002.

Introduction*

The government's use of the Internet to communicate is increasing. Hiller and Bélanger (2001) observe that this type of communication is characterized by the intersection of the differing types of relationships and stages of government that exist. Governments can use the Internet to interact with other government agencies, government employees, businesses, and individuals. To these constituents, the government can provide information, exchange communication, provide transactions, and integrate services. Currently, the Internet is used primarily to support the government to business relationship in ways such as providing regulatory information and accepting tax payments. To a lesser extent, the Internet is also used to support the government to individual relationship (e.g., automobile registration). Political participation (i.e., voter registration and voting) is the most important government to individual relationship but has received the least attention. In the political process, the government can and does use the Internet to provide online information about election dates and voter registration, but until recently the use of the Internet to support elections was limited to speculation.

The 2000 Arizona Democratic presidential primary was the first binding political election to include Internet voting. The election began with an extensive education and outreach program for voters. The election also faced legal challenge and claims that Internet voting effectively discriminates against ethnic minorities, but the election was allowed to proceed. Voters were able to cast their ballots from home, work, or wherever they had Internet access. Voters were also able to cast ballots by mail and at regular polling places.

This unique election provides the opportunity and empirical data needed to examine the benefits and issues of Internet voting, especially in comparison to the 1996 Arizona Democratic presidential preference election. The 2000 election illustrated the use of Internet technology in the voting process, the effect it could have on voter participation, and issues that must be resolved for future Internet elections. As the first of its kind, it is likely to be the focus of future discussions of Internet voting.

* *The author would like to thank The PricewaterhouseCoopers Endowment for The Business of Government for its support of this research, and Suzanne Cummins, George Powers, Valorie Hanni Rice, and Christine Salterio for their invaluable assistance.*

The 2000 Arizona Democratic Presidential Preference Election

In March 2000, the Arizona Democratic presidential preference election became the first binding political election to include Internet voting. Beyond that critical difference, the 2000 primary election was similar in many ways to the 1996 primary election. Both presidential preference elections were run by the Arizona Democratic Party rather than the Arizona secretary of state. Although the Arizona secretary of state does run presidential preference elections for political parties, the Democratic National Committee rules on election timing precluded the presidential preference elections from being conducted by the Arizona secretary of state. In both primary elections, there was effectively only one candidate. In 1996, Bill Clinton ran unopposed. In 2000, both Al Gore and Bill Bradley campaigned in Arizona, but Bill Bradley withdrew from the election, leaving only one candidate on March 7, the first day of voting. The goal of Internet voting was to increase voter turnout. "The last time we held a primary, only 12,000 out of 880,000 registered Democrats turned out. We need to do something to change that," said then Democratic Party Chair Mark Fleisher (Salkowski, 2000). The similarities between the two elections make Internet voting, the primary difference between them, easier to evaluate.

The educational outreach, legality, process, and technology used in the 2000 Arizona Democratic presidential preference election were reported on during and after the election (e.g., Mohen & Glidden, 2001). The election process began weeks before polls opened with an extensive outreach effort to educate voters, followed by increasing other opportunities to vote (e.g., mail), and providing voters with ample time and support to cast their ballots. Concerns about the digital divide resulted in a lawsuit that attempted to preclude Internet voting. Less obvious to voters was the array of hardware, software, and cryptography that were used to ensure the secrecy and security of their votes. The outreach, legal challenge, process, and technology used in the election are detailed in this section.

2000 Arizona Democratic Presidential Preference Election Milestones

January	Education and outreach begins. Voting Integrity Project files suit.
February	Court declines to prohibit Internet voting.
March	Ballots cast on Internet and paper.

Outreach and Education

An extensive educational outreach program was launched two months before the election. The program began in January 2000, with the mailing of a notice printed in both English and Spanish to all registered Democrats in Arizona. The notice announced the upcoming presidential preference election and described how and when voters could participate in the election. Voters were provided guidance on how to vote by mail, vote on the Internet from any location, or vote at a polling place using the Internet or paper ballots. Election information was also promoted in 20 target publications and more than 170 print, television, and radio outlets.

A special outreach effort was directed at African-American, Hispanic, and Native-American communities and those with limited Internet access. The number of polling places was increased by 35 percent over the 1996 Arizona Democratic presidential preference election, and 30 Internet voting sites were identified in communities with limited Internet connectivity. And in cooperation with the Arizona Intertribal Council, special voting sites were established on reservations and off reservations in communities with Native-American populations. Election information was also posted on African-American, Hispanic, and Native-American websites.

Legal Challenge

In January 2000, the Voting Integrity Project filed suit in U.S. District Court to prohibit Internet voting in the 2000 Arizona Democratic presidential preference election. The Voting Integrity Project is a nonprofit organization that monitors election integrity and intervenes in instances of perceived voting impropriety. The focus of the suit was the extent of the digital divide and the disenfranchising effect it would have on ethnic minorities in an Internet election. The suit claimed that white voters are more likely to have Internet access from home than African-Americans and Hispanics have from any location. Moreover, African-American and Hispanic voters together were only 40 percent as likely as white voters to have Internet access at home. The U.S. attorney general did not oppose the Internet election, and the court ruled against the Voting Integrity Project.

Election Process

Votes were cast by mail, over the Internet, and at polling places using paper ballots or the Internet. The information that was mailed to all registered Democrats contained an application that could be returned in

Voting Alternatives in the 2000 Arizona Democratic Presidential Preference Election

- **Off site**—ballots cast on the Internet from outside the polling site
- **On site**—ballots cast on the Internet from inside the polling site
- **Paper**—ballots cast on paper at the polling site
- **Mail**—ballots cast by mail

exchange for a mail-in ballot. All registered Democrats were also mailed a random seven-digit alphanumeric personal identification number (PIN) to validate their eligibility to vote on the Internet. Remote Internet voters were required to affirm their eligibility to vote and were advised of the felonious nature of providing false information. Voters also had the option of voting at polling places (at any polling location within the state) using traditional paper ballots or personal computers with Internet access located at polling places. Even unregistered voters were permitted to register at the polling place and then vote on the same day. The same ballot could not be cast both on the Internet and at a polling place because the Internet voting server tracked whether or not an individual ballot had been cast and polling places did not open until off-site Internet voting had stopped.

The initial notices were mailed several weeks before the election to give voters time to consider their voting alternatives and to request a mail-in ballot if desired. Internet voting was open during the four-day period beginning on Tuesday, March 7, at 12:01 a.m. and ending at midnight on Friday, March 10. Polling place voting, for both paper and Internet ballots, was held on Saturday, March 11. Help desk support was available to voters who needed assistance in finding the website, configuring their computers, and navigating the ballot. A variety of observers were invited to monitor the election process, including citizens, the Big Five accounting firm KPMG, and the National Association for the Advancement of Colored People (NAACP), among others. This context of time, support, and oversight was the capstone of the voting process.

Technology

Remote Internet ballots were cast from a wide variety of personal computers and web browsers. Most combinations of computers and browsers proved to be compatible with the voting system, but some older browser versions did not support the security and privacy features required by the

Security Measures

- **Voter Identification**—personal identification numbers (PIN) required to vote on the Internet were mailed to voters.
- **Ballot Validation**—ballot validity was authenticated by the Internet voting server.
- **Data Encryption**—data were encrypted to ensure ballot secrecy.
- **Intrusion Protection**—hardware and software were protected against intrusion.
- **Audit Trails**—access to ballot data was automatically documented.

voting system. Free distribution of the latest versions of the most common web browsers permitted Internet voters to upgrade their browsers if necessary. A secure socket layer communication link between the voting server and the remote Internet voting clients was established with digital signatures. Secure socket layer technology is the same type of connection used for most banking and commercial Internet transactions. The voting system was protected by a series of redundant servers and electrical power systems. A network router failed shortly after the polls were opened, but it was repaired in less than one hour.

The highest levels of internal and external security were maintained during the election. Individual votes were protected by personal identification numbers, ballot validity control, and ballot encryption. At a higher level of aggregation, the database tables containing the votes were protected against insider malfeasance by encryption that prevented anyone except KPMG from knowing the content of the cast ballots. The computers that contained the tables were housed in an undisclosed location, and access to the computers was controlled by key card and biometric security systems. Denial of service attacks are a simple but effective means of overloading a server with more Internet traffic than it can handle, causing all communication to stop. Given the relative ease of mounting a denial of service attack, it is not surprising that the election was the target of multiple denial of service attacks. All of these attacks were defeated, and intrusion-detection applications protected against virus and Trojan horse attacks to cripple or otherwise manipulate the process or the votes.

The secrecy and security of the election was supported by the database design, cryptography, oversight, and audit trails that were built into the voting process. The database containing the ballots had separate tables for voter identification and ballot content. Once the voting system received a ballot cast by a voter, the system detached the identification from the content and stored this information in separate tables that could not be merged. Both tables were then encrypted, but only the ballot content table was

Voting Turnout in the 1996 and 2000 Arizona Democratic Presidential Preference Elections

Ballot Type	1996	2000
Off-site Internet	N/A	35,768
On-site Internet	N/A	4,174
Paper	12,651	14,217
Mail	233	32,748
Total	**12,884**	**86,907**

provided to KPMG for decryption and tabulation. Audit trails were used to monitor access to the data, hardware, and software. Audit logs recorded those who voted (but not for whom they voted), who accessed the database sever, and versions and changes of the software. Thus, secrecy and security of the votes were protected by a series of technical and procedural checks and balances.

The combination of outreach, legal argument, process, and technology used in the election achieved the goal of the Arizona Democratic Party, which was to increase voter turnout. More votes were cast from off-site Internet locations than any other location. The outreach effort increased voter awareness of different voting options, the window of opportunity, and the number of polling places. The court was not convinced that the extent of the digital divide would substantially impact the election results. Polling places were opened after remote Internet voting was closed so that any voter who tried unsuccessfully at the last minute to vote on the Internet would still have the opportunity to vote at a polling place the next day. The array of technology used in the election protected the secrecy and security of votes, and hardware malfunctions resulted in less than one hour of downtime in the 96-hour Internet voting period. Thus, the unique nature of the event was matched with an equally unique combination of outreach, legal support, process, and technology that resulted in a successful election.

Efficiency and Effectiveness

As older voting systems are replaced with more current technology, issues of efficiency and effectiveness will be important to election officials. The grim picture of Florida election workers interpreting the remnants of chads on punchcard ballots will be especially salient in the search for new equipment. Besides the absence of chads, Internet voting could result in other efficiency and effectiveness improvements. The 2000 Arizona Democratic presidential preference election experienced a dramatic increase in Internet voter participation without the need for additional precinct polling sites and workers to staff them. Moreover, this increased voter participation required no additional voting booths or printed ballots.

The efficiency and effectiveness of the voting technology that election officials adopt will also be important to voters. The number of remote Internet votes as compared to traditional votes cast in the 2000 Arizona Democratic presidential preference election suggests that efficiency and effectiveness are important considerations to voters. The savings in time and reduction of pollution produced by that level of increased voter participation on a national basis would be immense, even if voters spent only one hour and drove only one mile to vote. If just 1 percent of votes actually cast in the 2000 U.S. presidential election had been cast on the Internet, the nation would have saved more than 26,000 hours and thousands of pounds of auto emissions.

Thus, data from the 2000 Arizona Democratic presidential preference election and the follow-up survey suggest that there is indeed ample opportunity to improve the voting process. Survey responses suggest that 62 percent of the unregistered voting age population would register on the Internet, increasing registered voters to over 90 percent of the voting age population. Similarly impressive increases could be found with Internet voting. At a national level, Internet voting would have resulted in ballots from more than 71 percent of the voting age population in the 2000 U.S. presidential election. Also important are the increases in efficiency and effectiveness that would reduce pollution and the use of natural resources.

Arizona Citizen Attitudes toward Internet Voting

On November 7, 2000, the Arizona secretary of state and the Maricopa County recorder sponsored an Internet voting pilot demonstration in Phoenix. Voters were allowed to cast mock votes at a polling place on an Internet voting demonstration system and were then surveyed about their experience. Of the 116 respondents, only 3 percent preferred the existing voting system over Internet voting and 85 percent believed the Internet voting system to be at least as secure as the existing system.

In the spring of 2001, a survey conducted at the University of Arizona on Internet voting was sent to a sample of Arizona residents. The survey was mailed to 4,000 Arizona residents randomly selected from driver and identification license records, and completed surveys were returned by 495 respondents. Sampling from driver and identification license records provided better selection than voter registration records would have because the former includes people who are not currently registered to vote. The resulting sample reflected the characteristics of the Arizona and U.S. populations, except that respondents reported somewhat higher levels of education than average. More information on the sample characteristics can be found in the Appendix to this chapter.

The survey included sections containing items on voter registration, voter participation, computer technology, the 2000 Arizona Democratic presidential preference election, and demographic identifiers. Registered voters were asked to identify their political party affiliation, and those who were not registered voters were asked if they would use the Internet to register if they could do so. Respondents who voted in the 2000 presidential election were asked what method they used to vote and the candidate for which they voted, and those who did not vote were asked which candidate they would have selected if they had voted. Respondents were asked if current or future computer technology could provide secure and reliable Internet voting. Finally, respondents were also asked if they would have voted on the Internet in the 2000 U.S. presidential election if it had been an option and the method (including the Internet) they would prefer to use in the next presidential election.

The survey contained a section for registered Democrats eligible to vote in the 2000 Arizona Democratic presidential preference election. Respondents were asked if and how they voted in this election. Respondents were also asked about the extent of their Internet access at the time of the election and if they received their voting PIN while the polls were open. A series of questions were directed at those respondents who voted on the Internet during this election. These respondents were asked if they experienced any technical difficulty with their computers or the voting website. They were also asked if they were able to successfully cast their ballot on the Internet. Finally, they were asked if their Internet voting experience was easier, faster, more economical, or made the difference between voting or not as compared to the traditional voting process.

The last part of the survey contained items on demographic identifiers and Internet connectivity. Respondents were asked to identify their sex, age, ethnicity, education, and range of household income. Respondents were also asked about their access to the Internet at home, school, work, public libraries, or other places (e.g., church, club, etc.). Respondents who did not have access to the Internet at any location were asked if they expected to get access within three, six, or 12 months, or if they ever expected to have Internet access.

Voter Registration

When those respondents who were not currently registered to vote were asked if they would register if able to do so on the Internet, 62 percent indicated that they would register to vote (see Table 7.1). Equal proportions (62 percent) of men and women would register on the Internet, and age was not a significant predictor of willingness to register on the Internet. A majority of all ethnic groups reported that they would register on the Internet. White respondents were the most likely to register on the Internet, but they were also the most likely not to register on the Internet. Education increased the likelihood of Internet voter registration, but the majority of respondents in all income groups reported that they would register on the Internet.

Table 7.1: Currently Unregistered Arizona Voters Who Would Use Internet for Voter Registration (percent)

		No	Not Sure	Yes
Total		**23.2**	**14.8**	**62.0**
Gender	Female	28.4	9.5	62.1
	Male	17.6	20.6	61.8
Ethnicity	Native American	0.0	0.0	0.0
	Asian	0.0	42.9	57.1
	Black	0.0	33.3	66.7
	Hispanic	21.7	17.4	60.9
	White	25.0	12.0	63.0
Education	Grade School	33.3	22.2	44.5
	High School/GED	21.8	18.2	60.0
	College	23.4	10.4	66.2
Income	Prefer not to answer	28.6	25.7	45.7
	Less than $30,000	14.3	25.0	60.7
	$30,001–$60,000	18.4	10.5	71.1
	$60,001–$90,000	20.0	0.0	80.0
	More than $90,000	29.4	5.9	64.7

(N = 495)

The survey results suggest that the Internet could dramatically increase voter registration across all sex, age, ethnicity, and education groups. These results undermine the claim that voter registration would effectively benefit only white voters. White respondents were more likely than any other ethnic group not to register on the Internet. In the context of the entire voting age population in the United States, if just half of the 24 percent of the unregistered voting age population actually did register on the Internet, there would be an additional 25 million registered voters.

Voter Participation

About 42 percent of all survey respondents indicated that they would have voted on the Internet in the 2000 U.S. presidential election if it had been an option (see Table 7.2). What people report that they would do is not always what they actually would do, so it is striking that almost the same percent (41 percent) of all votes in the 2000 Arizona Democratic presidential preference election were cast on the Internet. In addition, the number of traditional paper ballots cast in the 1996 and 2000 Arizona Democratic presidential preference elections was about the same. The survey results revealed that education and income increased somewhat the likelihood of Internet voting and are consistent with findings reported by Solop (2001).

In the 2000 Arizona Democratic presidential preference election, the number of off-site Internet votes was more than two and one-half times the number of paper ballots cast at polling places. In 2000, more than 105 million votes were cast for U.S. presidential candidates. If Internet voting had been available and resulted in the same increased participation as it did in the 2000 Arizona Democratic presidential preference election, then about 71 percent of the voting age population would have voted. This result contradicts speculation (e.g., Internet Policy Institute, 2001; Mohen & Glidden, 2001) that Internet voting would have little effect on voter participation.

Internet Access

Although the 2000 Arizona Democratic presidential preference survived legal challenge, the extent of the digital divide is crucial to the propriety of Internet voting. Data from the follow-up survey did not support the extent of the digital divide suggested by the Voting Integrity Project. Taken together, 89 percent of African-American and Hispanic respondents had Internet access at some location, as compared to 79 percent of white respondents who reported having Internet access at home. In addition, African-American and Hispanic respondents together were 81 percent as

Table 7.2: Would Have Voted on the Internet in 2000 (percent)

		No	Not Sure	Yes
Total		**38.3**	**19.5**	**42.2**
Gender	Female	38.4	19.0	42.6
	Male	38.2	20.0	41.8
Ethnicity	Native American	33.3	33.3	33.3
	Asian	30.8	30.8	38.4
	Black	50.0	16.7	33.3
	Hispanic	36.6	22.0	41.5
	White	38.4	18.8	42.8
Education	Grade School	43.8	31.2	25.0
	High School/GED	43.7	15.2	41.1
	College	35.2	21.3	43.5
Income	Prefer not to answer	45.0	19.5	35.5
	Less than $30,000	40.0	21.3	38.7
	$30,001–$60,000	41.2	18.4	40.4
	$60,001–$90,000	29.5	17.9	52.6
	More than $90,000	22.4	23.9	53.7

(N = 495)

likely as their white counterparts to have Internet access at home. Although a digital divide still exists, it appears to be narrowing with time.

Potential Advantages of Internet Voting

The Internet presents an opportunity for improving democracy and the process by which it is achieved. The registration and participation of voters that is essential to a healthy democracy could be increased with Internet technology. The digital divide between those who do and do not have computers and access to the Internet decreases every day as Internet technology becomes more affordable. Internet voting could also create gains in efficiency and effectiveness for voting technology, democracy, and the voting process. Despite the controversy and delay created by punchcard ballot technology in the 2000 U.S. presidential election, most jurisdictions do not have the resources to replace their punchcard ballot devices or other outdated voting equipment. As a remedy, the Ney-Hoyer bill (H.R. 3295, "Help America Vote Act of 2001," passed the House in December 2001) provides $2.65 billion over three years for jurisdictions to improve voting equipment, voter registration lists, and poll worker training. Included in the bill is $400 million to fund the replacement of punchcard voting machines. Internet technology could replace some of the voting machines in use today on a more cost-effective basis than simply replacing them with other poll site voting machines. In this section, each of these opportunities is discussed in more detail.

Easing Voter Registration

In 2001, the National Commission on Federal Election Reform published its report on recommendations to improve the federal election process. The first of 13 recommendations was the development and implementation of a computerized voter registration system that provides access to any jurisdiction within a state and shares information with other states. Internet voter registration could efficiently and effectively accomplish this and could also increase overall voter registration, especially among young people, who have always had the lowest levels of voter registration. Among registered voters there are millions of record changes each year and a substantial number of duplicate registrations. The opportunity for Internet voter registration to improve these conditions is described below.

Estimates of voter registration are based on the voting age population, which is the number of people in the United States who are at least 18 years of age. Because this population includes many people who are not eligible to vote (e.g., non-citizens, convicted felons, etc.), the percentage of the voting age population who are registered to vote is not accurate. However, it remains the basis for voting analyses and can be considered to yield conservative estimates of voter registration. That is, the true percentage of registered voters should be no less than the estimate and probably higher. In the 2000 U.S. presidential election, approximately 76 percent of the voting age population was registered to vote. Currently, an increase in registered voters equal to just 1 percent of the voting age population would result in over 2 million more registered voters.

The National Voter Registration Act of 1993 (NVRA) was designed to:

- Establish procedures to increase the number of registered voters for elections for federal office;
- Assist all levels of government in increasing voter registration and participation;

- Protect the integrity of the electoral process; and
- Ensure the accuracy and currency of voter registration rolls.

The NVRA also requires the Federal Election Commission (FEC) to maintain a voter registration form that does not require notarization or formal authentication and to report to Congress every two years on the effect of the NVRA. Internet voter registration could help accomplish all four goals of the NVRA by increasing the ease of registering and updating for voters and the efficiency of maintenance and validation for election officials.

The FEC reports to Congress on voter registration and ways to improve the process. From 1995 to 1998, in 43 states and the District of Columbia almost 77 million voter registration transactions were processed (FEC, 1997, 1999). About 59 percent of those transactions were first time or inter-jurisdictional changes, and the remaining 41 percent were intra-jurisdictional changes of name and address. During this time, there were more than 4 million duplicate voter registrations. The FEC also recommends that voter registration be maintained on statewide computer systems with online access by all local jurisdictions. Even if all first-time registrations were manually processed, subsequent updates processed on the Internet could decrease the enormous administrative burden and duplicate registrations currently experienced.

Thus, the Internet could increase voter registration, further the goals of the NVRA, and increase the speed and accuracy of voter registration transactions. Internet voter registration may be especially appealing to 18- to 20-year-old voters, who have had the lowest rates of voter registration since 1971, when the voting age was lowered from 21 to 18 years. Beyond advancing the goals of the NVRA, Internet voter registration would fulfill the FEC's consistent recommendation that voter registration records be maintained on a computer network with access at every jurisdiction office. The flexible nature of the Internet would allow voter registration records to be maintained at the national, state, or local level yet remain available to users at any location who need access to those records.

Increasing Voter Participation

The Internet can create an opportunity to convert increased voter registration into increased voter participation. In 2000, about 50 percent of the voting age population cast ballots in the presidential election, and that number could have been much higher with Internet voting. The close results of the 2000 presidential election illustrate how important individual votes can be (even in an electoral college system), and Internet voting could answer the demand for increased voter participation in future elections. Historically, rates of voter participation are generally stable across gender, age, and ethnicity. Rates of voter participation for various demographic groups and the effect Internet voting could have on voter participation among some of those least likely to vote are reviewed in this section.

Voting patterns in U.S. presidential elections are largely stable, but do shift occasionally. Slightly more than 50 percent of the voting age population voted in the 2000 election, down from an average of 57.6 percent of the voting age population who voted in the years 1972–1996. In the 1970s, men voted at slightly higher rates than women, but that trend reversed in 1980 and since then women have participated at slightly higher rates than men. Rates of voter participation consistently increase with age, except that in the years 1972–1984 rates of participation were lower for retirement-age voters than for those who were approaching retirement. But since 1988, rates of voter participation have been the highest among those who are 65 and older. Voter participation is weakest among 18- to 20-year-olds, whose participation rate of 37 percent is about half that of those who are 65 and older. A more constant pattern is the ethnic distribution of voter participation, which is led by whites (61 percent), followed by blacks (52 percent), and Hispanics (31 percent). Internet voting could increase levels of voter participation among everyone, especially those in the 18–20 age group.

Internet voting could increase rates of voter participation for those who are or will become part of the voting age population by increasing opportunities to vote, especially from home. According to 2000 census data, almost 54 million households had at least one computer and 81 percent of those also had access to the Internet. Men have slightly more computer and Internet access than women. Computer and Internet access increases with age until 44, after which it drops sharply. Patterns of computer and Internet access for ethnic groups mirror those of voter participation, with the highest levels of computer and Internet access reported by whites, followed by blacks and Hispanics.

Internet voting could have a balancing effect on voter participation because some of these computer and Internet access trends complement those of voter participation. For example, slightly more women vote than men, but men have slightly more computer and Internet access than women. Similarly, the youngest possible voters have the most computer and Internet access while the oldest voters have the least access. Internet voting would not only increase opportunities to vote from home, but also from school, work, public libraries, Internet cafes, and any other place around the world where the Internet can be accessed.

Increasing voter participation is the most often cited benefit of Internet voting. Because of increasing access to and use of the Internet, many people rely on it for personal and business transactions. The demographic characteristics of the current voting age population suggest that with Internet voting, the lower voter participation of men and young people could be improved because of their higher computer and Internet access. In addition, many of tomorrow's voters are currently exposed to and learning about Internet technology. About 70 percent of children in the 12–17 age group have a computer at home and about 69 percent of those also have Internet access, beyond what access they might have at school or other locations. By the time Internet voting could be possible, this group may not remember life without the Internet.

Improving Efficiency and Effectiveness

While the most obvious and perhaps most desirable benefits that the Internet could provide to the election process are increases in voter registration and voter participation, less obvious increases in efficiency and effectiveness are also desirable. One of the older forms of voting technology, mechanical lever machines, are no longer in production, and individual jurisdictions are considering newer voting technology to replace these machines. At the national level, increases in the efficiency and effectiveness of the democratic process could result in a more active and inclusive political process that could inspire higher rates of voter participation. The economic costs of elections could also be reduced with Internet voting. In this section, these opportunities for increased efficiency and effectiveness are examined.

Internet voting should not eliminate current voting technology, but rather complement it by improving the efficiency and effectiveness of balloting. Currently, five types of voting technology are used in the United States. The oldest form is the paper ballot, which is often used in smaller communities. Mechanical lever machines do not mark ballots but simply total the votes cast. Punchcard systems provide voters with a ballot in which holes are punched to identify their vote. Optical scanners can be used to tabulate ballots marked by voters. More recently, direct recording electronic systems have been used, which are an electronic version of the mechanical lever machine. Internet voting would be a distributed version of direct recording electronic systems, with a voting booth at every point of Internet access in the world.

Internet voting could increase the efficiency and effectiveness of the democratic process. For example, one reason that potential voters might not vote is that they feel removed from the process by relatively infrequent elections. Internet voting would allow elections to be held more frequently and thus allow voters to maintain a higher baseline level of participation in the process. Internet voting would also require elected officials to be more responsive to their constituents. One reason for this is that more frequent elections would require elected officials to maintain more frequent communication with their constituents, rather than just at election time. Another reason is that incumbents who do not represent the will of their constituents could no longer rely on the difficulty of mounting a recall election to maintain their position.

Internet voting could also reduce the cost of elections to society. As worthwhile as elections are, they represent a significant investment in time, money, and natural resources. Voting may take employees away from their jobs, which not only reduces productivity at the national level but may also require hourly employees to take time off at their own expense. A national voting holiday, as recommended by the National Commission on Federal Election Reform (2001), might increase voter participation but could result in even more lost productivity and wages than is currently experienced. Internet voting could also reduce the amount of natural resources consumed by elections. For example, the amount of paper used for ballots would be reduced, as would petroleum used to make special trips to polling places.

Thus, the Internet could create a more efficient and effective voting process. The Internet would be an efficient and effective voting technology, and is not far removed from the direct recording electronic voting systems in use today that do not use ballots but simply record votes in an electronic medium. Increased levels of democratic activity made practical by the efficiency and effectiveness of the Internet could lead to higher levels of participation by voters and accountability by elected officials if elections became more commonplace. This would be especially true for referendum elections. The efficiency and effectiveness of Internet voting could also result in increased voter participation while at the same time reducing income losses for employees who must take time off from work to vote and productivity losses for the organizations that employ them.

Clearly, there are numerous opportunities to improve voter registration, participation, efficiency, and effectiveness, and the Internet could deliver improvements in all of these areas. In concert with the recommendations of the National Commission on Federal Election Reform (2001) and the Federal Election Commission (1997, 1999), the Internet would create a computerized voter registration system that might not only increase voter registration but also increase the accuracy of the voter registration rolls. Internet voting could also increase rates of participation among those in the voting age population who have been the least likely to vote. The economies of scale that can be achieved with the Internet could also make the voting process much more efficient and effective. However, while the Internet could yield many benefits to the democratic process, there are three key sets of issues that must be overcome to achieve those benefits.

Key Issues to Be Resolved

The primary challenges facing Internet voting systems come from technical, legal, and social domains. Advances in Internet technology now allow commerce and banking to be securely transacted on the Internet, but even more advanced technologies would be required to maintain the security and secrecy of Internet voting at the client, server, and communication levels. Equally stringent will be the legal tests that Internet voting must pass so that it does not result in discrimination in voter registration or voting. At the societal level, Internet voting would require the integration of a sophisticated information system into a population with widely varying knowledge, skills, abilities, and attitudes toward computers. In this section, each of these challenges to Internet voting is discussed in more detail.

Technological Issues

The function of Internet voting systems requires them to be founded on unprecedented technology. This technology must meet the demands of providing the utmost security and secrecy for voters while remaining a viable voting alternative. Security must be maintained at the individual level (e.g., precluding ineligible voters) and at the systemic level (e.g., precluding computer viruses). To achieve this level of security, advancements will have to be made in areas such as identification and cryptography. In general, the technical issues of Internet voting are in the domains of the client, server, and communication path (Internet Policy Institute, 2001).

The Internet voting client is the platform of hardware and software used by the voter to cast a ballot and may be the most likely point at which a malicious object (e.g., software virus) may enter the voting system. For remote Internet voting, the Internet voting clients are the computer systems at home, work, and other locations that may be accessed by multiple users and have various points of entry (e.g., floppy disk, CD-ROM, or Internet link) for malicious objects such as computer viruses. Remote Internet clients

Key Technology Concepts

- **Client**—combination of hardware and software used by voters to cast ballots
- **Server**—combination of hardware and software used to receive, decrypt, tally, and archive ballots
- **Communication Path**—route and medium used to link the client with the server

could also include other points of Internet access, such as Internet appliances, WebTV, and cell phones. For kiosk Internet voting, the voting client is the voting terminal or booth that would be located in a public place (e.g., shopping mall) and would require constant monitoring to maintain adequate security. Computer-enabled kiosks are currently used in airports, shopping malls, and other locations to provide customer service. Finally, for poll site Internet voting, the Internet voting client is the voting terminal or booth that would be located in the polling place, similar to a traditional voting booth, and it would provide the least opportunity for the introduction of a computer virus. These clients could be identical to the kiosks but located at the poll site.

The Internet voting server is the system of hardware and software that receives, decrypts, tallies, and archives the votes. The server is vulnerable to various types of penetration attacks that could corrupt the voting process. One type of penetration attack is the Trojan horse, which spreads like a virus throughout the system and could permanently delete or alter votes. Another type of penetration attack is a remote control program, which can turn the target into a computer zombie that operates normally for legitimate operators but also provides complete access and control to illegitimate operators who, operating from anywhere in the world, could stuff or loot the electronic ballot box. Another type of server-based attack on Internet voting could be mounted with spoof servers, which are impostors designed to lure voters away from authentic Internet voting servers. Votes cast at these spoof servers could be lost forever—or, even worse, modified and passed on to an authentic Internet voting server.

The communication path refers to the route and medium used by the client to send the vote to the server. A secure communication path must maintain encrypted data and an authenticated communication link between the client and the server. With current technology, votes could be encrypted but an authenticated communication link between the client and server cannot be guaranteed. The most likely threat to the communication link is an attempt to simply disrupt the link rather than to alter the communication, a technique referred to as a denial of service attack. This type of attack occurs when the server is overwhelmed with more requests than it can handle and shuts down until the attack is over, thereby disrupting the voting process. Currently, denial of service attacks cannot be defended against without shutting down the communication link and effectively accomplishing the goal of the attacker.

Two important technical issues were illustrated in the 2000 Arizona Democratic presidential preference election. The first is the identification and validation of voters. Voters must have a valid registration and that registration must be verified by the Internet voting system. The challenge here is to provide voters with a unique identifier that can be used in the ballot

Internet Voting Client Access

- **Remote**—access from any Internet location
- **Kiosk**—access from public places (e.g., shopping centers)
- **Poll Site**—access at traditional polling places using personal computers

authentication process. The second issue is to maintain the security and reliability of the Internet voting system so that the voting process is not disrupted or delayed. The security of the system must withstand sabotage from both internal and external forces, and the reliability of the system must be ensured with redundant resources.

In the 2000 Arizona Democratic presidential preference election, voters were mailed a randomly generated seven-digit alphanumeric code to be used when voting from remote Internet locations. With about 2 billion permutations of such a code and additional challenge questions to establish the identity of the voter, the identification of voters was not as much an issue as the communication of that identification to the voters. Some voters did not receive their code during the window of remote Internet voting opportunity. Internet voting server security was maintained with biometric identification and firewalls. The vulnerability proved to be with the reliability of the system when a router failed and redundant equipment did not respond.

Although the technical issues of Internet voting are not likely to be insurmountable, they are significant. Under current technological conditions, remote Internet voting would create the greatest risk to the security and secrecy of votes while kiosk and poll site Internet voting would create less risk with monitoring. Servers may be vulnerable to sophisticated viruses or simplistic denial of service attacks. The communication path, which may be international, could also be compromised. Thus, the technical issues that must be resolved before Internet voting can be implemented in public elections are challenging, but no less so than the legal and social issues.

Legal Issues

Although the initial ruling on Internet voting was favorable, Internet voting must face review by the two agencies primarily responsible for regulating election process and technology in the United States, the Department of Justice and the Federal Election Commission. The Department of Justice enforces the Voting Rights Act, which prohibits voting processes and procedures that discriminate based on race or color. The Federal Election Commission maintains voting system performance and test standards to ensure the technical integrity of elections. Internet voting is a change in the democratic process that both of these agencies must address before it could be implemented in public elections.

The Voting Rights Act

The Voting Rights Act of 1965, together with amendments in 1970 and 1982 and numerous interpretations, consists of three main parts. The first part was designed to enforce the 15th Amendment and contains basic provisions against racial discrimination in voting, the application of dissimilar standards, disqualification by immaterial irregularities on voter registration, and qualification testing. The second part, known as Section 2, specifically prohibits any qualification or process that denies or abridges the right to vote on account of race or color. Finally, the third part, known as Section 5, prohibits changes in voting process or procedure that result in more racial discrimination in voting than currently exists.

> **Voting Rights Act**
>
> Voting Rights Act prohibits discriminatory:
> - Standards
> - Processes
> - Changes

Department of Justice

The Department of Justice is responsible for protecting voting rights through the enforcement of the Voting Rights Act. Under Section 2, the Department of Justice takes legal action on behalf of those whose voting rights are currently being violated on the basis of race or color. Under Section 5, proposed changes in existing voting process or procedure must be reviewed and approved by the Department of Justice before the changes can be implemented. Internet voting would be a change in voting process or procedure that the Department of Justice must review and approve before it could be implemented in public elections.

Federal Election Commission

The Federal Election Commission develops and implements performance and test standards for voting technology and equipment. In 1975, the first report on computerized voting technology was issued. During the 1980s,

> **Changes in Voting Standards and Processes**
>
> Changes in voting standards and processes must be approved by either:
> - U.S. attorney general, or
> - Federal court in the District of Columbia

more standards were developed, and in 1990 the first performance and test standards were issued for computerized voting systems. The performance standards describe the functional and technical requirements for voting systems while the test standards describe the process and criteria for evaluating voting systems. The Federal Election Commission, in collaboration with the National Association of State Election Directors, assists voting jurisdictions in the application of voting system performance and test standards.

The updated voting system performance and test standards include guidelines for Internet voting systems to assure that they are as accurate, reliable, and secure as other voting systems. The new standards, reflecting the issues raised in the Internet Policy Institute (2001) report, address Internet voting at poll sites, supervised remote sites, and unsupervised remote sites. The standards provide guidelines for hardware components (e.g., computer equipment used for poll site as well as supervised and unsupervised remote sites), software modules (e.g., encryption, decryption, and security) and communication (e.g., privacy, reliability, and durability). These standards will naturally evolve as Internet technology continues to develop.

Thus, Internet voting will have to face the regulatory challenge of the Department of Justice and the Federal Election Commission. The objective of voting laws enforced by the Department of Justice is to ensure that voters are able to participate in elections without discrimination based on race or color. The objective of the voting system standards developed by the Federal Election Commission is to ensure that all votes are validated and counted. These two agencies, responsive to the complementary needs for elections that are legally and technically viable, are vital in protecting the integrity of the democratic process.

Key Legal Issues

- Does increasing the opportunity to vote for some effectively reduce the opportunity to vote for others?
- Does the digital divide substantially follow ethnic distributions?

Social Issues

Advances in technology and favorable legal rulings would not necessarily make the Internet a socially appropriate addition to the voting process. If protected classes (i.e., ethnic minorities) of the voting age population do not have ready access (e.g., at home) to the Internet, this could be a violation of the Voting Rights Act. A more complicated issue is the prospect of a digital divide that isolates those who are not protected by the Voting Rights Act. One possibility would be to enact special laws that regulate Internet voting, but that solution lacks parsimony. Another possibility would be to increase the number of protected classes under the Voting Rights Act, but that could create more problems than it solves. The solution to this issue is not clear.

Data from the follow-up survey reveal that about 92 percent of the respondents reported having Internet access at home, school, work, public libraries, or some other location. Since Internet voting from home is likely to be the most convenient voting location, an examination of home Internet access is most relevant. Equal proportions of men and women reported having Internet access at home, and ethnic background was not a strong determinant of Internet access at home. However, those who were younger, more educated, and reported higher incomes were more likely to have Internet access at home than their counterparts. However, age, education, and income are not protected classes under the Voting Rights Act.

Several social aspects of Internet voting must be explored to evaluate the compatibility of Internet voting with society. As with any new information technology system, a wide variety of individuals and government agencies would need to learn how to operate an Internet voting system. One of the most, if not the most, important social impacts of Internet voting is the effect it could have on voter participation. However, if Internet voting had no impact on voter participation or a race-differentiated effect, then it would be ineffective if not illegal. These important social considerations are considered below.

There are a number of individual and organizational factors that can impact the ability of governments to use information technology in general. Dawes, Bloniarz, Kelly, and Fletcher (1999) note that individuals learn and adapt to information systems to varying degrees. They also suggest that more than 80 percent of information systems fail to be implemented or fail to achieve their objectives when they are implemented. One reason for this high failure rate may be that individuals may be inside the organization (e.g., employees) or outside the organization (e.g., clients), but both must interact with information systems to achieve the goals of the organization.

At the organizational level, Dawes et al. (1999) observe that organizations in the Information Age are much more fluid and dynamic than the structured hierarchy that characterized organizations in the Industrial Age. In more contemporary organizations, information technology may be used to enable individuals (both inside and outside the organization) rather than to control them. Although information systems can permit organizations to rapidly respond to the demands of the environment, the organization must also value needed change. Because of their size, complexity, and inertia, government agencies may face perhaps the most challenge in designing and utilizing information systems.

There are also several social issues specific to Internet voting systems (Internet Policy Institute, 2000). Some of these issues are or can be addressed by law or regulation. For example, access to the Internet for voter registration may fall under the auspices of the National Voter Registration Act. Similarly, the demographics of voter access to the Internet might effectively discriminate against protected classes identified in the Voting Rights Act. Internet voting could also impact the process and administration of elections, currently guided by voting system performance standards. No less important is the impact Internet voting could have on the roles of federal, state, and local government in the election process.

Perhaps more difficult to address are the social issues of Internet voting that are not informed by law or regulation (Internet Policy Institute, 2000). Previous attempts to increase voter participation by lowering barriers to voting have not inspired disaffected voters. But more important than just casting votes is casting informed votes, and the proliferation of dubious information on the Internet could result in misinformed voters. Alternatively, decreasing barriers to voters (however informed) could increase the number of referenda, thus undermining the deliberate and representative nature of the U.S. political system. Furthermore, remote Internet voting could similarly undermine the social cohesion that results from traditional voting.

The development of Internet voting systems will require an investment of years and millions of dollars. Before such an investment is made, the social aspects of Internet voting should be explored to determine how it can generate the highest social return. This return on investment may be weakened by the challenges of implementing large-scale information systems, monolithic voter apathy, or the relative disenfranchisement of certain voters. Ultimately, while it is almost certain that public Internet voting system technology can be developed, it is much less certain that the effects of such technology will be socially effective or even desirable.

Thus, the technical, legal, and social challenges to Internet voter registration and voting are formidable. New levels of information technology secrecy and security will have to be achieved before Internet voter registration and voting would be possible, but advances in cryptography and secure web transactions suggest that achievement of these new levels is not impossible. Legal structures that are designed to protect against discrimination in voter registration and voting must be applied to the Internet just as they would be applied to any other proposed change in the electoral process. Social structures, which are often difficult if not practically impossible to change, must also adopt or adapt to Internet voter registration and voting to make such an investment worthwhile. The failure of Internet voter registration and voting to meet any one of these challenges will eliminate any possibility of success.

Conclusion and Recommendations

The Internet was successfully used as a voting technology in the 2000 Arizona Democratic presidential preference election. This success was due in part to the considerable effort invested in voter outreach and education, and similar efforts would be important in future elections that include Internet voting. The Internet voting servers experienced no breach of security and only minimal downtime. The original goal of the Internet voting, increasing voter participation, was clearly achieved. More votes were cast on the Internet than any other means and were about three times the total number of votes cast in the 1996 Arizona Democratic presidential preference election.

Based on the results of the 2000 Arizona Democratic presidential preference election and the follow-up survey conducted at the University of Arizona, the future of Internet voting systems appears promising. It seems likely that voter registration and participation would increase on the Internet, and the entire voting process would be more effective and efficient than it currently is. In addition, technical, legal, and social challenges were met and may set a precedent for future online elections. However, these preliminary findings on the success and effectiveness of Internet voting must be followed by additional exploration, such as the research agenda cogently outlined by the Internet Policy Institute (2001) and the following recommendations.

Recommendation 1: State and local jurisdictions should continue to experiment with Internet voting.

The development of Internet voting system technology should be tested in binding political elections whenever possible. The development of this kind of technology should not be undertaken in the social vacuum of a test laboratory. Ideal elections for this kind of testing are local elections of limited scope such as for school board and city council members. Internet voting systems should not be afforded any technological quarter. Rather, the voting should be vetted under real world conditions to determine what improvements, if any, would result in an Internet voting system reliable and secure enough for a national election.

Recommendation 2: In concert with state and local experimentation, the level of research and development to improve Internet transaction security should be increased.

The experience of the 2000 Arizona Democratic presidential preference election illustrates the importance of robust Internet voting technology. Resistant to security threats, the Internet voting system used in that election was disabled, if only temporarily, by an internal hardware malfunction. Additional research by information technology experts in academia and industry is needed to develop Internet voting servers that are secure while accommodating as many different voting clients as possible. Refinements in encryption and secure Internet transmission are also needed to communicate the ballot intact without revealing the identity of the voter.

Recommendation 3: Social scientists should study the effect of Internet voting.

Voter Participation

Social science must study the individual and social effects of an Internet voting system. The voting age population consists of individuals, and research must continue to study the effect of an Internet voting system on voter registration and participation. Individual characteristics such as age, income, education, attitudes toward computers, and access to the Internet can contribute to the likelihood of registering and voting on the Internet. Research must determine whether an Internet voting system will increase voter registration and participation or if it would decrease, perhaps through increased suspicion by voters.

Democratic Process

Social science research must also study the societal effects of Internet voting systems. Currently, the white voting age population does have more Internet access than most other ethnic minorities, so the effect of the digital divide on social equality in the political process remains a critical research topic. The economies of scale created by an Internet voting system have direct implications for democracy. Social and political scientists must consider the effect that cost-effective elections will have on the frequency of elections. Similarly, research must address the changing role of federal, state, and local governments in a centralized voting structure.

Ultimately, these issues can be resolved, and Internet voter registration and voting may prove to be the catalyst that includes the isolated, inspires the disaffected, and motivates the apathetic people in the voting age population who do not currently participate in the democratic process. It may also be the agent that drives the accountability of elected officials to levels that eliminate and preclude those who do not represent their constituency. Internet voting systems should be neither accepted nor rejected out of hand. Instead, the opportunities and challenges they present should be the focus of vigorous research that can assist policy makers as they consider the role of the Internet in the democratic process.

Appendix: Research Methodology

This study relied in part on a survey research methodology. The survey was mailed to 4,000 people randomly selected from the best database available of Arizona residents. The survey contained items on voter registration, voter participation, Internet voting, and demographic characteristics. Completed surveys were returned by 495 respondents who generally characterized—but reported higher education and income than—the Arizona and U.S. populations.

Sampling

A database of 5.6 million driver and identification licenses from the Arizona Department of Transportation, Motor Vehicle Division, provided the basis for the sample. This source of records was selected over voter registration files because the latter does not reflect those who are not registered to vote but who might in the future. Moreover, the license database is likely to provide the most robust representation of Arizona residents that can be obtained because of the ubiquitous requirement for government-issued identification for transactions such as cashing checks and purchasing tobacco and alcohol. The complete database was transferred to the University of Arizona mainframe computer, and a random sample of 4,000 Arizona residents at least 18 years of age was selected to receive the survey.

Survey

The survey was printed on University of Arizona letterhead and included a cover letter that described the purpose of the study as one on voting and computer technology. The survey instrument measured a variety of variables on voter registration status, voter participation, and likelihood to vote on the Internet. A special section for those who were eligible to vote in the 2000 Arizona Democratic presidential preference election contained items on voting behavior during that election. The final part contained items measuring demographic characteristics. The survey and a postage paid business reply envelope were mailed to the 4,000 randomly selected residents, and the completed surveys were coded and subjected to statistical analyses.

Sample

Completed surveys were returned by 495 respondents that generally represent the voting age population in Arizona and the United States. The sample consisted of 53 percent women and 47 percent men, as compared to 51 percent women and 49 percent men in Arizona and the United States. The age of the respondents ranged from 18 to 94 years, with a median age of 51 years. The median age of the Arizona and U.S. populations are 34 and 35 respectively, but this includes those who are under 18 years old. About 87 percent of the respondents reported being of white ethnicity, more than the 75 percent white composition of Arizona and the United States. However, about 23 percent of the respondents considered themselves to be multi-ethnic, considerably more than the approximately 3 percent of the Arizona and U.S. populations who consider themselves to be multi-ethnic. About 31 percent of the respondents reported having completed a high school education, slightly more than the 26 percent of the Arizona population and 30 percent of the U.S. population. More than 65 percent of the respondents reported having at least a bachelor's degree, which is considerably more than the 20 percent of the Arizona and U.S. populations. About 21 percent of the respondents reported household incomes of less than $30,000, somewhat less than the 53 percent and 50 percent of the Arizona and U.S. populations reporting similar incomes. About 32 percent of the respondents were registered Democrats and 46 percent were registered Republicans, as compared to the 38 percent of registered Democrats and 43 percent of registered Republicans in Arizona. Thus, the respondents in this study were generally characteristic of the Arizona and U.S. populations, but reported somewhat higher levels of education.

Bibliography

Dawes, S. S., P. A. Bloniarz, K. L. Kelly, and P. D. Fletcher. (1999). *Some Assembly Required: Building a digital government for the 21st century.* Albany, N.Y.: University at Albany, SUNY, Center for Technology in Government.

Federal Election Commission. (1997). *The Impact of the National Voter Registration Act of 1993 on the Administration of Federal Elections.* Washington, D.C.: Author.

Federal Election Commission. (1999). *The Impact of the National Voter Registration Act on the Administration of Elections for Federal Office 1997-1998.* Washington, D.C.: Author.

Hiller, J. S., and F. Bélanger. (2001). *Privacy Strategies for Electronic Government.* Arlington, Va.: The PricewaterhouseCoopers Endowment for The Business of Government.

Internet Policy Institute. (2001). *Report on the National Workshop on Internet Voting: Issues and research agenda.* Washington, D.C.: Author.

Mohen, J., and J. Glidden. (2001). "The Case for Internet Voting." *Communications of the ACM* 44: 72, 74-85.

National Commission on Federal Election Reform. (2001). *To Assure Pride and Confidence in the Electoral Process.* New York: The Century Foundation.

National Voter Registration Act, 42 U.S.C. § 1973 et seq.

Phillips, D. M., and H. A. Von Spakovsky. (2001). "Gauging the Risks of Internet Elections." *Communications of the ACM* 44: 73-85.

Salkowski, J. (2000, March 5). "Local Hispanic Leaders Assail Internet Vote." *The Arizona Daily Star,* p. A1.

Solop, F. I. (2001). "Digital Democracy Comes of Age: Internet voting and the 2000 Arizona Democratic primary election." *PS: Political Science and Politics* 34: 289-293.

Voting Rights Act, 42 U.S.C. § 1971 et seq.

PART IV

Challenges Facing E-Government

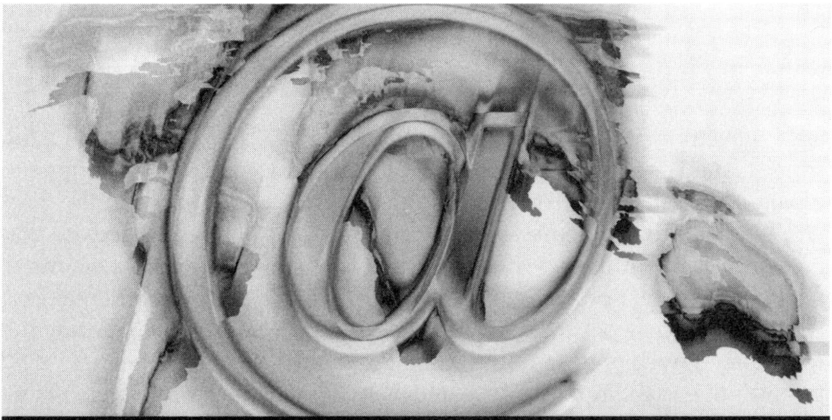

CHAPTER EIGHT

Financing and Pricing E-Service

Craig L. Johnson
Associate Professor of Public Finance and Policy Analysis
School of Public and Environmental Affairs
Indiana University-Bloomington

This report was originally published in January 2002.

Introduction

State government web portals are an indispensable component in the sophisticated delivery of electronic services by government: e-government. Ideally, the web portal serves as the face of digital government, the front end of a fully integrated system of databases and business processes that cross government agency lines and levels of government in a seamless fashion. The web portal should be designed emphasizing user-friendliness, convenience, and personal service. As Diana Gant and Jon Gant describe in chapter 3, web portals should exhibit four characteristics: openness, customizability, usability, and transparency. It will require substantial planning and money for state governments to infuse these characteristics throughout their web portals. Moreover, the movement from simply having a web presence and e-mail communications with the public to a system that provides a broad array of online transactions and actually transforms the way government and constituents interact is a complex, multi-year endeavor that requires substantial resources and an ongoing funding stream.

The construction of a web portal is an expensive undertaking and presents a significant financial and administrative challenge, even for state governments. Because of the expense and technological challenges, many state governments are turning to public/private ventures to construct, host, and operate their web portals. Such arrangements offer promise, but many issues critical to their ultimate success have yet to be resolved. This chapter addresses issues associated with web portal public/private partnerships and provides suggestions for strengthening such web portal projects.

Based on a survey of state governments, this research describes and analyzes the financing and pricing structures of state government web portals. Between April and July of 2001, the Indiana University research team conducted a telephone survey of state government officials responsible for their state's web portal. The survey asked respondents questions about capital planning and budgeting practices, spending and costs, financing and funding sources, description and pricing structure of online services, citizen adoption rates, and cost savings. The interviews were supplemented with additional information from annual reports, board meeting minutes, strategic e-government reports, and information on web portal sites. Our sample consists of information from 33 states.

The next section discusses the web portal as a capital investment. Then state web portal financing and pricing policies are analyzed, and the final section provides recommendations and concluding remarks.

Is the Web Portal a Capital Investment?

The government web portal infrastructure is a capital asset and should be designed, financed, developed, deployed, and managed as a capital investment. Government capital investments involve spending money on physical assets that are expected to provide benefits over an extended period of time. Often the physical assets provide the basic facilities and installations, the physical infrastructure, of an important governmentally provided service, like water supply and distribution.

Government capital projects are financed, managed, and accounted for in fundamentally different ways from operating activities. Most capital projects have several common elements:

- Substantial expense
- Long-term duration
- Infrequent occurrence
- Limited irreversibility
- Significant, extended impact on the target community

Capital projects are very expensive. The capital investment decision is a long-run production decision. Capital costs are large, up-front fixed costs; they are distinct from operating costs, which are associated with the use of a facility or installation over the short run. A small portion of capital costs may be generated from operating funds, but the bulk of the financing usually comes from long-term financial instruments. Most capital costs, once incurred, are sunk costs invested in project-specific assets. The sunk costs can't be recouped, and the assets, once purchased, have limited, if any, resale value.

Capital projects are long term along three dimensions. First, it takes a long time to bring a project to completion. Capital projects are complex endeavors that typically go through a series of capital planning and budgeting processes, and require an extended project construction period. Major capital projects are not built often and, therefore, the planning that goes into a project is substantial and vitally important. Substantial up-front planning costs must be incurred before construction gets under way. But once construction starts, physical infrastructure projects are difficult and expensive to halt or reverse. Second, the investment is expected to last a long time; capital projects commonly have an expected useful life of dozens of years. In addition, the investment is intended to have a significant effect on the long-term well-being of the organization and target community. Third, capital projects often involve the transfer of resources over time. Capital expenditures usually occur at the beginning of the project, while most project benefits accrue over the intermediate and long term. Because of their futuristic nature, benefits are much more difficult to estimate than up-front accounting costs, particularly tangible and intangible social benefits.

Because of the nature of capital projects described above, capital investment decisions are made with great care. A variety of sophisticated project evaluation techniques are used to systematically evaluate the return on capital investments, such as Benefit-Cost Analysis, Net Present Value Analysis, and Cost-Effectiveness Analysis.[1] Each of these techniques can provide useful information for decision makers, helping them make rational capital investment decisions based on the careful determination and consideration of the costs and benefits to all major stakeholders.

The Web Portal Infrastructure

The web portal infrastructure involves approaching IT development from a new, constituent-service orientation. Rather than simply adding bits and pieces to the present labyrinth of independent information management structures and systems, web portals should be developed with an enterprise-wide structure in mind, creating a unified technological infrastructure that presents a common and easy-to-use interface to the public. The web portal infrastructure consists of an enterprise architecture including user workstations, multiple routers, and load balancers; multiple web, application, and database servers; software applications for security and privacy programs; interfaces with legacy systems and payment systems; and custom applications for personalized technologies, such as messaging, scheduling, and online transactions. In addition, there are the costs involved in implementing networks, integrating databases, and, often, upgrading the telecommunications infrastructure.

Web Portal Developers

Currently, state government web portal projects are typically developed and implemented by either a government agency, such as the Information Technology Department in the state of Iowa, or by private vendors in partnership and/or under contract with a government-sponsored governing board or agency. The governing board or agency is usually vested with the authority to make all policy and contracting decisions. In Virginia, for example, the Virginia Information Providers Network Authority, VIPNet, is responsible for the development and expansion of Virginia's portal.[2] VIPNet is a legal authority with an 11-member board of directors and approximately 20 full-time employees. VIPNet is responsible for setting portal policies, overseeing operations, and approving all online services and charges. VIPNet contracts portal services from Virginia Interactive, a subsidiary of National Information Consortium, Inc. (NIC).

Web Portal Development

Agency Developer: Government agency acts as prime contractor and builds and operates portal internally.

Vendor Developer: Government contracts out portal development and operations to private sector firm(s).

Joint Government/Vendor Development: Government works in concert with private firm(s) to design, build, and operate portal. Often a government agency will be the prime contractor and be solely responsible for overall project design and implementation. The agency works with multiple vendors to build the portal, and individual vendors are subcontracted for building, and possibly operating, particular aspects of the portal, but are not contracted to build and operate the entire portal.

Table 8.1 provides information on the distribution of government agency and private vendor developers. State officials report that 11 (33 percent) of their web portals are agency developed, 14 (43 percent) are vendor developed, and 8 (24 percent) are jointly developed by government and the private sector. The state of New Jersey's web portal provides an example of an agency-developed web portal. New Jersey's Office of Information Technology (OIT) provides a wide range of web-based services and products for its "customers"[3]—New Jersey's departments and agencies—including application development, web-enabling legacy applications, and data integration and warehouse solutions. According to OIT, they have developed and currently maintain 90 percent of the applications used throughout state government. In most states, agencies must fund, build, and maintain their own applications.

Table 8.1: Distribution of State Web Portal Developers
N=33

	Number	Percentage (%)
Government Agency	11	33
Private Firm	14	43
Joint—Government & Private Firm	8	24

An example of joint portal development is provided by California. California hired approximately 15 different vendors to work on various pieces of the portal. While Deloitte Consulting was the project manager responsible for integrating all of the portal pieces, a government official stressed that California's Office of eGovernment maintained oversight of the design of the portal throughout the project. The government official emphasized that they specifically did not want long-term contracts with any vendor to develop the whole portal, and that they contracted out each piece in short-term contracts, helping them to retain full control over the portal.

Many governments contract with a private firm to develop their portal. NIC is the most frequent private contractor, representing 63 percent of state government portal contracts.[4] This figure is for general portal contracts. It should be noted that some firms are pursuing a strategy of bidding for specialized (unbundled) applications, such as State Department of Motor Vehicle Services or payment engines, rather than a general portal contract.

Table 8.2 provides information on spending for 16 enterprise portal projects.[5] State governments report spending an average of $2 million on enterprise portals, from a low of $303,250 to a high of $6,500,000. These figures should be considered low estimates because they do not include private vendor software development costs, which can be substantial. For example, NIC estimated their software development costs at $3.5 million for their subsidiary, Indiana Interactive. If software development costs were included for states with a private portal developer, the average cost would be higher.

Table 8.2: Web Portal Spending Costs
N=16

Average Cost	Standard Deviation	Minimum	Maximum
$2,055,000	$1,828,000	$303,250	$6,500,000

A few additional caveats regarding portal spending figures are in order. Many states surveyed could not separate portal from other e-government spending, so their figures are not included. States that expended funds for very limited website purposes, not a potentially enterprise-wide portal, are also not included. Our intention is to present an accurate picture of spending for comprehensive, enterprise web portal projects. In addition, many governments, or their vendors, would not release portal spending information, stating that it is proprietary, and some states reported that they did not keep track of aggregate portal costs.

Planning and Budgeting for Web Portal Projects

Over 85 percent of web portal projects, like most traditional IT budgets, are currently funded as operating expenditures in the annual operating budget with little centralized tracking of expenditures. IT agencies often use a charge-back system to bill agencies for multiple IT services, and only a few states report itemizing and separately tracking and reporting web portal expenditures. States that have established a budgetary line item for annual web portal expenditures report an average annual budget of $730,000.

It is not uncommon for expenditures to be commingled across different activities, functions, and agencies in government operating budgets. In capital budgets, in contrast, expenditures are accounted for separately for each project, which enables the government to better manage spending on particular projects over time. No state in our sample explicitly funds all portal expenditures from a capital projects fund. A few states use the capital projects fund to account for most expensive IT hardware purchases. Two states, Georgia and Washington, have established enterprise funds for portal spending. Using an enterprise fund approach is an important step forward because it acknowledges that portal spending will be ongoing and that funded projects should be self-sustaining.

Enterprise funds are used to account for activities for which a fee is charged to users to cover service-related costs, including capital costs such as depreciation and debt service.[6] Fees or charges of activities accounted for in enterprise funds should include depreciation expenses, and are commonly levied at a rate to cover debt service costs, as well as operations and maintenance. Therefore, portal fees and charges accounted for in enterprise funds should be derived from real costs.

National Information Consortium (NIC)

NIC was formed in 1997 to combine under common ownership individual companies operating in the states of Kansas, Indiana, Nebraska, and Arkansas, and the National Information Consortium USA, Inc. NIC has become a national leader in the provision of Internet-based, electronic government services. NIC's services include the development and management of official government web sites (portal outsourcing); document management, filing, and ethics and elections reporting systems; and web-based supply chain and e-purchasing services. Portal revenues accounted for 66 percent of total NIC revenues in 2000.

Source: National Information Consortium 2000 Annual Report.

Since web portal projects are rarely accounted for in the capital budget, they usually do not go through a capital planning process where their return on investment is calculated and directly compared to other potential investment projects. Only one state reported conducting a benefit-cost or return-on-investment analysis *prior* to investing in a web portal project. The annual (incremental) operating budget approach makes it difficult for state governments to fully invest in web portal initiatives that have an expected high return in the future, but require substantial up-front funding and long-term, cross-agency collaboration. Government officials are often hesitant to highlight expected savings for fear of having the savings cut from their base budget. Budgeting systems should provide incentives for administrators to make cost-saving portal investments. Officials should be allowed to reinvest the savings into expanding the portal infrastructure, especially for portal services that are demanded by constituents and provide significant social benefits.

Enterprise Funds and Internal Service Funds

While enterprise funds and internal service funds are both classified as proprietary funds (fiscal and accounting entities used to account for governmental activities that are operated as quasi-businesses), they differ in their focus. Traditionally, most IT activities have been accounted for in internal service funds, recognizing the traditional role of the IT unit as a service provider within government. Internal service funds are used to report activities where an agency provides goods or services to other funds, departments, or agencies of the government on a cost-reimbursement basis.

With the advent of web portals and online transactions, a new orientation toward enterprise fund accounting is appropriate and reflects the new external, programmatic orientation of many IT activities. Enterprise funds are used to report activities for which a fee is charged to external users for goods or services. According to the Governmental Accounting Standards Board, activities are required to be reported as enterprise funds if:

1) debt is secured by a pledge of net revenues from fees and charges of the activity;
2) the cost of providing services, including capital costs such as depreciation or debt service, are to be recovered with fees and charges, rather than with taxes or similar revenues;
3) pricing policies establish fees and charges to recover costs, including capital costs.

Source: Governmental Accounting Standards Board, Statement No. 34 of the Governmental Accounting Standards Board: Basic Financial Statements—and Management's Discussion and Analysis—for State and Local Governments, (June 1999).

Indicative of the lack of long-term planning, only a few states have developed procedures for projecting future portal spending. This lack of long-term planning is disconcerting for two reasons. First, one of the main benefits of the portal is that new applications can continuously be fitted to the portal infrastructure, adding more value to the initial investment. A web portal is a dynamic, not a static, investment; it is designed to be able to grow to provide new and improved content and services. Therefore, future costs, beyond mere maintenance costs, and future benefits are integral aspects of any web portal investment.

Second, many portals in operation today are really enhanced pilot projects, and are not yet fully scaled portals providing multiple online communications and transaction services linked to back-end legacy systems.[7] Many states have chosen to launch "something" very quickly, adding infrastructure improvements and applications piecemeal overtime, rather than plan and construct a full-scale portal initially. Such portals are built with the foreknowledge that future development costs will be substantial and recurring. Despite these planning shortcomings, a clear advantage from contracting with an established private vendor is the rapid speed with which they are able to bring a basic, scalable, portal architecture online. Moreover, unbundling segments of the portal infrastructure and applications into separate contracts makes economic sense provided it is implemented within an overall strategic plan and vision of what the final product will look like. The vast majority of portals were reported to be up and running within one year. Some private vendor projects were completed even sooner; North Carolina's @Your Service portal was reportedly completed in six weeks.[8]

How State Governments Finance Web Portal Projects

Most websites were initially financed and developed from internal government resources, often using the labor of motivated employees. This was sufficient when the web was primarily used to display information on government offices and officials. But now that the web can be effectively used for collaborative commerce (i.e., transacting business, delivering services, facilitating communications and interaction between citizens and government, and between levels and types of governments), the *traditional* financing and development strategies are no longer robust enough to produce a sufficient amount of capital on a timely and regular basis. Therefore, new financing strategies for web portal projects should be adopted.

State governments employ two basic financing approaches: 1) government financed; and 2) private vendor-financed (the so-called self-funding model). The notion that portals developed by private firms—without any major appropriations from the state government—are "self-funded" is a misnomer. In such a case, the private firm simply puts capital up front in the expectation of receiving cash flows from the portal. The vendor makes a business decision that the discounted value of expected future net cash flows from portal operations will be greater than the up-front investment. Those future cash flows, however, come from citizens and firms. Private vendors attempt to recoup their investment by generating revenue from two basic sources: 1) charging users for the "convenience" of transacting business over the web rather than through traditional channels such as over-the-counter and mail-in; and 2) charging businesses for "enhancing" the value of basic government information. These two added-value approaches form the primary funding streams behind the *Internet-based model.*

Despite the long expected useful life of the web portal infrastructure, most state governments do not use a long-term financing strategy. Most portal contracts are from three to five years, indicating that vendors are willing to supply state governments a form of intermediate-term finance. Bond proceeds were used in only one state, and only two states report using a special technology fund. As implemented, these special technology funds set aside funds for portal projects, but they are not revolving funds.[9] Revolving funds are set up to recycle funds in order to make the fund self-sustaining. The revenues from current and seasoned projects flow back into the system to provide money for new projects. State revolving funds have proven successful at financing major physical infrastructure programs, but even the most successful revolving funds received public start-up funding in the form of federal grants and matching state government debt proceeds.

The charge-back system used to support many IT budgets does not provide, by itself, a sufficient and sustainable amount of revenue to implement full-scale portal development in a comprehensive fashion. However, a financing strategy that couples an enterprise-based charge-back system with some form of intermediate or long-term financing from state government bonds may be effective. A bond financing program can generate a large, flexible pool of funds for multiple capital investment projects over an extended period of time. Such an *infrastructure-financing model* has proven successful at financing a wide variety of major capital improvements and can be an effective and efficient financing mechanism to support the next wave of web portal development, along with other e-government investments. An enterprise-based charge-back system, with charges established at rates based on the marginal cost of service provision, can provide an incremental revenue stream to support debt service (or lease rental) payments.

Taxes, Fees, or Charges?

Ultimately, all state government web portals are paid for by some combination of general revenues (mostly taxes), user fees, or user charges from constituents doing business with the state. According to Mikesell,[10] user fees involve the sale of licenses by government to engage in otherwise restricted or forbidden activities. User charges, in contrast, are prices charged for voluntarily purchased services. While user-charge based services may benefit specific individuals or businesses, they are provided to fulfill basic governmental responsibilities.

The distinction between fees and charges is important for online services provided by government, since most government services currently provided online are also provided, for a fee, through traditional mechanisms. For example, the cost to renew a vehicle registration is a user fee. The vehicle registration is a necessary condition for operating the vehicle simply because the government requires a payment for granting people the privilege of driving a car. The additional charge for the option of renewing a vehicle registration online is a user charge, provided there are alternative ways of renewing the registration. A critical element of a user charge is that it's voluntary, implying that consumers are not legally required to purchase the service, or, if they are, that there are alternative providers. Therefore, most so-called convenience fees are user charges.

User charges have several benefits. First, they enable government to make the people who benefit from the service pay for the service; conversely, people who do not benefit do not have to pay. This improves equity because non-users are not forced to subsidize users. Secondly, they help officials gauge constituent preferences and estimate demand for a service. This can enhance operational efficiency and improve internal resource allocation decisions because services need only be provided for users at the level they demand. In addition, user charges make more economic sense when demand is price elastic, implying user demand is price sensitive. The more price elastic demand, the greater the potential for inefficiency if users do not face true costs.

User charges, however, may not be appropriate when the services intentionally subsidize low-income or otherwise disadvantaged households, or when the services provided generate substantial social benefits. User charges are commonly set based on both the benefit derived from usage and the cost of service provision. The basic rule for efficient economic pricing requires marginal benefit to equal marginal cost. For services that primarily benefit the direct user, the price charged should equal marginal cost. When social benefits are also generated from providing a service, then aggregate social benefits need to be considered. In cases where benefits can be separated into those enjoyed by direct users and those by society in general, prices should be divided among users (a user charge) and all of society (general revenues).

Indeed, user charges make more economic sense when direct users enjoy most of the benefits. User charges should be based on marginal benefits, not total benefits. For example, it may be argued that as more people become comfortable with using web portals, and more services are put online, the benefits from individual online usage will spill over to all of society by reducing the digital divide and making government more constituent-centric. In such a case, direct user charges should be based only on their marginal benefit, not the entire social benefit. Direct users should cover marginal operating costs, but capital costs that provide societal benefits can be covered with general revenues.

User-charge pricing also makes sense when it can reduce congestion, which may require charging different prices at different times. There should be a difference between demand at peak times and off-peak times. This implies that web portal charges should not be fixed, but should vary based on congestion. Higher prices are appropriate at peak times, and lower prices—perhaps zero charge—at off-peak times. Internet resources, such as bandwidth, are limited; once the service becomes crowded, additional users impose congestion costs on other users. Therefore, another role of the user charge can be to reduce overcrowding during peak hours, which should increase constituent satisfaction and overall usage.

The Structure of Portal Revenue and Prices

The amount of web portal revenue produced from online services is a function of price and quantity. Revenue is generated from the delivery of services over the Internet such as renewing motor vehicle registrations online. Price is the charge for purchasing government services online, and quantity is the number of online transactions. Obviously, the higher the prices charged and the greater the number of online transactions, the greater the revenue. Equally obvious, governments *should not* charge citizens or businesses a price that maximizes portal revenue—it is the business of government to provide services with a social demand at a price that covers a portion, if not all, of the costs of provision. But it is not governments' business to maximize revenue. Moreover, governments should not charge a price that reduces demand below socially optimal levels, especially for G2C services. High prices for online services may increase revenue, but at the cost of fewer transactions and lower adoption rates. Such a policy is not socially optimal if web portal services provide substantial social benefits.

Indiana Interactive, Inc.

Indiana Interactive, Inc., was created in 1995 to develop, operate, maintain, and expand an electronic government portal for the Access Indiana Information Network, a State of Indiana government instrumentality created by the Indiana General Assembly for the purpose of providing access to state, county, and local information for Indiana citizens and businesses. Indiana Interactive, Inc., is responsible for funding up-front investment and ongoing operating costs, and managing and marketing the portal.

Source: Indiana Interactive, Inc., and subsidiary, Consolidated Financial Statements for the Years Ended December 31, 1999 and 1998.

The special nature of information provision makes this especially important. State government web portal pricing policies and practices should be consistent with sound information pricing principles. The cost structure of an information technology supplier generally involves high fixed costs and very low marginal costs. Therefore, producers, especially private vendors, have an incentive to create a virtual monopoly, limiting competition and controlling supply.

One way suppliers attempt to limit competition is to control the flow of information. Information on revenues generated by web portals is very limited because most web portals have only recently begun to bring services online, and current public disclosure and reporting practices need improvement. Most states do not record and report portal revenues centrally. More states should consider establishing the web portal, or the governing board, as an accounting entity for financial reporting and public disclosure purposes. In cases where officials believe this to be overly burdensome, they should nevertheless do so to enhance the public's trust of their e-government efforts. While many states that contract with private vendors were very forthcoming with information, including audited financial reports and contracts, some states responded that the information was proprietary, indicating that some states need to implement procedures for publicly disclosing web portal finances and other activities. Even when the portal is operated under contract by a private firm, its activities and finances should be disclosed to the public in a full and timely manner, just like other governmental activities.

Despite the limitations mentioned above, our inquiry indicates that state government web portals have substantial revenue-generation potential. One important aspect of a revenue structure is its ability to produce a stable revenue stream. Indiana is widely acknowledged to have established one of the first portals with a broad array of online transactions. Table 8.3 shows Indiana Interactive, Inc.'s financials from 1996 to 1999.

The data show steadily increasing revenues from $11.65 million in 1996 to $14.57 million in 1999. Gross profit increased sharply between 1996 and 1998, dipping slightly in 1999. But net income has decreased sharply since 1997, because of increasing operating expenses. The "cost of revenues" fluctuated between 76 percent and 82.5 percent of revenues, indicating that prices for online services remained steady over this period. The cost of revenues in web portal accounting terminology refers primarily to the contractual amount of fees remitted to government agencies from online transactions. Another example of the revenue potential of web portal services is provided by Virginia, which realized a gross profit of $3.9 million in 2000, based on $21 million in revenues. The revenue figures from the early deployment of online services and transactions in Indiana and Virginia indicate that the portal and its applications have substantial revenue potential.[11]

Portal revenue is a function of online transaction volume (not merely hits, accesses, sessions, or any other measure that does not involve an exchange of funds for a service or product); the more online transactions, the more revenue generated. While aggregate data on transactions is currently scant, early data from Texas is illustrative of the transaction volume potential. In the first quarter of 2001, Texas collected $8,062,159 on 11,632 payment transactions, which were mostly generated from a few agencies with applications that went live in July 2000.

Table 8.3: Indiana Interactive, Inc., Financials

	1996	1997	1998	1999
Revenues	$11,658,194	$12,524,065	$13,850,258	$14,574,808
Cost of Revenues	$9,623,884	$10,040,041	$10,601,849	$11,402,941
Gross Profit	$2,034,310	$2,484,024	$3,248,409	$3,171,867
Operating Expenses	$1,309,734	$1,671,922	$2,862,963	$2,880,120
Operating Income	$724,576	$812,102	$385,446	$291,474
Net Income	$711,223	$803,777	$279,411	$118,435

Source: Indiana Interactive, Inc., and subsidiary, Consolidated Financial Statements for the Years Ended December 31, 1995, 1996, 1997, 1998, and 1999.

What Online Services Are Provided?

States now provide a variety of online services to citizens (G2C) and businesses (G2B). These new developments involve both opening up new distribution channels for traditional services, and the creation of new information-related services. The services offered to businesses and those offered to citizens should be viewed as distinct services with different demand and other relevant characteristics. Business organizations have a better technological infrastructure, and business users have more technological knowledge than the average citizen. In addition, businesses have a demand for different services, and probably a greater ability and willingness to pay for services that are comparable to G2C services in terms of production costs. As a result, different pricing structures are appropriate for G2B and G2C commerce.

The most frequently reported G2C online services involve motor vehicle agencies—vehicle registration renewal, specialty plates, and driver's license renewal. Many states enable citizens to obtain other licenses online for hunting and fishing, real estate, and other professional occupations. Other frequently provided online services include state park reservations and personal income-tax filing.

States report providing many G2B added value services for authorized businesses involving searching records and generating reports for driver's records, vehicle titles, liens, and registrations; business certificates of existence, entity name, and principals. Other business services include Uniform Commercial Code (UCC) filings and searches, tax payments, business registration and renewal, and license verification. Most states offering added value business services have designed a two-part pricing structure, charging firms a fixed annual "premium service" subscription fee of $50 plus a per search or report fee. States now appear to be modestly increasing the premium subscription fee: Tennessee now charges $75, and Montana is proposing to charge $75. Despite the increase, G2B services may still be underpriced, both in terms of recovering the full cost of provision and their marginal benefit to businesses. For example, for the $50 annual subscription fee *accessIndiana* provides businesses with 10 accounts covering 21 services, including monthly billing and online account management services. A rigorous demand analysis would likely find that a $50 or $75 annual premium service fixed fee plus a small variable cost per search or record substantially undervalues the premium service, given:

1. the substantial fixed and variable costs incurred to design and build the portal infrastructure;
2. annual operations and maintenance costs, including the non-trivial cost of providing monthly billing and online account management services; and

3. the likelihood that businesses have an inelastic demand for most premium services, such as motor vehicle and title lien searches.

State governments, not just their private vendors, need to rigorously analyze the demand for current and prospective G2B services. A two-part pricing structure lends itself to fixed and variable cost recovery, where the fixed charge is set to cover fixed (capital) costs, and the variable charge is set to cover operating costs. States should also distinguish between mandated versus non-mandated services. Services that are demanded by private firms but are not mandated by the state should be priced based on firms' willingness to pay, and revenues generated above costs can be used to subsidize portal activities that provide substantial social benefits. On the other hand, services that are mandated by the state, like vehicle registration renewals, should not be priced above the cost of provision.

The Pricing Structure of Online Services

When private vendors operate the state portal, G2C and G2B service charges are under the authority of a governing board. In practice, the vendor proposes a fee structure that the governing board usually approves without making substantive changes. In states where portals are run by the government agency, it is not clear that there is an economic basis used to derive portal charges. States report that their charges are not based on a formal breakeven analysis or similar methodology. In most cases the convenience fee is established like other fees in the budgetary process, where the agency through the executive branch recommends a fee structure and the legislature enacts it into law, sometimes with modification.

Most states, around 80 percent, impose some type of charge for online services. The total charge for online services (TOC) includes the statutory fee for service provision through traditional channels. It may also include a convenience fee (CF)—a usage-based charge imposed on citizens to use the system—or a convenience discount (CD), where the cost to the public is lower for services transacted online. Only two states in our sample, 8 percent, use convenience discounts. States appear reluctant to use CDs despite anecdotal evidence that demand is price elastic. In Arizona, for example, adoption rates skyrocketed for online vehicle registration renewals once the $6.95 charge was eliminated in 1998.[12] For online services with an elastic demand, sharp CD programs may translate into substantial administrative savings if properly planned and implemented.

Over half of the states charge a convenience fee (CF), which is placed on top of the fee for services delivered through a traditional venue. Since customers still have the option of using the service through a traditional venue (e.g., over the counter), the CF is actually a user charge and is referred to herein as a convenience charge (CC). In most states, the portal charge consists of the convenience charge (CC), or convenience discount (CD), and the electronic payment processing (EPP) fee.[13]

Electronic Payment Processing (EPP) Fees

Some states that impose an additional cost for using online services do not impose a CC, but they do pass along the EPP fee. Often electronic payment processing fees frequently constitute the largest part of the price of doing business online, and are clearly viewed by policy makers as an impediment to the growth of online service delivery. However, officials should not view electronic payment processing costs in isolation; rather they should be compared to check-processing costs. A recent study reports that, per transaction, check-based payment is more costly than electronic payment for payees receiving point-of-sale and bill payments, $1.25 to $0.23.[14]

States report three basic ways credit card processing charges are structured for online services: 1) as a single rate percentage of the transaction; 2) as a percentage range; and 3) as a single rate percentage of the transaction plus a fixed transaction fee. For single percentage rates, credit card processing charges per transaction range from 1.50 percent to 2.28 percent; ranges vary from 1.7–3.5 percent to 2.5–4 percent per transaction; and single percentage plus fixed fees vary from 1.614 percent + $0.24 to 2.35 percent + $0.10 per transaction. Generally, these figures are substantially higher than the CCs states are charging.

In many states the credit card processing fee paid to the merchant bank is not transparent, because it's folded into the transaction fee. However, in other states, the EPP fee is clearly designated as a separate charge. Some states have comprehensive agreements with merchant banks, but commonly the state will negotiate a separate agreement for online services, and private vendors have negotiated agreements on behalf of the government in a few states.

In some states, around 20 percent of our sample, the government cannot, or does not, impose an additional charge, so the agency must absorb the cost of online transactions, whether the service is provided in-house or by a vendor. Arizona vehicle registration renewals provide a case in point. Arizona contracts with IBM for their vehicle registration renewal portal operations. But the state is prohibited from levying an additional portal charge on citizens for vehicle registrations and licenses. The charge for each vehicle registration renewal that IBM processes over the web has three components: a $1.00 fixed charge, plus 2 percent of the vehicle tax (or $4, whichever is greater), plus up to 1.7 percent of total transaction costs for merchant (EPP) fees. Arizona reimburses IBM up to 1.7 percent of total transaction costs for merchant (EPP) fees. IBM gets to keep $1.00, plus 2 percent of the vehicle tax (or $4, whichever amount is larger). Therefore, IBM is guaranteed a minimum of $5 per transaction and an indeterminate maximum amount, but the maximum could be substantially higher since Arizona uses an ad valorem system, not a fixed registration fee, to determine the vehicle registration renewal fee, and uses $363 as a typical registration amount on their website. For specialty plates, Arizona levies a $4 portal charge on top of the $25 fee, and the entire $4 goes to IBM. The agency is, however, responsible for absorbing up to 1.7 percent of the EPP fee.

Advertising as a Revenue Source

State government officials have put thumbs down on the advertising revenue model. Only 12.5 percent of state government portals offer any form of advertising, and even these states do not use advertising to generate revenue. Iowa recently contracted with govAds to sell web advertising, referred to as "sponsorships," on its portal. Iowa's strategy of selling advertising comes as a direct response to the 50 percent budget cut in its e-government initiatives by the Iowa General Assembly. According to Iowa officials, the state retains the right to remove advertisements and incurs no up-front expense. govAds is responsible for setting up the advertising operation and receives revenue through a negotiated split in revenues from the advertisements. Iowa provides a test case of the appropriateness of advertising on state government web portals, as well as advertising's ability to generate a sufficient and stable revenue stream.

State governments probably can't generate substantial revenue from advertising, even when they want to. But they may be able to generate enough revenue from benign advertising, like the tourism advertising links on the Minnesota web portal, to largely offset EPP and other costs. State officials should follow Iowa's lead and re-evaluate the revenue potential of benign, non-controversial advertising. Clearly, there are a myriad of issues that states will have to work through in order to establish a viable advertising revenue model, but such impediments can be surmounted. States should assertively tackle the obstacles because it will only increase their ability to expand the benefits of e-government to their constituents. In addition, many citizens may view advertising more favorably than state government officials believe. In Texas, for example, almost 75 percent of state residents reportedly view advertising as either an entirely or somewhat acceptable e-government funding method.[15]

Recommendations

The web portal has the potential to change how government is organized and how it interacts with its constituents. But in order to move forward effectively, IT professionals must work together with budgeting and finance experts to find solutions to financial and management problems associated with the development and operation of web portals and online transactions. Government officials and private vendors should build upon the best traditional ways of funding portals by incorporating proven techniques from infrastructure finance coupled with unique Internet-based funding mechanisms.

While the empirical data is not yet sufficiently developed to provide solid evidence on complex public policy issues like the efficacy and cost efficiency of portal vendor development and financing, it is clear that government officials and private firms should view the ultimate end users of the portal as customers with a demand for new services and improved service delivery. These new and improved services must be designed based on the needs and capacities of users, not merely traditional organizational structures and inter- and intra-governmental relationships. They must be priced in a way that maximizes social, not just private, benefits, which in many cases should lead to charging no price at all. The changes described in this report, if implemented, will go a long way toward alleviating the underfunding problem in web portal development, while simultaneously maximizing adoption and usage. Specifically, we recommend that decision makers consider the following:

Recommendation 1

Web portal projects are capital projects and should be classified and accounted for as such. Web portal expenditures should be viewed as a capital investment, classified as capital expenditures, accounted for in the capital budget, and reported distinctively and comprehensively in budgetary and financial reports.

Recommendation 2

Web portals are long-term capital investments and should be financed like other long-term capital investments. Web portal projects should be supported with long-term financing that is repaid from multiple funding sources. User charges are appropriate but should not be relied on to finance capital costs for services generating significant social benefits. The capital financing approach produces stable and substantial longer-term funding, and facilitates an optimal portal and online transactions development process.

Recommendation 3

Governments should conduct studies that analyze the benefits and costs of developing web portals and applications for online transactions.[16] Such rigorous studies should be used to guide portal and application development decisions, particularly in terms of estimating potential cost savings, social benefits to stakeholders, and the demand for particular online services. Before setting user charges for G2B services, governments should estimate the demand for G2B services since such services may significantly reduce a firm's cost of business. And before imposing user charges for G2C services, governments should understand the potential intermediate and longer-term cost savings from the strategic use of convenience discounts.

Recommendation 4

Within G2B online services, states should distinguish between mandated versus non-mandated services. G2B services that are demanded by private firms but are *not* mandated by the state should be priced based on firms' willingness to pay. Revenues generated above costs can be used to subsidize portal activities that provide substantial social benefits. On the other hand, G2B services that are mandated by the state, like vehicle registration renewals, should not be priced above the cost of provision.

Recommendation 5

Government officials should not allow electronic payment processing costs to prevent the establishment of new online transaction services. EPP costs, while substantial, should be evaluated in terms of the potential savings from lower check-processing costs. Governments should re-evaluate the option of raising a limited amount of revenue from benign, non-controversial web portal advertising or sponsorships, which may help offset EPP costs.

Recommendation 6

More states should consider establishing the web portal or the governing board as an accounting entity for financial reporting and public disclosure purposes. States should record and report portal revenues centrally, preferably in an enterprise-type fund. In cases where officials believe central tracking and reporting to be overly burdensome, they should nevertheless do so to enhance the public's trust of their e-government efforts. Even when the portal is operated under contract by a private firm, its activities and finances should be disclosed to the public in a full and timely manner, and in a manner that enables the public to track and evaluate the operations of the portal and the delivery of online services.

Recommendation 7

Government budgeting systems, including charge-back systems, should provide incentives for administrators to make cost-saving portal investments. Budgeting systems should enable programmatic savings generated from web portal investments to be enjoyed by line agencies. Administrators should be encouraged to reinvest the savings into expanding the portal infrastructure, especially for portal services that are demanded by constituents and that provide significant social benefits. In addition, chargeback systems should be based on real costs, and savings from portal investments should be credited to IT units when appropriate.

Appendix I: Web Portal Funding and Financing Models: Traditional, Infrastructure-Finance, and Internet-Based

TRADITIONAL MODEL	**FUNDING STREAMS—General revenues:** monies appropriated from the general fund. **Charge-back pricing:** internal assessments that allocate costs to individual agencies or departments for centralized and distributed operations and services. **FINANCING MECHANISMS—None.**
INFRASTRUCTURE-FINANCE MODEL	**FUNDING STREAM—Debt proceeds:** funds generated from the sale of state or local government notes or bonds. **FINANCING MECHANISMS—Debt securities:** state governments sell short-term notes and long-term bonds in the municipal securities market to raise money to pay for capital improvement projects. There are three basic types of debt securities: general obligation, revenue, and lease rental. *General obligation (GO) bonds* are full faith and credit debt secured by the general taxing power of the issuing government. GO bond debt service is repaid from general governmental revenues. *Revenue bonds* are sold to finance projects that are intended to be "self-sustaining"; that is, they are expected to generate enough revenue through user charges and other non-tax sources to meet debt service payments and cover operations and maintenance activities. *Lease rental securities* are supported by leasing contracts that include an annual appropriation requirement that is structured to cover rental payments. Lease rental securities, sometimes also referred to as certificates of participation (COP), are often sold by general service agencies to finance intermediate-term equipment purchases.

INFRASTRUCTURE-FINANCE MODEL (cont'd)	**Revolving funds:** funding programs that recycle loanable funds to finance successive generations of projects over an extended period of time. Using dedicated capital from various sources including grants, asset sales, borrowing, and equity contributions, revolving fund managers employ portfolio management techniques to lend funds to projects at low or zero cost, and recycle the incoming funds into future lending or granting activities. Leveraging is commonly used to expand the resources available to the fund. Leveraging involves using fund assets to provide additional security for debt repayment, enabling the fund to generate financing that is a multiple (e.g., 4-to-1) of fund assets.
INTERNET-BASED MODEL	**FUNDING STREAMS—Advertising:** revenue generated from the sale of advertising space, or "sponsorships," on web portal pages. **Portal Access and Transaction-Based Revenue:** *Subscription fees*: fixed, up-front charges for access to additional (premium) services. Typically, the subscription fee is an annual fee that is coupled with a variable charge for services such as information searches and report printouts or downloads. *User fees:* revenue from the sale of licenses by government to engage in otherwise restricted activities. A hunting license fee, for example, that is levied by the government as a condition for the individual to exercise the "privilege" of hunting. *User charges:* prices charged for voluntarily purchased services. Prices levied for online service transactions are convenience charges. User charges are established on an exchange market model where a good or service is traded for funds. Individual consumers or firms can be identified and charged for the good or service, and non-payers can be excluded from consumption. **FINANCING MECHANISM—Vendor Finance:** intermediate-term financing where private vendors pay for start-up costs, commonly using internal funds or equity proceeds, and intend to recoup their investment through online transaction charges and subscription fees.

Appendix II: More on the Pricing of Online Services and the Impact on Agency Budgets

The basic pricing structure for online services can be illustrated with the following equation:

Total Online Service Charge (TOC) =

Statutory Fee (SF) + Convenience Charge (CC) – Convenience Discount (CD) + Electronic Payment Professing Fee (EPP)

(Eq. 1)

The total charge for online services (TOC) includes the statutory fee for service provision through traditional channels. When imposed, the convenience fee is placed on top of the fee for services delivered through a traditional venue. Since customers still have the option of using the service through a traditional venue (e.g., over the counter), the convenience fee is actually a user charge—a usage-based charge imposed on citizens to use the system—and is referred to here as a convenience charge (CC). TOC can also include a convenience discount (CD), where the cost to the public is lower for services transacted online. Some states that impose an additional cost for using online services do not impose a convenience charge but pass along the EPP fee. In most states, the portal charge (PC) is an additional charge, where:

Portal Charge (PC) = CC (– CD) + EPP

(Eq. 2)

An example of a PC is provided by electrical contractor license renewals in Idaho. The statutory electrical bureau fee (SF) is $100 for obtaining a license renewal on site. The portal charge (PC) for online service is $5. Therefore, the total charge for an online (TOC) license renewal is $105. The $5 portal charge has two components: 1) the Access Idaho transaction fee of $2.35, plus the EPP fee of $2.65. The EPP fee is paid to a merchant bank for processing credit card payments. Notice that the EPP fee is larger than the Access Idaho transaction fee. This is not uncommon, especially for higher TOCs, since the merchant bank fee is commonly a percentage of the transaction.

Table 8.A.1 provides an example of online service delivery transactions from the government agency's perspective. Table 8.4 presents agency revenue (AR) as a function of several variables already discussed—SF, CC, CD, EPP—and a new variable PV, the amount of the charge allocated to the private vendor. It illustrates the revenue impact on the agency for three basic scenarios: 1) the agency receives new net revenue; 2) the agency receives no new revenue, but incurs no new costs; 3) the agency receives no new revenue and incurs new costs.

In the online service new revenue scenario, the agency receives \$2.35 in new revenue per online transaction (line 1) because the agency imposes a CC greater than the EPP fee. (Note that the agency receives \$100 for delivering the service on site.) In this case the agency is responsible for the

Table 8.A.1: An Illustration of the Impact of an Online Service Delivery Transaction on an Agency Budget

Agency Revenue (AR) = Statutory Fee (SF) + Convenience Charge (CC) – Convenience Discount (CD) – Electronic Payment Processing Fee (EPP) – Portal Vendor Fee (PV)

1.	New Revenue	AR	=	SF	+	CC	–	CD	–	EPP	–	PV
		\$102.35	=	\$100	+	\$5	–	\$0	–	\$2.65	–	\$0
2a.	No New Revenue, but Agency Breaks Even (no vendor)	AR	=	SF	+	CC	–	CD	–	EPP	–	PV
		\$100	=	\$100	+	\$2.65	–	\$0	–	\$2.65	–	\$0
2b.	No New Revenue, but Agency Breaks Even (with vendor)	AR	=	SF	+	CC	–	CD	–	EPP	–	PV
		\$100	=	\$100	+	\$5	–	\$0	–	\$2.65	–	\$2.35
3a.	Net Revenue Loss (no vendor)	AR	=	SF	+	CC	–	CD	–	EPP	–	PV
		\$97.35	=	\$100	+	\$0	–	\$0	–	\$2.65	–	\$0
3b.	Net Revenue Loss (with vendor)	AR	=	SF	+	CC	–	CD	–	EPP	–	PV
		\$95.00	=	\$100	+	\$0	–	\$0	–	\$2.65	–	\$2.35

development and operation of the portal, not a private vendor. The CC, however, is non-trivial. While covering the EPP fee and providing additional revenue for new investment, it may create a disincentive for constituents to use the online system.

In the second scenario (lines 2a and 2b), the agency receives no new revenue, but incurs no additional costs. The agency imposes a CC sufficient to cover the EPP fee (line 2a), and does not contract with a private vendor. This has the advantage of a lower portal charge and helps to expand in-house IT capacity. When contracting with a vendor, the agency can charge a CC equal to the EPP fee plus vendor's fee (line 2b). This has the benefit of a quick launch, but the portal charge to the constituent is greater.

In the third scenario, the agency loses revenue directly from the online transaction. In line 3a, the loss is due to the EPP fee; in line 3b it is due to both the EPP fee and the private vendor fee. While ostensibly an entirely negative result for the agency, this situation may provide agencies with a strong incentive to realize the commonly "hypothesized" savings from bringing transactions online. Moreover, it enables the agency to bring applications online quickly, maximizes constituent adoption, and may increase social benefits.

No scenario presented in Table 8.4 has a CD, which would reduce agency revenue directly, at least initially, but would likely increase usage quickly and broadly. States that provide CDs have the agency absorb the cost. If substantial cost savings result from moving services online, then these initial costs should be viewed as an investment in future savings.

Endnotes

1. Dr. David Audretsch, Dr. Jon P. Gant, and Dr. Craig L. Johnson, *A Return on Investment Framework for Evaluating E-Government.* (Bloomington: Indiana University School of Public and Environmental Affairs, 2001).

2. See *Virginia Information Providers Network Authority Annual Report 2000.*

3. The term "customer" is the official language used by the OIT to describe its services rendered to state government organizations. See http://www.state.nj.us/oit/services_do.html, accessed July 26, 2001.

4. The following private vendors are listed as a percent of vendor-developed portals found in our sample: National Information Consortium, Inc. (63 percent), Accenture (16 percent), IBM (11 percent), KPMG (5 percent), Perpetual Plus Technology (5 percent).

5. The states are Arizona, California, Delaware, Indiana, Massachusetts, Michigan, Missouri, Montana, Nebraska, New Mexico, North Carolina, Oklahoma, Pennsylvania, Rhode Island, South Carolina, and Texas.

6. See Governmental Accounting Standards Board, Statement No. 34 of the Governmental Accounting Standards Board: *Basic Financial Statements—and Management's Discussion and Analysis—for State and Local Governments,* (June 1999).

7. Pilot projects are basically controlled experiments or development projects. They can demonstrate the feasibility of a larger, full-scale project, and should be designed for scalability and full integration. In addition, a pilot project should include evaluation procedures that include user feedback, and raise and answer major operational support questions.

8. See Report for the General Assembly, *E-Government: Using Technology to Transform North Carolina's Governmental Services and Operations in a Digital Age.* (Information Resource Management Commission, February 2001).

9. For a description of the successful state clean water and safe drinking water revolving fund programs, see: United States Environmental Protection Agency, *SRF Fund Management Handbook,* (Office of Water, April 2001). For an analysis of the necessary financing components of revolving fund programs, see: Craig L. Johnson, "Managing Financial Resources to Meet Environmental Infrastructure Needs: The Case of State Revolving Funds," *Public Productivity and Management Review,* (Spring 1995, Vol. 18, No. 3).

10. John Mikesell, *Fiscal Administration: Analysis and Applications for the Public Sector,* (fifth edition, 1999).

11. Similarly, Nebraska Interactive generated positive net income in both 1998 and 1999. (Nebraska Interactive, Inc., Financial Statements for the Years Ended December 31, 1999 and 1998).

12. Ellen Perlman, "No Free Lunch Online," *Congressional Quarterly, Inc.* (2000).

13. See Appendix for more discussion on the pricing of online services and the impact on agency budgets.

14. See Kirstin E. Wells, "Are Checks Overused?" Federal Reserve Bank of Minneapolis, *Quarterly Review,* (Vol. 20, No. 4, Fall 1996); and David Humphrey, et. al., *Cost Recovery and Pricing of Payment Services.* (Policy Research Working Paper, 1833, The World Bank, October 1997).

15. See Texas @nline Electronic Government Task Force, *Texas Online: A Feasibility Report on Electronic Government* (November 1, 2000).

16. For a discussion of the importance of conducting an assessment of the costs and benefits of providing web-based government services, see Steven Cohen and William Eimicke, "The Use of the Internet in Government Service Delivery," chapter 2 in *E-Government 2001,* edited by Mark A. Abramson and Grady E. Means (Rowman & Littlefield Publishers, Inc., 2001).

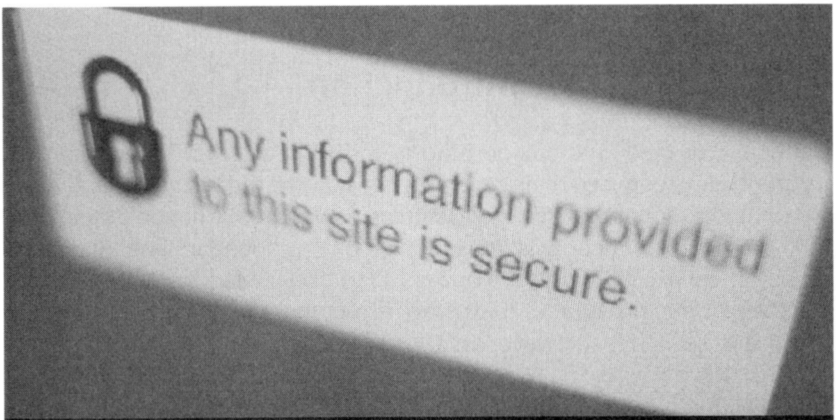

CHAPTER NINE

Public-Sector Information Security: A Call to Action for Public-Sector CIOs

Don Heiman
National Association of State Chief Information Officers
(NASCIO)

This report was originally published in July 2002.

Introduction

Public-sector chief information officers (CIOs) at all levels operate on the boundary line between their governments' internal organizations and those external forces that threaten their systems—some of our nation's most critical infrastructure. Security is implemented on this boundary line. At the end of this chapter (Appendix II), you will read about Mark's story. Mark is a state senior technologist, and his story is a composite of collective experiences and scenarios. However, in a larger sense, it is a story for all public-sector CIOs, a story both prophetic and sobering. Deep in this story, however, there is also a message about the satisfaction and enjoyment that comes from meeting difficult challenges.

Security is more than a principle or a right. If implemented properly, security is a way of life. It protects basic values that underpin our culture and liberties. This report is about security of information technology (IT), our way of life, and the values that lay deep in the core of our American culture. These values include rights to personal privacy, assurance of liberty, mutual and self-protection, and basic economic and social freedoms central to our democracy. This report is oriented toward a special audience of government CIOs in local, state, and federal jurisdictions. More than anything else, this report is a call to action, written with a sense of urgency and dedicated to the victims and families of the September 11th attacks on America.

Today government is uniquely accessible and federated. The federation of hundreds of agencies and their accessibility makes it difficult for governments to adopt common IT architectures and management (audit) standards. In addition, many states do not have security-confidentiality laws. This inhibits information sharing about security breaches and unwelcome intrusions across branches of government and jurisdictions. Also, states do not have security risk assessments on all their critical IT assets. This thwarts their ability to develop metrics and report on security performance. Finally, few states have a security portal to coordinate IT and emergency-management responses across jurisdictional boundaries. We simply need a better approach for assessing risk, managing IT assets, reporting on security performance, setting architecture, and sharing resources. We also need a governance structure for IT that clearly defines roles and accountabilities.

The Scope of the Problem

Today there are 109.5 million Internet hosts on the World Wide Web. Five years ago there were 6.6 million hosts. Looking back only three years, there were 2.1 million high-level domain names. Today there are 29.9 million

Table 9.1: Reported External and Internal Security Threats
Percentage of respondents experiencing these security breaches.

Category	2000	2001
Outsider/External Breaches	%	%
Virus/Trojans/Worms	80	89
Attacks on bugs in web servers	24	48
Denial of service	37	39
Buffer overflow attacks	24	32
Exploits related to active program scripting/mobile code	37	28
Attacks related to protocol weaknesses	26	23
Attacks related to insecure passwords	25	21
Insider/Internal Breaches	%	%
Installation/use of unauthorized software	76	78
Illegal or illicit use of computing resources (i.e., porn surfing, harassment)	63	60
Personal profit from computing resources (e.g., investing, e-commerce)	50	60
Abuse of computer access controls	58	56
Physical theft, sabotage, or intentional destruction of computing equipment	42	49
Installation/use of unauthorized hardware/ peripherals	54	47
Electronic theft, sabotage, or wrongful disclosure of data or information	24	22
Fraud	13	9

Source: Reproduced with permission from Information Security.

high-level names. Sixty-two percent of all U.S. households are now online. In the U.S. alone, 73.1 percent of all Internet users visit e-commerce sites.[1]

Just as the world is becoming more tightly interconnected via the Internet, the world is also accelerating IT automation with computers. For example, last year 7.4 million information appliances were shipped. By 2005, 51.8 million will ship annually. Even more staggering are the statistics on the shipment of personal computers. In 2000, over 49 million personal computers were shipped, and this will continue to increase dramatically each year for the next four years and beyond.[2] Parallel to these developments, a recent study by the National Governors' Association (NGA) reveals that this year states will spend $4 billion on homeland security.[3] A significant portion of this expenditure will go toward cyber-security. The Gartner Group reports that last year governments at all levels spent 6.4 percent of their revenues on IT. This spending level was 5.4 percent just a year earlier.[4] Clearly government has a strong commitment to digital government and IT infrastructure.

Digital government has many direct advantages for citizens and businesses. At the same time there are profound security risks and vulnerabilities, which must be managed. Digital government requires proactive IT governance and a robust infrastructure, which we know can be compromised by cyber-attacks, system failures, and natural disasters. If our electronic infrastructure is compromised at key points, the operations of government will be shut down with disastrous consequences. Recent global intrusions and virus attacks underscore this concern. The Code Red, Goner, and Qaz worms cost the private sector more than $13 billion in 2001.[5] Precise figures are not available for government specifically, but it is reasonable to assume that the costs are at least equal to that of private-sector organizations. It is very common for small- and medium-sized states to see 4,500 intrusion attempts per week.

Information Security magazine published the results of an October 2001 survey of 2,545 security specialists in both private and public-sector organizations. The following table shows the percentage of survey respondents reporting external as well as internal security breaches. The numbers speak volumes about the security risks to critical assets and the need for coordinated action.[6]

Across our nation, thousands of technologists work tirelessly to discover, repair, and recover from the hundreds of attacks that penetrate IT infrastructures every day. We simply need a better approach.

A Holistic Approach

Security involves more than *just IT.* Holistic security is about physical security, disaster preparedness, emergency response, and critical infrastructure protection. Security requires multi-level cooperation and coordination of military, law enforcement, and subject-matter experts. Security touches auditors, facilities managers, and maintenance workers.

Security management begins with the adoption of security policies that have legitimacy within the enterprise. Security policies come from a process that builds consensus among many key stakeholders. This includes elected officials and other policy makers as well as end users, government employees, and citizens. Security policies should embody standard practices that everyone in the organization must follow. These standard practices include an understanding of specific outcomes or goals the enterprise is committed to achieve. These goals are critical to security planning and critical to assessments about how well the organization protects its assets.

Once security policies and standard practices have been agreed upon, the organization is ready to conduct a security risk assessment. The assessment documents the "as is" and compares the "as is" to the standard practices embodied in policies. The comparison yields a gap. Gaps are important because they point to initiatives. These "gap closing" initiatives are prioritized and become a part of the enterprise's long- as well as short-range security plans. After the initiatives are implemented, audits should be done to make sure the gaps are closed and the standard practices are followed. These audits also help organizations stay compliant to policies and standard practices. In addition, security audits and standard practices are key to creating IT enterprise security architectures. These architectures include design principles for building highly integrated and secure IT infrastructures and applications. Also, standard practices, audits, and security "gap" analysis are critical for establishing IT performance metrics. In fact, the best way to determine if security gaps have been closed and stay closed is through the use of metrics.

Finally, intrusions and vulnerabilities should be closely monitored via automated and manual security technologies. Effective IT security cannot be managed with "guess-timates" or in an environment where responsible parties are too afraid to admit shortcomings. Once standard practices and metrics are in hand, the public-sector CIO is in a position to develop a compelling business case that points from the "as is" to the "to be" state of security, which will assure policy makers and stakeholders that security investments will be effective.

Many government systems provide essential services that touch citizens in a highly direct and personal way. These essential services are part of the nation's critical infrastructure. This makes IT security a key aspect of our nation's homeland security. Therefore, as metric data is gathered, it should be shared confidentially among the states and their federal partners. This will require a forum that fosters open sharing of case studies and lessons learned. We must develop a community of public-sector cyber-emergency responders to work with public safety, health, and emergency-management professionals.

Again, security done well is a way of life. For each of us to be secure, we must radically alter the way we live and the way we conduct our affairs. Radical—that is, fundamental—change is difficult because it challenges our traditional paradigms and our assumptions surrounding the way we live and work. Radical change for the ancient Greeks required a *metanoia*—a deep change of heart. September 11th made apparent the need to change our way of life, and the events of that day call us to a new epistemology—a *metanoia* that redefines what we mean by security and personal responsibility. Government leaders must set aside the "federated" cultures that foster agency autonomy and "my turf" thinking. We must share information, be more watchful, and become more disciplined in how we manage our affairs in community. We must also change our language about security. Security is more than "being safe." It is about justice and self-worth. It is about our dignity. Security is a way of life. This chapter will serve as a high-level guide for this new way of living.

Recommendations

Management

Recommendation 1: Implement an IT Governance Structure That Ensures Everyone Is at the Table

Develop an IT governance structure that is inclusive of all stakeholders. The structure should include security governance at the enterprise level and it should bring to the policy table emergency response and audit leadership. All branches of state government and local units of government should be represented in order to develop policies, set standards, and establish enterprise-level security plans.

Leavitt's Diamond

In 1965, Harold Leavitt, the Walter Kenneth Kilpatrick Professor of Organizational Behavior and Psychology (Emeritus) at Stanford University's Graduate School of Business, created a simple diamond graphic to depict the four key components of any organization.[7] Leavitt pointed out that all organizations are made up of people, structure, task, and technology.

In 1994, Open Framework, a division of International Computers Limited of England, used Leavitt's Diamond to build a representation of how organizations exist within the context of their external social and technological

Figure 9.1: Leavitt's Diamond

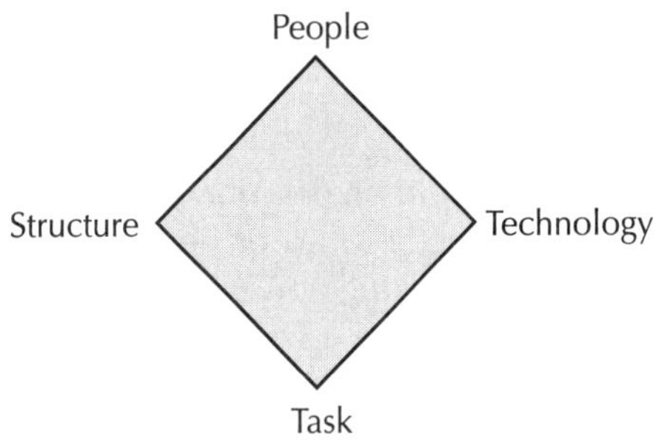

environments.[8] Open Framework used this model to develop a highly popular methodology for enterprise IT architecture.

The Open Framework model defines "culture" to include individual roles and structure. The core values underpin management processes, which lay at the heart of organizational culture. CIOs live on the boundary line between the external and internal environment of the organization. On this boundary line, CIOs balance the four components of an organization against the constant pressures from the external social, economic, and political forces that press on the enterprise. The Open Framework model also is designed to align management processes to business strategy and technology. The alignment occurs through structure and individual role responsibilities.

Figure 9.2: Open Framework Model

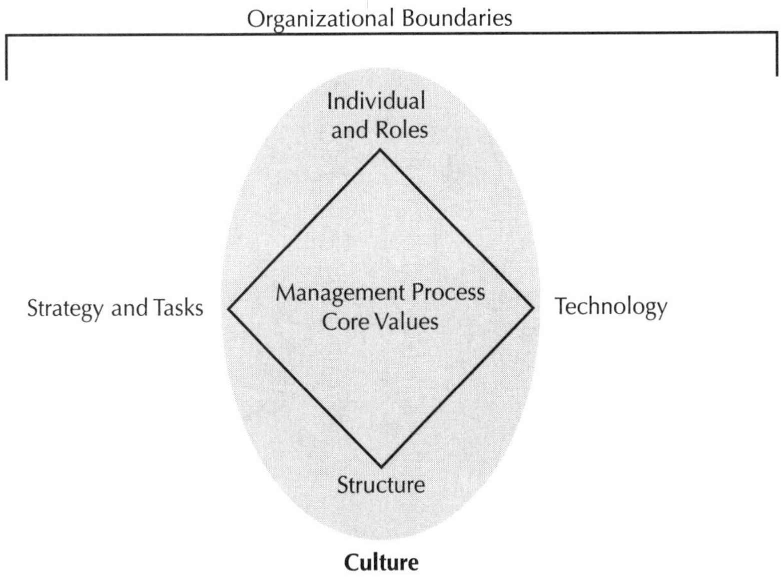

IT Governance Models

IT governance is critical to effective security policy making and implementation. In the U.S., public-sector IT governance arrangements reflect one of three distinctive patterns.

Collegial Model

Many states use a CIO arrangement that could be described as "collegial." In this arrangement, the CIO reports directly to his or her governor and draws positional authority from the policy-making power of the governor and the cabinet. Collegial governance looks like a web with the CIO (and the governor) in the center and lines of influence and direction radiating outward toward agencies, commissions, and communities of interests. Since each state enterprise is uniquely structured, the lines of influence vary from state to state. Some lines are solid while others are dotted.

The collegial web grows over time, and the relationships—along with organizational affinities—change constantly. The CIO manages the context of IT through long-range planning, funding incentives, policies, and relationships. The CIO's staff is generally small but politically significant to the

Figure 9.3: An Example of the Collegial Governance Arrangement

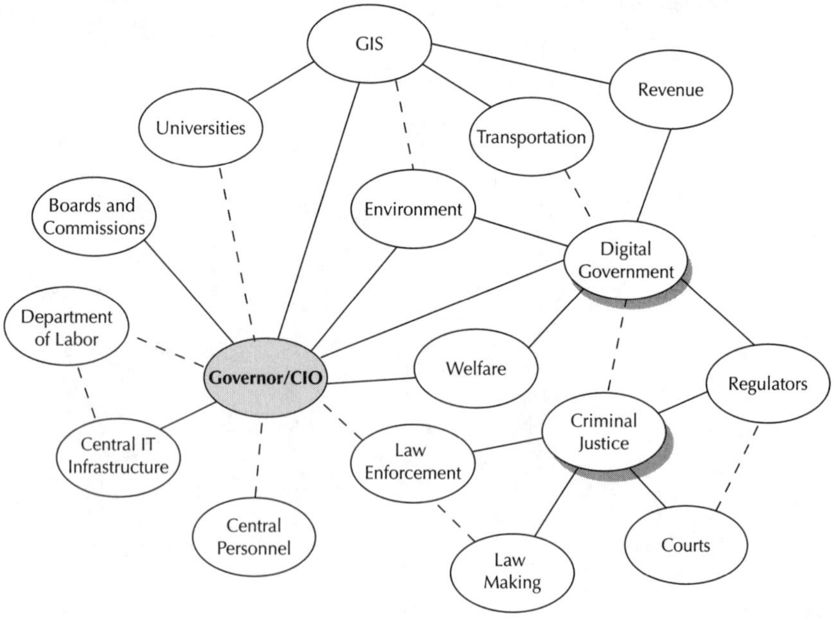

federation. Whenever there is a new governor or internal realignments (and conflicts) occur, the CIO, who relies on warm, professional relationships and reciprocal alliances throughout the enterprise, is at peril.

Rules-Based Arrangement

Almost as many states use a rules-based governance arrangement. These states have mature organizational linkages and laws, which come from active legislative oversight. Rules-based structures generally have an executive council, which performs primary oversight through approval reviews, policy making, standards setting, and planning. The CIO staff is larger than those found in collegial organizations. The rules-based CIO staff develops enterprise reporting procedures, scorecards, and exception reports. The structure has a graduated, or hierarchical, structure. Rules-based structures are top down and rely on committees to achieve significant initiatives.

Often, rules-based structures do not cover all branches of government. Educational institutions, courts, and legislative oversight are more loosely coupled to the executive branch. In addition, concerns about separation of powers constrain the governance model because of the model's reliance on rules and exception reporting.

Figure 9.4: An Example of a Rules-Based IT Governance Arrangement

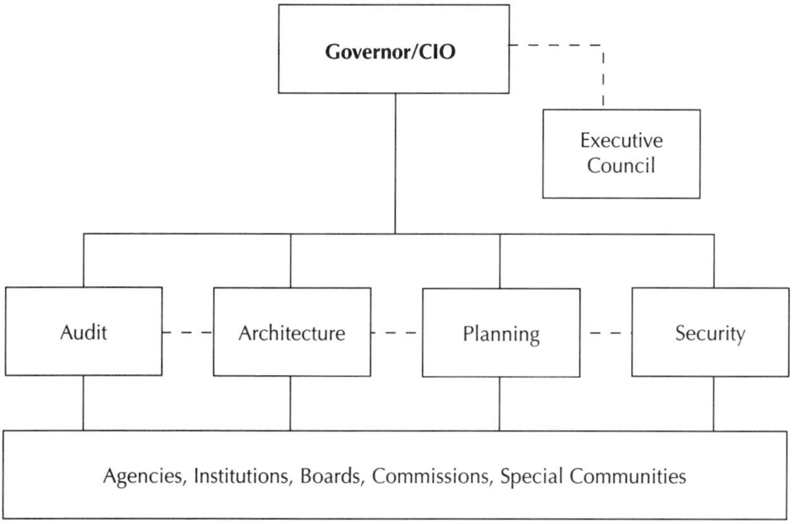

Roles-Based Arrangement

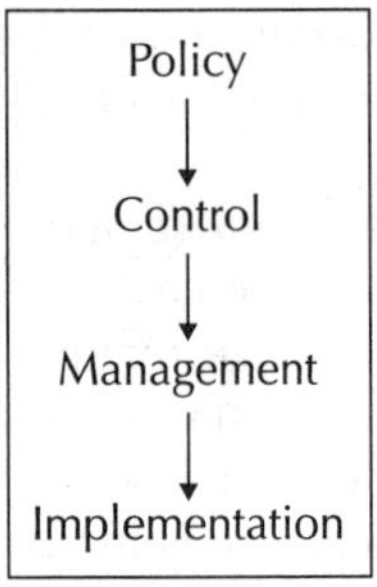

A growing number of states are moving toward a roles-based arrangement. This model follows the traditional hierarchy of an organizational structure.

The policy role is high level and enterprise-wide in its focus. All branches of government are under the same enterprise policies while the individual branches of government retain their policy-making authority for the organizations and agencies under their jurisdiction. In order to strike a balance between the branches and the enterprise, the IT-governance statute must clearly specify the enterprise policy-making authority.

The roles-based model usually has a central executive council with broad-based representation. The representation includes all branches, educational leadership, local units, and private sector. The chief information technology architect for the state supports the council. The council is responsible for policies, long-range plans, project-management standards, and enterprise architecture. Enterprise security is also under the council's watchful eye. The governance model is modular in its design.

Figure 9.5: An Example of a Roles-Based IT Governance Arrangement

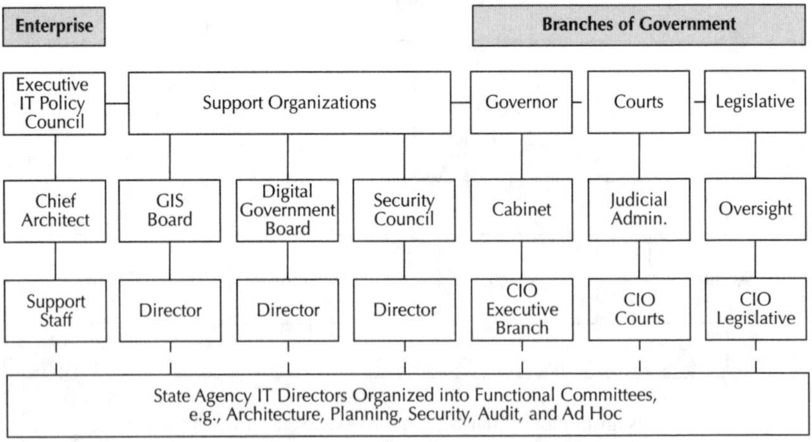

[Note: In some states the executive branch CIO position might be a cabinet-level position or attached as an adjunct to the governor's office.]

The state chief information technology architect, working with state agencies, prepares architectures, long-range plans, policies, and project management standards. The executive, legislative, and judicial branch CIOs manage and implement these enterprise plans, policies, and project management standards. The branch CIOs also approve projects, establish directions and plans influence funding, and implement architectures (for their branches of government). The branch CIOs are voting members of the enterprise executive council, and the executive-branch CIO sits in the governor's cabinet or occupies a similar cabinet-level position reporting to the governor. The support organizations depicted in Figure 9.5 work at the enterprise level as well as at the governmental-branch level.

Security in a roles-based IT governance model is often handled through a subcommittee of the executive council for oversight. This subcommittee has policy authority over a security council representing all branches of government. The chief security officer reports to this council and draws staffing resources from the state agency-level IT directors. NASCIO's Enterprise Architecture Working Group has done some excellent research into roles-based governance, which is contained in its "Enterprise Architecture Development Kit, Version 1.0." The toolkit is available for free download at NASCIO's website at www.nascio.org/hotissues/ea.

The three governance models are rarely as pure as described here. Local, state, and federal governments use variants of each of the models. For this reason, a roles-based model may also use collegial- and rules-based substructures to achieve enterprise goals.

Despite the need for hybridized arrangements, local, state, and federal governments should create an IT governance model that allows the enterprise to set policies, standards, and practices for protecting critical infrastructures.

Figure 9.6: An Example of Security in a Roles-Based IT Governance Arrangement

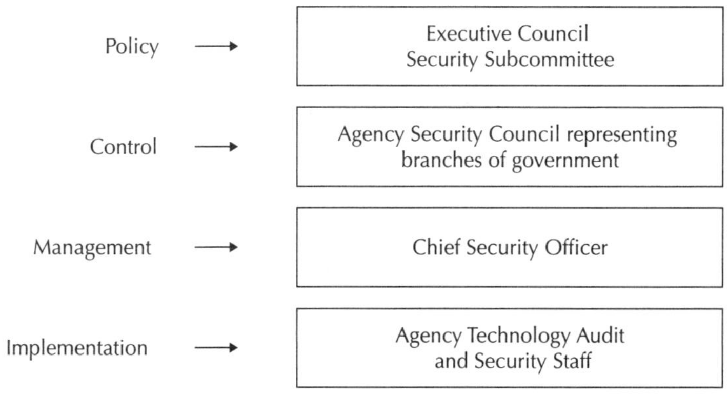

At the state level, the IT governance model should include all the branches of government and clearly identify a security authority and an oversight body to monitor performance against policies and directions. All branches of government should subscribe to an enterprise architecture and shared infrastructure, project management standards, IT metrics, and audit standards for external and internal review of controls.

Finally, IT security must be integrated with emergency response at the state and local levels. State governments are uniquely postured to lead the integration because they are positioned between local units and the federal government. Also, the states' posture is enhanced with an IT infrastructure that touches cities, townships, counties, and other jurisdictions where people live and work. For this reason, state governments should realign their IT governance structure to fully involve local and federal government entities.

Recommendation 2: Implement Enterprise Planning for Outcomes to Measure Enterprise Success

Implement enterprise planning for outcomes, including measures for success and best practices for setting and performing tasks, and commit to sharing resources for the good of the whole.

People Are Key

Security relies on people, their expertise and their cooperation. In large government organizations there are many IT technologists as well as subject-matter experts who are IT literate and active in building systems. At any given period there can be 25 to 50 major IT systems under development. This is especially true for governments that are highly active in digital government initiatives.[9] Coordinating such a large and diverse labor force is very challenging for CIOs. Shared IT infrastructure and large application portfolios further complicate the challenge. In order to meet this challenge, CIOs seek to develop a coherent set of design principles, standard practices, and technology choices that are well grounded in the disciplines of information management. Moreover, a core team of at least four key players needs to be involved.

The CIO's job is more technical and managerial, while the CTO (chief technology officer) focuses more on the business case for IT. The central-infrastructure provider is technical and focused on shared resources, and the architect is focused on technical standards. Large government bodies have separate specialists for each of the four roles, while medium-sized organizations tend to combine roles. For example, medium-sized government organizations (i.e., 25,000 to 40,000 employees) might combine the CIO and CTO roles. Smaller jurisdictions could also benefit from combining

Figure 9.7: The Core Team

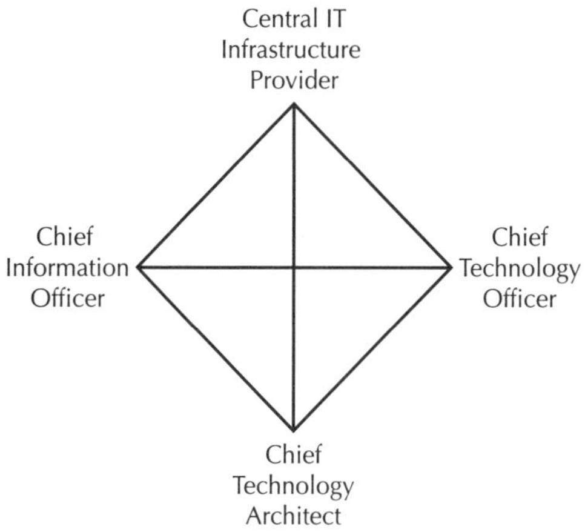

the IT central infrastructure provider role with this position. As a general rule, it is best to keep the technology architect separate from the CIO role. This separation provides a check and balance. Here the architect plans and sets enterprise standards, while the CIO implements and manages to the architectures and standards. The two roles frequently overlap in the planning functions.

Enterprise Security Planning

Security Planning requires a clear understanding of enterprise plans and architecture and an understanding of IT technology and trends. The plans and architecture are based on guiding design principles, attributes, and standard practices and technologies that comprise the shared enterprise IT infrastructure. The guiding design principles must penetrate the organization in forming a "common will." The design principles form evaluation criteria and can be used as an enterprise "scorecard" against which to measure successes and set initiatives. Clearly the workforce must be properly trained in these guiding design principles, standard practices, and the technologies that comprise the shared enterprise IT infrastructure. Communication and Coordination are key aspects of Enterprise Security Planning.

Strategic long-range plans set priorities for the enterprise. When determining enterprise priorities, it is essential to include stakeholders. Leveraging expertise of many participants to understand unique requirements and constraints can result in "win-win" shared IT infrastructure choices. Figure 9.8 depicts the Planning Cycle showing the relationship between enterprise long-range planning, short-range planning, projects, enterprise budgets,

Figure 9.8: The Planning Cycle

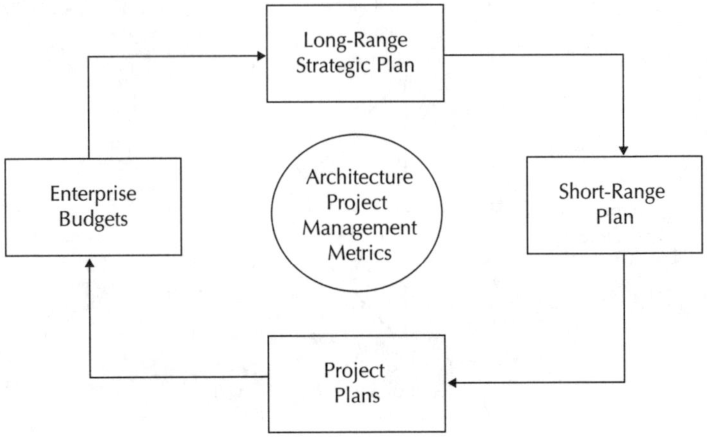

and shared enterprise architecture and infrastructure. Security planning is part of this overall planning cycle.

The planning model above moves from strategy in long-range and short-range plans to tactics in individual project plans and enterprise budgeting. Enterprise Architecture drives and supports formation of an enterprise infrastructure. Project management, and metrics are crucial to measuring success of individual projects for both conformance to the enterprise architecture and infrastructure as well as contributing to the evolution of the enterprise architecture and shared infrastructure. Security is addressed as a sub-architecture and in the metrics used to measure progress. The security gaps identified in this process are addressed in project plans and budget considerations.

Recommendation 3: Adopt IT Control Objectives

Adopt IT control objectives to manage, implement, and maintain IT systems.

COBIT®[10]

Developed by the IT Governance Institute and the Information Systems Audit and Control Association and Foundation (ISACA/ISACF), COBIT—Control Objectives for Information and Related Technologies—provides a framework designed to assess how well internal controls support the business processes and requirements of the enterprise. The objectives cover information technology effectiveness, compliance, integrity, and efficiency. The standards also address key planning and organizing practices, acquisition and implementation of IT resources, delivery and support, and monitoring performance against standards. The CobiT "Executive Summary" consists of an Executive Overview that provides a thorough awareness and understanding of CobiT's key concepts and principles for management awareness.

At the heart of the CobiT framework are assessment instruments for evaluating application systems, technologies, facilities, data, and people. The CobiT framework, which explains how IT processes deliver the information that the business needs to achieve its objectives, divides IT into 34 high-level control objectives, one for each of 34 IT processes, contained in four domains as follows:

- **Planning and Organization**—covers strategy and tactics, and concerns the identification of the ways IT can best contribute to the achievement of the business objectives.
- **Acquiring and Implementing**—deals with identifying IT solutions as well as implementing and integrating them into the business process. Life-cycle issues such as changes and maintenance of existing systems are also covered by this domain.
- **Delivery and Support**—addresses the delivery of required services, ranging from traditional operations over security and continuity aspects to training. This domain also includes the actual processing of data by application systems.
- **Monitoring**—guides management's oversight of the organization's control process and independent assurance provided by internal and external audits, as IT processes must be regularly assessed for their quality and compliance with control requirements.

The framework also takes into account fiduciary, quality, and security needs for the enterprise and provides for seven information criteria (i.e., effectiveness, efficiency, availability, integrity, confidentiality, compliance, and reliability) that can be used to generically define what the business requires from IT as well as which IT resources (i.e., people, applications, technology, facilities, and data) are impacted. In addition, 318 detailed control objectives have been established for IT management and practices.[11] Also, CobiT contains audit guidelines that provide suggested audit steps corresponding to each of the 34 high-level control objectives.

As shown in Figure 9.9, the Management Guides are composed of the following:

- **Maturity Models**—to help determine the stages and expectation levels of control and compare them against industry norms.
- **Critical Success Factors**—to identify the most important actions for achieving control over the IT processes.

Figure 9.9: Hierarchy of CobiT Framework Materials

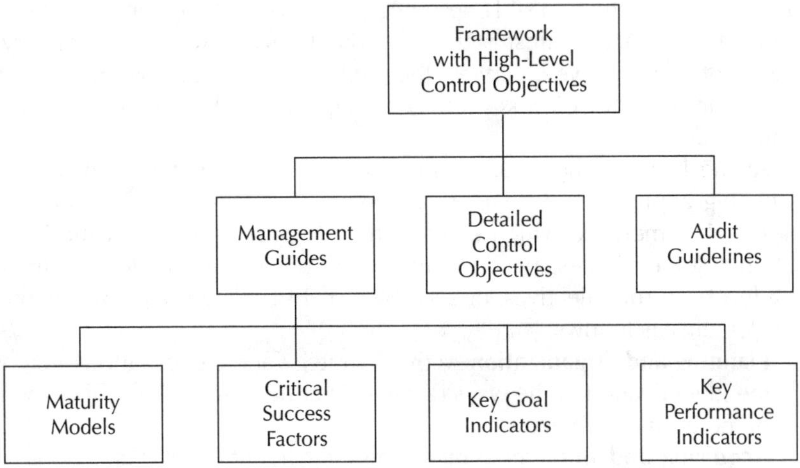

Source: Reprinted with permission of ISACA.

- **Key Goal Indicators**—to define target levels of performance.
- **Key Performance Indicators**—to measure whether an IT control process is meeting its objective.

These Management Guidelines help answer the questions of immediate concern to all those who have a stake in enterprise success.

CobiT was founded in the belief that successful enterprises, such as states, must manage the effective union between business processes and information systems.[12] The model depicts central functions as a driver of enterprise activities. The controls help ensure that business objectives are met through vigilance to best practices and effective as well as efficient use of resources. CobiT emphasizes security and helps the organization better control the task dimension of Leavitt's Diamond.

FISCAM

Some states use the "Federal Information Systems Control Audit Manual: Volume I Financial Statement Audits" (FISCAM) developed by the U.S. General Accounting Office (GAO). The body of standards presented in the manual "...provides auditors guidance in evaluating internal controls over the confidentiality, integrity, and availability of data maintained in computer-based information systems,"[13] (FISCAM cites CobiT as a key reference in each of its sections addressing evaluating and testing of these controls.) It takes an enterprise perspective and can be used to integrate IT architecture, governance, and planning activities across all branches of state government. It also ties in nicely with a number of key federal directives and initiatives to include:

- Presidential Decision Directive 63: "Protecting America's Critical Infrastructures" at www.fas.org/irp/offdocs/pdd-63.htm
- Presidential Decision Directive 67: "Enduring Constitutional Government and Continuity of Government" at www.fas.org/irp/offdocs/pdd/pdd-67.htm
- NIST Special Bulletin 800-14: "Generally Accepted Principles and Practices for Security of Information Technology Systems"at http://csrc.nist.gov/publications/nistpubs/ (See "SP 800-14.")
- NIST Special Bulletin 800-18: "Guide for Developing Security Plans for Information Technology Systems" at http://csrc.nist.gov/publications/nistpubs/ (See "SP 800-18.")
- NIST Special Bulletin 800-26: "Security Self-Assessment Guide for Information Technology Systems" at http://csrc.nist.gov/publications/nistpubs/ (See "SP 800-26.")
- NIST Special Bulletin 800-34: "Contingency Planning Guide for Information Technology Systems" at http://csrc.nist.gov/publications/nistpubs/ (See "SP 800-34.")

The GAO and the National State Auditors Association (NSAA) have jointly published a companion manual, the Management Planning Guide for Information Systems Security Auditing (www.gao.gov/special.pubs/mgmtpln.pdf) to help organizations implement FISCAM reviews. (See GAO's "Special Publications: Computer and Information Technology" web page at www.gao.gov/special.pubs/cit.html for more information, including "Federal Information System Controls Audit Manual: Volume I Financial Statement Audits," "Information Security Risk Assessment: Practices of Leading Organizations," and "Information Technology: An Audit Guide for Assessing Acquisition Risk.")

Many public- and private-sector organizations provide assurance services, including security reviews, control assessments, and policy guidance. These organizations include the Centers for Medicaid and Medicare Services (CMS) (http://cms.hhs.gov) and the American Institute of Certified Public Accountants' (AICPA) SysTrust (www.aicpa.org/assurance/systrust/princip.htm), just to name a few.

Recommendation 4: Develop Security Metrics

Develop security metrics that accurately measure unwanted intrusions, security breaches, penetrations, and vulnerabilities. The reporting should be shared at a summary level with the executive, legislative, and judicial branches of state government as well as with other governmental organizations. The reports should be confidential to government communities.

In order for security to permeate the plans and culture of an organization, the CIO needs to develop a set of reporting metrics that clearly show whether security requirements are being satisfied. The metrics flow from several important sources.

Audit Findings

Internal and external auditors evaluate general and application controls in order to determine the level of test work required to confirm the accuracy and reliability of financial statements. Audits identify weaknesses in management practices and in security. Auditors, who evaluate specific controls related to IT systems and security, are a rich source of information for CIOs, IT infrastructure providers, chief security officers, and chief technology officers, as well as technology architects.

Intrusion Attempts and Penetrations

IT security officers are very interested in the count of intrusions that appear in scanning reports, as well as penetration counts, the level of penetrations, and the nature of the penetrations. Finally, security officers are highly sensitive to the count of attacks that come from internal as well as external sources. This information should be gathered at the department level of the organization and reported at the enterprise level through the CIO and into the IT governance structure.

Virus Alerts and Recovery

A constant readiness center, intrusion response team, or an equivalent must know when viruses infiltrate the organization, how the viruses negotiated their way through security, and the resources used—measured in elapsed time and cost—to recover from the viruses. Distributed denial of service (dDoS) attacks, viruses, worms, hacks, sloppy users, breaches of physical security, and software failures are part of the normal conduct of business. The important point here is that CIOs know when these events are increasing beyond a baseline. Also, it is very important that the CIO knows what caused the spike. Basic systems should have 99.9 percent ("three nines") availability. However, mission-critical systems require an availability baseline as high as 99.999 percent ("five nines"). This higher level is required in mission-critical criminal justice, payment, and payroll applications, to mention only a few. When availability drops below these levels, the CIO must be informed.

National Alerts

National alerts are important sources of information for CIOs and chief security officers. There are many national organizations that report alerts and provide subscriber services to customers who need technical help to protect core systems or processes. NASCIO's Security and Reliability Team assembled the following descriptions of some of the many IT security resources that operate on a national and international scale and are available to all public-sector CIOs and security chiefs.

- **CERT/CC**—The Software Engineering Institute (SEI) at Carnegie-Mellon University established the CERT/CC in 1988. SEI is a federally funded research and development center with a broad charter to improve the practice of software engineering. It is also an excellent source for incident statistics. (www.cert.org/nav/index.html)
- **National Infrastructure Protection Center (NIPC)**—An operational entity of the FBI, NIPC serves as a national critical infrastructure threat assessment, warning, vulnerability, and law-enforcement investigation and response entity. It is an excellent source for critical alerts emanating from the federal government. (www.nipc.gov)
- **Critical Infrastructure Assurance Office (CIAO)**—An agency of the U.S. Department of Commerce, CIAO was created in response to Presidential Decision Directive 63 (PDD-63) in May 1998. CIAO assists states and local units of government on critical infrastructure protection strategies. Their services are also available to industry sectors. (www.ciao.gov)
- **Partnership for Critical Information Security (PCIS)**—Also originating from PDD-63, PCIS is a nonprofit entity providing public-private collaboration. It operates out of the U.S. Chamber of Commerce. (CIAO leads federal government participation in PCIS activities.) It coordinates outreach to the eight national critical infrastructure sectors, which include information and communications, electric energy, gas/oil production and storage, banking and finance, transportation, water supply, emergency services, and government services. PCIS also addresses sector interdependencies, vulnerabilities, information sharing, and public awareness. (www.pcis.org)
- **System Administration, Networking and Security Institute (SANS)**—Founded in 1989, SANS is a cooperative research and education organization of system administrators, security professionals, and network administrators. The institute is a unique partnership of government agencies, private corporations, and universities from around the world. It is also an excellent source for vulnerability reports and global trends in cyber-threats. (www.sans.org/newlook/home.php)
- **National State Geographic Information Council (NSGIC)**—Members of NSGIC include senior geographic information system (GIS) managers representing state government, federal agencies, local government, the

private sector, and education. The association provides research, best practices information, and technical training, including uses of GIS for homeland security. (www.nsgic.org)

Intra-State Security Information Sharing and Analysis Centers

Many state, federal, and local units of government rely on the organizations profiled above. However, the resources of these organizations alone are not targeted enough to effectively handle the growing incidents of intrusions, viruses, and hacks seen by a particular enterprise. As a result, a number of states have developed internal security information sharing and analysis centers or ISACs, to help their security officers analyze and parse intrusions. These *intra-state* ISACs are frequently linked to a constant readiness center, which is the coordinating center for state government enterprise response and recovery.

Some intra-state ISACs consist of inter-agency listservs that allow a state's security chief to push alerts to the agency IT directors. They also allow the list membership to collectively analyze incidents and suggest responses. As they mature, intra-state ISACs will be staffed with specialists who have expertise in hardware, software, networks, and physical security. The ISACs will also have emergency response specialists trained in emergency management disciplines and well versed in techniques for IT disaster preparedness and recovery. ISAC specialists will work side by side with certified IT disaster recovery experts. In addition, the ISAC's staff should be trained in audit standards such as those in the IT Governance Institute's CobiT (Control Objectives for Information and Related Technologies) or the U.S. General Accounting Office's Federal Information System Controls Audit Manual (FISCAM), depending on that state's audit approach. Also, they should be familiar with generally accepted security standards such as ISO/IEC 17799 ("Code of practice for information security management").

Recommendation 5: Develop Enterprise-IT Security Architectures and Establish a Shared/Common Security Technology Infrastructure

Develop state enterprise-IT architectures using accepted architecture-setting methodologies. Define the security domain of the architecture based on guiding design principles and standard practices. Establish an enterprise shared infrastructure by defining a common set of technologies and approaches that can be leveraged across the enterprise.

Stephen Covey says that effectiveness begins with the "end in mind."[14] The "ends" for organizations are commonly referred to as "goals." Five key qualities should be considered when decisions are made about system goals and their effectiveness. The system must have:

Figure 9.10: System Architecture Qualities

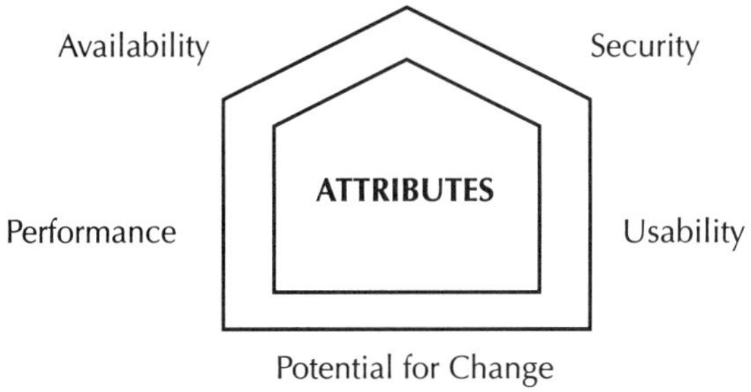

- Potential for change
- High availability
- High usability
- Adequate performance
- Reliable security (i.e., trustworthiness)

Each of these five qualities must be in balance. For example, security affects system availability, and it can also degrade performance and usability. It is a tradeoff. As systems become more difficult to access, the usability of the system will decrease. Security also adds overhead to the system, which in turn adversely affects performance. The tradeoffs require an understanding of risks, user/stakeholder needs, current costs, staff skills, and the business demands for each system. These business demands, which can be categorized by attribute, are key. They drive total cost of ownership and determine staffing skills required to balance the tradeoffs. Table 9.2 presents key factors related to each attribute.

These attributes flow through the business, application, information, and technical architectures. They permeate the sub-architectures that describe information technology from different perspectives—from the point of view of the application developer, end user, service provider, and IT manager. Many specialists are involved and their perspectives are critical to system integrity, reliability, and, ultimately, performance. Again, security, a key architectural component, is about people and how well they are able to blend perspectives and talents.

Recommendation 6: Develop a Business Case for Security

Develop a business case for security. The business case should be based on a full risk assessment of critical-infrastructure vulnerabilities. The risk assessment should include a complete inventory of critical systems and assets. The assessment also should involve a gap analysis between actual and ideal security levels for the identified systems and assets.

It is natural to ask: "How do I begin building a secure environment?" As mentioned earlier, Covey reminds us "to begin with the ends in mind."[17] The ends he refers to are the targets we want to hit. Risk assessment helps us define the targets for a secure environment. Risk assessment also helps us know where we stand today. The following recommendations outline a simple approach that can be used to perform risk assessments. The approach has a start-up phase and five follow-on steps.

Step 1. Determine Actual "As Is" Risk

There are many risk-assessment methodologies. However, the best methodologies share a core logic that starts with an inventory, determines criticality, and analyzes the number of people affected if a given asset is lost. These three processes are used to create an Impact-Risk Index. Next, the analysis examines the time required to recover if the asset is lost. This information is also indexed and multiplied by an estimate of the probability of losing an asset. This is called the Recovery-Loss Index. An actual risk assessment index is then calculated by multiplying the Impact-Risk Index by the Recovery-Loss Index. The result is an Actual Risk Index expressed as a percentage.

Impact-Risk Index x Recovery-Loss Index = Actual Risk Index

Table 9.2: Business Demands Attributes

Availability	Usability	Performance	Security
Reliable components Error detection Fault tolerance Repair Preventive maintenance Distribution, installation, and activation	User testing and evaluation Requirements capture and analysis Ergonomics Consistent user interface Support services, training, and documentation	System predictability Comparability and benchmarks Manageability, control, and monitoring	Confidentiality Integrity Availability to authorized users Accountability Non-repudiation

Figure 9.11: Simplified Risk Assessment

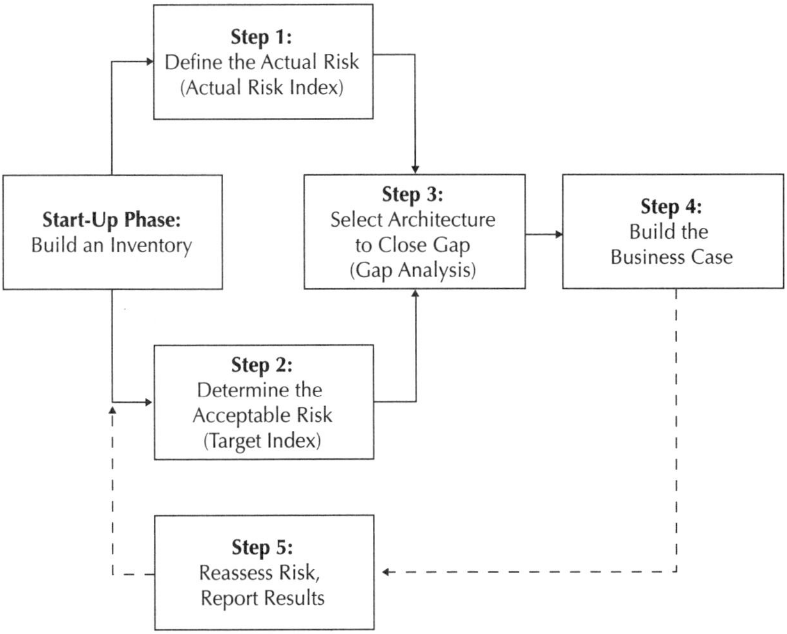

Step 2. Determine the Target or "To Be" Risk Index

The security council and asset owners should meet and, using the most reliable data available, develop a target risk index acceptable to the enterprise. The target risk index is expressed as a percentage. Some assets with low criticality might have a high target-index number, such as 10 percent, while highly critical assets might have a low target-index number, such as 1 percent. The target index represents the amount of risk an organization is willing to accept against various types of cyber-threats. When the index is high, more risk is accepted; a low index number means only minimal risk is acceptable.

Step 3. Determine and Close the "Gap"

Risk assessment methodologies also include gap analysis. The analysis compares the acceptable risk ("to be") with the actual risk level ("as is"). The difference is called the "gap." It is oftentimes expressed as a positive or negative percentage. Negative gaps indicate the enterprise is at risk, while positive gaps mean security for an asset meets or exceeds expectations.

Acceptable Risk Index - Actual Risk Index = Risk "Gap"

In addition, popular methodologies include a process for closing the gap. This process uses the enterprise architecture to select security subassembly architectures that best fit the criticality and recovery time for the asset or system. The goal is to select a security architecture that produces a positive "gap" score.

Step 4. Build the Business Case

The fourth step in risk assessment involves building the business case for security. The security council and asset owners should estimate the cost for the security architecture selected to reduce the gap. This cost is compared to economic and qualitative losses if the security architecture is not implemented. This represents a cost-avoidance benefit and is central to determining the feasibility for implementing security initiatives. This benefit is called an exposure to loss reduction.

Step 5. Implement, Reassess, and Report Results

The last step is often not done, yet it is the most important. Security is organic in the sense that security must adapt to changing conditions caused by technology advances as well as changing threats upon the enterprise. For example, the events of September 11, 2001, dramatically changed the exposures to loss and the probabilities that affect security indices. Such events also drive innovations in architecture. For these reasons, the security council needs to evaluate the implementation of new security initiatives on at least a quarterly schedule. These evaluations involve refreshing the risk assessment and reporting the results to asset owners and to the IT governance authority. Finally, CIOs should make sure all security initiatives comply with change management disciplines and that the inventory of assets is updated to reflect security architectures and current risk assessments.

The inventory is more than a listing of assets and systems. The inventory should include an estimate of the number of people affected by the systems along with the risk assessment for "as is" and "to be" risks. Also, the inventory should properly report the "gap" index for each asset or system.

Technology

Recommendation 7: Deploy Security Technologies

Define security controls and deploy automated and manual security technologies based on asset inventories and application criticality, including security levels derived from the enterprise architecture for IT.

The following recommendation covers methods organizations use to select appropriate security technologies. In the following example, IT security architectures are grouped into three levels. The choice of a security level to protect an asset depends on the asset's importance, vulnerability, and value. There must be a current and accurate inventory of IT assets to drive the security-level selection process.

Level 1—Basic

This lowest level contains the minimum architecture for security. Basic security includes control over physical access to data centers and enterprise networks. Documented entry systems such as key-card entry and log reports are required for physical access to the data center and other secure areas. Also, passwords are required for electronic access to IT systems. Passwords should be at least nine characters with capital and lowercase letters, numbers, and symbols. Software should be able to deny password changes that repeat or are closely related to historic passwords used by individuals. Password changes should be forced every two to four weeks. Finally, network scans and virus protection disciplines are critical to basic security practices.

Basic security also requires a complete understanding of LAN segments. The understanding includes server placement as well as application assignments on the LAN segments. In addition, firewalls and basic encryption using a Secure Sockets Layer (SSL) are required. Applications should also have password protection and forced-change procedures as mentioned above. Finally, the applications should have a full array of edits, exception reporting, check digits, and balance confirmations like batch-control totals and transaction controls. Confirmation of application controls is the independent responsibility of functional users who own the application. Here separation of duties is very important.

Basic security also requires frequent reviews of system logs, strong controls over administrator rights, and a robust procedure to manage system-level patches, fixes, and emergency upgrades. Technical support owns the system-level software and the security process to properly control deep system-level changes, such as those to operating systems or utilities.

In order for general and application controls to exist, three criteria must be satisfied. First, control must first be established. Second, it must operate. And, third, the operation must be supervised through independent confirmation by management. If any of these three requirements is missing, control—by definition—does not exist. Finally, basic security requires control over system-level changes and application changes. These changes must be subject to version control, documentation, and recovery disciplines. Change management is fundamental to security.

Level 2—Medium

The medium level of security requires an architecture that emphasizes complete authentication of those who access IT systems. The authentication can include public key infrastructure (PKI), biometrics, cryptographic-card technology, or variants thereof that confirm that a given user is, in fact, the person whom he or she claims to be. Also, callback technologies are frequently used to confirm that certain devices are authorized to access certain networks.

For mission-critical applications, managers are responsible for passwords that are used to perform emergency fixes. These passwords are kept in sealed envelopes under lock and key. They can be used only once. All passwords are encrypted using at least 256-bit encryption algorithms. Finally, users are barred from a system after two failed attempts to properly enter the correct password and/or user identity. All exceptions are logged and independently reviewed by system administrators as well as system owners.

Cryptographic-card technologies allow users to have unique passwords for each session. This technology is frequently used in law enforcement applications. The password exists only for enough time to allow log-on. Also, the passwords are fully encrypted and security administrators closely monitor the use of the cards. More sophisticated network scans, transaction sheathing (such as tunneling technologies), and request-callback techniques are also used to secure systems that require medium-level security. Finally, critical data that passes through networks at this level should be fully encrypted.

Level 3—High

This highest security level moves from defense to offense. The network should know who is seeking access to a given system and sound the alarm when unauthorized access is attempted or gained. Knowledge of the user is ascertained by full authentication, confirmation based on application security profiles, and full authorization.

The highest level of security also includes active system scanning, random "white hat" hack attempts by security officers and auditors, and masking of infrastructure through the use of "honey pots" that entice hackers to false targets where they can be monitored and "tar pits" that bog down the spread of viruses and worms within a system. Security technologists use tar-pit logs to reverse-engineer attacks and to trace the identity and source of intrusions. Finally, security officers notify organizational partners when that partner's infrastructure has been compromised, thus exposing the state's systems. Security officers work closely with law enforcement and, with help from the legal staff, are empowered to press legal charges against those who attempt to compromise systems.

Organizations must have policies for monitoring unauthorized installation of software by employees in violation of security protocols and license agreements. System administrators should frequently examine the software operating on PCs and servers to confirm that the software is appropriate and that software versions conform to organizational standards. Also, security officers and local campus administrators must have current procedures for responding to virus attacks. The procedures should give the officers and administrators the authority to disconnect devices that threaten the stability of LANs, metropolitan area networks (MANs), and wide area networks (WANs). Security is not for the fainthearted; it is hard work and it has costs. As mentioned earlier, regardless of level, effective controls exist when three criteria are satisfied. First, control must be established. Second, it must operate, and, third, the operation must be supervised through independent confirmation by management. If any of these three requirements are missing, control—by definition—does not exist.

Recommendation 8: Develop a State Security Portal

Develop a state security portal that integrates with emerging technologies for emergency responders such as intelligent roads and radio-frequency infrastructure. The state security portal should have a public access site as well as a private, enterprise site for coordinating emergency response.

Earlier we discussed the key people involved in setting enterprise standards. Remember the core team graphic.

These four positions form the core team for setting enterprise design principles, standard practices, and technology choices for the shared enterprise infrastructure. However, the core team requires help to develop security sub-architectures. For this reason, the core team needs to add

Figure 9.12: The Core Team (Revisited)

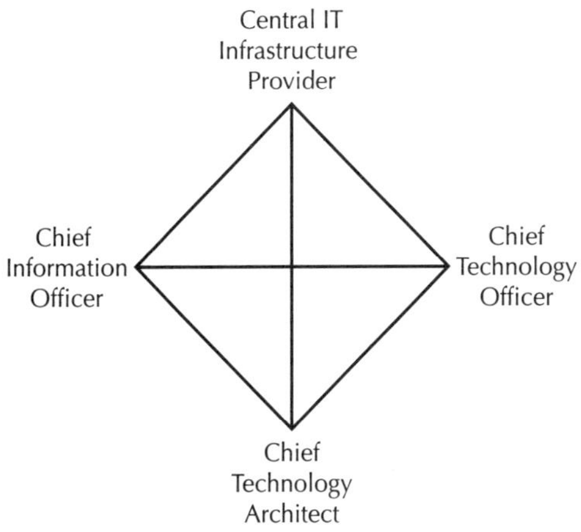

Figure 9.13: The Expanded Core Team

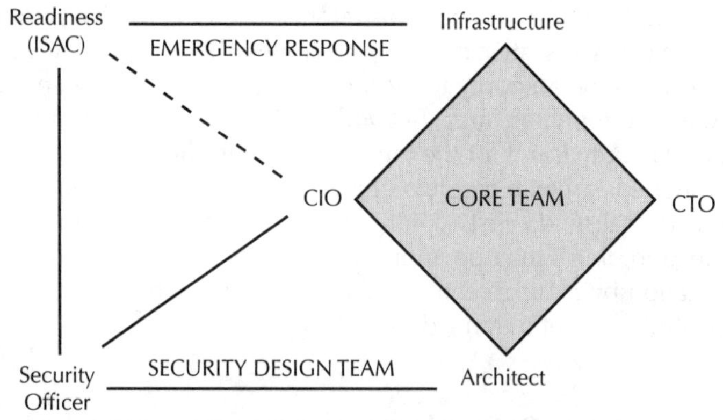

emergency response team specialists. These specialists include the chief security officer and the director of the constant readiness center.

Also the core team should include a security design team to assist those who manage the constant readiness centers and ISACs. This computer emergency/incident response team (CERT or CIRT) should include the state CIO, director of the readiness center/ISAC, chief security officer, and the director(s) of the shared data center and network infrastructures. The CIO is the linchpin for core, design, and response teams.

In addition to managing emergency response, the CERT is responsible for managing a security portal used by the enterprise, citizens, and businesses that rely on state services. The portal has a secure as well as public access site. The portal should be designed to help emergency management notify and assist citizens in time of crisis. It should also help coordinate the enterprise's response to disasters and major security breaches. The portal site relies heavily on geographic information system (GIS) technologies. GIS is a key technology for integrating security response and applications that support these responses.

The portal provides controlled private access to applications that include 511-truck routing, ambulance responses, 911 services, criminal-justice information-system alerts, and Federal Emergency Management Agency (FEMA) response. The public security portal also includes placeholders to report critical infrastructure alerts such as water contamination sites, power failure locations, road closings, fires, and telecom outage areas. The site also shows civil defense facilities, schools, hospitals, and related support service locations critical at the time to emergency response.

The secure site is designed to push critical-infrastructure information, including maps locating assets valuable to law enforcement and emergency management personnel. The portal should also be designed to coordinate FEMA response teams, the National Guard, and IT specialists.

In its most sophisticated form, the security portal is more than a website. The portal should be tied to intelligent highway systems to include electronic signs and disparate emergency radio broadcast frequencies. Citizens should be able to view critical-infrastructure messaging from roadside electronic billboards and hear these messages on home and car radios. True integration is more than a web page and requires leveraging common enterprise infrastructure to full benefit.

Homeland Security

Recommendation 9: Establish an Interstate ISAC

Establish an interstate security information sharing and analysis center (interstate ISAC) funded at least partially by the federal government. The interstate ISAC, building on the federal-sector ISAC model, will assist states in analyzing security breaches, repairing affected systems, reporting security alerts, providing clearinghouse services for progressive practices, and interfacing with appropriate federal entities.

Many states will not have the resources to staff and fund their own intrastate ISAC. States realize that the cost of these services is high and the level of talent required to unravel hacks is difficult to find. It takes highly specialized skills to handle a hack in deep infrastructure. An *interstate* security information sharing and analysis center (interstate ISAC), built on the federal-sector ISAC model, could provide these skills and aggregate state incident data to support national strategic cyber-security planning. NASCIO should continue its effort to answer the recent call by Howard Schmidt, vice chairman of the President's Critical Infrastructure Protection Board, to coordinate the creation of an interstate ISAC to supplement individual states' efforts.[16]

Also, the interstate ISAC could help states coordinate their responses to cyber-attacks and serve as a liaison to law enforcement and national defense entities. Coordination also includes dissemination of best practices for meeting audit exceptions and for implementing security standards promulgated by oversight bodies, internal auditors, and federal agencies that have issued mandates such as the Health Information Portability and Accessibility Act (HIPAA) security rules. As with intrastate ISACs, an interstate ISAC must have staff trained in generally accepted audit and security standards. These standards cover basic disciplines for how states manage IT resources. The standards also establish a context for setting security architectures and initiatives.

The interstate ISAC will:

- Assist states and local units in their efforts to thwart unwanted penetrations
- Identify sources of attacks
- Help in repairing affected systems
- Scan for unwanted intrusions
- Develop strategies and tactics for being more offensive in protecting systems and critical infrastructure, including IT strategies for identifying and prosecuting perpetrators
- Advise on security architecture
- Serve as a clearinghouse of high-level information and statistics about security risks and violations
- Provide early warning and notice
- Partner with laboratories and corporations for testing new technologies such as honey pots and tar pits for deployment in the states

Recommendation 10: Develop Model State Legislation for Information Sharing

Develop model state legislation that allows local, state, and federal entities to confidentially share security incident reports among themselves and with other ISACs supporting the nation's critical-infrastructure owners and operators.

In order to coordinate response, understand critical infrastructure, develop national strategies, and disseminate best practices in cyber-security, governments must share sensitive security information among themselves. However, this information can be a powerful weapon in the wrong hands. For this reason, sharing will not occur unless there is an assurance of confidentiality against state open records/sunshine laws and the federal Freedom of Information Act (FOIA). Interstate sharing has been limited because states fear that their security activities could become a part of another state's open records when information is shared across state boundary lines or with local or federal units of government. Also, it is difficult for CIOs to coordinate the sharing of security information that is highly sensitive to an agency, board, or commission. Nonetheless, coordination and sharing information is crucial to protecting critical infrastructure. Legislation is required at the state and national levels to provide the necessary assurances that inter-governmental security reports will be held in confidence. Security, privacy, and open records must be in balance. Finally, the legislation should prohibit private-sector firms from disclosing sensitive security information acquired in the normal course of business with governments.

Conclusions

Security is a tough business. It is intellectually challenging and emotionally draining. It is simply wrong to place the burden of security solely on the shoulders of security officers, technologists, and IT executives. Security is a shared responsibility across the entire enterprise, to include subject-matter experts, functional users, and oversight professionals. Secure organizations are built on a culture that is open, resource sharing, and focused. Secure organizations do not happen by accident.

For security to be effective, governments should teach all their employees control standards and build the standard practices into their planning and measuring processes. They should provide clear feedback through audit reports and metrics to confirm that security is properly practiced. Good security comes from a highly trained and motivated workforce. In his theories about motivation, Vic Vroom, John G. Searle Professor of Organization and Management at Yale University, created a simple model about what drives individual and corporate behavior. He said people must know what is expected. They also need to know how to meet the expectations. Armed with this knowledge, employees need to understand rewards and actually value the rewards. Finally, this knowledge must come from direct and fair feedback. Vroom said that if any of those key ingredients are missing, then motivation to act breaks down.[17] Vroom's theories are as valid today as ever.

Our children want a world that is more advanced and, at the same time, more "user friendly" than the one we have today. They want an online world that is less bureaucratic and more "life-event" driven. In this world, online government information and services are organized around significant events such as getting married, obtaining a driver's license, opening a business, coping with the loss of a loved one, or responding to a public emergency. They want a world that is "one stop" with "no wrong door." In that world the boundary lines of government will be seamless. In essence, our children want a virtual government—meaning anything done in the presence of government can be done electronically without regard to time and location. Security in that world will be non-intrusive, reliable, confidential, and available. Security in that world is tailored to the needs of citizens and businesses.

There is an epistemology—that is, specific theories and knowledge—that underlies security and IT. It is soulful—deeply personal, virtuous, and mindful of others' needs. This chapter calls public-sector CIOs to take up this epistemology. It calls for a metanoia that radically changes the way governments interact by creating new ways to share resources in order to protect vital interests. CIOs are called to develop IT governance structures that are open, sharing, and highly secure. They should follow Vic Vroom's advice about motivation, clearly plan security outcomes, teach security best practices, build security responsibilities into all position descriptions, provide feedback though metrics and scorecards, and reward employees for practicing security. These rewards include special recognition, bonuses for hitting targets, and promotion opportunities.

CIOs must also assess risks and build security portals for emergency response. In addition, the state CIOs should develop model state legislation to protect confidentiality in reporting security breaches and responses to them. The legislation should allow for the sharing of information among government entities. There also should be federal support for establishing an interstate ISAC.

The 10 recommendations that comprise this call to action reflect the belief that we cannot simply declare that everything has changed since September 11th. We must *take action* to change some of the ways we live and conduct business. We must build a world that protects our loved ones and the critical assets we all require to sustain our way of life.

Appendix I: Report from the NASCIO Forum on Security and Critical Infrastructure Protection

by Chris Dixon, NASCIO Digital Government Issues Coordinator
November 13-14, 2001
Dulles Airport Marriott
Washington, D.C.

Introduction

Security as it relates to information technology (IT)—often referred to as cyber-security—represents the ability of electronic-information owners to assure the following aspects of information systems.

- Confidentiality—information is accessible only to authorized parties.
- Integrity—information is accurate and complete at all times.
- Availability—systems are accessible and can deliver information when needed.

Secure information systems are as vital to citizen trust in digital government transactions as they are to consumers in electronic commerce. Moreover, governments attempting to do business online must comply with complicated privacy laws that can treat multiple instances of the same citizen information differently in various contexts depending on where the information is collected and how it is used. This adds to the complexity of security measures to defend information systems against the following threats.

- Insiders—accidental or malicious compromises of security protocols by authorized users
- Crackers/Virus Writers—random individuals seeking to penetrate or disable systems for personal satisfaction
- Activists—issue-oriented individuals seeking to penetrate or disable systems on behalf of a cause
- Organized Criminals—groups seeking to penetrate or disable systems for profit
- Terrorists—groups seeking to penetrate or disable systems in order to exacerbate the effects of violent acts
- Spies—intelligence operatives seeking to penetrate or disable systems on behalf of commercial or political interests
- Information Warriors—military forces seeking to penetrate or disable systems as part of a larger conflict among nation states

Toward addressing these goals and issues, the National Association of State Chief Information Officers (NASCIO) sponsored the Forum on Security and Critical Infrastructure Protection. More than 80 individuals participated in the day-and-a-half event. Participants included state CIOs and security chiefs representing 35 states. Other participants included representatives of local and federal government IT management as well as staff from other agencies and branches of state government. (Forum presentations can be found online on NASCIO's website at www.nascio.org/2001/11/securityforum011113-14.cfm.)

State CIOs have found that cyber-threats to state-government IT systems, including cyber-terrorism, have not become more pronounced since the recent War on Terrorism began in response to the September 11th attacks. (This is likely due to the fact that Islamic jihadists have not invested resources in this area.) However, thanks to sources such as Carnegie Mellon's CERT/CC, state CIOs are acutely aware of the fact that, over time, all types of cyber-threats are likely to increase in frequency and sophistication, with different threats emerging at different times from disparate sources worldwide. Fortunately, public interest in assuring the availability of government services (and, thus, the IT that supports them) has risen along with interest in assuring other aspects of the nation's critical infrastructure such as power, water, communication, financial, and transportation services, among others. Additionally, public officials are increasingly aware of the need to share reliable information as part of defense and emergency management efforts in times of crisis.

This chapter is the product of the forum. It provides a series of recommendations and action items under the headings of architecture, assessment, business alignment, education and communication, funding, governance, and legislation. Some of the action items are directed toward the states and others will be carried out by NASCIO and its organizational partners, including the National Governors' Association (NGA) and the federal government, among others.

Governance

Assuring public safety and the reliability of public services is a fundamental function of government. Toward that end, security oversight must be formally and permanently installed at the executive level of state government. Furthermore, the IT security governance structure must span the branches of government and include city and county participation.

State Action:

- Define and implement an adaptable governance structure for IT security.
- Link local governments into the governance process.

NASCIO Actions:

- Collect progressive governance practices for use by the states.
- Serve as an active voice for the states at the federal level.
- Coordinate efforts with the National League of Cities (NLC), the National Association of Counties (NACo), and NGA to aggressively promote governance models and best practices.

State and NASCIO Actions:

- Promote the fact that (1) IT is integral to prevention and response, (2) citizens hold government to a higher standard of privacy/security than the private sector, and (3) security can no longer be "delegated" to IT exclusively.
- Articulate a vision of what needs to be accomplished.

Legislation

Establishing a permanent, high-profile role for cyber-security will require legislative action and statutory authority. A governance body will have to be formally established. Security standards will have to be assessed and enforced. All of this will require the sponsorship of governors and key legislators who have to educate their peers on the nuances of cyber-security and technology. (Biometrics are not a cure-all!) State CIOs and their security chiefs will have to impress upon policy makers that cyber-security is an integral part of physical security and homeland defense.

State Actions:

- Statutorily identify an entity with compliance and enforcement authority over enterprise IT management, including security.
- Support the passage of legislation that would exempt state cyber-security communications with the federal government and ISACs from FOIA/Open Access laws—and encourage states to pass similar legislation to foster appropriate internal sharing and interchange with private partners regarding critical infrastructure.
- Keep all cyber-security legislation broad in regard to cyber-threats, not limited to cyber-terrorism.
- Champion legislation that creates real penalties for cyber-crimes of all varieties.

NASCIO Actions:

- Circulate examples of IT-management legislation that establishes security compliance and enforcement authority through a variety of centralized and decentralized arrangements.

- Conduct a grassroots campaign among the states to support federal cyber-security legislation that benefits the states.
- Educate governors, state CIOs, legislators, and commissioners of uniform state laws about the need for cyber-security legislation.
- Work with the National Conference of Commissioners of Uniform State Laws (NCCUSL) to draft model legislation that allows appropriate and confidential internal sharing of security-related information within and among the branches of state government and with private partners.
- Issue a background paper and talking points with the National Center for State Courts (NCSC), the National Conference of State Legislators (NCSL), NCCUSL, and NGA apprising policy makers of the need for legislation.

Business Alignment

In order to make security more than just an afterthought, or a series of procedures and technologies that are merely bolted on to existing operations, state CIOs and other policy makers will have to recognize it as an integral element of any digital-government rollout. Officials must be able to point to a specific set of critical business offerings—for example, public safety, education, human services, finances, and e-commerce—that depend on reliable computing and communication systems and assign security resources accordingly. These essential services will also be seen as the juiciest targets for attack, as bringing them down will deliver the heaviest blows to governments and citizens. Moreover, as citizens seek a more unified digital-government presentation that spans all the levels of government, state CIOs and their security chiefs will need to coordinate with local and federal service providers to eliminate seams that invite cyber-threats to divide and conquer with attacks on the weakest link.

State Actions:

- Collaborate with local and federal government on issues of continuity and security.
- Include security as a part of planning for IT systems.
- Synchronize security and business-continuity plans across jurisdictions and levels of government.
- Act with a sense of urgency!

NASCIO Actions:

- Ensure federal, state, and local collaboration.
- Facilitate public-private relationships that will help identify the best solutions for security and business continuity.
- Facilitate communication to the public at large.

Assessment

Establishing standards for security and incorporating them into the enterprise architecture will be only an intermediate step in the process. Determining those security standards will require an assessment of the likely threats to state IT assets along with the corresponding risks—that is, the pain that will be suffered as a result of a particular violation. This will, in turn, allow security architects to prescribe particular security standards that meet at the intersection of a likely cyber-threat and the level of risk a given owner can reasonably (or legally) tolerate. Moreover, assessments will have to be conducted periodically to check and enforce compliance with security standards across the enterprise if these standards are to be more than just friendly suggestions.

State Actions:

- Adopt a common state-federal methodology for identifying and assessing critical assets—for example, the Critical Infrastructure Assurance Office's U.S. Project Matrix. This methodology, focusing on mission-critical business processes, should identify interdependencies among internal and external systems and identify risks and vulnerabilities.
- Conduct assessments utilizing a joint state-federal assessment tool.
- Develop a business case to drive response to identified risks and vulnerabilities—quantify the cost of not acting in order to make inaction untenable.
- Coordinate state and federal homeland security efforts toward critical infrastructure assurance.
- Report best practices and success stories back to NASCIO.

NASCIO Actions:

- Act as a clearinghouse for progressive practices and success stories.
- Develop a business case for assessment.
- Help to align national assessment efforts among states and across the levels of government.
- Work with NGA to present a common voice in pursuit of federal funding support.
- Encourage the federal government to coordinate intergovernmental assessment efforts through the Office of Homeland Security.

Architecture

An adaptive, enterprise information architecture provides a set or framework of agreed-upon principles and standards, based upon business processes, that enable information sharing and interoperability across the enterprise. These enterprise-wide standards, incorporating fundamental security and privacy concerns, allow numerous departments and agencies to develop systems that meet universal requirements without forcing them to deploy a particular product or a specific technology type. Enterprise-wide adoption of architectural standards is an ongoing process of definition and education. It is not a one-time project or initiative. Over time, the coherent development of dispersed systems will facilitate sharing of information, and it will permit security personnel to better manage ever changing systems and capitalize on what should be a real home-field advantage against cyber-threats.

State Actions:

- Endorse the forthcoming NASCIO *Enterprise Architecture Toolkit* and commit resources to make architecture a high priority.
- Define your enterprise and identify your stakeholders, recognizing that stakeholders are not just internal, but span disciplines, jurisdictions, and branches of government.
- Establish a governance structure that effectively manages the architecture.
- Provide real leadership, not just mandates, in architecture for local units of government.

NASCIO Actions:

- Publish *Enterprise Architecture Toolkit* for the states.
- Promote the development of compatible architecture among the states that will enable information sharing and interoperability.
- Play a leadership role with respect to awareness, education, and adoption of architecture.
- Serve as a repository of effective architectural practices from government and private industry.

Education and Communication

Long-term cyber-security will require education to raise America's consciousness of cyber-threats and prevention. Targeted messages and instructions will have to be delivered to everyone from citizens (who should be able to recognize and report cyber-crimes) to state employees (who must be vigilant against lapses and violations of procedures and systems) to policy makers (who must be apprised of the nature and limitations of various security strategies and technologies before implementing them). State CIOs and their security chiefs should be prepared to formulate internal security education programs and champion external security education programs. Specific cyber-security and critical-infrastructure-protection campaigns will have to be developed for the different levels of government as well as for citizens and other private-sector partners. Over time, messages should be tailored to address immediate and emerging threats as identified through intergovernmental communication (horizontal and vertical) of incident-related data and alerts.

State Actions:

- Identify key stakeholders.
- Develop a cyber-security and critical-infrastructure-protection education curriculum.
- Develop information sharing mechanisms between the state, local governments, and private entities.

NASCIO Actions:

- Develop a cyber-security and critical-infrastructure-protection education framework.
- Act as a conduit to the federal government, allowing the states to speak with one voice.
- Establish a state security information sharing and analysis center (interstate ISAC) to facilitate communication among the states and the federal government.

Funding

As security is a fundamental concern for IT, funding for security must reflect its importance to the reliability of citizen-centric digital government. This will mean the strategic and rapid deployment of expertise, training, and technologies to secure critical business processes across the enterprise. Funding must be deployed flexibly within an enterprise, not a stovepipe, view, allowing resources to flow to where they are needed most immediately. Ongoing research and development will also play a key role in countering immediate and emerging cyber-threats. State government will routinely call upon existing resources at the universities and in the private sector to supplement internal resources.

State Actions:

- Include funding for certification and validation of cyber-security, disaster-recovery, and business-continuity standards.
- Assign responsibility for enterprise cyber-security funding within the state IT governance structure.

NASCIO Actions:

- Work with NGA to identify a single federal contact who can help eliminate barriers in federal stovepipe funding.
- Explore all potential sources of funding and technical assistance.
- Act as a clearinghouse for funding strategies at state, local, and federal levels.

Forum Participants

Steve Akridge
Georgia

Kim Bahrami
Florida

Claire Bailey
Arkansas

David Ballard
Kentucky

Jean Bogue
NASCIO/NSR

Howard Boksenbaum
Rhode Island

Dave Boyer
U.S. Department of Justice

Mike Boyer
Montana

Andy Cannon
Alabama

Mary F. Carroll
Ohio

Joe Christensen
Georgia

Keith Comstock
West Virginia

Steven Correll
NLETS

Elias S. Cortez
California

John Curley
NASCIO/NSR

Sharon Dawes
Center for Technology in Government

Matthew R. DeZee
South Carolina

Chris Dixon
NASCIO

Allen L. Doescher
Louisiana

Otto Doll
South Dakota

Greg Dzieweczynski
Minnesota

Cheryl Edwards
NASCIO

Donald Evans
Public Technology, Inc.

Bob Feingold
Colorado

David Fisher
Minnesota

Frank Galeotos
Wyoming

Ann Garrett
North Carolina

Charles F. Gerhards
Pennsylvania

Danielle M. Germain
ITAA

Curt Haines
Pennsylvania

Lynn Harris
New Mexico

Ron P. Hawley
North Carolina

John Hohl
Wyoming

Laura Iwan
New York

Leon Jackson, Jr.
District of Columbia

Thomas M. Jarrett
Delaware

Larry G. Kettlewell
Kansas

George Kohut
Public Technology, Inc.

Laura Larimer
Indiana

Erin Lee
National Governors' Association

Steven Lee
West Virginia

Vic Mangrum
Tennessee

Chad C. McGee
Louisiana

Valerie J. McNevin
Colorado

Scott McPherson
Florida

Michael McVicker
Washington

Elizabeth Miller
NASCIO

Amy Moran
Wisconsin

Gail A. Morris
Missouri

Kym Patterson
Arkansas

William F. Pelgrin
New York

Holli I. Ploog
DynCorp Management Resources, Inc.

R. D. Porter
Missouri

Jim Pritchett
National Center for State Courts

Susan Puntillo
Wisconsin

Carolyn T. Purcell
Texas

Wendy W. Rayner
New Jersey

Rock Regan
Connecticut

Mark Reynolds
Connecticut

David J. Roberts
SEARCH

Gary Robinson
Washington

Beth Roszman
NASCIO

Thom Rubel
National Governors' Association

Terry Savage
Nevada

Steve Schafer
Nebraska

N. Jerry Simonoff
Virginia

Dan Sipes
North Dakota

Craig Stender
Arizona

Marianne Swanson
NIST

Matthew Trail
NASCIO

Donald W. Upson
Virginia

Aldona K. Valicenti
Kentucky

Randall von Liski
Illinois

Richard C. Webb
PricewaterhouseCoopers, LLP

Gerry Wethington
Missouri

Mary Gay Whitmer
NASCIO

Rick Zelznak
Arizona

Appendix II: Mark's Story: A Hypothetical Case Study

The CIO Responds

It was winter in the heartland. Mark, a senior technologist for his state government's Unix-derived operating systems, was ready to go home. Before leaving, he decided to conduct one last check of the operating system that supports the state's Department of Natural Resources' server applications. The department's system was recently moved to Mark's central server farm. While checking the health of the system he noticed that an obscure operating system file had been updated only an hour earlier. Mark was puzzled, as he had not applied any fixes or patches that day.

When Mark examined the changed file, he saw that the code was capable of spying on password traffic that moved across a local area network (LAN) segment. The code was thin and looked like a dormant agent. Mark realized the system had been hacked. This hack was deep and the intent was clear. The LAN segment included a central payment system. If this system was compromised, Mark knew vital state operations could be seriously impaired.

He immediately notified his management, the state CIO, and the state chief security officer. The departmental owners of the systems were also notified. In short order, the LAN segment was reconfigured and the affected systems were re-certified by the owners. Mark and the chief security officer documented the intrusion and attempted to understand how the hacker was able to penetrate the state's security infrastructure. The State Bureau of Investigations (SBI) was called in to assist in the analysis. More than 10 days of investigation passed with no clear results.

As it turned out, the hack Mark discovered was particularly nasty. Ron, the state's CIO, was concerned that the initial investigation of the hack yielded no information about how it occurred. Ron was hoping for additional information before he briefed the state's Security Council. Immediately after the hack, Ron met with the state's chief IT architect and the chief security officer to discuss the hack and the steps that would be followed to flush the hack and investigate how it happened. During the meeting, the chief security officer commented, "A hack of this nature is worth about $8,000." Ron was taken aback. "Are people selling these hacks?" he asked. The answer was swift and direct, "Yes."

As Ron worked on his briefing for the IT Security Council, he wondered to himself: *Are there agents inside our operations and we just don't know about them? Maybe I am dealing with a much larger problem here.*

Fortunately, Ron worked in a state that has a strong IT governance structure. The structure includes an executive-level policy council for IT as well as support organizations for e-government, geographic information systems, and security. The Security Council is a key support organization with IT stakeholder members from the audit community, emergency management, and security staff in state agencies. Ron is very proud of the council's work and its enterprise representation. Nonetheless, he knew the briefing would be difficult.

The Enterprise Responds

Before Ron briefed the Security Council, he asked Mark to re-platform the Department of Natural Resources application on a new server and leave the old server intact for the investigation. This proved to be a very important decision.

Ron then hired a security consultant to investigate the server and application. The consultant learned that the hack occurred in two stages. The first stage happened before the server was moved to Mark's server farm. During this stage the hacker created a back-door path to the server. After the server moved to Mark's area, the hacker came back and created a routine to spy on LAN traffic. The consultant also discovered how the hacker navigated to the server when it was located in the Department of Natural Resources and he discovered how the hacker got into Mark's LAN. The security holes he discovered were immediately closed. Ron included this information in his security briefing notes.

He also included in his notes information from the security log kept by Mark. A day before the briefing, Ron met with the consultant to discuss how well the agencies document security breaches and how well they follow the state's IT security architecture. The meeting was disappointing. Agencies do not always follow the architecture for old infrastructure and applications. However, they meticulously follow the architecture for new infrastructure and applications. Also, the consultant confirmed that agencies do not keep meaningful metrics on security intrusions, successful penetrations, down time, and the like. The Security Council briefing was scheduled for 1:00 p.m.

The Security Council was formed the previous year in response to Ron's concerns about the growing number of intrusions the state was observing in the network. The number increased an alarming 25 percent in a three-month period. Ron also wanted the state to take a more aggressive approach to handling viruses and spams. He created a Constant Readiness Center to handle disaster recovery, and he wanted the center to expand its role to include coordination of emergency responses to viruses and other homeland security cyber-threats. Emergency management staff from the Adjutant General's Office was formally invited to join the Security Council and to provide staff for the Constant Readiness Center.

Ron knew the Security Council and the Constant Readiness Center staff would have many questions about Mark's hacker and would wonder about how many undetected agents could conceivably be residing in the state's systems. During the meeting, the council talked about security risks, noting that half of the security violations reported to the FBI and the Systems Administration, Networking, and Security Institute were violations perpetrated by insiders. The council asked Ron how the state controls against insider attacks and how the state protects itself from outsiders "social engineering" key staff to disclose security passwords, architectures, and techniques for safeguarding critical infrastructure.

When Ron told the council that agencies were following the security architecture for new infrastructure but not always using it for old infrastructure or applications, Janet, the chief security officer for the Department of Labor, made an important observation. "We need to conduct a statewide inventory of all our systems," she said. "We can use our Y2K inventory and update it with a security assessment." Janet volunteered to head a subcommittee to develop a "simple and practical" assessment methodology. "The methodology will point to our vulnerabilities. We can then use our architecture to fix the most critical vulnerabilities."

This discussion extended into a dialogue about security audit standards. The council decided to explore national audit standards and craft a policy statement for consideration by the executive IT policy council to train state employees on the standards. The council also drafted a recommended policy for building the standards into position profiles and job class specifications. The council reasoned that IT audit standards, risk assessments, and architecture can drive security metrics, since they are all tied together. A second subcommittee was created to recommend the audit standards that would be adopted by the entire enterprise.

Ron then told the council how the state had failed when it moved the Department of Natural Resources server to Mark's area. Ron explained that when the server was moved, it was placed on the next available LAN segment without regard to other systems on the segment. Mark did not do the move. Instead, a unit that performs facilities management services did the move. The technologist who handled the move assumed the security infrastructure on the LAN segment would protect against outside intrusions, and was not aware a back door existed prior to the move. Also, the server was not evaluated for abnormalities before it was moved and management did not oversee the move. The meeting with the Security Council lasted over four hours.

Lessons Learned

After briefing the Security Council, Ron—the state's CIO—scheduled a meeting with the Constant Readiness Center staff. Ron knew that it was impossible to parse every intrusion. His staff was small and his budget limited. The Readiness Center team understood Ron's money concerns; however, they felt providing security analysis services to state agencies and local units of government for a subscription fee could solve the problem. Also, they felt Ron could seek federal help through emergency management grants to cover start-up costs. Ron was intrigued with the suggestions. Clearly an analysis center would help disseminate information, provide technical security support to agencies, and serve as a clearinghouse and reporting organization for metrics and vulnerability assessments. The Readiness Center staff agreed to review their mission and propose an expanded role. The staff also recommended that the Readiness Center create a security lab to investigate emerging technologies, especially those that are more offensive in nature.

Ron knew the recommendations from the Security Council and Readiness Center would be expensive. He remembered back a year ago when he contracted with a national firm for a full-time network engineer. The engineer was an expert who for one year worked on site directly with state network technologists to develop a highly hardened network infrastructure. While the expert cost $155,000 per year, he was worth every cent. Ron's network up-time reports exceeded "four nines" (i.e., 99.99 percent)—quite an accomplishment in an 830-router network. Ron's customer satisfaction ratings were equally impressive—more than meeting expectations on performance, communication, price value, and understanding customer business needs. Ron remembered back four years when the satisfaction scores were only 78 percent of expectation. However, when the budget reductions came, Ron decided to cut the expert. This was a hard choice to make, but he saw few alternatives. The hacker and funding concerns were constantly on Ron's mind.

Mark—the state senior technologist—and Ron faced a unique challenge. They never caught the hacker, but they did safeguard their state's critical systems. Ron implemented a security analysis center, adopted COBIT audit standards, and built the audit standards into all IT position profiles and job class specifications. He leveraged his governance structure to help fund the security initiatives. Over 150 professionals were trained in COBIT, and the agencies gladly paid for the training. The state auditors developed a security risk assessment methodology and used it in their agency audit work. The audit standards, risk assessment, and analysis center work drove performance metrics. Funds were raised to begin work on a security portal, and legislation was passed to protect the confidentiality of security breaches and unwelcome intrusions. Most importantly, for over six months there have been no reported security breaches in any of the state agencies.

It was snowing in the heartland when Mark first encountered the hacker. Today, it is spring in the heartland, about 3:30 in the afternoon. Ron's phone is ringing. It is Mark and he is excited. "Ron, the hacker is back and I can see him trying to get into my honey pot." Ron laughed the low kind of laugh that comes when you are satisfied. "This is great," Ron declared. "Go get him!"

It took some time for Ron to completely realize the full significance of Mark's experience with the hacker. Ron was aware of the thousands of hits reported each week from intrusion-detection software. However, few hits ever materialized into a hack or penetration. Over time the thousands of hits were only bumps in the night to Ron. Yet one of the bumps was very real and serious. Ron wondered: *What about all those other bumps?* As Ron reflected he came to a new understanding. He realized the bumps are all real. *People want to get into my state's systems. They are out there and they are probing us.* Ron thought: *Each bump has a purpose.* This realization gave Ron pause and he experienced a metanoia: *I am part of a larger world, bigger than just my state. How many other states have been exploited in this way? How many exploits like this have gone unnoticed until it was too late? How could CIOs share and learn from experiences like this?*

Catching Mark's hacker before he does damage is a single success—a loud bump in the night. Ron had a change of heart. He realized that his state needed to help and to receive help from other states. Ron realized that security is a way of life that demands aggressive action tempered by humility and a willingness to share.

Appendix III: Recommended Resources

Center for Technology in Government (State University of New York at Albany)

- Project: "Sharing the Costs, Sharing the Benefits: The NYS GIS Cooperative" (www.ctg.albany.edu/projects/gis/gismenu.html)

Computer Science and Telecommunications Board (The National Academy of Science)

- Publications—Topic: Security, Assurance and Privacy (www4.nas.edu/cpsma/cstb.nsf/web/topic_security)
- "Summary of a Workshop on Information Technology Research for Crisis Management" (www4.nationalacademies.org/cpsma/cstb.nsf/web/pub_crisismanagement)

Dartmouth College

- Institute for Security Technology Studies (www.ists.dartmouth.edu)

IT Governance Institute

- "Board Briefing on IT Governance" (www.itgi.org)
- "Information Security Governance: Guidance for Boards of Directors and Executive Management" (www.itgi.org)

National Institute for Standards and Technology (NIST)

- Computer Security Resource Center csrc.nist.gov

RAND

- "Research on Mitigating the Insider Threat to Information Systems—#2: Proceedings of a Workshop Held August, 2000" (www.rand.org/publications/CF/CF163)
- "Security Controls for Computer Systems" (www.rand.org/publications/R/R609.1/R609.1.html)

U.S. Commission on National Security/21st Century (The Hart-Rudman Commission)

- Final Phase III Report—"Road Map For National Security: Imperative for Change" (www.nssg.gov)

Endnotes

1. Jeffery Eisenach, Thomas Lenard, and Stephen McGonegal, *The Digital Economy Fact Book* (3rd edition, 2001), (Washington, D.C.: Progress and Freedom Foundation), 1-9.

2. Ibid., 24-27.

3. National Governors' Association, "Homeland Security: The Cost to States for Ensuring Public Health and Safety," *Issue Brief*, 5 December 2001, <http://www.nga.org/center/divisions/1,1188,C_ISSUE_BRIEF^D_2915,00.html> (20 March 2002).

4. Barbara Gomolski, Jeremy Grigg, and Kurt Potter, "2001 IT Spending and Staffing Survey Results," *Gartner Group Strategic Analysis Report* R-14-4158, 19 September 2001, 9.

5. James Middleton, "Major viruses cost industry $13bn in 2001," *vnunet.com*, 10 January 2002, <http://www.vnunet.com/News/1128147> (20 March 2002).

6. Andy Briney, "Cover Story: 2001 Industry Survey," *Information Security*, October 2001, <http://www.infosecuritymag.com/articles/october01/images/survey.pdf> (21 March 2002), 34-43.

7. Harold Leavitt, "Applied Organizational Change in Industry: Structural, Technological, and Humanistic Approaches," *Handbook of Organizations* (J.G. March, ed.), (Chicago: Rand McNally, 1965), 1144-1170.

8. Allen Hutt, *Open Framework: Transforming Your Business with Information Technology* (Issue 1), November 1994, (Bracknell Berks, England: International Computers Limited), 1-8.

9. For a broad discussion of the attributes of digital government, see NASCIO's publication "Creating Citizen-Centric Digital Government: A Guide for the States" at <http://www.nascio.org/hotissues/dg>.

10. Thanks to John W. Lainhart IV, the first Inspector General of the U.S. House of Representatives, a member of the COBIT Steering Committee, for his assistance in editing the following section on COBIT.

11. John W. Lainhart IV, "Assuring Service Improvements and Systems Modernization," slide presentation for PricewaterhouseCoopers, LLP, October 2001.

12. IT Governance Institute, "Executive Summary," *COBIT Governance, Control and Audit for Information and Related Technology* (3rd ed.), July 2000, <http://www.itgi.org/resources.htm> (20 March 2002), 6.

13. NIST, "Federal Information Technology Security Assessment Framework" 28 November 2000, <http://www.cio.gov/Documents/federal_it_security_assessment_framework_112800.html> (16 April 2002).

14. Stephen R. Covey, *The Seven Habits of Highly Effective People* (New York: Simon and Schuster, 1990).

15. Ibid., 95-144.

16. William Welsh, "IT security regulations unlikely, Bush official says," *Washington Technology*, 8 April 2002, <http://www.washingtontechnology.com/news/1_1/state/18080-1.html> (30 April 2002).

17. Victor H. Vroom, *Work and Motivation* (New York: John Wiley and Sons, 1964).

CHAPTER TEN

Preparing for Wireless and Mobile Technologies in Government

Ai-Mei Chang
Professor of Systems Management, Information Resources Management College, National Defense University

P. K. Kannan
Safeway Fellow and Associate Professor of Marketing
The Robert H. Smith School of Business
University of Maryland

This report was originally published in October 2002.

Introduction*

"Hopefully, high-speed access will come over the air as opposed to fiber optics."

—President George W. Bush

"The greatest challenge we face is to get a handle on how new technologies have created new opportunities, and to reconfigure government accordingly."

—Senator Joseph Lieberman

In the last five years, we have seen a phenomenal increase in initiatives and efforts toward reinventing government with the help of information technology (IT). This trend has been fueled by the dot.com era and the changing expectations of citizens and government employees, and by the desire of government leaders to capitalize on the emerging technologies to make government processes more efficient and effective. Part of the current excitement of this trend is the emergence of the wireless channel. The wireless channel is being viewed as the extension of the Internet-based e-channel, a paradigm shift from the static terminal of the personal computer (PC) to the flexible "anytime, anywhere" context of the mobile environment.

Although the enthusiasm has been dampened a bit by the dot.com bust, the concept of enabling enterprise, commerce, and service applications for citizens, businesses, and employees anytime, anywhere is being viewed as the next big technology-enabled breakthrough looming over the horizon. Many mobile devices, such as notebook computers and personal digital assistants (PDAs), are already being used as extended enterprise tools. This mobile suite is now being supplemented by digital telephones with Internet and wireless data access capabilities. The extended enterprise applications are closely followed by wireless commerce applications directly to the customer and consumer via these wireless devices.

The growth of wireless technology and its potential for enterprise applications have already galvanized private-sector organizations to focus on system designs and business models that can render the applications a reality. There is a similar growing interest in the government sector as evidenced by agency-level projects that seek to leverage the wireless technology for e-government applications: Department of the Interior's emergency response systems, Army Corp of Engineers' support of the mobile workforce, and the

---

* *The authors would like to thank Ranapratap Chegu and Mark Abramson for their critical review of earlier drafts and for their many suggestions and contributions of content to improve the exposition of this chapter.*

wireless portal services of the Defense Information Systems Agency and the United States Postal Service (USPS), to name a few. Whereas these efforts can be viewed as taking advantage of the low-hanging fruit, it is important to identify and understand the nature of the wireless/mobile technology and its appropriateness for different enterprise applications, the key drivers of successful adoption and application, and, most important, the technology readiness of the government workforce and citizens. These are precisely the objectives of this chapter as we outline the context and research issues in the following sections.

Era of E-Government

The coming decade is clearly the era of e-government. Societies in each city, state, and country are increasingly interconnected, and citizens and customers who have experienced the improvements and efficiency that the Internet facilitates are demanding more from their governments—at the federal, state, and local levels. In fact, a recent study by the University of Maryland's Center for e-Service and Rockbridge Associates (Federal Computer Week, 2002) reveals that government websites in the United States attract more visitors than commercial websites, underlining the emerging importance of e-government. This trend is not confined to the United States. All over the world, governments are increasingly leveraging connectivity to provide citizen services electronically; the list includes Australia, the United Kingdom, Germany, Taiwan, Singapore, and Malaysia.

In the United States, e-government is thriving at all levels of government. It has been reported that more than 60 percent of all Internet users in the United States interact with government websites (OMB, E-Government Strategy, 2002). State and local governments, given their closer proximity to citizens, have taken the lead in many cases to provide direct service through the Internet channel. At the federal level, with a view to making government more focused on citizens and results, President Bush has made "expanding e-government" a priority in his Management Agenda. The E-Government Strategy report of the Office of Management and Budget (OMB) (February 27, 2002) points out that the primary focus of the "expanding e-government" initiative is on citizen service—to make it easy for citizens to obtain services and interact with the federal government, to improve the government's responsiveness to citizens, and to improve government efficiency and effectiveness. The report further points to suboptimal technology leverage and resistance to change as two key reasons, among others, for the federal government's inability to increase productivity. In the 1990s, government agencies used IT to automate existing processes rather than to create efficient solutions through process redesigns. Moreover, agency culture, fear of reorganization, and fear of technology created resistance to integrating work and sharing use of systems across agencies. Our study is specifically relevant in this context because it focuses on understanding technology and assessing its fit to applications and processes, and understanding the technology readiness of employees to help identify appropriate implementation of technology and successful adoption.

Wireless/Mobile Technology Trends

In this study we use "wireless" and "mobile" interchangeably, while being fully cognizant that mobility does not always equate to the wireless space, and wireless does not always equate to mobility. However, there is significant overlap in applications of these technologies, so it makes sense to treat them together for the purpose of this study. However we define the basic technology, it is inarguable that the technology is diffusing at one of the fastest paces witnessed among personal technology products all over the world (see Figure 10.1).

Figure 10.1: Wireless and Mobile Technology Trends

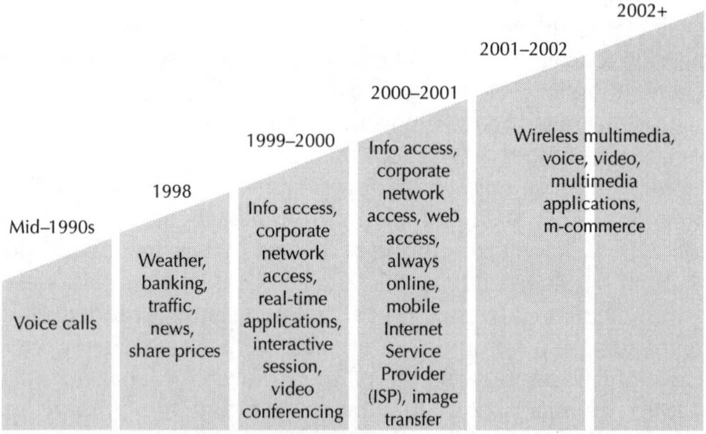

State of Technology	First Generation Systems (1G)	Second Generation Systems (2G–2.5G)	Third Generation Systems (3G)
Features	Analog voice service, no data	Digital voice and data, 9.6–14.5 Kbps data, enhanced calling features, not always on data connection	Superior voice quality, up to 2 Mbps always on data, broadband data services

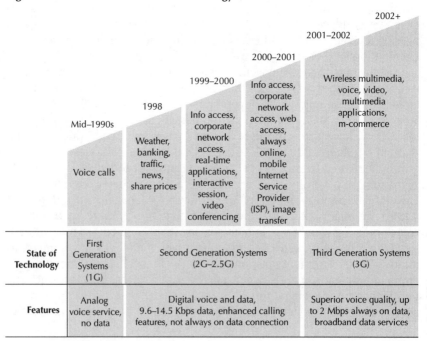

Source: PricewaterhouseCoopers Consulting

Studies by various market research firms lend credibility to this trend. Gartner predicts that by 2004, 60 percent of office productivity workers will carry or own at least three mobile devices, and 80 percent of all new applications for consumer use will permit access from wireless devices (Casonato, 2002). International Data Corporation (IDC) has estimated that pervasive computing devices, which include PDAs, wireless phones, pagers, and global positioning systems (GPSs), will exceed 6 billion (Caldow, 2001). By 2003, wireless phones will be as common as television sets. This applies not only to the United States but also across third-world countries, where consumers are directly adopting wireless phones, completely bypassing wired connections. In countries like Japan and Finland, wireless devices have become a social phenomenon—users play games, send and receive instant messages, access data, and use them as substitutes for PCs.

The growth in device sales is also spurring commerce. The market potential for wireless commerce is quite significant. Market researchers predict that by the end of 2005, there will be almost 500 million users of wireless devices, generating more than $200 billion in revenues (Ovum Online, 2000). By 2004, more end users will access the Internet via handheld mobile terminals than wired connections (ARC Group, 2002). And by 2006, the global m-commerce market will be worth $230 billion (Strategy Analytics, 2002).

The current generation (second generation or 2G) of wireless/mobile technology includes cellular phones, pagers, wireless-enabled laptop computers, PDAs, wireless local area networks (WLANs), and GPSs, with the wireless service providers' technology enabling transmittal of voice and text/data (at 9.6 to 14.5 Kbps) working fairly well. With the advent of third generation (3G) wireless networks and broadband in the near future, wireless devices can be content rich, enabling transmittal of content-rich graphics, video, and other information at speeds up to 2 Mbps. Currently, technology such as Bluetooth can provide short-range wireless connectivity that can link several types of devices enabling seamless interactions among various devices. 3G technology can further extend the similar functionality and coverage. There is consensus, however, that 3G services require resolution of several factors such as spectrum allocation, technical development, and significant network build-up before their potential can be realized. Although this may take several years, telecommunications companies are rolling out 2.5G services such as general packet radio service (GPRS) that can provide significant improvements over 2G services.

With the rapid penetration and adoption of personal technology worldwide and with the impending expansion of network functionality and capacity to provide rich content in a mobile environment, wireless/mobile technology has significant potential for providing commercial applications, especially in the business-to-consumer (B2C) domain, which we call "m-commerce" (see Figure 10.2). At the moment, wireless and mobile technologies are being adopted significantly in the business-to-employee (B2E) realm because their benefits (such as productivity gains) are easily quantifiable and therefore their adoption is justifiable. We call this domain "m-business."

Although this trend is significant in private-sector applications, it is also quite visible in the public sector. At the state and local government levels in the United States, there is greater emphasis on using wireless/mobile technology for public safety and emergency response applications, such as supporting field personnel, sharing information, locating personnel, and maintaining network communication. At the federal level, wireless applications are prominent among the 24 initiatives that OMB's E-Government Task Force has identified as priority e-government implementations. For example, the Department of the Treasury will manage the Wireless Public Safety Interoperable Communications (SAFECOM) project aimed toward achieving interoperable wireless infrastructures among all levels of government. It is clear that against this backdrop, the time is right to examine the role that wireless and mobile technologies could play in e-government.

Figure 10.2: Difference between M-Commerce and M-Business

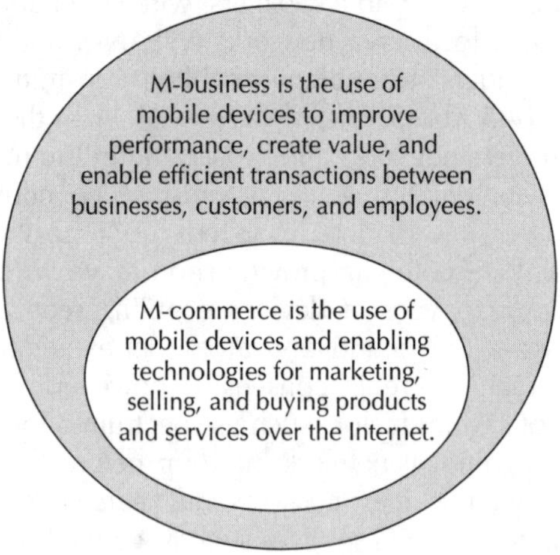
M-business is the use of mobile devices to improve performance, create value, and enable efficient transactions between businesses, customers, and employees.
M-commerce is the use of mobile devices and enabling technologies for marketing, selling, and buying products and services over the Internet.

Research Issues

Our study has four important goals with regard to understanding how to leverage wireless technologies for e-government applications:

- Understanding the unique characteristics of the wireless/mobile environment and the use of wireless/mobile technology
- Mapping the characteristics and usage for enterprise applications based on studies of successful adoption of the technology in private-sector settings
- Understanding the role of wireless/mobile technology in e-government based on the findings of the first two goals
- Assessing the technology readiness of the government workforce for wireless/mobile applications and increasing the likelihood of technology acceptance

Understanding the unique characteristics of wireless technology and its usage is a prerequisite to a successful wireless strategy at the enterprise level. In this context, our research focuses on understanding how the characteristics drive the usage of the technology under different situations—both from a customer/citizen viewpoint and from an enterprise usage situation viewpoint. Our prior research in this area (Chang et al., 2002; Kannan et al., 2001) has uncovered interesting insights into how consumers use this technology and how it affects their behavior. We extend this work in the domain of enterprise users and in the context of enterprise application.

The second goal of this study is to map the characteristics of the wireless environment and application orientation in the enterprise context. This is accomplished using studies of initiatives and implementations in private-sector organizations. The focus is on identifying the underlying common factors that are related to mapping wireless characteristics with application orientations. Identification of such factors will help in a normative way to understand what types of applications can be successful in leveraging wireless technology and under what specific usage situations. We develop a prescriptive matrix that managers can use to evaluate the application of wireless technology to specific applications.

Based on the findings of the first two parts of the research and the prescriptive matrix, the third part of the study examines emerging e-government applications and potential applications in which wireless technology can be successfully leveraged. The focus is on both intra-governmental applications as well as upstream channel applications such as procurement and downstream channel applications such as service provision through portals and websites. We also examine the pros and cons of adopting wireless technology within an e-government setting.

The fourth goal of the study is to illustrate the assessment of technology readiness of the workforce with regard to adopting wireless technology and to provide steps for increasing employees' likelihood of accepting new wireless and mobile technologies. Wireless devices are *personal* devices, carried by employees, customers, and citizens on their person. The usage of wireless devices and the ultimate success of the projects will depend on the technology readiness of the employees of an organization with respect to wireless technology.

The study includes a survey that collected responses from a group of federal employees on multiple-item scales (some developed by Rockbridge Associates to measure consumer technology readiness) to understand how the technology readiness of employees relates to their attitudes toward adoption of wireless applications and perceptions of their usefulness. Students from several government agencies who attend classes at the National Defense University, Information Resources Management College (IRMC), were surveyed for the study. The survey offers insights into understanding perceptions of employees toward wireless technology and formulating appropriate implementation strategies. We also provide suggestions that a government agency can use to increase its employees' technology acceptance.

In the context of fast-paced developments in wireless technology and widespread consumer adoption of the technology, it is imperative that public-sector organizations focus on integrating the wireless channel as part of their multi-channel effort to reach businesses and citizens as well as use mobile technology within their business processes. Adoption of the wireless environment by citizens and private-sector organizations creates an expectation among citizens and businesses toward such integrated channels of communication and commerce. However, public-sector organizations should not rush into premature applications of the technology without understanding the technology, its usage, and their workforces' readiness. Our study focuses on helping government-sector organizations understand the dynamics of wireless adoption.

Understanding Wireless/Mobile Technology

In this section, we focus on key characteristics of the wireless/mobile devices and technology and the characteristics of the environment within which the applications are embedded. It is necessary to remember that devices vary in processing capability from cell phones and pagers, to PDAs and laptops. We will focus mostly on cell phones, pagers, and PDAs, and when necessary address issues regarding laptops separately. The characteristics we discuss are relevant to both G2C (B2C) and G2E (B2E) applications.

Device Characteristics

The key characteristic of the wireless environment is "ubiquitous interactivity" (see Figure 10.3), as opposed to "interactivity" of the Internet environment, because the wireless device is one that is always handy and available to an individual. These characteristics distinguish wireless devices from PCs and laptops, which are not generally handy or easy to use at a moment's notice, although they may be available at all times. Second, a wireless device is distinctly *personal,* and its usage can be tracked to an individual rather than to a household, as is the case with PCs and other devices. Third, wireless technology is "location aware"; that is, it is easy to track where the user is physically as long as the wireless device is on. These characteristics have important implications.

The first implication is the issue of accessibility. A wireless device enables a citizen to access government services at any time and from any place. It also allows employees and organizations (government agencies) to access each other at any time and from any place. The second implication is that a citizen can be targeted specifically and reached by a government agency instantaneously because a wireless device can be associated with a particular consumer rather than a household or Internet protocol (IP) address. This may allow a government agency to be proactive in providing services and reaching citizens at their points of need. (In the B2E context, this implies that a government agency can contact a specific employee—who is telecommuting, for example—at a moment's notice.) This enables the organization to interact quickly with citizens and employees.

Location awareness also implies that an organization can pinpoint where the citizen or consumer is using the wireless device. This has implications for the types of applications being considered for wireless deployment. It is

Figure 10.3: Ubiquitous Interactivity

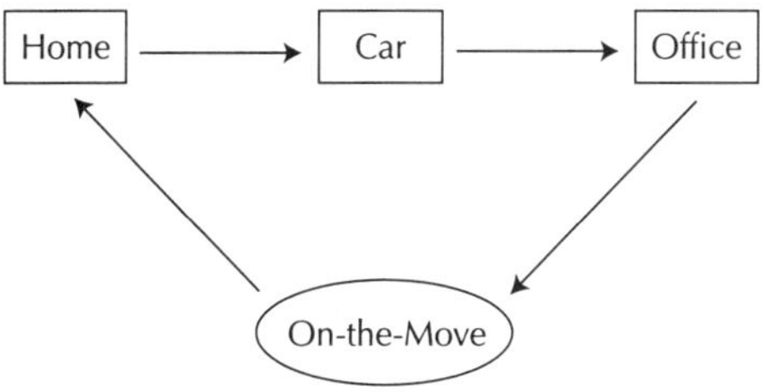

Adapted from Chang et al., 2001

advantageous in an emergency situation when the caller needs to be located and rescued. However, it might imply an unnecessary invasion of privacy.

Usage Characteristics

Given the near-term limitations in information processing capabilities and information transmission capabilities, the usage of wireless/mobile devices in their current form and technology is an important factor to consider in any development of applications. Given the constraints of its size for handy usage, the user interface of a wireless device is quite limited and cannot display information-rich content in a useful way. (This is not the case for laptops, but then laptops are not very handy.) This constraint limits the clients' capabilities for processing and storing information and data. Most important, the bandwidth over the air for wireless transmission is also a constraint in the near term. These constraints limit the use of wireless technology to predominantly text-based, less information-intensive exchanges and interactions.

This limited usage implies that a consumer's (or citizen's) search for information in the wireless environment may be limited, and customers may be constrained in their search behavior (Kannan et al., 2001). This may also imply that there are higher switching costs in moving away from an organization with which a consumer is transacting business in the wireless environment. This may suggest that there could be first-mover advantages for an organization using the wireless channel to retain customers through implementation of customer relationship management (CRM). This is aided by four factors: (1) the ability to provide truly personalized content and service by tracking personal identity, (2) the ability to track consumers across media and over time, (3) the ability to provide content and service at the point of need, and (4) the capability to provide highly engaging content. In the case of service provision from a government-agency viewpoint, this constraint has implications on how such services may be provided. Also, in the B2E domain, the interaction and transfer of content may be quite limited in nature. The technology can be used for sending alerts and for short interactions but not for transferring large amounts of enterprise data.

Another usage-related issue is consumers' *compulsion to use* wireless technology. The convenient nature of the wireless device has made it easy for consumers to use the technology for interactive purposes such as "chats." Experiments have shown that consumers who use wireless devices for making commercial transactions (such as trading stocks) tend to use the same devices even when alternative channels (Internet, telephone, etc.) are available for making those transactions (Chang et al., 2002). This tendency may indicate that as costs decrease and bandwidth increases, the wireless channel can significantly substitute other channels for service delivery to the extent that customers adopt the technology. As the technology advances, the most significant potential lies in the delivery of services over wireless devices, including interactive games; gambling; banking; stock trading; and booking and ticketing for travel, hotels, and events. This tendency will also create expectations regarding services obtained from government agencies.

The compulsion-to-use aspect of the wireless technology also implies, in the case of B2E applications, that identification of user technology readiness can pay rich dividends. If employees are already significant users of the technology, their compulsion to use the technology can facilitate the adoption of wireless applications. This also points to the advantage of launching pilot programs within organizations to study the use of wireless for enterprise applications—it prepares employees and organizations for easier transitions when the technology starts delivering on its potential.

Environmental Characteristics

Three important issues need to be addressed in the context of the characteristics of the wireless/ mobile environment: security, privacy, and application platforms. These three characteristics, in addition to the other characteristics, play an important role in determining the success of wireless/mobile applications.

Security

Security in a wireless/mobile environment must be addressed at several levels. The most commonly addressed level in a cursory analysis is the over-the-air security of content being transmitted. However, security can exist at different levels: at the network infrastructure level, at the software application level, and at the device level. The security of the overall application is a function of security at each of these levels.

Let us first examine the issue of over-the-air security, which becomes a popular issue whenever a "drive-by" hack attack is reported in the press. It is undeniable that despite encryption of content that is transmitted, the over-the-air security can be breached with sophisticated hacking. Although encryption technologies are useful, there are many of them, and the problem for a single-service provider is how to accommodate all of them. The lack of standards has left the issue of end-to-end encryption for all traffic still a distant objective. But it is also true that over 85 percent of the security breaches occur at the device level—breaches involving lost or stolen devices, passwords, and lax authentication procedures and access control. In this context, wireless/mobile applications should be treated as any other

IT enterprise application. The security issues are the same: having an effective security policy, authentication and access control, firewalls, and virus protection. The only additional issue will be over-the-air security. In the context of enterprise applications, depending on the coverage and application, security concerns can be minimized. Also, individual organizations can use proprietary solutions for end-to-end security without much problem, thereby eliminating many of the problems that arise from lack of standards in the B2C context. But this does create the problem of lock-in with one vendor for the organization adopting the technology.

The implication of concerns regarding over-the-air security for B2C (or G2C) applications can be two-fold. One is the issue of an actual security breach, which can result in increased risk of economic loss and potential litigation from consumers. The second and more serious issue is negative security perceptions that consumers/citizens may have regarding the wireless/ mobile environment that may affect their adoption of the technology for critical applications. Extant research (e.g., Frels and Kannan, 2002) has shown that security concerns can increase customers' perceptions of risks in conducting transactions in the e-channel and affect their behavior. For example, in a recent interview, a senior vice president of a wireless security services firm remarked, "I personally would not buy stocks and check bank accounts using my cell phone or mobile laptop today." (Stone 2001). Therefore, it is conceivable that over-the-air security will remain an important obstacle in the short term.

When wireless/mobile applications are used in the WLAN environment, the security issues are similar to any other IT enterprise application. The 802.11b WLANs, the common WLAN standard (see Appendix II), suffer from several problems: Wireless signals meant for enterprise use can still be intercepted from public areas; interoperable implementation can lead to less secure networks; and rogue access points can be set up with an enterprise network. However, improvements to security standards, proprietary solutions offered by vendors, and the use of "sniffers" to discourage rogue elements can provide a relatively "safe" environment for WLAN enterprise applications. Using security protocols such as the Wired Equivalent Privacy (WEP) specified in the IEEE Wireless Fidelity (Wi-Fi) standard, 802.11b can provide a level of security and privacy comparable to what is usually expected of a wired LAN. Other applications such as remote wireless access into corporate networks (without the use of a laptop) are prone to security breaches. Implementations of Bluetooth (for local, short-coverage wireless network applications) are designed to operate with as many devices as possible and thus do not have strong authentication schemes to prevent rogue elements from entering the network.

The Computer Security Resource Center within NIST provides many publications that list the benefits and security risks of many of the wireless devices, such as Bluetooth, handheld devices, and WLANs. These publications also provide practical guidelines and recommendations for mitigating the risks associated with these technologies (see http://csrc.nist.gov/publications/draft.html). There are many vendors and service providers who provide security solutions at various levels, and they should be used if vendor lock-in is not a concern. If the application is piecemeal or a pilot, which is the common type of implementation today, then end-to-end solutions provided by vendors can be used.

Privacy

The location-aware property of the wireless/mobile devices can lead to privacy concerns, especially for consumers/citizens who do not wish be to be tracked geographically. In the B2C market, organizations are excited about the prospect of communicating and interacting with consumers and persuading them at the point-of-need or point-of-purchase. For example, if a consumer were tracked walking in a shopping mall, then personalized messages can be transmitted to his/her wireless device with regard to a product or service. Such tracking can be extremely invasive, however. Similarly, cell phones, PDAs, and pagers can be tracked as they are used. Location awareness is now being used to track citizens during emergencies. However, if "emergency" were to be defined as "state emergency," then the technology can be used for tracking private activities. The potential for such applications can lead to serious privacy concerns and can severely impact the usage of the technology. In the case of enterprise applications, one can make a case that employees can be monitored at work (whether or not through wireless devices), but if personal boundaries are violated in such monitoring activity, it could lead to serious litigation problems.

Application Platforms

Another characteristic of the current wireless/ mobile environment is the multitude of application platforms for end-user and client applications. These range from Wireless Application Protocol (WAP) 1.2 and Global Systems for Mobile Communications (GSM), to DoCoMo's (Japan) I-Mode, Windows CE, Palm OS, and Nokia's open middleware. WAP is an open platform, whereas I-Mode is a proprietary platform. The challenge with the presence of a plethora of platforms is to understand who the winner will be and what platforms will enjoy a large user base. Given the current state of flux in client-side platforms, rolling out applications in the B2C domain is risky. In the case of enterprise applications, the impact of this will be to render the wireless strategies of organizations quite fluid and oriented toward the short term.

Table 10.1 provides a summary of the various characteristics of the wireless/mobile technology and how they impact B2C (G2C) applications and B2E (G2E) applications.

Mobile and Wireless: Aren't They the Same?

While these two words are often used interchangeably, there is a definite and logical difference between the two:

Wireless: "without wires." As a rule, almost all mobile devices are wireless, but wireless devices may not always be mobile. For example, a desktop PC can wirelessly be connected to a cable modem or a LAN to access the Internet but does not have mobility.

Mobile: "capable of moving or being moved." In terms of IT and communications, "mobile" refers to devices that are portable and can be carried by an individual to (almost) any place and still satisfy the communications needs. Some of the most prevalent mobile communication devices include:

- *Mobile phone:* Wireless hand-held phones with built-in antennas, often called cell, mobile, or PCS phones.
- *Laptop computer:* Also known as a notebook personal computer. This is the most common type of mobile computing device, having all the features available in regular desktop computers, with the additional advantage of mobility.
- *Personal Digital Assistant (PDA):* A hand-held computer that allows you to store, access, and organize information. Basic PDAs allow you to store and retrieve addresses and phone numbers, maintain a calendar, and create to-do lists and notes. More sophisticated PDAs can run word processing, spreadsheet, money manager, game, and electronic book reading programs, and also provide e-mail and Internet access.
- *Pocket personal computer:* Brainchild of Microsoft Corp., it is similar in functionality to the Palm PDA but based on the Microsoft Windows operating system. It has in-built versions of Microsoft Word and Excel software.
- *Tablet personal computer:* A hybrid of a PDA and a notebook PC. Some of its distinguishing features include the latest Microsoft XP operating system and the option of having an integrated or docking keyboard. Users can write directly on the screen using a digital pen; notes can be saved as they are or converted to text to be used by other applications. These are relatively lightweight, with longer battery life as compared to notebook computers.
- *One-way pager:* Fits easily in a shirt pocket; some are as small as a wristwatch. A miniature, short-range wireless receiver captures a message, usually accompanied by a beep. The simplest one-way pagers display the return-call telephone number of the person who sent the message.
- *Two-way pager:* Allows you to send data as well as receive it. It works much like a mobile phone, except text rather than voice is exchanged. In some cases, a two-way pager can serve as an alternative to a cellular phone.
- *Global Positioning System (GPS):* A "constellation" of 24 well-spaced satellites that orbit the Earth, making it possible for people with ground receivers to pinpoint their geographic location. The location accuracy is anywhere from 100 to 10 meters for most equipment.

Table 10.1: Wireless/Mobile Characteristics and Implications

Characteristics		Implications for:	
		B2C/G2C	B2E/G2E
Device	Ubiquity—handy, available at all time, user friendly	Citizen/consumer accessible at all times, demand for 24/7 service	Employee accessible, work accessible
	Personal	Marketed to consumer at individual level	Individual employees accessed
	Location-aware	Consumer/citizen tracked by location	Employees can be tracked by location
Usage	Search/information download—limited storage and processing capacity	Limits application to text-based, short messages, e-mail, and voice mail; search limited	Alerts employees, interacts with databases, updates information
	Compulsion to use	Implications for multi-channel design to service consumers/citizens	Easy to roll out B2E applications and easier adoption
Environment	Security—limited over-the-air security	Security risks exist, suitability varies by application	Need for proprietary solutions for end-to-end reliable security, switching costs increase
	Privacy	Consumers/citizens can be tracked, privacy standards are needed	Employee privacy must be ensured
	Application platform—too many standards	Difficult to roll out applications impacting a large market, uniformity in service could be a problem	Piecemeal applications based on standard/interoperable platforms is the way to go

Understanding Enterprise Applications

Many factors must be considered in making a decision to adopt wireless/mobile technology for B2C/G2C and B2E/G2E applications. Extant studies (e.g., Casonato, 2002) have shown that in the B2E/G2E realm, the primary reason for adopting a wireless technology was to increase employee productivity, followed by cost containment. Some organizations also consider such initiatives as experiments to launch a new information channel. In the B2C/G2C realm, service improvements and competitive advantage seem to be the main reasons for adopting wireless initiatives. Enterprises must take a proactive approach to leading the deployment of wireless/mobile technology. With the advent of sophisticated devices and the rapid adoption at the personal level, both employees and citizens/customers will be demanding that more services and access be available in handheld devices at "anytime, anywhere" environments. An enterprise will have to control the adoption of the technology on its own terms rather than fully acceding to customer/employee demands or fully banning the use of such devices. The six critical factors that enterprises should consider in adopting the technology are discussed below.

Employee/Customer Mobility

It is understandable that with the increase in mobility of the workforce, customer/citizen demand for mobile access technology will be higher. In the B2E/G2E realm, many enterprise functions require the workforce to be mobile. One example is sales and service teams, which can be frequently on the road. In addition, in some industries, workforces tend to be very mobile—for example, the construction industry, news media, transportation and logistics organizations, other organizations in the supply chain link, insurance industry, health-service industry, and retail and other service industries. In such cases, where information access or alerts are needed, wireless applications tend be the low-hanging fruit. In the B2C/G2C realm, a certain segment of consumers (who could be mobile employees of other companies or those living in large metropolitan areas) could be compulsive users of mobile technology and may demand service in that channel. Thus, it is not surprising that many financial services industries are adopting wireless/mobile technology as a complementary channel to reach and service consumers. Additionally, organizations that focus on meeting customer demand at the point-of-need or point-of-purchase can seriously consider the use of wireless technology to communicate and interact with customers based on their locations. Thus, a simple rule of thumb would declare that the larger the fraction of employees/customers that are mobile, the greater the case for wireless/mobile technology, although the following factors could play considerable roles in moderating this need.

Information Needs

This critical factor usually determines the value of wireless/mobile applications in a given context. Information needs cover four main areas:

- How intensive is the information needed in a mobile environment
- How urgent is the information requirement in the mobile setting
- How reliable should the access be in the context of the application
- The degree of interactivity desired

We have observed that content-rich information (animation and video) is inherently unsuitable for the 2G and 2.5G applications. The wireless environment is more suitable for text-based information. Even with text-based information, applications such as database access and updating in real time and such synchronization activities can render the information requirement intensive.

The second issue is how urgent the information requirement is. If it is not needed immediately for an application (such as in emergency situations) and can be downloaded and used later, then wired laptop-based applications could be used in place of wireless technology.

The third important issue is the reliability with which the information and access is acquired. Wireless networks are quite unreliable in their current state: Coverage is spotty, latency could be high, and there could be frequent disconnects. In the case of data applications, static could lead to unreliable information being transmitted. Or because data applications use algorithms to prevent transmittal of faulty data, static could lead to repeated, automatic re-transmission of data and thereby create delays in mobile applications. Given the limited processing and storage capacities, using information-intensive applications in such an unreliable context could be challenging. The same argument could be extended for the degree of interactivity desired. If the interactivity is voice based or involves sporadic interactivity of other types, then the reliability issue may not be significant. However, continued interactivity required for data synchronization and replication activities could pose a significant problem. Figure 10.4 provides a summary overview of the suitability of wireless/mobile applications as a function of the component of information needs.

In the context of B2E/G2E applications, the mobile workforce can easily use applications such as contact information for clients, address databases, calendar functions, basic personal information management (PIM), e-mail, voice-mail functions, and messaging. These activities are Level 1 activities (see Table 10.2), which we classify as *access and alert* activities

Figure 10.4: Suitability of Wireless Applications as a Function of Information Needs

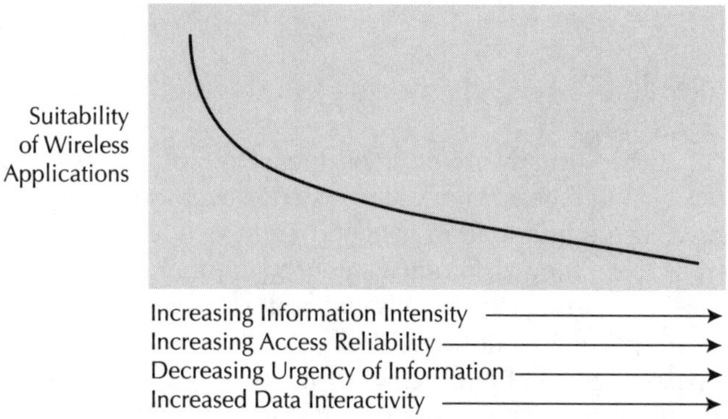

Table 10.2: Levels of Information Intensity and Types of Applications

Degree of Information Intensity	Examples of Applications
Level 1 *Access and Alert Activities*	E-mail (desktop, server-based), voice mail, PIM, messaging, and calendar
Level 2 *Access and Update Activities*	Real-time data access (checking prices, inventory, credit status), file and content distribution, basic data synchronization applications (data collection, forms, inventory)
Level 3 *Access and Transact Activities*	Advanced data synchronization applications (sales force automation, supply chain management, customer relationship management, marketing communications)

(Lemon et al., 2002). These are also the most common activities for which wireless/mobile technology is currently being used. Messaging/e-mail is seen as the key application in terms of revenue in the next five years. The Level 2 activities involve access and updates and require more reliability in connection. Level 3 activities involve access and transaction, and they require continued interactivity. Office applications such as WLANs could fall in the Level 2 and Level 3 category of applications.

Security Requirements

The security needs for the application may further constrain the use of wireless and mobile technology for the Level 1 through Level 3 activities. In general, the security requirements for messaging/e-mail applications may not be very high, but this depends on the context within which the application is set. In the government context, it has been reported that military applications have a much higher security requirement for Level 1 applications (Intergovernmental Advisory Board [IAB], 2001). In the context of B2C/G2C applications, security risk assessments have to be carefully made given the generally poor security features of the wireless environment.

Extent of Cost/Revenue Impact

The extent of cost reduction (and/or revenue increase) from Level 1 activities is usually marginal. Generally, as applications move from Level 1 to Level 3, the cost reduction opportunities from process *changes* (rather than process *automation*) and revenue increases from productivity improvements are much more significant. In fact, many enterprises have embarked on Level 3 activities with a view toward improving their bottom line in a significant way (Anonymous, 2001). This obviously implies that the organizations can quantify the cost reductions and revenue increases through the use of wireless/mobile technology. However, there are also instances of adoption of wireless technology at Level 1 applications with a view toward experimenting with the technology and gaining valuable experience before rolling out enterprisewide deployment. This is the reasoning behind many pilot projects being carried out in enterprises—the experience allows one to evaluate the suitability of technology and its adoption to less risky processes. The learning will be useful for later deployment on larger projects.

Competitive/Strategic Advantage

There are times when an organization must deploy wireless/mobile applications because competitive pressures demand it. This is the case in the financial services industry in the B2C domain. Many full-service and discount brokers offer wireless-based transaction capabilities for their clients as a means of providing them the advantages of e-service and thereby retaining them as customers. Given the competitive pressures in the industry, the deployment of wireless technology is motivated primarily not by productivity gains or cost containment (which may certainly be by-products) but by the need to move fast and stay ahead of the competition. Many of the wireless deployments in the transportation and logistics industry have occurred for this same reason. This suggests that strategic needs and pressure for significant returns may override security concerns that may be inherent in wireless/mobile usage.

Technology Readiness

Technology readiness of users (consumers/citizens and employees) plays an important role in the decision to deploy wireless/mobile technology. We focus on this issue specifically in the upcoming sections of this chapter, although we have highlighted this factor here for the sake of completeness.

A Prescriptive Matrix

Based on our analysis, we provide a prescriptive matrix that considers all the relevant factors in deciding whether a specific wireless application should be deployed (see Table 10.3). In the next section, we illustrate the usage of the matrix in considering e-government applications.

Table 10.3: A Prescriptive Matrix for Wireless Adoption

<table>
<tr><td colspan="2" rowspan="2"></td><td colspan="2">Degree of Sophistication of Technology*</td></tr>
<tr><td>High</td><td>Low</td></tr>
<tr><td rowspan="2">Technology Readiness of Target Segment</td><td>High</td><td>Stars
High-impact projects
Mission-critical applications of high strategic advantage should be undertaken; high-level commitment needed for success</td><td>Low-Hanging Fruit
Go for immediate wireless deployment
High probability of successful adoption</td></tr>
<tr><td>Low</td><td>Future Potentials
Wait and see
Applications more complex; go forward with pilots; educate/train employees; wait for mature technology</td><td>Near Harvests
Educate/train target segment
Wireless deployment with extensive training; significant chance of success</td></tr>
</table>

* Factors influencing degree of sophistication of technology: Information intensity, reliability of access, interactivity intensity, and security/privacy requirements. Each factor ranges from high to low.

Applying Wireless/Mobile Technology to Government

The potential for wireless/mobile applications within government is immense. It is estimated that at least 30 percent of the government workforce has traditionally been mobile (Caldow, 2001). With the advent of e-government and high-tech device use that allows telecommuting, it could easily be much higher in the coming decade. Thus, the extent of mobility in the target employee segment can be significantly high, setting the stage for widespread wireless/mobile deployment. Given that governments, by their very nature, have a segment of the workforce involved in law enforcement and compliance enforcement, transportation and logistics, and health and social services, there are many instances of low-hanging fruit—this involves the police force, traffic enforcement, firefighters, health-care workers, social workers, inspectors of all kinds, transportation officials, emergency management workers, and maintenance workers. This indicates that the potential for deploying wireless technology for *intra-governmental* applications is significant.

However, the potential does not stop there. As seen in Figure 10.5, e-government activities encompass not only intra-governmental processes but also the interface between businesses (G2B/B2G interface) and the interface with citizens (G2C interface). Wireless applications in these interfaces, although less common at present, also have a bright future. We first

Figure 10.5: The Scope of E-Government

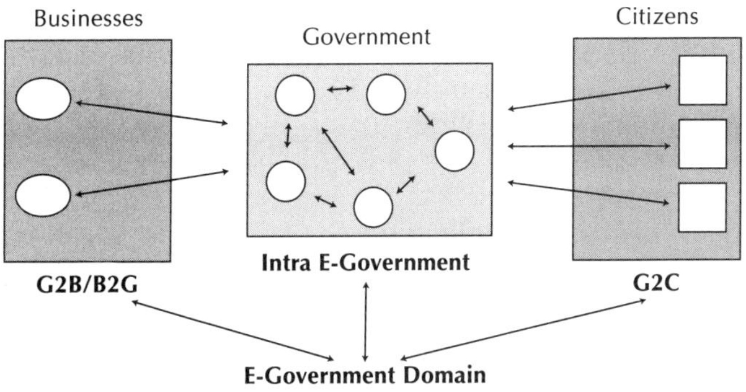

Adapted from Rust and Kannan, 2002

discuss the most common applications seen in e-government (the low-hanging fruit quadrant of our prescriptive matrix, Table 10.3) and then examine the wireless/mobile potential in other quadrants.

The Low-Hanging Fruit

A plethora of intra-governmental applications at the state, local, and city and municipal levels fall within this category. Most of them are characterized by the following features: high mobility of the workforce, which highlights the productivity-enhancing potential of wireless and mobile technology; low security or privacy concerns (at least currently) or operations in protected band spectrum; required urgency of access; and quick employee buy-in because of the evident gains in productivity and simplification of job functions. These applications include (see Table 10.4) police applications in Sacramento, California, and in Pasco, Washington; use of BlackBerry handheld devices in Seattle's transportation hub and Boston's Logan Airport to increase security against terrorism; integrated network links between Colorado Springs and El Paso County to share communications infrastructure for police, fire, and public utility agencies; and so on. One of the main characteristics of these projects is that the productivity improvements are immediately quantifiable and easily measured. In fact, not only have there been reports about productivity gains, process simplifications, and increases in program effectiveness through the use of mobile technology in the police force, but literature also suggests improvement in job satisfaction and employee morale (Agrawal et al., 2002). Another observation concerning these projects is that they are spread over all levels of government—local, state, and federal—indicating that such opportunities exist at all levels. Also, it is interesting to note that in some instances, wireless access acts as a substitute for wired access, especially in cases of emergency and situations of unreliable wired connections. All these opportunities are intra-governmental applications.

Government-to-Citizen Applications

These applications generally tend to fall within the "low-hanging fruit" quadrant as well as the "near harvests" quadrant. As seen in Table 10.5, there are not as many examples of G2C services through wireless. At the local government level, IBM's Total Web-Government project involves small cities and municipalities belonging to the National League of Cities and National Association of Counties to set up information portals that could be accessed by wireless devices. Such services aimed at the general

Table 10.4: Examples of Low-Hanging Fruit Wireless Applications

	Government Agency	Application Description
1.	Sacramento, CA, Police	800 MHz radio network allows data networking and helicopter video downlink possibilities.
2.	Pasco, WA, Police	Incident reports are directly transmitted to police headquarters by wireless from incident locations.
3.	Houston, TX, and New Jersey Parking Enforcement	Handheld devices print tickets and send information directly to database using wireless.
4.	Seattle International Airport and Seaport Boston's Logan Airport	Research in Motion (RIM) BlackBerry pagers tap into National Crime Information Center (NCIC) databases, and allow e-mail and networking with other officers for crime prevention.
5.	City of Edmonton, Alberta	Building inspectors use mobile devices to enter inspection reports directly into database.
6.	Colorado Springs, CO, and El Paso County	800 MHz radio network deployed to connect 51 agencies through a shared infrastructure, including police, fire, EMS, and public utility agencies.
7.	Fire Management, Southern California	GIS systems are used to map and track moving fires for fire management.
8.	Military and Government Hospitals	Use computerized physician order entry (CPOE) for mobile tracking of patients and patient care.
9.	Biomedical Research in Mali, West Africa, by U.S. NIAID	Uses NIAID's microwave radio communication to access Internet instead of phone lines to overcome wired infrastructure problems (expensive, unreliable, and experiencing frequent outages).
10.	Department of Justice and Department of the Treasury—Wireless Public Safety Interoperability	Resolving wireless interoperability to provide seamless, coordinated, integrated public safety communications for the safe and efficient protection of life and property.
11.	Centers for Disease Control and Prevention, Atlanta, GA	Plans using GPS-equipped devices to collect data in bioterrorism-related incidents.
12.	U.S. Marine Corps	Field warehouse sites are using handheld wireless computers and special warehousing software to track inventory.

Source: Government Technology (www.govtech.net) and IAB, 2001

Table 10.5: Examples of Government-to-Citizen Applications

	Government Agency	Application Description
1.	National League of Cities (NLC) and National Association of Counties (NACo)	Broadband satellite connectivity to rural and remote areas to access local government websites and information portals for checking on community events and for sending e-mail to municipal officials.
2.	King County Metro Transit, WA	Bus riders use wireless devices to access information portals to check real-time schedule information on bus arrivals and departures.
3.	State of Virginia	"Lobbyist in a Box," an interactive application, allows citizens, lobbyists, and legislators to access information on the status of bills moving through the legislative process.
4.	City of Buffalo, MN	Provides broadband data services accessible through wireless devices for citizens and businesses as a subscription-based service.
5.	University of Texas at El Paso Various State Universities	Local wireless access to the Internet and student services are becoming more common in such captive environments.

Source: Government Technology (www.govtech.net) and IAB, 2001

public are especially useful where a wired network infrastructure does not exist (as in remote and sparsely populated communities) because they enable citizens to access the portals to check on community events and send e-mail to legislators. The other applications involve accessing information portals using wireless devices: bus riders checking on bus schedules, citizens checking on the status of bills, and students at universities accessing portals and the Internet through wireless devices. The universities, especially, have gained significant experience in rolling out services for students that can be accessed in the mobile mode. The advantages they possess include promoting a homogeneous population and relatively tech-savvy, enclosed, small environments that allow deployment of reliable wireless technology and easier troubleshooting.

There are many issues that need to be resolved in the G2C domain before the applications catch on. First is the issue of urgency of access: Are government services ever needed in such an urgent access mode? Except for emergency situations, this is generally not the case. Citizens could well use wired access through the Internet or telephone to access the services. However, as we have seen in some applications, if the wired infrastructure is nonexistent or expensive, then the wireless infrastructure becomes a viable alternative. In such cases, government needs to look at this service channel seriously. Second is the issue of security and privacy. For extensive rollout of services using wireless technology, an adequate level of security and privacy must be ensured. Finally, there is the issue of user acceptance of technology: Is a significant portion of the user group sufficiently tech savvy to appreciate the value of the service? This is a question of cost versus benefit that needs to be critically analyzed before a wireless deployment is contemplated.

Mobile Collaboration Applications

These government applications tend to fall within the "stars" quadrant based on their security requirements and the need for collaborative interactivity. Some examples include WLAN applications in U.S. Navy destroyers and the U.S. Air Force, wide area network (WAN) applications in the city of Blacksburg in Virginia and the town of Enfield in Connecticut, and the two-way messaging systems of the Department of Energy in the Nevada Operations Office. The common feature in these applications is that they are all in the intra-governmental domain, all requiring effective security features, and all requiring a good deal of interactivity in applications.

Most of these applications are also mission critical. For example, in the U.S. Navy application, sailors aboard the U.S.S. Howard use wireless devices to access the ship's wired LAN from wherever they are on the ship. The technology helps in the critical maintenance operations aboard the ship. The WAN application of Blacksburg uses wireless to connect the city's government agencies to help provide integrated services to the community.

These applications are "stars" in the sense of their potential revenue/cost impact, which can be of an order of magnitude larger than those in the low-hanging fruit quadrant. Sometimes, competitive pressures can lead to the deployment of "star" applications, even within the government, without much regard to potential cost/revenue impact. A case study at one branch of the U.S. military has been reported (Anonymous, 2001) where competition for potential recruits is quite fierce between branches of the armed forces. This branch, which traditionally used form-based tracking of potential recruits, switched to using wireless-based applications to facilitate the process and reduce lead times in recruiting, and to help field recruiters react quickly to the market.

Future Potentials

Many potential applications in the e-government realm can become a reality with maturing technology, increased security, and increased bandwidth. These include applications such as e-learning through wireless technology, wireless WAN applications, CRM applications based on service portals accessed by citizens in a secure and private mode using their wireless devices, and so on. Although the potential is seemingly limitless, it is necessary to understand that wireless is but another alternative channel that can be used for services. Therefore, wireless/mobile technology should not be adopted for the sake of the technology itself. Rather, the adoption should be driven by the needs that we have identified in the prescriptive matrix. There are many who suggest deploying wireless pilot programs for accessing information from government portals. The key question is whether such access is needed (now or in the future) for the target segment that accesses the information. This will play a key role in determining the "future potentials."

Other Issues Relevant to E-Government

In addition to the factors presented in the prescriptive matrix (Table 10.3), a few more issues are relevant in the case of e-government. These factors moderate the impact of the other factors in Table 10.3 in determining whether to deploy wireless/mobile technology and, if so, how to deploy it.

Substitute for Wired Networks

In some examples we have discussed, wireless technology was deployed as a substitute for wired technology. Although it is generally not recommended, there are special instances in which wireless is actually a better option than wired technology. These are cases in which the areas of operation are remote and the wired infrastructure is very expensive. In many developing countries, the wired networks are unreliable, expensive, and experience frequent outages (as in the case of the National Institute for Allergy and Infectious Diseases' [NIAID's] deployment in Mali, West Africa). In some developing countries, technology has skipped a generation and thus, while the wired telecommunication infrastructure is spotty and sporadic, one may find extensive wireless coverage. In such cases, wireless technology is an obvious choice for e-government applications.

Multi-Channel Strategies

E-government is accomplished through providing multiple "touch points" to citizens and businesses. The wireless channel is but one of them. It is important to understand that the application of the prescriptive matrix

Wireless and Mobile Statistics

- Analysts estimate 17% compound growth over the next five years in wireless communications (both services and equipment) spending. (Cahners In-Stat Group)
- There will be over 650 million cellular/PCS subscribers worldwide by 2003, more than tripling from nearly 210 million subscribers at year-end 1997. (*iSky* magazine)
- The growth in the number of users (worldwide) for the various wireless services will be as follows (ARC Group):

	Number of users in millions					
	2000	2001	2002	2003	2004	2005
Messaging (SMS, e-mail, fax)	100	230	399	611	916	1,268
E-commerce and retail	12	36	107	195	318	469
Financial services	50	123	225	357	529	798
Intranet (corporate)	5	20	49	81	129	206
Internet browsing, WAP	4	20	85	183	344	614
Entertainment	61	143	246	372	554	775
Navigation/location	47	146	239	345	488	785

- Spending for e-government (including federal, state, and local) will grow from $1.5 billion in 2000 to more than $6.2 billion by 2005. In 2005, the G2G and G2B segments will top $4 billion. The G2C segment is forecast to reach $455 million in 2000, and it will grow to $2.2 billion in 2005. (Gartner Group)
- President George W. Bush's FY 2003 budget request includes $3.5 billion in support of first responders. The single biggest portion of that amount, $1.4 billion, is designated for enhancing communications. (PRIMEDIA Business Magazines + Media)

is done with a multi-channel strategy to provide services to citizens and businesses. The impact and role of wireless technology on e-government ought to be examined within the context of a multi-channel strategy.

Impact on Digital Divide

Given the penetration of wireless technology among citizens, its social acceptability, its user-friendliness, and its cost as compared with the PC-based Internet, the use of wireless technology may be a significant way to reduce the impact of the digital divide and provide e-government services that more citizens can access other than through the PC-based Internet. This is one of the key reasons that may drive the deployment of pilot programs in many government agencies that currently provide portal-based e-service to its citizens. We believe that local and state governments can take a proactive role in bridging the digital divide through the use of wireless technology because they are in closer contact with the citizens than the federal government is.

Impact of Competition

It is obvious that government should not be looking at wireless technologies from the point of view of return on investment (ROI) and cost containment alone. This is an era in which governments compete. Local governments, state governments, and even national governments compete in today's global economy for business investments, a skilled workforce, good jobs, and so on. Governments need to view wireless/mobile technology as a means of gaining competitive and strategic advantage in a crowded field. Thus, some wireless applications may not make much sense from an ROI viewpoint but may make good sense from a strategic viewpoint.

Getting Users Technology Ready

As we have seen in the context of the prescriptive matrix, user technology readiness plays an important role in determining whether to go for immediate deployment of wireless/mobile technology and in determining the strategy for deployment. In this section, we formally define technology readiness as a construct that can be measured and the role it plays in the acceptance of wireless technology by employees. We also focus on the factors that affect technology acceptance of employees and how organizations can influence employees' technology acceptance through concrete measures, with a particular focus on wireless technology acceptance.

Technology Readiness Defined

The construct of technology readiness has been defined as "people's propensity to embrace and use new technologies for accomplishing goals in home life and at work" (Parasuraman, 2000, p. 308). The construct pertains to "an overall state of mind resulting from a gestalt of mental enablers and inhibitors that collectively determine a person's predisposition to use new technologies" (Parasuraman, 2000, p. 308). It is important to emphasize that technology readiness is an overall state of mind and not a measure of technology competency. Thus, "it is a combination of technology-related beliefs that collectively determine a person's predisposition to interact with technology-based products and services" (Parasuraman and Colby, 2001, p. 27).

Many researchers (Mick and Fournier, 1998, for example) have found that people's views and attitudes toward technology are a mixture of positives, which push them to adopt and use technology, and negatives, which pull them away from technology. A person's technology readiness, therefore, is determined by the combination of these pushes and pulls. Thus, technology readiness consists of four dimensions: two positive dimensions called "contributors" and two negative dimensions called "inhibitors."

The first contributor is "optimism"—a positive view of technology and a belief that it offers people increased control, flexibility, and efficiency in their lives. The second contributor is "innovativeness"—a tendency to be a technology pioneer and thought leader. The first inhibitor is "discomfort"—a perceived lack of control over technology and a feeling of being overwhelmed by it. The second inhibitor is "insecurity"—a distrust of technology and skepticism about its ability to work properly (Parasuraman, 2000).

Technology readiness is a composite of these four dimensions. Employees' technology readiness can be measured using a multiple-item scale, which, in turn, can be used to construct an index called the Technology Readiness Index (TRI). In Appendix I, we provide a study that illustrates how employees' TRI can be measured. (The full list of items and the survey administration kit are available from Rockbridge Associates, which holds the copyright for TRI.)

A key reason why employees' technology readiness is one of the important dimensions of our prescriptive matrix (Table 10.3) is due to the linkage between TRI scores and technology-related behaviors. Research by Parasuraman (Parasuraman, 2000) and Rockbridge Associates (Parasuraman and Colby, 2001) has shown that the TRI is able to (1) distinguish between users and non-users of high technology services; (2) identify, between two groups, the stronger one in terms of acceptance of more complex and more futuristic technologies; and (3) identify specific groups of users for whom discomfort and insecurity is likely to be significant. TRI scores correlate well with consumers' ownership of technology-based products and services (people who own technology-based products and services have a significantly higher TRI score) and with people's use of technology-based services (as compared with those who have no plans to use the services, those who do plan to use the services in the next 12 months or have used the services in the past 12 months have significantly higher TRI scores).

Technology Readiness and Wireless Technology Adoption

In Appendix I we show, based on our empirical study, that TRI scores also predict employees' attitudes toward wireless technology and adoption. Specifically, we find that those employees with higher TRI scores (1) feel that wireless technology has an important role to play in e-government, (2) have a more positive attitude toward adopting wireless technology in general, and (3) have a more positive attitude toward adopting wireless technology in their specific work processes. Employees with higher TRI scores also have fewer security concerns about using wireless/mobile technology for personal work as well as enterprise applications. More important, those employees with higher TRI scores were already owning/using a significantly higher number of distinct wireless/mobile devices than those with lower TRI scores, a clear indication of their level of comfort with the technology. The study thus provides a clear motivation for using technology readiness as an important dimension to consider when deciding to adopt wireless/mobile technology.

In the context of adopting wireless technology, measuring employees' technology readiness is necessary for three important reasons:

- First, TRI scores of the employees provide insights into using the prescriptive matrix (Table 10.3), where the mean TRI values of the employee group can be used to classify employees on the technology readiness scale.
- Second, the individual scores of employees can be used for screening those employees for specific technology assignments, training programs, and education.
- Third, the individual scores on the specific dimensions of optimism, innovativeness, discomfort, and insecurity can be used to group employees into segments based on their scores (Parasuraman and Colby, 2001) so that training and education programs can be tailored for the different segments with a view toward easing the process of wireless technology adoption.

We view TRI not as an end in itself in using it for the prescriptive matrix, but as a starting point for influencing employees' technology acceptance so that wireless technology adoption is smooth and efficient. In attaining this objective, TRI scores provide the current state of technology readiness of employees and indicate means to improve technology acceptance where TRI scores are low.

Factors Influencing Technology Acceptance

Employees' acceptance of new technology and intention to use the new technology for work processes depend on three main factors: (1) the perceived usefulness of the technology, (2) the perceived ease of use, and (3) the perceived availability of resources for technology use (Davis, 1989; Mathieson et al., 2001).

- Perceived usefulness is defined as the extent to which an employee believes that using a particular technology will enhance her or his job performance—the higher the perceived usefulness, the higher the technology acceptance and technology adoption. The implication is that as long as the use of wireless technology is expected to explicitly increase their productivity or make their job easy and increase their job effectiveness, its perceived usefulness is high. However, if the usefulness is not evident, the government organization must make efforts to educate its employees about the technology.
- Perceived ease of use is defined as the degree to which a person believes that using a technology will be free from effort. Perceived ease of use is a catalyst to increasing the likelihood of user acceptance. The advantage of wireless technology on this dimension is that the technology plays an important role in consumer/ personal applications. Thus, employees are likely to be familiar with the technology and be at ease with it.
- Perceived availability of resources includes resources such as time available for performing or learning to perform a task, level of support available from other staff (particularly information services [IS] staff), and technology attributes such as system availability, cost of access, documentation, and perceived level of control over the technology. The higher the perception of the availability of these resources, the higher the technology acceptance. This factor is particularly relevant if the wireless/mobile application is complex.

Other significant external factors also play a role in determining technology acceptance by moderating the influence of the above three factors on technology acceptance. The most important of these other factors is employee gender. Researchers (Venkatesh and Morris, 2000) have shown that men consider perceived usefulness to a greater extent than women in making their decisions regarding the use of a new technology, both in the short term and the long term. However, perceived ease of use was more salient to women, as compared with men, after initial training with the technology and over time with increasing use of that technology. Other research (e.g., Agarwal and Prasad, 1999) has established that individual-level differences such as education, similar prior experience, and beliefs about IT also have an impact on the acceptance of technology. These individual-level differences are precisely what we see reflected in the individual-level TRI scores. These differences also affect how employees learn to use the technology over time and have important implications for developing training programs. This is particularly relevant when mean TRI scores of employees are low and the management is embarking on programs to increase the probability of acceptance of the new wireless/ mobile applications.

Planning for Technology Acceptance

Government agencies can take the following steps to increase employees' acceptance of wireless/mobile technology.

- *Train and Educate Employees.* Training programs, which include formal classroom education and hands-on job training, are essential for employees to understand the role wireless technology can play in their jobs. Given the gender differences, these training/education programs must emphasize the productivity benefits for men and the process/usability issues for women. Testimonials from peer groups and superiors can play an important role in the acceptance of specific applications.
- *Create Peer Support.* One of the advantages of using TRI scores is that an organization can identify employees who are most receptive to wireless/mobile technology and use them as the "lead-user" group in providing support for their peers. Lead-users can be selected for training programs first and then play a critical role in helping/supporting their peers through similar training programs.
- *Implement Pilot Applications.* In many situations, the usefulness of applications may not be evident explicitly before implementing the applications. In such situations, pilot programs are excellent ways to introduce the wireless technology and its benefits to employees. Such programs, in addition to resulting in employee buy-in, may also identify the potential inhibitors to successful applications so that the negatives can be minimized before a full-scale launch.
- *Provide Excellent IS Staff Support.* It is critical that employees perceive and make use of support from IS staff early in the adoption process, especially when technology readiness is low. This helps employees overcome the inhibitors of discomfort and insecurity through liberal help and support from IS staff as they use the technology. An organization cannot provide too much help at the start of the adoption cycle.

- *Encourage Wireless/Mobile Technology for Personal Use.* One advantage of wireless technology is that it also has significant personal applications. To increase employees' comfort level with the technology and increase its perceived ease of use, employees can be encouraged to use wireless technology for their personal and work use. Government agencies can provide subsidies or incentives for buying wireless phones, PDAs, and other handheld devices, as they are quite inexpensive as compared with other types of technology. Employees can be encouraged to check their voice mail and e-mail using wireless devices. This benefits the organization, too, as employees use their personal time to get comfortable with wireless technology, thereby reducing the overall training duration.
- *Recruit, Train, and Assign Using TRI.* TRI can be used as an effective screener to recruit and assign technology-savvy employees to the applications that demand a high level of technology acceptance. The training can also be tailored based on the TRI profiles of employees.
- *Create a Learning Culture in the Organization.* Employees should be encouraged to experiment with new wireless technology and new applications. Incentives should be provided to them for helping in designing applications and for suggesting improvements to the processes and applications. This enhances their involvement in the use of wireless technology, providing a sense of ownership and thereby improving the chances of successful adoption and potential productivity gains.

Application Development—The Next Steps

Since our focus in this chapter is on understanding the *role* of wireless and mobile technology in e-government and not on the *process of applying* the technology, we have stopped short of the critical next steps: the wireless application development approach and methodology. However, it is imperative that successful implementation of wireless and mobile technology depends on the risk management approach and the selection of appropriate methodology. In Figures 10.6 and 10.7, we provide an overview of the risk management approach and the critical factors to consider in wireless application development. These next steps should provide a smooth transition from understanding the need and role of wireless technology in e-government to successfully implementing the technology in e-government processes.

Figure 10.6: PricewaterhouseCoopers' Risk Management Approach to Application Development

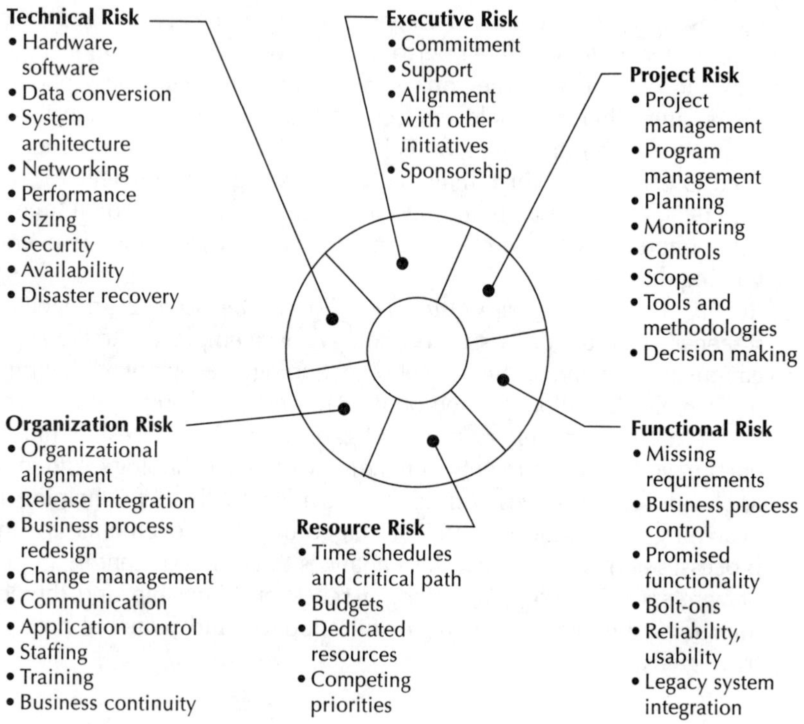

Source: PricewaterhouseCoopers Consulting

Figure 10.7: Factors to Consider in Wireless Application Development

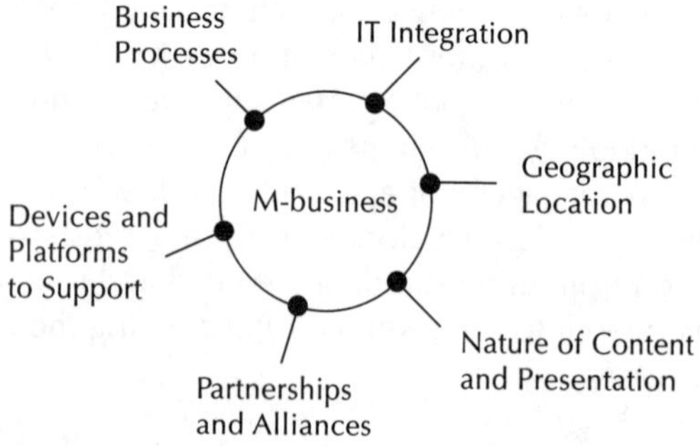

Source: PricewaterhouseCoopers Consulting

Findings and Recommendations

We introduced this chapter with four important goals with regard to leveraging wireless technologies for e-government: (1) understanding the unique characteristics of the wireless/mobile environment and technology usage, (2) mapping the characteristics and usage for enterprise applications based on studies of successful adoption of the technology in private-sector settings, (3) understanding the role of wireless/mobile technology in e-government, and (4) assessing the technology readiness of the government workforce for wireless/mobile applications and increasing the likelihood of technology acceptance. The summary of our findings and recommendations based on the four goals is as follows:

Key Findings

- Wireless and mobile devices are user-friendly personal devices with a significant penetration among citizens and consumers. Wireless/ mobile technology provides an alternative channel to reach consumers and citizens. Because of its widespread use and personal nature, its potential for B2E/G2E and B2C/G2C applications is significant. However, due to limited security/privacy features and a plethora of incompatible standards, it is more suitable, currently, for B2E/G2E applications rather than B2C/G2C applications. G2B (vendors/system integrators/contractors) applications also have significant potential.
- Strategies for successful wireless adoption depend on four important factors: extent of mobility in the target segment, information access needs, security/privacy requirements of the application, and technology readiness of the target segment.
- Most of the current applications of wireless/ mobile technology in government fall within the low-hanging fruit quadrant. A few citizen-centric applications are motivated by the need to reach out to geographically remote communities or by the lack of wired access. With maturing technology and developments, governments should be able to roll out citizen-focused services through the wireless channel.
- Measuring employees' technology readiness is a key component of the wireless technology implementation process. Employees' TRI scores are good predictors of their attitudes toward wireless technology adoption in their work processes and their ultimate acceptance of wireless/ mobile applications.
- Employees' acceptance of wireless technology can be influenced through technology training and other programs. These can have a positive impact on employees' perceptions of the usefulness of wireless

applications, the ease of use of wireless applications, and the availability of necessary resources.

Recommendations

Although this chapter has outlined many of the technology's characteristics and potential, it also holds out a warning. As with any technology, adoption of wireless/mobile technology should not be pursued for the sake of having a new technology; rather, the adoption should be motivated by the needs of the organization or the government agency. We have described many of these needs and how they affect an organization's wireless strategy through the prescriptive matrix. The following are the specific recommendations for government agencies:

- *Measure Technology Readiness, and Educate and Train Employees.* The organization must determine where its employees stand with respect to technology readiness and technology acceptance. An important first step, based on this measurement, is planning for formal education and training focusing on wireless/mobile technology basics, specifics, and role in government. Case studies of government agencies that have implemented wireless programs could contribute toward this end. IT partners could also provide help in training and education.
- *Harvest the "Low-Hanging-Fruit."* Once the low-hanging fruits are identified based on the prescriptive matrix, government organizations should go for quick and full deployment to take advantage of the productivity improvements. Agency budgeting should reflect funding for these deployments, and these projects should be put on the fast track for immediate implementation.
- *Plan for the "Stars."* Stars are high-impact projects that have complex requirements in terms of security/privacy needs and information interactivity and reliability needs. These projects should form part of strategic plans, and budgets should be allocated for experimentation and pilots. As wireless/mobile technology matures, these projects will pay off significantly. However, care should be taken in selecting the technology platform and infrastructure so that the organization does not get locked into proprietary technology, especially in the realm of G2C applications.
- *Launch Pilot Programs.* Government organizations should think creatively in identifying opportunities for wireless and mobile implementations. Wireless may be a good substitute for wired technology in geographically remote areas where citizen access is important. Wireless may play a significant role in bridging the digital divide, given its wide usage. Launching pilot programs focusing on these areas is especially

important as employees and citizens learn using the technology for mutual benefit. Creation of a central testing environment, such as the DISA or NIST laboratories, may help significantly in launching pilots.

- *Encourage Employees' Wireless/Mobile Use.* Increasing employees' comfort with the technology and increasing their perceptions of ease of use are the best ways to prepare them for technology acceptance. Government agencies should encourage, through incentives, employees' use of PDAs, wireless devices, and handheld devices both for work and personal use. Wireless LANs could replace wired LANs in some locations as a means of experimenting with technology and moving up the learning curve.

We also saw that, in addition to the factors in the prescriptive matrix, other issues may have an impact on the decision to adopt wireless technologies in the government context. For example, governments work in competitive environments, just like private business organizations. So sometimes wireless adoption can be motivated purely from a strategic viewpoint rather than from ROI considerations. Governments should be proactive in designing systems and applications with this goal in mind.

It is clear that much needs to be done if wireless applications are to deliver on their potential. Some of these efforts rest with the federal government. The supply of spectrum available to wireless carriers for rolling out broadband initiatives is fast dwindling. This calls for broadband-friendly policies and stimuli to encourage building a wireless infrastructure. The second issue is the confusion over prevailing standards. Market forces will determine and solve much of this eventually, but until then, widespread deployment and adoption of wireless technology can be risky. The third issue is that of security. Widespread G2C applications are possible only when a secure and private environment is ensured. This will also happen eventually, and until then, governments should roll out successive pilot programs to gain experience and expertise for large-scale applications.

Appendix I: Technology Readiness Index and Attitudes toward Wireless Technology Adoption

In this appendix, we explain the measurement of the Technology Readiness Index (TRI) with an illustrative measurement of TRI using a survey administered to a group of government employees. We also relate their technology readiness with their attitudes toward wireless adoption, their perceptions on the role that wireless can play in government applications, and their wireless usage.

The TRI scale consists of four dimensions:

- Optimism—a positive view of technology and a belief that it offers people increased control, flexibility, and efficiency in their lives
- Innovativeness—a tendency to be a technology pioneer and thought leader
- Discomfort—a perceived lack of control over technology and a feeling of being overwhelmed by it
- Insecurity—distrust of technology and skepticism about its ability to work properly

Each dimension is measured using multiple-item scales. Examples of the multiple-item scale include:

- For optimism: "Products and services that use the newest technologies are much more convenient to use." "Technology gives you more freedom of mobility."
- For innovativeness: "Other people come to you for advice on new technologies." "You keep up with the latest technological developments in your areas of interest."
- For discomfort: "Technology always seems to fail at the worst possible time." "Sometimes you think that technology systems are not designed for use by ordinary people."
- For insecurity: "You do not consider it safe giving out a credit card number over a computer." "You worry that information you send over the Internet will be seen by other people."

Each item is responded to on a 5-point scale ranging from strongly agree (5) to strongly disagree (1). (The full list of items and the survey administration kit are available from Rockbridge Associates, which holds the copyright for the TRI). The TRI is the composite score derived from averaging the four dimensions, after reverse coding the scores on the discomfort and insecurity components. Thus, a high TRI score represents a high level of technology readiness. TRI as a measurement scale has been shown to have high reliability, good content, and discriminant validity and to be convergent.

Attitudes toward Wireless Adoption

In addition to the TRI items in the survey instrument, we included several items that measured (1) respondents' perceptions of the role of wireless/ mobile technology in e-government settings, (2) their attitudes toward adopting wireless technology in government in general, (3) their attitudes toward adopting wireless technology for their specific work, (4) their usage of wireless technology for personal work, and (5) a number of other related issues. The specific items used are listed in Table 10.A.1. All items were measured on a 5-point scale ranging from strongly disagree (1) to strongly agree (5), with 3 being neutral. The items were developed based on pilot studies, and the multiple-item measures were factor analyzed using confirmatory techniques to ensure unidimensionality. The reliability of the multiple-item scales is also high (as indicated by the coefficient alpha values ranging from 0.72 to 0.84). The survey instrument included information on whether the respondent owned wireless devices such as cellular phones, pagers, PDAs, wireless PDAs, and wireless access to the Internet. Gender, age, and education information along with government agency affiliation were also elicited.

Respondent Information

In all, 204 government employees, half of whom were taking courses at the National Defense University, participated in the survey. Three surveys had to be discarded because they were only partially filled out. The government agencies represented include the U.S. Army, U.S. Navy, U.S. Air Force, Department of Defense, Defense Intelligence Agency, DISA, Internal Revenue Service (IRS), Department of State, U.S. Coast Guard, Department of the Treasury, U.S. Customs Service, General Services Administration (GSA), Department of the Interior, Environmental Protection Agency (EPA), Federal Aviation Administration (FAA), and a few other agencies. Based on the responses to the demographic questions, approximately 61 percent of the respondents were male and 39 percent were female. About 44 percent were between the ages of 45 and 55, 46 percent between 35 and 45, and 10 percent under 35. In terms of education, 22 percent had postgraduate degrees, 47 percent had graduate degrees, 26 percent had undergraduate degrees, and 5 percent had completed high school.

In terms of the composition of the respondents, our sample is biased toward the more educated and more IT-oriented employees (some of whom were attending IT-oriented classes at the university). The sample was chosen deliberately for two reasons: We were trying to relate TRI with attitudes toward wireless deployment. If such relationships were significant in this

Table 10.A.1: Items Related to Wireless/Mobile Technology

1.	Role of Wireless Technology (ROLE) (Coefficient Alpha = 0.82)	a. Wireless/mobile technology can play a very useful role in government IT practices. b. Wireless/mobile technology has a limited role to play in government processes (reverse coded).
2.	Attitude toward Adoption (General) (ATTADOPT) (Coefficient Alpha = 0.79)	a. Adoption of mobile technology in government processes is a good thing. b. Adopting wireless/mobile technology at work in government organizations can create more problems than good (reverse coded).
3.	Attitude toward Adoption (Work) (ADOPTWK) (Coefficient Alpha = 0.84)	a. You will actively use mobile/wireless technology for collaborative work if provided the option. b. You will strongly support the adoption of wireless/mobile enterprise applications in your work. c. Wireless/mobile technology can play a very useful role in your work processes.
4.	Personal Usage of Wireless (PERUSAGE) (Coefficient Alpha = 0.72)	a. You often use wireless/mobile technology for personal financial activities such as stock trading or banking. b. You often use wireless/mobile technology for personal work.
5.	Personal Optimism (PEROPTM)	Using wireless/mobile technology gives people more control over their daily lives.
6.	Security in Personal Context (PERSECU)	You do not consider it safe giving out a credit card number over a wireless phone or other mobile devices.
7.	Comfort in Personal Usage (PERCOMFT)	You are not very comfortable using wireless/mobile technology for your personal work.
8.	Security Enterprise Context (ENTRSECU)	Using wireless/mobile devices to access enterprise data has significant security risks as compared with using wired devices.
9.	Wireless as a Substitute for Wired (SUBSTITUT)	If wireless/mobile technologies were adopted in my organization, it will substitute wired technologies.
10.	Wireless Limited Role (LMTDROL)	Wireless/mobile technology is appropriate for voice and e-mail but not for other work processes.
11.	Wireless Is Hyped (HYPE)	The benefits of wireless/mobile technology are often grossly overstated.

population (where the TRI values are likely to be quite high with low variance across the sample), then it is much more likely to be replicated at a general population level, where variances in the TRI are likely to be much higher. Second, IT employees are more likely to be part of the "lead-user" segment of wireless device users, and it was important to establish the relationships at their level.

Survey Results and Implications

As seen in Table 10.A.2, the respondents as a group scored significantly high on the technology optimism dimension (mean = 4.02) and high on the innovativeness dimension (mean = 3.77). It is interesting to note that although the mean value for the discomfort dimension is around the neutral range, the mean value for the insecurity dimension is higher than that (mean = 3.27). Overall, the mean for the TRI is 3.36, with the minimum TRI value at 2.3 and the maximum at 4.2. The mean TRI is much higher for this group as compared with the general consumers owning technology-based products and services (as analyzed by Parasuraman, 2000) where the means ranged from 2.90 to 3.12. It is also comparable to the TRI scores obtained by consumers using technology-based services such as purchasing e-tickets and other items online. This indicates that, as a group, the respondents have high technology readiness, while there are some individuals with low TRI values (2.3), with the range of TRI values being 1.9.

Table 10.A.2: Scores on TRI and Its Component Dimensions

Scale	Optimism	Innovativeness	Discomfort	Insecurity	TRI
Mean	4.02	3.77	3.08	3.27	3.36
Standard Deviation	0.46	0.70	0.51	0.69	0.40
Minimum	3.00	1.70	2.00	1.90	2.30
Maximum	4.90	5.00	4.40	4.90	4.20
Range	1.90	3.30	2.40	3.00	1.90
Sample Size	199	199	199	199	199

Tables 10.A.3 and 10.A.4 provide the mean scores of the respondents on their attitudes toward wireless adoption and perceptions of wireless technology. As a group, these government employees with high TRI scores feel very positively about the role of wireless technology in government processes (mean on ROLE = 3.75). They view that the adoption of wireless technology in government processes is a good thing and that it can do more good than harm in government applications (mean on ATTADOPT = 3.54). This attitude is not just confined to generalities; this group also feels positively about adopting wireless technology to their own work processes (mean on ADOPTWK = 3.51).

Table 10.A.3: Scores on Role and Attitude toward Adopting Wireless and Usage

Scale/Variable	ROLE	ATTADOPT	ADOPTWK	PERUSAGE	PEROPTM
Mean	3.75	3.54	3.51	2.49	3.64
Standard Deviation	0.96	1.02	1.04	1.21	1.11
Minimum	1.00	1.00	1.00	1.00	1.00
Maximum	5.00	5.00	5.00	5.00	5.00
Range	4.00	4.00	4.00	4.00	4.00
Sample Size	199	199	198	201	200

Table 10.A.4: Scores on Security, Comfort, and Substitute Perceptions

Variable	PERSECU	ENTRSECU	PERCOMFT	SUBSTITUT	LMTDROL	HYPE
Mean	2.60	1.97	3.22	2.23	2.33	3.40
Standard Deviation	1.40	1.01	1.32	0.97	1.13	0.96
Minimum	1.00	1.00	1.00	1.00	1.00	1.00
Maximum	5.00	5.00	5.00	5.00	5.00	5.00
Range	4.00	4.00	4.00	4.00	4.00	4.00
Sample Size	199	201	201	200	200	200

In terms of their wireless usage for personal work and activities, although they are quite optimistic about wireless technology providing them more control over their daily lives (mean on PEROPTM = 3.64) and somewhat comfortable about using wireless technology for personal work (mean on PERCOMFT = 3.22), they do not use wireless technology often to do their personal work or financial activities (mean on PERUSAGE = 2.49). This implies that although they have mobile devices, such as a mobile phone, those devices might be intended more for social activities (chatting) than for personal work. This might also reflect their attitudes toward security of using wireless/mobile devices.

The respondents as a group tended to disagree with the statement that they do not consider it safe giving out a credit card number on a wireless/mobile device (mean on PERSECU = 2.60). They also tended to disagree with the statement that using wireless/mobile devices to access the enterprise had significant security risks as compared with using wired devices (mean on ENTRSECU = 1.97). This might indicate that security concerns become more pronounced when personal work is involved than when enterprise work is involved, although the absolute scores reveal that this group has a positive perception of wireless security overall.

The group did not think wireless is a substitute for wired technology (mean on SUBSTITUT = 2.23) and did not feel that wireless use is limited to voice and e-mail (mean on LMTDROL = 2.33). However, they did somewhat agree that the benefits of wireless/ mobile technologies are often overstated (mean on HYPE = 3.40).

The wireless industry has galvanized itself after the events of September 11, 2001, as a possible role player in homeland security. The respondents also answered questions on this issue. As a group, they were close to neutral when it was stated that wireless/mobile technology has a greater role to play as compared with other technologies in providing homeland security (mean = 3.12). They also indicated that the events of September 11 did not in any significant way affect their likelihood of adopting wireless technology either for their work processes or for their personal use.

In terms of ownership of mobile/wireless devices, the respondent group could be termed as early adopters of technology: 87 percent owned a mobile phone, 37 percent had a PDA and 20 percent had a PDA with wireless capabilities, 29 percent owned pagers, and 13 percent had wireless access to the Internet. This correlates well with the high TRI scores that the group obtained.

Although we have seen that as a group the respondents have high TRI scores and positive attitudes and perceptions regarding wireless technology and its adoption in work processes, a better test would be to correlate these scores at the individual level. Table 10.A.5 provides the correlations between individual TRI scores and the individual attitude scores and perception scores on the various dimensions. As seen in the table, the correlations are quite positive (ranging from 0.32 to 0.47 for the attitude toward adoption scores). The other correlations are also in the expected directions. Interestingly, the number of wireless devices that respondents own is correlated positively with their TRI scores. This is a clear indication that TRI scores can predict individual attitudes and perceptions toward wireless technology and adoption. This exercise also shows why we have chosen technology readiness as an important dimension of our prescriptive matrix. It plays a major role in determining user acceptability of technology, which is a key factor in the successful adoption of wireless initiatives.

Table 10.A.5: Correlation between TRI and Wireless Attitudes and Perceptions

Scale/Variables	TRI Correlation
ROLE—Wireless Role in Government	0.42
ATTADOPT—Attitude toward Adopting (General)	0.46
ADOPTWK—Attitude toward Adopting at Work	0.47
PERUSAGE—Personal Usage	0.46
PEROPTM—Personal Optimism	0.34
PERSECU—Security Perception Personal	0.44
ENTRSECU—Security Perception Enterprise	0.32
PERCOMFT—Comfort in Personal Usage	0.35
SUBSTITUT—Wireless as Substitute for Wired	-0.03
LMTDROL—Wireless Has Limited Role	-0.16
HYPE—Wireless Benefits Hyped	-0.41
Number of Distinct Wireless/Mobile Devices Owned	0.37

Appendix II: IEEE Wireless Communication Standards

1. The 802.11 Working Group for Wireless Local Area Networks

The IEEE 802.11 specifications are wireless standards that specify an "over-the-air" interface between a wireless client and a base station or access point, as well as among wireless clients. The 802.11 standards can be compared to the IEEE 802.3 standard for Ethernet for wired LANs. The IEEE 802.11 specifications address both the Physical (PHY) and Media Access Control (MAC) layers and are tailored to resolve compatibility issues between manufacturers of wireless LAN equipment.

802.11aOFDM in the 5GHz Band

802.11a is a Physical Layer (PHY) standard (IEEE Std. 802.11a-1999) that specifies operating in the 5GHz UNII band using orthogonal frequency division multiplexing (OFDM). 802.11a supports data rates ranging from 6 to 54Mbps. 802.11a-based products became available in late 2001.

802.11bHigh Rate DSSS in the 2.4GHz Band

The task group for 802.11b was responsible for enhancing the initial 802.11 DSSS PHY to include 5.5Mbps and 11Mbps data rates in addition to the 1Mbps and 2Mbps data rates of the initial standard. 802.11 finalized this standard (IEEE Std. 802.11b-1999) in late 1999. Most wireless LAN installations today comply with 802.11b, which is also the basis for Wi-Fi certification from the Wireless Ethernet Compatibility Alliance (WECA).

802.11c—Bridge Operation Procedures

802.11c provides required information to ensure proper bridge operations. Product developers utilize this standard when developing access points.

802.11d—Global Harmonization

In order to support widespread adoption of 802.11, the 802.11d task group has an ongoing charter to define PHY requirements that satisfy regulatory bodies/laws[?] within additional countries. This is especially important for operation in the 5GHz bands, because the use of these frequencies differs widely from one country to another.

802.11e—MAC Enhancements for QoS

The 802.11e task group is currently refining the 802.11 MAC (Medium Access Layer) to improve QoS for better support of audio and video (such as MPEG-2) applications. The 802.11e group should finalize the standard by the end of 2002, with products probably available by mid-2003.

802.11f—Inter Access Point Protocol

802.11f is currently working on specifying an inter access point protocol that provides the necessary information that access points need to exchange to support the 802.11 distribution system functions (e.g., roaming). The 802.11f group expects to complete the standard by the end of 2002, with products supporting the standard by mid-2003.

802.11g—Higher Rate Extensions in the 2.4GHz Band

The charter of the 802.11g task group is to develop a higher speed extension (up to 54Mbps) to the 802.11b PHY, while operating in the 2.4GHz band. 802.11g will implement all mandatory elements of the IEEE 802.11b PHY standard. The FCC still needs to approve the use of OFDM in the 2.4GHz band, a generally necessary action when messing with the PHY. As a result, it will likely take a relatively long period of time before 802.11g products appear on the market.

802.11h—Spectrum Managed 802.11a

802.11h addresses the requirements of the European regulatory bodies. It provides dynamic channel selection (DCS) and transmits power control (TPC) for devices operating in the 5GHz band (802.11a). Through the use of DCS and TPC, 802.11h will avoid interference in a way similar to HiperLAN/2, the European-based competitor to 802.11a. 802.11h hopes to have its standard finalized sometime before the end of 2003.

802.11i—MAC Enhancements for Enhanced Security

802.11i is actively defining enhancements to the MAC Layer to counter the issues related to wired equivalent privacy (WEP). 802.11i will incorporate 802.1x and stronger encryption techniques, such as AES (Advanced Encryption Standard). The standard will likely not have IEEE ratification before mid-2003.

2. The 802.15 Working Group for Wireless Personal Area Networks

The IEEE 802.15 Working Group, in the IEEE 802 family, provides standards for low-complexity and low-power consumption wireless connectivity. In March 1998, the Wireless Personal Area Network™ (WPAN™) study group was formed. In May 1998, the Bluetooth Special Interest Group (SIG), Inc. was formed, and in May 1999, the IEEE WPAN Study Group became

IEEE 802.15, the WPAN Working Group. In July 1999, Bluetooth™ released the Bluetooth Specification v1.0a.

IEEE 802.15 WPAN™ Task Group 1 (TG1)

Bluetooth is an industry specification for short-range RF-based connectivity for portable personal devices. The IEEE has reviewed and provided a standard adaptation of the Bluetooth Specification v1.1 Foundation MAC (L2CAP, LMP, and Baseband) and PHY (Radio).

IEEE 802.15 WPAN™ Task Group 2 (TG2)

TG2 is developing recommended practices to facilitate coexistence of Wireless Personal Area Networks™ (802.15) and Wireless Local Area Networks (802.11). The Task Group is developing a coexistence model to quantify the mutual interference of a WLAN and a WPAN™.

IEEE 802.15 WPAN™ Task Group 3 (TG3)

TG3 is chartered to draft and publish a new standard for high-rate (20Mbit/s or greater) WPANs™.

IEEE 802.15 WPAN™ Task Group 4 (TG4)

TG4 is chartered to investigate a low data rate solution with multi-month to multi-year battery life and very low complexity. It is intended to operate in an unlicensed, international frequency band. Potential applications are sensors, interactive toys, smart badges, remote controls, and home automation.

3. The 802.16 Working Group for Broadband Wireless Access Standards

IEEE 802.16 specifications support the development of fixed broadband wireless access systems to enable rapid worldwide deployment of innovative, cost-effective, and interoperable multi-vendor broadband wireless access products.

Sources: www.80211-planet.com/tutorials, www.ieee802.org/15/pub

Bibliography

Agarwal, Ritu, and Jayesh Prasad, "Are Individual Differences Germane to the Acceptance of New Information Technologies," *Decision Sciences,* Vol. 30, No. 2, Spring 1999, pp. 361-391.

Agrawal, M., H. R. Rao, and G. L. Sanders, "Impact of Mobile Computing Terminals in Police Work," *Journal of Organizational Computing and Electronic Commerce* (forthcoming, 2002).

Anonymous, "The Future of Enterprise Mobile Computing," Synchrologic White Paper, Synchrologic, Inc., Alpharetta, Ga., 2001.

ARC Group, Future Mobile Handsets: Worldwide Market Analysis & Strategic Outlook 2002-2007, published April 2002, www.the-arc-group.com.

Baum, Christopher, "Key Issues in E-Government-to-Citizen Connections," Gartner Report, Note Number K-11-3758, June 27, 2000.

Caldow, Janet, "e-Gov Goes Wireless: From Palm to Shining Palm," White Paper, Institute for Electronic Government, IBM Corporation, August 2001 (www.ieg.ibm.com).

Casonato, Regina, "Gartner Predicts 2002: Wireless and Mobile," Gartner Report, Note Number LE-16-1709, February 1, 2002.

Chang, Ai-Mei, P. K. Kannan, and Andrew B. Whinston, "Consumer Behavior in the Wireless Environment: Implications for M-Commerce," Working Paper, University of Maryland, College Park, Md., 2002.

Davis, Fred D., "Perceived Usefulness, Perceived Ease of Use, and User Acceptance of Information Technology," *MIS Quarterly,* Vol. 13, No. 3, pp. 318-339.

E-Government Strategy: Implementing the President's Management Agenda for E-Government, White Paper, Office of Management and Budget, Washington, D.C., February 27, 2002.

Federal Computer Week, "Study: Government Web Sites are Big Hit," January 10, 2002. Available at http://www.fcw.com/geb/articles/2002/0107/web-study-01-10-02.asp.

Frels, Judy, and P. K. Kannan, "Consumers' Perceptions of Privacy and Security Risks on the E-Channel: Implications of Customization, Reputation and Size of User Base," Working Paper, Smith School of Business, University of Maryland, College Park, Md., June 2002.

Giacomelli, Dan, "Bridging the Gap Between Innovation and Early Adoption: CSC Explores Mobility with a Client," White Paper, Computer Sciences Corporation, October 2000.

Government Technology, Mobile Government, August 2002, available at http://www.govtech.net/ magazine/channels.phtml?channel=14.0.

Intergovernmental Advisory Board, "Wireless Technology in Government," IAB Report, November 2001. Available at http://gsa.gov/intergov under the Intergovernmental Advisory Board section and Reports and Presentations.

Jones, Nick, "Will Mobile Phones Bridge the EU Digital Divide?" Gartner Report, Note Number SPA-14-5463, January 31, 2002.

Kannan, P. K., Ai-Mei Chang, and Andrew B. Whinston, "Wireless Commerce: Marketing Issues and Possibilities," in *Proceedings of the 34th Hawaii International Conference on System Science,* January 2001.

Lemon, Katherine, Fredrick Newell, and Loren J. Lemon, "The Wireless Rules for e-Service," in *e-Service: New Directions in Theory and Practice* by Roland Rust and P. K. Kannan (editors). New York: M. E. Sharpe, July 2002, pp. 200-234.

Mathieson, Kieren, Eileen Peacock, and Wynne Chin, "Extending the Technology Acceptance Model: The Influence of Perceived User Resources," *The Database for Advances in Information Systems,* Vol. 32, No. 3, Summer 2001, pp. 86-112.

Mick, David Glen and Susan Fournier, "Paradoxes of Technology: Consumer Cognizance, Emotions, and Coping Strategies," *Journal of Consumer Research,* 25 (2), 1988, pp. 123-143.

Ovum Online, Mobile E-Commerce: Market Strategies, May 2000, www.ovum.com.

Parasuraman, A., and Charles L. Colby, *Techno-Ready Marketing: How and Why Your Customers Adopt Technology.* New York: The Free Press, 2001.

Parasuraman, A., "Technology Readiness Index (TRI): A Multiple-Item Scale to Measure Readiness to Embrace New Technologies," *Journal of Service Research,* Vol. 2, No. 4, May 2000, pp. 307-320.

Rust, Roland, and P. K. Kannan (editors), *e-Service: New Directions in Theory and Practice.* New York: M.E. Sharpe, July 2002.

Sood, Rishi, "State and Local Government: A Peek at 2002," Gartner Report, Note Number ITSV-WW-DP-0218, December 20, 2001.

Stone, Adam, "Wireless Security: An Oxymoron?" *M-Commerce Times,* May 15, 2001. Available at www.mcommercetimes.com/Solutions/125.

Strategy Analytics, Latest Research and Insights, 2002, available at http://www.strategyanalytics.com/.

Venkatesh, Viswanath, and Michael G. Morris, "Why Don't Men Ever Stop to Ask for Directions? Gender, Social Influence, and Their Role in Technology Acceptance and Usage Behavior," *MIS Quarterly,* Vol. 24, No. 1, March 2000, pp. 115-139.

About the Contributors

Mark A. Abramson is executive director of the IBM Endowment for The Business of Government, a position he has held since July 1998. Prior to the Endowment, he was chairman of Leadership Inc. From 1983 to 1994, Mr. Abramson served as the first president of the Council for Excellence in Government. Previously, Mr. Abramson served as a senior program evaluator in the Office of the Assistant Secretary for Planning and Evaluation, U.S. Department of Health and Human Services

He is a Fellow of the National Academy of Public Administration. In 1995, he served as president of the National Capital Area Chapter of the American Society for Public Administration. Mr. Abramson has taught at George Mason University and the Federal Executive Institute in Charlottesville, Virginia.

Mr. Abramson is the co-editor of *Transforming Organizations, E-Government 2001, Managing for Results 2002, Innovation, Human Capital 2002,* and *Leaders*. He also edited *Memos to the President: Management Advice from the Nation's Top Public Administrators* and *Toward a 21st Century Public Service: Reports from Four Forums*. He is also the co-editor (with Joseph S. Wholey and Christopher Bellavita) of *Performance and Credibility: Developing Excellence in Public and Nonprofit Organizations,* and the author of *The Federal Funding of Social Knowledge Production and Application*.

He received his Bachelor of Arts degree from Florida State University. He received a Master of Arts degree in history from New York University and a Master of Arts degree in political science from the Maxwell School of Citizenship and Public Affairs, Syracuse University.

Ai-Mei Chang is a Professor of Systems Management and director of the Center for eGovernment Education at the Information Resources

Management College (IRMC) of the National Defense University. Her current teaching and research focuses on e-government, e-business, and e-service, with a particular focus on understanding and using technologies such as the Internet and wireless/mobile channels for government processes and services. As director of the Center for eGovernment Education, she provides direction and guides the activities of the center. The center provides education and research in e-government, and shares e-government concepts and best practices with interested parties.

Dr. Chang has been on the program advisory board of e-government conferences for the past four years, co-chaired tutorial sessions, and given tutorials and lectures focused on e-government and e-business. She has been a technical reviewer for the National Science Foundation and the National Institute of Standards and Technology in these areas. She has also worked on projects dealing with software maintenance within U.S. Army organizations. She has received grants from the National Science Foundation for her work that focused on cooperation support systems and intelligent agents. She is the recipient of the President's Award of Merit for Superior Individual Effort in Scholarship at the National Defense University in July 2001.

Dr. Chang has a Ph.D. degree in Management Information Systems and a bachelor's degree in computer science and mathematics, both from Purdue University. She has published articles in scholarly journals including *Information Systems Research; Communications of the ACM; IEEE Transactions on Systems, Man, and Cybernetics; Decision Support Systems;* and *The Journal of Organizational Computing.* She is an associate editor for *Decision Support Systems and Electronic Commerce* and is on the editorial board of *The Journal of Organizational Computing and Electronic Commerce.*

Robert S. Done is an Assistant Research Professor of Management and Policy at the Eller College of Business and Public Administration, University of Arizona, where he conducts research on public policy issues and manages the Decision Behavior Laboratory.

Dr. Done's primary research interests are issues that intersect the public and private sectors. He regularly presents his work at national conferences such as the Academy of Management and has published his findings in journals such as *Psychology, Public Policy, and Law.* His teaching experience includes courses in management, public administration, and statistics. In addition, his other interests include Internet technology, distance learning, and data mining. Prior to his academic career, Dr. Done worked for more than a decade in county government. In addition to research and teaching, he provides information technology consulting services to public and private sector clients.

Dr. Done holds an M.P.A. (1992) and a Ph.D. in management (2000), both from the University of Arizona.

Barry Fulton is a Research Professor at George Washington University and Director of the University's Public Diplomacy Institute. He teaches public diplomacy at the State Department's Foreign Service Institute and recently served as a Yale-Stimson Senior Fellow. He is an expert consultant to the under secretary of state for management and serves periodically in the State Department's Office of the Inspector General.

He is an associate of Global Business Access, a member of the Board of Directors of Info/Change—a nonprofit consortium founded to expand affordable access to information and communication technologies in developing countries—and a member of the Washington Institute of Foreign Affairs. He recently served on the Defense Science Board Task Force on Managed Information Dissemination.

Professor Fulton was associate director of the United States Information Agency (USIA) from 1994 to 1997, when he joined the Center for Strategic and International Studies to direct a project on "Reinventing Diplomacy in the Information Age." Prior to his presidential appointment, he was acting director of USIA's Bureau of Educational and Cultural Affairs. During a 30-year career with USIA, he served in diplomatic assignments in Brussels, Rome, Tokyo, Karachi, and Islamabad. He retired from the Foreign Service with the grade of Minister-Counselor.

He established and directed the American Forces Radio and Television Service in Turkey, where he served as a lieutenant in the U.S. Air Force. He has been an adjunct professor at American University; has taught part-time at the University of Maryland, University of Illinois, San Antonio College, and the Pennsylvania State University; and has lectured at numerous universities and organizations.

Professor Fulton holds a Ph.D. in communications from the University of Illinois, and an M.A. in broadcasting and B.S. in electrical engineering from Penn State. He is the recipient of the Presidential Meritorious Honor Award, the Vice President's Hammer Award for Reinvention in Government, and the Edward R. Murrow Award for Excellence in Public Diplomacy from the Fletcher School of Law and Diplomacy.

Diana Burley Gant is an Assistant Professor of Information Management in the School of Information Studies at Syracuse University. Dr. Gant teaches courses on electronic commerce and the management of information systems.

She earned her B.A. (1990) in economics from The Catholic University of America and is a graduate of Carnegie Mellon University, where she received an M.S. in management and public policy (with a concentration in management information systems) from the H. John Heinz III School of

Public Policy and Management (1992), an M.S. in organization theory (1995), and a Ph.D. in organization science and information technology (1998). In addition, she was a Woodrow Wilson Foundation Public Policy Fellow (1990-1992).

Dr. Gant's research examines the extent to which new information and communication technologies (ICTs) influence changes in individual behavior and organizational action. Dr. Gant has presented her work at several national and international conferences, and she has published a variety of articles and book chapters on ICTs and e-commerce. Several granting bodies including Indiana University, the National Science Foundation, Bell Atlantic Mobile Systems, and the Natural Hazards Research Center have funded her work. Dr. Gant has worked and consulted with a wide array of public, private, and nonprofit agencies seeking to inform management and public policy, and to advance public understanding of how these technologies will impact society.

Jon P. Gant is an Assistant Professor of Information Management and Public Administration at the Maxwell School of Citizenship and Public Affairs, Syracuse University. Dr. Gant teaches courses on the management of information systems, database management, systems analysis and design, and geographic information systems. He also teaches executive education courses in managing government operations for the U.S. Department of the Navy.

He earned his B.G.S. (1987) from the University of Michigan and is a graduate of Carnegie Mellon University, where he received both an M.S. (1992) and a Ph.D. (1998) in public policy and management (with a concentration in management information systems) from the H. John Heinz III School of Public Policy and Management.

Dr. Gant's research examines how information technology enables new models of collaboration, and strategies for enhancing the information technology capabilities of organizations. He has worked on research projects funded by The Sloan Foundation, the U.S. Department of Labor, the National Science Foundation (NSF), and the Central Banks of the Caribbean. His work has appeared in a variety of both academic and practitioner journals. Dr. Gant speaks internationally to academic and practitioner-based audiences on information technology, productivity, and public sector service delivery.

He is currently working on research focusing on digital government initiatives in partnership with the Center for Technology in Government at the State University of New York at Albany. This National Science Foundation-funded study investigates new models of collaboration for delivering government services across the United States, Canada, Europe, and Asia. Dr. Gant is also collaborating with the Korean Institute for Public Administration on a study evaluating e-government initiatives by the city government of Seoul, Korea.

Don Heiman recently retired from the State of Kansas, where he served four years as the chief information technology officer for the executive branch and chief information technology architect for the three branches of government. During his tenure, Kansas was widely regarded as a national leader in digital government innovation and implementation. For the past seven years, Heiman also directed the state's central data center and the wide area network used by Kansas state agencies. He began his career in state government in 1976 with the Kansas Legislative Division of Post Audit, where he directed the performance and IT audit staffs.

Prior to joining the state, Heiman worked for Midwest Research Institute in Kansas City, Missouri, as an industrial economist. He also worked as a personnel officer and later as Board of Trustees consultant for North Kansas City Memorial Hospital. He was drafted into the U.S. Army in 1971. During his active duty at Fort Gordon, Georgia, he served in the Army's medical corps as a social work specialist E-5.

He is the author of numerous articles and papers in academic journals both in the United States and England. He served seven years on the editorial board for the *Journal of Organizational Change Management.*

Heiman holds an undergraduate degree in business from Rockhurst University in Kansas City, a master of science in business from the University of Kansas, a master of arts in pastoral studies from Loyola University (New Orleans), and master of public administration from the Edwin O. Stene School of Public Administration at the University of Kansas.

Craig L. Johnson is Associate Professor of Public Finance and Policy Analysis at the School of Public and Environmental Affairs, Indiana University-Bloomington.

Since arriving at Indiana University in 1992, Dr. Johnson has won three teaching awards, authored numerous articles and research reports in the area of public financial management and financial markets, and has recently co-edited *Tax Increment Financing and Economic Development.*

Dr. Johnson is the director of the Minority Achievers Program/Mathematics and Science Scholarships at Indiana University-Bloomington, which provides scholarships and support services to high-achieving, academically talented undergraduate students.

He has experience as a budget analyst for the New York State Division of the Budget and as a legislative policy analyst for the Office of the Deputy Speaker of the New York State Assembly. Dr. Johnson has also served as a financial management consultant to a wide array of public, private, and nonprofit agencies.

Dr. Johnson received his Master of Public Administration and Ph.D. degrees from the University at Albany, State University of New York, in the area of public finance. He holds a Bachelor of Arts degree from San Jose State University, where he graduated first in his class.

P. K. Kannan is Safeway Fellow and Associate Professor of Marketing at the Robert H. Smith School of Business, University of Maryland, where he currently researches and teaches in the area of e-service, online customer loyalty, e-channels of distribution (including wireless channels) and marketing of information products. He is also the associate director of the Center for e-Service, which is designed to help partner companies and government agencies research and develop e-service strategies. He is a co-editor (with Roland Rust) of the book *e-Service: New Directions in Theory and Practice* (M. E. Sharpe, 2002). He is currently working with IBM in testing an online promotion system and with National Academy Press on the pricing of online digital content. He has received grants from the National Science Foundation (NSF) and Mellon Foundation for his current research.

Professor Kannan has consulted for companies such as SAIC, IBM, Proxicom, and Fannie Mae, focusing on the marketing of products and services in high-technology environments. He also has consulted for Frito-Lay, PepsiCo, and Giant Food. He has developed and delivered executive programs focusing on e-channels of distribution for NorthropGrumman, ARINC, and FAAP, Brazil. Professor Kannan is the recipient of the Krowe Award for Teaching Excellence at the Smith Business School for the year 2001. He was also a panelist in the NSF Workshop on Research Priorities in e-Commerce (1998) and a Fellow of the American Marketing Association Consortium on e-Commerce (2001).

Professor Kannan holds a Ph.D. in management from Purdue University (1988) and a master's in industrial engineering from NITIE, Bombay. He has published his research in many of the leading marketing and information systems journals including *Marketing Science* and *Communications of the ACM*. He is an associate editor for *Decision Support Systems and Electronic Commerce* and serves on the editorial board of the *Journal of Service Research* and the *International Journal of Electronic Commerce*. He is the past chair of the American Marketing Association Special Interest Group on Marketing Research.

Julianne G. Mahler is Associate Professor of Government and Politics in the Department of Public and International Affairs at George Mason University. She has worked extensively in the area of organization theory and public management, conducting research on organization culture in several federal government agencies. Her most recent research is on agency learning and the evolution of policy technologies.

Dr. Mahler has published numerous articles on decision making, measuring customer satisfaction, and organization culture and learning. She is co-author of *Organization Theory: A Public Perspective* with Hal Gortner and Jeanne Nicholson. She currently directs the master's program in political science at George Mason University. Her B.A. in political science is from Macalester College and her M.A. and Ph.D. are from the State University of New York at Buffalo.

M. Jae Moon is assistant professor at the George Bush School of Government Affairs and Public Service in Texas A&M University. Before joining the Bush School, he was at the Graduate School of Public Affairs at the University of Colorado at Denver (1998–2002), where he was named Teacher of the Year in 1999 and 2001. He also taught several summer classes (in organization and management) to MPA and JD students at the Maxwell School of Citizenship and Public Affairs at Syracuse University. He has taught master's and doctoral courses in public management, organizational change and management, globalization and public policy, technology and environmental program management, and research methodology.

His research interests include public management, information technology, and comparative public administration. His research has recently appeared in major public administration and policy journals, including *Technology Forecasting and Social Change, Governance, Public Administration Review, Journal of Public Administration Research and Theory, Public Performance and Management Review, International Review of Public Administration,* and *Administration and Society.*

Dr. Moon earned a B.A. in political science from Yonsei University, Korea (1988), an M.A. in international politics from Kyunghee University, Korea, and a Ph.D. in public administration from Syracuse University.

Therese L. Morin is responsible for leading the IBM Information Technology Solutions practice area within the Public Sector Group. In that capacity she leads over 600 IT professionals. Her responsibilities include leading thought leadership for the group and increasing the number of IT professionals.

Ms. Morin has served as the engagement partner on some of the practice's leading e-government and financial management projects for the federal government. Her most recent projects involve work with FirstGov, U.S. Agency for International Development, Military Sealift Command, NAVSEA TeamSub, and General Services Administration.

She is the author of the book *Information Leadership: A Government Executive's Guide*. The book outlines a new approach to leveraging information by working as an executive team, guided by organization-wide strategy and information management principles.

Ms. Morin holds an M.B.A. from Concordia University and a Bachelor of Commerce from McGill University.

Priscilla M. Regan is an Associate Professor in the Department of Public and International Affairs at George Mason University. Prior to joining that faculty in 1989, she was a senior analyst in the Congressional Office of Technology Assessment (1984-1989) and an Assistant Professor of Politics and Government at the University of Puget Sound (1979-1984). Since the mid-1970s, Dr. Regan's primary research interest has been the analysis of the social, policy, and legal implications of organizational use of new information and communications technologies.

Dr. Regan has published over 20 articles or book chapters, as well as *Legislating Privacy: Technology, Social Values, and Public Policy* (University of North Carolina Press, 1995). As a recognized researcher in this area, she has testified before Congress and participated in meetings held by the Department of Commerce, Federal Trade Commission, Social Security Administration, and Census Bureau. Dr. Regan received her Ph.D. in government from Cornell University in 1981 and her B.A. from Mount Holyoke College in 1972.

Dr. Genie N. L. Stowers is a Professor and Director of Public Administration at San Francisco State University, where she teaches courses on financial management, program evaluation, and managing information in the nonprofit and public sectors.

Dr. Stowers has worked in the area of government Internet applications and online teaching since 1995. Her research interests include information management and electronic government information, policies and management of human service and nonprofit organizations, urban policy and politics, and policies and politics affecting women and ethnic/racial minorities. She has published articles in *Government Finance Review, Public Productivity and Management Review, Public Administration Review,* and *Journal of Public Affairs Education*. Dr. Stowers is writing a book about innovation in e-government, and her current projects cover the information architecture of public-sector websites, e-procurement, and e-government initiatives.

Dr. Stowers has also been a Visiting Scholar at the Institute for Governmental Studies at the University of California, Berkley. She was also a Professor in the Department of Political Science and Public Affairs at the University of Alabama at Birmingham, where she directed the Women's Studies Program.

Dr. Stowers received her undergraduate degree from the University of Florida and her Ph.D. from Florida State University.

About the IBM Endowment for The Business of Government

Through grants for research, the IBM Endowment for The Business of Government stimulates research and facilitates discussion of new approaches to improving the effectiveness of government at the federal, state, local, and international levels.

Research grants of $15,000 are awarded competitively to outstanding scholars in academic and nonprofit institutions across the United States. Each grantee is expected to produce a 30- to 40-page research report in one of the areas presented on pages 405-407. Grant reports will be published and disseminated by the Endowment. All the chapters presented in this book were originally prepared as grant reports to the Endowment.

Founded in 1998, the Endowment is one of the ways that IBM seeks to advance knowledge on how to improve public sector effectiveness. The IBM Endowment focuses on the future of the operations and management of the public sector.

Who is Eligible?

Individuals working in:

- Universities
- Nonprofit organizations
- Journalism

Description of Grant

Individuals receiving grants will be responsible for producing a 30- to 40-page research report in one of the areas presented on pages 405-407. The research paper should be completed within a six-month period from the start of the project. Grantees select the start and end dates of the research project.

Size of Grant

$15,000 for each research paper

Who Receives the Grant

Individuals will receive the grant, unless otherwise requested.

Application Process

Interested individuals should submit:

- A three-page description of the proposed research
- A résumé, including list of publications

Application Deadlines

There are two funding cycles annually, with deadlines of:

- The 15th of April
- The 15th of November

Applications must be postmarked or received online by the above dates.

Submitting Applications

Hard copy:

Mark A. Abramson
Executive Director
IBM Endowment for The Business of Government
1616 North Fort Myer Drive
Arlington, VA 22209

Online:

www.businessofgovernment.org/apply

Program Areas

E-Government

Specific areas of interest:

- Government to Business (G2B)
- Government to Citizen (G2C)
- Government to Employees (G2E)
- Government to Government (G2G)
- Capital investment strategies for e-government
- Enterprise architecture

Examples of previous grants in this area:

State Web Portals: Delivering and Financing E-Service by Diana Burley Gant, Jon P. Gant, and Craig L. Johnson (January 2002)

Leveraging Technology in the Service of Diplomacy: Innovation in the Department of State by Barry Fulton (March 2002)

Federal Intranet Work Sites: An Interim Assessment by Julianne G. Mahler and Priscilla M. Regan (June 2002)

Financial Management

Specific areas of interest:

- Cost accounting and management
- Financial and resource analysis
- Financial risk management and modeling
- Internal controls
- Financial auditing
- Contract management
- Reconciliation
- Erroneous payment recovery
- Asset management
- Systems modernization

Examples of previous grants in this area:

Credit Scoring and Loan Scoring: Tools for Improved Management of Federal Credit Programs by Thomas H. Stanton (July 1999)

Using Activity-Based Costing to Manage More Effectively by Michael H. Granof, David E. Platt, and Igor Vaysman (January 2000)

Audited Financial Statements: Getting and Sustaining "Clean" Opinions by Douglas A. Brook (July 2001)

Human Capital

Specific areas of interest:

- The components of human capital management required to accomplish an organization's mission (such as knowledge, skills, abilities, attitudes, and experience)
- Employee recruitment and retention
- Workforce planning and analysis
- Pay for performance

Examples of previous grants in this area:

Organizations Growing Leaders: Best Practices and Principles in the Public Service by Ray Blunt (December 2001)

A Weapon in the War for Talent: Using Special Authorities to Recruit Crucial Personnel by Hal G. Rainey (December 2001)

A Changing Workforce: Understanding Diversity Programs in the Federal Government by Katherine C. Naff and J. Edward Kellough (December 2001)

Managing for Results

Specific areas of interest:

- Policy, management, and resource allocation decisions that make use of performance and results information
- Balanced scorecards and measurement of customer service
- Collaboration between organizations to achieve common outcomes
- Performance-based budgeting

Examples of previous grants in this area:

Using Evaluation to Support Performance Management: A Guide for Federal Executives by Kathryn Newcomer and Mary Ann Scheirer (January 2001)

Managing for Outcomes: Milestone Contracting in Oklahoma by Peter Frumkin (January 2001)

Using Performance Data for Accountability: The New York City Police Department's CompStat Model of Police Management by Paul E. O'Connell (August 2001)

New Ways to Manage

Specific areas of interest:

- Contracting out
- Competition
- Outsourcing
- Privatization
- Public-private partnerships
- Innovations in management of public organizations

Examples of previous grants in this area:

Understanding Innovation: What Inspires It? What Makes It Successful? by Jonathan Walters (December 2001)

Making Performance-Based Contracting Perform: What the Federal Government Can Learn from State and Local Governments by Lawrence L. Martin (June 2002)

21st-Century Government and the Challenge of Homeland Defense by Elaine C. Kamarck (June 2002)

Transforming Organizations

Specific areas of interest:

- New organizational values in the public sector
- Changed public sector cultures
- Enhanced public sector performance
- Studies of outstanding public sector leaders

Examples of previous grants in this area:

Creating a Culture of Innovation: 10 Lessons from America's Best Run City by Janet Vinzant Denhardt and Robert B. Denhardt (January 2001)

Transforming Government: Dan Goldin and the Remaking of NASA by W. Henry Lambright (March 2001)

Managing Across Boundaries: A Case Study of Dr. Helene Gayle and the AIDS Epidemic by Norma M. Riccucci (January 2002)

For more information about the Endowment

Visit our website at: www.businessofgovernment.org
Send an e-mail to: endowment@businessofgovernment.org
Call: (703) 741-1077